Making the Modern South
David Goldfield, Series Editor

TROUBLED
COMMEMORATION
The American Civil War Centennial, 1961–1965

ROBERT J. COOK

LOUISIANA STATE UNIVERSITY PRESS

BATON ROUGE

Published by Louisiana State University Press
Manufactured in the United States of America
First printing

DESIGNER: Jenny Green
TYPEFACE: Minion Pro
TYPESETTER: Newgen–Austin
PRINTER AND BINDER: Edwards Brothers, Inc.

LIBRARY OF CONGRESS CATALOGING-IN-PUBLICATION DATA
Cook, Robert J., 1958–
Troubled commemoration : the American Civil War centennial, 1961–1965 / Robert J. Cook.
p.   cm. — (Making the modern South)
Includes bibliographical references and index.
ISBN-13: 978-0-8071-3227-2 (cloth : alk. paper)
1. United States—History—Civil War, 1861–1865—Centennial celebrations, etc.   2. United
States—History—Civil War, 1861–1865—Influence.   3. Memorials—Social aspects—United
States—History—20th century.   4. Public history—Political aspects—United States—
History—20th century.   5. Memorials—Political aspects—United States—History—
20th century.   6. Southern States—Race relations—History—20th century.   7. African
Americans—Civil rights—Southern States—History—20th century.   8. Civil rights
movements—Southern States—History—20th century.   9. Cold War—Social aspects—
United States.   10. United States—Social conditions—1960–1980.   I. Title.
E641.C76 2007
973.7'6—dc22
2006027281

For Doris Crandall
and to the memory of Max Crandall
with affection

CONTENTS

PREFACE

AFTER YEARS OF NEGLECT, the Civil War centennial is finally gaining the recognition it merits from historians—not so much because of the intrinsic importance of the event itself but for what it tells us about the diversity, pliability, and openness to manipulation of American memory at a time when elite and popular anxieties over change were rendered particularly acute by the country's ongoing battle against communism and the growing stridency of the African-American civil rights movement. Although I have been influenced by the recent surge in scholarly interest in historical memory, my desire to write what is, perhaps surprisingly, the first full-length study of the centennial derives primarily from my preoccupation with the Civil War itself and the wider black struggle for freedom and equality in the United States. Opting to devise a course on the modern civil rights movement when I arrived at the University of Sheffield in 1990, I was soon struck by the extent to which Civil War events—the focus of my doctoral and postdoctoral research at Oxford and Cambridge respectively—impinged on the actions and rhetoric of some iconic 1960s figures. Neither Martin Luther King's "I Have a Dream" speech in August 1963 nor President John F. Kennedy's contemporaneous public pronouncements on civil rights can be read effectively without recognizing that they were delivered a hundred years after the issuance of Lincoln's Emancipation Proclamation. In the midst of the faltering Civil War centennial, history provided both of these leaders with vital leverage in their efforts to promote racial equality in America. This book therefore was not conceived originally as another contribution to the growing corpus of literature on historical memory but, rather, as a more specialized investigation of the Civil War's continuing impact on the United States in the mid-twentieth century. While certainly it can be read as a test case of historical memory, it builds less on the work of theorists such as Pierre Nora than on that of empirical scholars such as David W. Blight and W. Fitzhugh Brundage, whose research and publications stem directly from a concern for racial justice in the nation as a whole and the South in particular. My principal hope is not that this study will alter the way sociologists, anthropologists, and historians define historical memory but that it will strengthen our understanding of how Civil War memory impinged upon the fight to defend and destroy the pernicious system of racial oppression that constricted the lives of so many southerners, white as well as black, in the tenacious reign of Jim Crow.

I have accrued numerous debts in the course of writing this book. Although I could begin with Bruce Catton, whose book *The Coming Fury*—checked out of my local public library in the early 1970s—was the first American history book I ever read, my primary debt is to Sylvia Frank Rodrigue, former editor-in-chief of Louisiana State University Press. It was Sylvia who suggested that I write this book after hearing me deliver a paper on the centennial at the Southern Historical Association meeting in Louisville in November 2000. Without her initial encouragement I would probably have confined my work on the subject to a handful of essays and articles. Rand Dotson and Lee Sioles at LSU Press saw the project through to completion. My thanks also go to them and to my efficient copyeditor, Glenn Perkins.

Studies like this require time and money. I am particularly grateful then, first, to the University of Sheffield for providing me with a semester of research leave in 2003 and grants for travel to Washington, DC, Virginia, and the Midwest and, second, to the British Academy for a small personal research grant that enabled me to undertake essential archival work in the southern and northeastern United States in the summer of 2002. For accommodation during these visits to North America I am indebted (not for the first time in several cases) to the kindness of many friends, most notably Barbara Holmlund and Julianne Borton in Silver Spring, Carole Bucy and Edward Harcourt in Nashville, Dan and Jane Carter in Columbia, Mary Beveridge in Kansas City, and John Zeller in Des Moines. Several veterans of the centennial period (I hope they'll forgive me for the appellation), Ed C. Bearss, James M. McPherson, Howard N. Meyer, William Garrett Piston, and James I. Robertson Jr., shared their memories of the centennial years with me. This book is all the richer for their generous assistance. I learned much from discussions with fellow scholars not only at the annual SHA meeting but also in research seminars at the universities of Leeds, London, Oxford, and Warwick. I also wish to register my thanks for the help provided by the efficient staff at the National Archives; the John F. Kennedy Presidential Library; the Rare Book and Manuscript Library at Columbia University; the Manuscript, Archives, and Rare Book Library, Emory University; the Earl Gregg Swem Library at the College of William and

Mary; and the state libraries and archives of Alabama, Georgia, Mississippi, New Jersey, New York, South Carolina, Tennessee, and Virginia.

I owe an enormous intellectual debt to a select group of people. I am especially grateful to David Blight and series editor David Goldfield for their detailed and constructive reports on the near-final manuscript. Four other historians, Fitz Brundage, Richard Carwardine, Richard King, and Hugh Wilford, gave up their time to read and comment critically on an early draft, and Andrea Bevan provided skilled help in the formating and indexing of this volume. Although regrettably I am compelled to follow convention and state that the mistakes are all mine, the ensuing analysis bears the imprint of many invaluable and insightful suggestions. Most authors, slaves to the word processor, would be certifiably insane without the support of their immediate family. My greatest debt, then, is to Andrea, Martha, and Daniel and to my parents, Margaret and John, for their priceless love and unstinting encouragement.

ABBREVIATIONS

ANC	African National Congress
ANECA	American Negro Emancipation Centennial Authority
ASNLH	Association for the Study of Negro Life and History
CWCA	Civil War Centennial Association
CWCC	U.S. Civil War Centennial Commission
GAR	Grand Army of the Republic
NAACP	National Association for the Advancement of Colored People
NEUM	Non-European Unity Movement
NPS	National Park Service
SAH	Society of American Historians
SCLC	Southern Christian Leadership Conference
SCV	Sons of Confederate Veterans
SHA	Southern Historical Association
SNCC	Student Nonviolent Coordinating Committee
SUV	Sons of Union Veterans
UDC	United Daughters of the Confederacy

Troubled Commemoration

Introduction

IN OCTOBER 1960, ninety-five years after his illustrious grandfather had accepted the surrender of Robert E. Lee's Confederate forces at Appomattox Court House in Virginia, Major General Ulysses S. Grant III trumpeted the approach of the one hundredth anniversary of the American Civil War. In spite of turning eighty in July, the retired army officer chaired a new federal commission that had been created by Congress to oversee a four-year commemoration of the country's most damaging conflict. The past, he reminded readers of *This Week Magazine,* could not be divorced from the present. "Like many still living," he wrote, "I was raised in an atmosphere filled with memories of the Civil War." He recalled visiting the home of his ailing grandfather at Long Branch, New York, in the mid-1880s and finding the one remembrance of the war to be "a drum surrounded by a sunburst of bayonets." Most Americans, averred the general, understood his "close feeling" for the Civil War because the experience had been a shared one. "The war did not divide us," he insisted. "Rather, it united us, in spite of a long period of bitterness, and made us the greatest and most powerful nation the world had ever seen." He ventured the hope that every American family would join in the exciting series of commemorative events that were being planned by local groups as well as his own agency. "Battles will be re-enacted, many on a huge scale. Colorful ceremonies will be held, exhibitions of war trophies and mementos organized. There will be memorials, parades, new historical markers and a great many special ceremonies." [1]

1. Ulysses S. Grant III, "Here comes the greatest centennial in U.S. history!" *This Week Magazine,* Oct. 16, 1960, 8, 9, 11. The former Union commander and president died of throat cancer on July 23, 1885, shortly after completing his two-volume history of the Civil War, *The Personal Memoirs of U. S. Grant.*

Although a myriad of centennial observances did take place between 1961 and 1965, the commemoration did not live up to Grant's lofty expectations. After an initial period in which many Americans demonstrated a keen enthusiasm for Civil War events, the centennial ran into serious trouble and never recovered its early momentum. Originally planned, as the general's consensual approach revealed, as an exercise in cold war nationalism, the centennial was soon mired in controversy—much of it generated by the renewed racial and sectional tensions of the era. In the wake of the U.S. Supreme Court's landmark desegregation decision in *Brown v. Board of Education* large numbers of southern whites once again resisted what they regarded as federal encroachment on their rights. The parallels between the 1960s and the 1860s, explicit in much of the media coverage of the civil rights movement, were not lost on contemporaries, and the centennial suffered accordingly. When the time came to mark Lee's surrender at Appomattox in April 1965, the American public's attention was no longer fastened on the kind of commemorative events that had proved to be so absorbing four years previously. Once diverted by parades and sham battles, Americans were now preoccupied by the black freedom struggle and growing evidence that their country was becoming embroiled in a divisive new war in southeast Asia.

Scholars have paid little attention to the Civil War centennial. Alongside the turbulent events of the early 1960s—the Cuban missile crisis, the March on Washington, the assassination of President John F. Kennedy—it seems to pale into insignificance. But while the centennial was patently not a major occurrence in the history of the United States, it remains a subject worthy of scholarly investigation. This is not primarily for the events themselves (though the most important of these will be related in the chapters that follow) but because of what this troubled exercise in public history tells us about the relationship between historical memory on the one hand and, on the other, the development of cold war culture, the successes and failures of the civil rights movement, and the progress of the modern South.

For all his failings General Grant was right about one thing: the past is always integral to the present. Several of those historians who have bothered to take note of the centennial have approached the topic from the vantage point of historical memory—widely regarded in these postmodern times as a legitimate object for scholarly concern. Over the past twenty years historians have drawn profitably on the work of psychologists, anthropologists, biologists, and sociologists to posit that memory has been, and remains, a primary tool in the construction of group and national identity. Perceiving historical memory as a manifestation of power relations within society as well as a tool of nation-building, they have introduced us to new and exciting readings, not only of traditional written sources but also of parades, entertainment shows, exhibitions, buildings, monuments, and commemorative events. Their principal contribution to scholarship has been to uncover the often hidden political content of objects, images, places, and events that, outwardly at least, appear to have been politically neutral. Different groups in society remember the past in different ways, and they do so for diverse purposes. The past is always elusive, highly contested, and selectively remembered (or selectively forgotten) by groups who have power and by those who do not. How that past is regarded is always conditioned by the exigencies of the present.[2]

As David W. Blight and other historians have shown, the Civil War furnishes abundant evidence for those who regard collective memory as inherently unstable, politically charged and processive. From the moment it started, the meaning of the great conflict was contested. Northern Republicans and pro-war Democrats believed they were fighting the "War of the Rebellion" to defeat a hellish revolt by treacherous slaveholders against the best government on earth. As the bloodletting grew worse so-called "Copperheads," northern Peace Democrats, rejected this analysis and contended that the Lincoln administration was trying to turn a limited struggle to save the old Union into an all-out war to abolitionize the country at the expense of white Americans. Confederate leaders maintained all along that their Republican enemies were plotting to seize national power by assaulting the South's constitutional rights, including the right to hold property in slaves. After Appomattox attempts to control the memory of the Civil War proceeded apace. Northerners who read books by Republican leaders like Horace Greeley and Henry Wilson did not doubt that the war had been started by a despicable Slave Power conspiracy; that it had been waged by brave Union men prepared to lay down their lives for the republic; and that the North's victory represented the triumph of representative government over the forces of anarchy, tyranny, and subversion.

2. The term "historical memory" originated with the sociologist Maurice Halbwachs in 1925. The scholarly literature on this topic is vast and growing rapidly. For an overview, see Jeffrey K. Olick and Joyce Robbins, "Social Memory Studies: From 'Collective Memory' to the Historical Sociology of Mnemonic Practices," *Annual Review of Sociology* 24 (1998): 105–40. Pierre Nora, a leading figure in the recent memory boom, has written insightfully on the distinction between memory and history in "Between Memory and History: Les Lieux de Mémoire," *Representations* 26 (1989): 7–24. For an early and fruitful excursion into the realm of historical memory in the United States, see Michael Kammen, *Mystic Chords of Memory: The Transformation of Tradition in American Culture* (New York: Alfred A. Knopf, 1991). Joy S. Kasson, *Buffalo Bill's Wild West: Celebrity, Memory, and Popular History* (New York: Hill and Wang, 2001), is an important case study.

While most former Confederates grudgingly accepted the finality of southern military defeat and the loss of slavery, they exhibited few signs in the immediate postwar years of repentance or a weakened commitment to white supremacy. Leading southern figures such as Jefferson Davis and Alexander H. Stephens helped to fashion the Lost Cause defense of the Rebellion by insisting that they had been defending states' rights, not slavery, and that ultimately the South had been defeated only by the numerical and economic superiority of the enemy.[3]

During the last two decades of the nineteenth century, these seemingly irreconcilable viewpoints were mediated by the memories of the veterans themselves. Former Union and Confederate soldiers began to forge common ground as they embarked on a collective search to locate meaning in their wartime service. Against a backdrop of rapid social and economic change, waning sectional animus, and the relatively humdrum nature of postbellum civilian life, Civil War soldiers sought not only to recapture the camaraderie of wartime service (for example by joining organizations like the Grand Army of the Republic [GAR] or the United Confederate Veterans) but also to confirm their own historical significance by writing about their military experiences in magazine articles. While the process of trying to establish the "truth" about their battlefield exploits often proved intensely frustrating, their efforts to emphasize the value of their own contributions in the field led them to a fraternal recognition of their opponents' courage. It was not uncommon to see former Union and Confederate soldiers gathering for reunions on the sites of major battles. As early as July 1887 several hundred southerners who had participated in Pickett's famous charge at the battle of Gettysburg were greeted spontaneously atop Cemetery Ridge by an even larger group of veterans from the Pennsylvania Brigade. The veterans' growing sense of the war as a shared experience between brave men provided an essential basis for sectional reconciliation—a complex and uneven process that was given added momen-

---

3. Matthew J. Grow, "The Shadow of the Civil War: A Historiography of Civil War Memory," *American Nineteenth Century History* 4 (2003): 77–103, is a comprehensive overview of recent studies of Civil War memory, but see also David W. Blight's important collection of essays, *Beyond the Battlefield: Race, Memory, and the American Civil War* (Amherst: University of Massachusetts Press, 2002). Generally speaking, interest in the Lost Cause and its connection to white supremacy has prompted greater coverage of southern than northern memory and of the half century after 1865 than the middle or late twentieth century. On the course of Civil War memory in the years immediately after Appomattox, see Thomas J. Pressly, *Americans Interpret Their Civil War* (Princeton: Princeton University Press, 1954), 28–51, 73–95, and David W. Blight, *Race and Reunion: The Civil War in American Memory* (Cambridge, MA: Harvard University Press, 2001), 31–170.

tum by the war against Spain in 1898 and the steady emergence of a consensual interpretation of the Civil War that received assent from white Americans on both sides of the Mason-Dixon line.[4]

The new nationalist orthodoxy (well established by 1918) represented an uneasy combination of northern and southern interpretations and would remain the principal popular narrative of the Civil War at least until the 1960s. The story ran as follows: the late conflict had been a tragic brothers' war brought on by the South's determination to defend the rights of the states against perceived encroachment by the North. Both sides had fought courageously in the war, but in the end the North's superior economic and manpower resources had carried the day. While the killing was unfortunate, the Union victory had been a blessing because it had laid the foundations of future American greatness. Postbellum northern attempts to impose Reconstruction on the defeated South, however, had been unnecessarily vindictive and ill-judged (not least because the emancipated blacks were in no fit state to receive the privileges of full citizenship). Northern and southern whites alike accepted that slavery had been a heavy encumbrance for the ruling race, but most concurred that it had been a relatively benign institution for African Americans.[5]

Evident most clearly in James Ford Rhodes's seven-volume *History of the United States from the Compromise of 1850* (1893–1906) and the burgeoning cult of the personally kindly and sectionally charitable Abraham Lincoln, the nationalist explanation of past events is most accurately described as dominant rather than hegemonic. In asserting in 1912 that "because I love the South I rejoice in the failure of the Confederacy," Woodrow Wilson certainly spoke for large numbers of his fellow southern whites.[6] However, the Lost Cause was a remarkably flexible ideology that could be utilized by both conservatives

4. Blight, *Race and Reunion*, 171–210. A number of recent works stress the instability of the veterans' memory as well as their growing tendency to engage in reconciliatory rituals with their former enemies. See esp. James A. Kaser, *At the Bivouac of Memory: History, Politics, and the Battle of Chickamauga* (New York: Peter Lang, 1996), and Carol Reardon, *Pickett's Charge in History and Memory* (Chapel Hill: University of North Carolina Press, 1997). Stuart McConnell, *Glorious Contentment: The Grand Army of the Republic, 1865–1900* (Chapel Hill: University of North Carolina Press, 1992), remains the best modern study of the GAR.

5. Pressly, *Americans Interpret*, 121–34, 187–92; Peter Novick, *That Noble Dream: The "Objectivity Question" and the American Historical Profession* (Cambridge: Cambridge University Press, 1988), 72–80.

6. Woodrow Wilson, quoted in John A. Thompson, *Woodrow Wilson* (Harlow, UK: Longman/Pearson Education, 2002), 16.

and progressive exponents of the New South like Wilson. It was not, therefore, entirely compatible with the consensual forces unleashed by the process of sectional reconciliation. In an age marked by civic voluntarism rather
than state activism, middle- and upper-class white women played a critical
role in conserving an authoritative memory of the Confederate experience
which, precisely because local whites accepted it as gospel, functioned as an
instrument of racial dominance.[7] Bitter at the sufferings caused by the Yankee
invaders and excluded from Blue-Gray bonding by their lack of battlefield experience, they forged a distinctive civic identity for themselves by educating a
new generation of southern whites about the glories of plantation culture, the
region's unified struggle to resist northern domination, and the manifold horrors of Reconstruction. Women who formed chapters of the United Daughters
of the Confederacy (UDC) after its founding in September 1894 raised funds
to build a rash of Confederate monuments across the South at the turn of the
century, monitored the region's school textbooks to ensure that children im-
bibed what they saw as the true interpretation of the Civil War, and pressured
state governments to take greater responsibility for preserving and disseminating an exclusive white memory of the late unpleasantness. Although they
welcomed signs that northerners were ready to accept large portions of the
Lost Cause narrative, the Daughters remained suspicious of Yankee motives
and watchful of any attempt by northerners to disparage the Confederacy.[8]

7. W. Fitzhugh Brundage, *The Southern Past: A Clash of Race and Memory* (Cambridge, MA:
Belknap Press of Harvard University Press, 2005), 15.

8. On the changing role of southern women in memorializing the Confederacy, see ibid.,
12–54, 105–37; Fred Arthur Bailey, "The Textbooks of the 'Lost Cause': Censorship and the Creation of Southern State Histories," *Georgia Historical Quarterly* 75 (1991): 507–33; Karen L. Cox,
*Dixie's Daughters: The United Daughters of the Confederacy and the Preservation of Confederate
Culture* (Gainesville: University Press of Florida, 2003); Jacqueline Glass Campbell, *When Sherman Marched North from the Sea: Resistance on the Confederate Home Front* (Chapel Hill: University of North Carolina Press, 2003), esp. 105–10; Cynthia Mills and Pamela H. Simpson, eds.,
Monuments of the Lost Cause: Women, Art, and the Landscapes of Southern Memory (Knoxville:
University of Tennessee Press, 2004). The Confederate experience was too painful and divisive for
some elite southern women, for example those involved in Charleston's incipient historic preservation movement after 1918. Importantly, however, artists like Alice Ravenel Huger Smith drew
heavily for inspiration on an idealized antebellum South. Smith's widely disseminated images of
happy "darkies" and benevolent masters bolstered Jim Crow by appealing to a national audience
during the 1930s. See Stephanie E. Yuhl, "Rich and Tender Remembering: Elite White Women
and an Aesthetic Sense of Place in Charleston, 1920s and 1930s," in W. Fitzhugh Brundage, ed.,

There were several reasons why northern whites were willing to meet southerners more than half way. First, sectional reconciliation was a necessary precondition for collective advancement in the closing decades of the nineteenth century. The nationalist orthodoxy may have required northerners to acknowledge the courage of their former enemies, but defeat required the latter to recognize the inviolability of the American republic. Second, the strains generated by industrialization, urbanization, and immigration caused many middle-class Yankees to reconceptualize their conquered province as an antidote to the social ills of the modern-day North. Increasingly, the cohesive plantation society of the Old South that was in large part a romantic invention of postbellum southern writers struck northerners as an attractive foil to their chaotic, plural society riven by ethnic tension and industrial warfare.[9] Third, and most important, northerners' disillusionment with Reconstruction combined with the imperatives of sectional reconciliation, the growth of a mass consumer society, and the rising popularity of social Darwinist thought to ensure that whiteness was a fundamental bulwark of the dynamic capitalist republic that soon emerged from the crucible of civil war. As Grace Elizabeth Hale contends, white Americans in all parts of the country found race to be extremely "useful in creating new collective identities to replace older, more individual, and local groundings of self."[10] With the nation safe and the torch of abolitionism extinguished, northern opinion-makers and ordinary people alike had little difficulty accepting that the former Confederates had been right all along about the innate inferiority of African Americans. The building of a segregated society in the South in the 1890s and early 1900s went hand in hand with the construction of Confederate monuments and the writing of Lost Cause histories. It would not have been possible without the acquiescence of northern whites.

The readiness of most northerners to embrace consensus-building myths about the Old South and Reconstruction was evident in the nationwide popularity of pro-southern movies such as D.W. Griffith's epic silent feature, the virulently racist *Birth of a Nation* (1915), and the most successful talkie of them

---

Where These Memories Grow: History, Memory, and Southern Identity (Chapel Hill: University of North Carolina Press, 2000), 227–48.

9. Nina Silber, *The Romance of Reunion: Northerners and the South, 1865–1900* (Chapel Hill: University of North Carolina Press, 1993), 66–92.

10. Grace Elizabeth Hale, *Making Whiteness: The Culture of Segregation in the South, 1890–1940* (New York: Pantheon, 1998), 7.

all, producer David O. Selznick's *Gone with the Wind* (1939).[11] However, while
this acceptance largely vindicated Winston Churchill's contention that "[t]he
victors forget, the vanquished remember," it concealed the existence of two oppositional narratives—what David Blight has termed counter-memories.[12] The
first of these, an uncompromising white Unionist memory of the Civil War as
the War of the Rebellion, was fostered principally by hard-line Republicans,
former abolitionists, and some of the veterans belonging to the GAR who regarded sectional reconciliation as a sell-out to the country's enemies. Lacking
contemporary political relevance (in marked contrast to the linkage between
the Lost Cause and segregation), this counter-memory virtually died out with
the passing of the wartime generation and the return of southern whites to
their allegiance to the Union by the time of America's entry into World War I.
It was kept alive mainly by the retention of Julia Ward Howe's stirring "Battle
Hymn of the Republic" in official rituals and by the activities of small groups
such as the Sons of Union Veterans (SUV) and the obscure Society for Correct Civil War Information. Run by two sisters whose father had been a Union
officer, the latter produced a mimeographed "Bulletin" which appeared at ir-
regular intervals between 1935 and 1941. In the first number the women set out
their agenda: "unmitigated opposition" to anyone who sought to undermine
"pride in the heritage left . . . by the Union soldiers, who conquered the most
powerful enemies our Nation has known."[13] Later issues assailed Rebel apolo-
gists like the UDC and the Sons of Confederate Veterans (SCV), denounced
the book and movie versions of *Gone with the Wind,* and attacked those who
described the Civil War as "the War Between the States." In November 1940
the "Bulletin" turned its fire on Franklin D. Roosevelt for hosting Confederate
veterans at the White House and criticized FDR's electoral opponent Wendell

11. Hugely controversial at the time of its release (it was subjected to a nationwide boycott
campaign by the National Association for the Advancement of Colored People), *Birth of a Nation*
had grossed around $20 million by 1921. According to Bruce Chadwick, its "biggest grosses came
from Northern and Western cities, where audiences were just as accepting of the film's racial slant
as those in the South." The same author notes that "just about every adult in the country" had
seen *Gone with the Wind* by 1945. Bruce Chadwick, *The Reel Civil War: Mythmaking in American
Film* (New York: Alfred A. Knopf, 2001), 132, 187.

12. Winston S. Churchill, quoted in Richard B. Harwell, "The Stream of Self Consciousness,"
in Frank E. Vandiver, ed., *The Idea of the South: Pursuit of a Central Theme* (Chicago: University
of Chicago Press, 1964), 23; David W. Blight, "W. E. B. DuBois and the Struggle for American Historical Memory," in Geneviève Fabre and Robert O'Meally, eds., *History and Memory in African-
American Culture* (New York: Oxford University Press, 1994), 46.

13. Robert R. Dykstra, "The Continuing War," *Civil War History* 9 (1963): 431.

Willkie for eulogizing Robert E. Lee. Impressive though such residual Unionist fervor may have been, the work of the Society and other similar bodies exerted little impact on most northern whites, who, by the time of Pearl Harbor, either had no interest in the Civil War whatsoever or regarded it as a tragic episode in the nation's distant past.

A second and, ultimately, far more potent counter-memory of the war was the variant nurtured by African Americans. As far back at least as Reconstruction blacks had understood the dangers posed by the advance of sectional reconciliation. Internecine strife between whites provided the necessary precondition for the abolition of slavery and the passage of two constitutional amendments extending the citizenship rights of the freedpeople. The late Rebels' refusal to accept black equality, however, placed further progress in jeopardy. The black abolitionist Frederick Douglass struggled to keep alive his race's oppositional memory of the Civil War—a pro-northern narrative that stressed not only southern white iniquity but also black support for the Union, the overriding significance of emancipation, and the thwarted promise of Reconstruction.[14] He struggled in vain. Increasingly eager for an end to sectional strife, a majority of northern whites came to endorse the view of their southern peers that African Americans should be left to the tender mercies of those who claimed to know them best. In July 1875 Douglass asked, "If war among the whites brought peace and liberty to the blacks, what will peace among the whites bring?"[15] By 1900 the answer was clear: disfranchisement and loss of dignity in a segregated South.

The feeble national purchase of the black counter-memory was painfully evident in the way whites began to gain control of public spaces across the United States. A plethora of Civil War commemorative exercises and monument building took place between 1870 and 1930. Only a handful of war memorials recognized the substantial black contribution to the Union war effort, the most significant of these being Augustus Saint-Gaudens's bronze monument to Robert Gould Shaw and his 54th Massachusetts regiment unveiled on Boston common in May 1897.[16] By this time, however, the U.S. Supreme Court

14. David W. Blight, *Frederick Douglass' Civil War: Keeping Faith in Jubilee* (Baton Rouge: Louisiana State University Press, 1989), 219–39.

15. Frederick Douglass, quoted ibid., 217.

16. Sixty-five black Union veterans attended the Shaw monument unveiling ceremony in Boston, but by 1897 the black counter-memory was fading rapidly from public view in the United States. David W. Blight, "The Shaw Memorial in the Landscape of Civil War Memory," in Blight, *Beyond the Battlefield*, 153–69.

had already provided constitutional justification for segregation in *Plessy v. Ferguson,* and virtually the only visible places black veterans could remember the Civil War were African-American parades (important memory sites for a people with very limited financial resources) and their own separate, dwindling encampments of the GAR. In July 1913 more than 55,000 Union and Confederate veterans attended the fiftieth anniversary commemoration of the battle of Gettysburg. There is no evidence that any black Union soldiers attended this landmark event in which speaker after speaker (President Wilson included) paid homage to the courage of the soldiers from both sides and vaunted the restored unity of the American republic.[17]

No less telling and poignant was the marginalizing of blacks at a ceremony to dedicate the Lincoln Memorial in Washington, DC, on May 30, 1922. Speakers at the event made few references to divisive topics and stressed the late president's contribution to saving the republic rather than freeing the slaves. Those blacks who did attend the ceremony were seated separately, and the only invited African-American speaker was Booker T. Washington's accommodationist successor at Tuskegee Institute, Robert R. Moton, who—in fairness—did at least observe that American history had been marked from the beginning by an, as yet, unfinished contest between freedom and bondage. The national press took little notice of Moton's words, and it was left to the crusading black newspaper the *Chicago Defender* to call for a boycott of the Memorial until "juster and more grateful men come to power and history shall have rebuked offenders against the name of Abraham Lincoln."[18] Although African-American scholars and their left-wing allies endeavored to sustain the black counter-memory in the 1920s and 1930s, their work had little impact on the way most Americans thought about the receding sectional carnage.

The established nationalist orthodoxy was buffeted after 1918 by a number of developments, notably the advent of two rival scholarly interpretations of the Civil War—a revisionist view, heavily influenced by the recent slaughter on the western front, which blamed irresponsible fanatics and a blundering generation of antebellum politicians for the outbreak of a needless conflict, and the

17. Blight, *Race and Reunion*, 7–13, 383–91. Although African-American veterans were not present at the ceremony in 1913, for twenty years before the Great War, black GAR members from Baltimore sponsored their own annual pilgrimage to Gettysburg in order to mark President Lincoln's preliminary Emancipation Proclamation. Black tourists were regular visitors to the battlefield in the late nineteenth and early twentieth centuries. See Jim Weeks, *Gettysburg: Memory, Market, and an American Shrine* (Princeton: Princeton University Press, 2003), 92–98.

18. *Chicago Defender,* quoted in Christopher A. Thomas, *The Lincoln Memorial and American Life* (Princeton: Princeton University Press, 2002), 158.

deterministic analysis of Charles and Mary Beard, who argued in 1927 that the Civil War was the inevitable result of an irrepressible conflict between an industrialized North and an agrarian South.[19] Ultimately, however, both of these interpretations bolstered the consensual, pro-southern line on the war: the revisionist by heaping much of the blame for the conflict on northern abolitionists and the Beardian by attributing the war to material factors rather than any debate over the morality of slavery. America's involvement in the antifascist and anticommunist crusades of the 1940s subjected both schools of thought to real pressure within the academy, but at mid-century the main props of the nationalist consensus remained in place outside it.[20] The durability of the old orthodoxy provided the context for General Grant's vision of the centennial as a truly national (that is, intersectional) commemoration. The federal commission which he chaired between 1957 and 1961 made few attempts to involve African Americans in the proceedings. The Civil War was deemed to have been primarily a white man's experience (just as it appeared to have been by the time the veterans gathered at Gettysburg in 1913), and blacks, as the southern writer Walker Percy put it, were to be "the ghost at the feast."[21]

A REPRESENTATIVE COMMEMORATION

Although Robert G. Hartje furnished a useful overview of the Civil War centennial as a salutary lesson in how not to plan the bicentenary of the American Revolution in the late 1960s and early 1970s, two of the most insightful evaluations of the event have been provided by Michael Kammen and John Bodnar.[22] Both of these scholars use the centennial as a case study to demonstrate the contested nature of the American past and to show how the federal

19. Pressly, *Americans Interpret*, 204–14, 257–85; Novick, *That Noble Dream*, 234–38.

20. Novick, *That Noble Dream*, 354–59.

21. Walker Percy, "Red, White, and Blue-Gray" (1961), in *Signposts in a Strange Land*, ed. Patrick Samway (New York: Farrar, Straus, and Giroux, 1991), 82.

22. Robert G. Hartje, *Bicentennial USA: Pathways to Celebration* (Nashville: American Association for State and Local History, 1973), esp. 60–93; Kammen, *Mystic Chords*, 590–610; John Bodnar, *Remaking America: Public Memory, Commemoration, and Patriotism in the Twentieth Century* (Princeton: Princeton University Press, 1992), 206–26. There are also two general essay-length treatments of the centennial: Robert Cook, "From Shiloh to Selma: The Impact of the Civil War Centennial on the Black Freedom Struggle in the United States, 1961–65," in Brian Ward and Tony Badger, eds., *The Making of Martin Luther King and the Civil Rights Movement* (Basingstoke, UK: Macmillan, 1996), 131–46, and Jon Wiener, "Civil War, Cold War, Civil Rights: The Civil War Centennial in Context, 1960–1965," in Alice Fahs and Joan Waugh, eds., *The Memory of the Civil War in American Culture* (Chapel Hill: University of North Carolina Press, 2004), 237–57.

government attempted to use that past to construct a strong sense of national identity in the twentieth century.

Bodnar's analysis is the more trenchant of the two, providing as it does rich evidence to support his thesis that "[p]ublic memory emerges from the intersection of official and vernacular cultural expressions."[23] Ever since the early nineteenth century, he argues, elites in America have had a vested material interest in promoting grassroots attachment to the nation-state through the manipulation of patriotic and historical symbols. But while ordinary Americans have generally acknowledged their loyalty to the nation, they have also used national symbols and patriotic events for their own purposes. He cites, for example, Frederick Douglass's assertion that "[w]e [blacks] have to do with the past only as we can make it useful to the present and the future" and shows how immigrant groups have used local commemorations to forge a strong sense of ethnic identity as well as to demonstrate their loyalty to the wider community.[24] The persistent tension between official and "vernacular" forms of historical memory, he argues, was particularly apparent during the years of the Civil War centennial when southern pride in the Confederacy, intensifying racial strife, and popular enthusiasm for sham battles undermined attempts by national authorities to make the centennial a dignified and consensual event.[25]

In *Mystic Chords of Memory,* his epic account of the ways that Americans have developed a sense of historical tradition, Michael Kammen acknowledges the significance of conflict in the country's past. However, he convincingly stresses the power of consensual modes of collective remembrance (and forgetting), asserting that "ultimately there is a powerful tendency in the United States to depoliticize traditions for the sake of 'reconciliation.'"[26] Although Kammen does not delineate the close connection between southern commemorations and the fight against integration, exaggerates the exceptional nature of historical memory in the United States, and misjudges the extent to which centennial officials eventually accommodated the wish of blacks to celebrate emancipation, his assertion that the Civil War centennial was "decentralized by design and enjoyed far more success in scattered localities" merits extended consideration.[27]

23. Bodnar, *Remaking,* 13.
24. Ibid., 43.
25. Ibid., 13–14, 206–26.
26. Kammen, *Mystic Chords,* 13.
27. Ibid., 572.

Richard Fried's entertaining and valuable assessment of cold war culture, *The Russians Are Coming! The Russians Are Coming!* (1998), locates the Civil War centennial in the context of official efforts to alert the American people to the dangers of the communist threat through the application of patriotic pageantry. Observing dryly that in the late 1940s and 1950s history was "long prescribed as cod-liver oil for civic irregularity," he convincingly depicts the centennial as a culmination of initiatives like the mobile Freedom Train exhibit, Loyalty Day, and the ongoing development of an idealized American community at colonial Williamsburg.[28] Like Bodnar and Kammen, Fried charts the contentious progress of the centennial—an event he regards as a critical stage in the decline of cold war pageantry. "No earlier observance," he remarks, "triggered so many resonances with the nation's global role or became so embroiled in politics, media and popular culture. All public rites are subject to competing uses and readings, but no mobilization of the past in support of the present prompted as much friction as the Civil War anniversary."[29]

This study offers not only a detailed narrative of the Civil War centennial but also an evaluation of the themes highlighted by Bodnar, Kammen, and Fried. It suggests too that an assessment of this underexplored event can contribute to a fuller understanding of the civil rights struggle and the role of historical memory in the development of modern America, especially the modern South. Chapter 1 probes the cold war origins of the commemoration as well as the formation and initial organizing activities of the United States Civil War Centennial Commission. Chapter 2 investigates white southerners' relatively enthusiastic response to the commemoration with particular emphasis on local celebrations of the Confederacy in Montgomery and Jackson. Such enthusiasm, it is suggested, was directly linked to the ongoing struggle against integration. By the spring of 1961 the centennial had run into trouble owing to the federal commission's tolerance of segregated accommodation in Charleston, South Carolina, the venue for the agency's fourth national assembly as well as a grand reenactment of the Confederate bombardment of Fort Sumter that had unleashed civil war one hundred years previously. The events and immediate consequences for the centennial of the Charleston fiasco are analyzed in Chapter 3, as is the Kennedy administration's handling of what was one of its first domestic crises. Chapter 4 considers the growing problems of the federal commission and the displacement of the existing leadership by

28. Richard M. Fried, *The Russians Are Coming! The Russians Are Coming! Pageantry and Patriotism in Cold-War America* (New York: Oxford University Press, 1998), 99.

29. Ibid., 122.

professional historians during the summer and fall of 1961. African-American efforts to contest the centennial are investigated in Chapter 5. Civil rights leaders like Martin Luther King Jr. and Roy Wilkins were hardly less aware than Frederick Douglass of the need to marshal a usable past in the service of contemporary objectives and viewed the centenary of the Emancipation Proclamation as a heaven-sent opportunity to wrest control of the centennial away from southern whites. Chapter 6 examines the last three years of the centennial. Public interest in the commemoration waned quickly, and the reasons for this are explored in some depth. But so are the main events of 1962–65, which included persistent efforts by segregationist leaders like Governor George Wallace of Alabama to turn Civil War memory to their own political advantage. Although the achievements of the commemoration were limited, the principal cultural productions of the centennial years—primarily in the areas of film, fiction, and historical scholarship—are assessed in Chapter 7. The conclusion stresses not only the significance of the centennial for historians interested in the evolution of cold war consensus ideology in the 1960s but also its relevance to an understanding of the strengths and weaknesses of historical memory in the second half of the twentieth century. For all their efforts, Americans inside and outside the centennial establishment—the government bodies overseeing the exercise—did little to alter the ways ordinary people thought about (or did not think about) what novelist-turned-historian Shelby Foote called "the cross roads of our being."[30] By the close of the centennial there were visible signs that the black emancipationist narrative of the war had made a return to the national consciousness and that some southern whites were prepared to reconsider the Confederate past. These developments, however, were a result not primarily of centennial-related events but of reconfigured power relations occasioned by the civil rights movement. If historical memories of America's bloodiest trauma often posed a formidable obstacle to racial equality in the mid-twentieth century, the evidence provided by the Civil War centennial suggests that they were not an insuperable barrier against progressive social change.

30. Shelby Foote, quoted in Gabor S. Boritt, "Lincoln and Gettysburg: The Hero and the Heroic Place," in Robert Brent Toplin, ed., *Ken Burns's "The Civil War": Historians Respond* (New York: Oxford University Press, 1996), 86.

Organizing a Cold War Pageant

THE IDEA FOR a national commemoration of the Civil War originated with private American citizens, primarily "buffs" who belonged to amateur discussion groups called Civil War round tables, and a body of interested professionals, many of them historians, who founded the Civil War Centennial Association in New York in 1953. However, efforts to encourage the creation of a federal agency to oversee the four-year event were strongly supported by the National Park Service (NPS), and these bore fruit in September 1957 when President Dwight D. Eisenhower signed into law a congressional joint resolution setting up the U.S. Civil War Centennial Commission (CWCC). In the late 1950s the new agency labored to make the planned commemoration a weapon of the cultural cold war—a popular heritage bonanza that would reinforce government calls for civic activism and vigilance by educating Americans about the brave deeds and deeply held values of their nineteenth-century precursors. The task proved to be a difficult one. Some people worried that any attempt to mark the Civil War would inflame sectional tensions at a time when racial issues were moving to the forefront of the nation's political agenda or feared that the centennial was just an excuse for arrogant Yankees to laud it over the white South once again. Others simply had no interest in the American past, whether it was intended for use as popular education or entertainment. But by January 1961 the federal commission's considerable efforts seemed to have paid off. Most states had set up their own centennial bodies which in turn had begun to encourage the development of local committees. Even though the marginalization of African Americans was a cause of concern to some observers, the prospects for a successful and genuinely grassroots commemoration seemed bright.

ORIGINS

Proposals for an official commemoration of the Civil War centennial had their origins in a discernible increase in popular interest in the conflict during the late 1930s and 1940s. It was no coincidence that the birth of the modern Civil War industry coincided with the final passing of the veterans themselves. Although a quarter of a million Americans assembled to watch the dedication of the Eternal Light Peace Memorial on the field on July 3, fewer than 1,400 former Union and Confederate soldiers actually attended the emotional seventy-fifth anniversary of the battle of Gettysburg in 1938. The average age of the veterans was 94.[1] By 1950 only a handful of the original protagonists were left alive, and Americans with a keen interest in the war cast around rather desperately to make contact with the survivors. A southern journalist, William D. Workman Jr., called at the home of 106-year-old General Howell, South Carolina's only living veteran, in June 1952. Hoping to record an authentic Rebel yell before it was too late, Workman, a committed segregationist, found the old soldier "too ill to make any effort other than a feeble 'hello.'" He subsequently discovered that the folklore section of the Library of Congress had made a previous assault on the general's vocal chords only to find its way barred by Howell's wife, who "refused to permit him to attempt the yell on the grounds that he might drop dead on the spot."[2]

Tragicomic though it was, this unsuccessful effort to recover the Civil War through the medium of one of its few survivors was symptomatic of a profound human desire to recapture a past event before all direct contact with that event vanishes with the remorseless passage of time. But William Workman was already too late. By the middle of the twentieth century, rapid modernization and the passing of the veterans had rendered the Civil War what Pierre Nora has labeled a *lieu de mémoire*. Most Americans had become so divorced from their past as a result of industrialization, urbanization, and mass immigration that the bitter conflict was no longer a genuinely felt memory—except perhaps for those in the South where, for reasons linked to the trauma of defeat, the relatively slow pace of economic development, and the desire to maintain segregation, the war continued to exert a greater pull on individuals. To a large extent the Civil War was now a value-laden memory site to be commemorated in official ritual or commodified by publishers and film studios rather than unselfconsciously remembered by ordinary people in their daily routines.

1. Edward Tabor Linenthal, *Sacred Ground: Americans and Their Battlefields* (Urbana: University of Illinois Press, 1991), 96–97.

2. William D. Workman Jr. to Luther H. Evans, June 20, 1952; Duncan Emrich to Workman, July 2, 1952, folder on "*The State*, Special Editions, The Burning of Columbia (1965—CWC), Confederate Material Gen. 1952–1969," unnumbered box, William D. Workman Jr. Papers, Modern Political Collections, South Caroliniana Library, University of South Carolina.

After surging in the late nineteenth and early twentieth centuries, popular interest in the Civil War waned in the 1920s as a consequence of the mass killing on the western front during World War I. However, in the next decade the nation's past offered Americans both a source of inspiration in the difficult present and a means of legitimizing the kind of change deemed necessary for a better future. Margaret Mitchell's novel, *Gone with the Wind,* an adept fusion of the plantation myth and Lost Cause advocacy, sold a million copies within six months of its publication in June 1936.[3] Readers identified with the central character, Scarlett O'Hara, a compound of Old South belle and New (South) Woman whose struggles mirrored not only those of her war-torn homeland but also those of Depression-era Americans. The book's message of deliverance through adversity reached an even wider domestic audience after Metro-Goldwyn-Mayer (MGM) released David O. Selznick's more racially liberal film version in 1939.[4] The book and the movie contributed to a growing audience for Civil War–era history, as did Douglas Southall Freeman's magisterial four-volume biography of Robert E. Lee (1934–38) and Carl Sandburg's widely read *Abraham Lincoln: The War Years* (1939), which depicted the martyred president as a model leader for a democracy in troubled times.

It is likely that the country's involvement in modern conflicts also stimulated grassroots interest in the events of the 1860s. Viewed as a positive experience by some Americans, the "good war" of 1941–45 against Germany and Japan fueled the popularity of military history in the United States. The concomitant impulse during the early stages of the cold war toward domestic consensus and 100-percent Americanism intensified the popular thirst for knowledge about the Blue and the Gray. Renewed prosperity not only helped to increase the readership for Civil War literature of all kinds but also contributed to the growth of automobile tourism in the late 1940s and 1950s. During this period growing numbers of American families visited the country's national parks to immerse themselves in scenic grandeur and authentic representations of their past. Civil War battlefields such as Gettysburg, Shiloh, and Vicksburg administered by the National Park Service witnessed an unprecedented surge in visitors—so strong, in fact, that by the mid-1950s Conrad

---

3. Jim Cullen, *The Civil War in Popular Culture: A Reusable Past* (Washington, DC: Smithsonian Institution Press, 1995), 67.

4. An estimated 120 million Americans had seen *Gone with the Wind* by the end of World War II. Bruce Chadwick, *The Reel Civil War: Mythmaking in American Film* (New York: Alfred A. Knopf, 2001), 187. On Selznick's attempts to render Mitchell's "absolution for the South" as inoffensive as possible to northerners and blacks, see ibid., 194–99.

L. Wirth, a former landscape architect who headed the NPS, responded to the new demand by seeking substantial increases in his agency's budget.[5]

Americans who wanted to sustain their interest in the Civil War could do more than simply read a book or visit battlefields. They could attend a meeting of their nearest Civil War round table. These lecture and discussion groups provided much of the impetus for an official centennial commemoration. The first chapter was founded in Chicago in 1940. The members were professionals who came from as far away as Texas and New Mexico to attend monthly meetings at the city's venerable University Club. By 1948 the group numbered 150 enthusiasts.[6] They included Ralph G. Newman, a dapper Chicago bookdealer; Carl Haverlin, a Lincoln buff who headed Broadcast Music Inc. in New York City; a local chemist-businessman and iconoclastic author, Otto Eisenschiml; the Lincoln bard Carl Sandburg; and several prominent historians including Lee's biographer Douglas Southall Freeman, Frank E. Vandiver of Rice Institute in Houston, and the leading revisionist Avery O. Craven of the University of Chicago.[7] Most rank-and-file members were not academics but professional businessmen (such as Monroe F. Cockrell of the Continental Illinois Bank) with an interest in the Civil War. The round table movement expanded rapidly throughout the United States after World War II. Around forty groups existed by 1958, three-quarters of them in the South and Midwest.[8] Like the Chicago original, they were predominantly urban and proved especially attractive to white male professionals, many of whom had served recently in the U.S. armed forces. Typically, members would meet every month to hear a

---

5. After declining during the Great Depression and World War II, the number of tourists visiting Gettysburg National Military Park rose from 659,000 in 1950 to 756,000 by 1956. Shiloh witnessed an increase of nearly 165,000 between 1954 and 1956. Jim Weeks, *Gettysburg: Memory, Market, and an American Shrine* (Princeton: Princeton University Press, 2003), 124; "Tabulation of Visitors to Areas Administered by the National Park Service," 1955, 1957, in folder on "National Park Service," box 27, subject files 1957–66, Records of the Civil War Centennial Commission, Records of the National Park Service, Record Group 79, National Archives (hereafter CWCCR).

6. *Chicago Sunday Tribune,* clipping, May 29, 1948, microfilm 1115, frames 683–84, reel 1, Stanley F. Horn Papers, Tennessee Historical Society Collections, Tennessee State Library and Archives.

7. Apart from Sandburg, Otto Eisenschiml was probably the most well known of these buffs. He had gained renown in 1937 by claiming in his *Why Lincoln Was Murdered* that U.S. Secretary of War Edwin Stanton had masterminded Lincoln's assassination. For an astute history of this ridiculous but influential thesis, see William Hanchett, *The Lincoln Murder Conspiracies* (Urbana: University of Illinois Press, 1986), 158–248.

8. Boyd B. Stutler, ed., "Notes and Queries," *Civil War History* 4 (1958): 199.

Civil War lecture (normally one with a military emphasis) and discuss recent books on the conflict. The New York round table, founded in 1950, proclaimed itself open to "everyone who shares an appreciation of and respect for the singular American qualities of conviction, rugged determination, and loyalty which so marked the majority of Union and Confederate soldiers during the furious tides of a Civil War." Active members who paid the requisite $10 fee ($5 for out-of-town residents) were presented in 1956–57 with a program that included talks by two of its own: Professor Allan Nevins of Columbia University on "A Realistic View of the Civil War Soldier as a Fighter" and Bruce Catton, a fellow historian, on "New Thoughts on the Civil War."[9]

Other evidence of what Edward Tabor Linenthal has called "a distinct Civil War subculture" was not hard to find.[10] The North-South Skirmish Association, an early battle reenactment group, was set up in 1950.[11] Five years later Ralph Newman founded the Civil War Book Club to give readers expert guidance on the rapidly growing output of relevant historical scholarship and provide authors with an even larger constituency for their work. "Popular interest in the Civil War, the Confederacy and the colorful personalities of the period," contended an early press release for the book club, "has been accelerated as new literature continues to appear, and even ardent enthusiasts are sometimes uncertain which books to buy."[12] Within a year Newman could boast some of America's most famous names among his 2,142 members, the most eye-catching being President Dwight D. Eisenhower, former presidents Harry S. Truman and Herbert Hoover, and Democratic idol Adlai E. Stevenson.[13] Whether any of these political grandees subscribed to *Civil War History*, the first specialized academic journal of its kind which also made its debut in 1955, is unclear.

Given the abundance of interest in the Civil War manifested by these initiatives, it was hardly surprising that the approaching centenary of secession

9. "The Civil War Round Table of New York, Inc.: Its History, Programs and Membership 1956–1957" (n.p., n.d.), folder on "Civil War Roundtable of New York," box 6, Records of the New Jersey Civil War Centennial Commission, New Jersey State Archives.

10. Linenthal, *Sacred Ground*, 98.

11. "General Information & Fact Sheet, North-South Skirmish Assoc., Inc." in folder on "North-South Skirmish," box 90, subject files 1957–66, CWCCR.

12. Civil War Book Club, undated press release encl. in Ralph G. Newman to Stanley F. Horn, July 11, 1955, frame 768, reel 1, Horn Papers.

13. Newman, "An Informal Report to the Stockholders of the Civil War Book Club, Inc.," n.d., folder on "Civil War Book Club," box 184, Bell I. Wiley Papers, Manuscript, Archives, and Rare Book Library, Emory University.

led many people to invoke the need for a formal commemoration. Prominent among those calling for such an event were the Civil War Centennial Association (CWCA) and the Civil War Round Table of the District of Columbia.

Incorporated in 1953 and based at an address on New York's Fifth Avenue, the CWCA was a small, nonprofit organization designed to function as "a vehicle for properly celebrating" the Civil War centennial.[14] Its avowed aim was not to control centennial proceedings but to act as "a general forum" for coordination in some fields and stimulation in others. Although little was heard of this group until Carl Haverlin announced its plans at the annual conference of the Southern Historical Association in Memphis in November 1955, the membership was a select one.[15] Important figures in the Chicago round table numbered among its leading lights, notably Haverlin (who served as president), Ralph Newman, and Carl Sandburg.[16]

Well-known historians of "the middle period" also belonged to the CWCA. They included Allan Nevins, Bruce Catton, and Bell Irvin Wiley, each of whom would play a major role in subsequent events. Significantly, the three men shared an interest in the wider dissemination of what they regarded as good scholarly history. Nevins, a gray-haired journalist-turned-academic, was one of the most distinguished historians of his generation. Born in Illinois and an active member of the Democratic party, he remained a prolific writer despite the fact that he was now approaching retirement from his position at Columbia University. His commitment to the development of an educated public in the United States prompted his decision to chair the Society of American Historians (SAH), a group of around 400 professional historians and writers dedicated to this end. The cold war import of the SAH was evident in its plans for a history agency to pool and disseminate historical scholarship for the majority of Americans seeking meaning and stability in their lives. "An

14. CWCA certificate of incorporation and by-laws, encl. in Carl Haverlin to Horn, Sept. 2, 1955, frame 31, reel 2, Horn Papers.

15. James W. Silver, "The Twenty-First Annual Meeting," *Journal of Southern History* 22 (1956), 62. The 1955 SHA conference was notable for "one of the most dramatic gatherings in the history of the Association"—a tense "integrated" evening session devoted to the subject of school desegregation. African-American educator Benjamin Mays insisted, to intermittent applause, that blacks would struggle ceaselessly for legal equality. The novelist William Faulkner, back from a world tour sponsored by the U.S. State Department, declared that opposing equality on racial grounds was "like living in Alaska and being against snow" and stressed the significance of civil rights in the propaganda war against communism (60–61).

16. See undated CWCA prospectus in folder on "General Correspondence, 1958," box 184, Wiley Papers.

enlightened citizenry," proclaimed a draft prospectus in March 1953, "is democracy's greatest strength. In this country, with its unparalleled facilities for mass communication, adult education is possible on a large scale; moreover, there is an increasing demand for books, articles and programs with depth and quality. Above all, many people are hungry for guidance, for orientation, since the very confusion of these times leads to the asking of questions and a search for understanding."[17]

Fifty-five-year-old Bruce Catton, like Nevins a midwesterner by birth and a journalist by training, was a thoughtful, gifted communicator and perhaps the country's best-known chronicler of the Civil War in the mid-twentieth century. He was better placed than any college professor to garner public attention for his writings, being senior editor of *American Heritage,* a magazine of popular history founded in 1954 under the partial sponsorship of the SAH. His reputation was cemented the same year when *A Stillness at Appomattox,* the final elegiac volume of his "Army of the Potomac" trilogy, won a Pulitzer Prize and the National Book Award for nonfiction.

The tall, bespectacled southern academic Bell Wiley possessed a lower national profile than Nevins and Catton, but he shared the two northerners' passion for good, accessible history. Born in rural west Tennessee in 1906 and reared by strict Methodist parents in straitened economic circumstances, he had spent his youth picking cotton and absorbing stories of the Civil War told by Union and Confederate veterans (his own maternal grandfather had fought against Sherman in the Atlanta campaign).[18] After a short period as a schoolteacher, he entered higher education, eventually completing a Yale Ph.D. under Ulrich B. Phillips, then the leading authority on slavery. Subsequently, he taught at several southern colleges before being appointed to a post at Emory University in Atlanta in 1949. Wiley's hardscrabble upbringing gave him a genuine empathy for common folk. He was a popular teacher who believed that "[m]any people of lowly background potentially are great people and if given an opportunity through education can reach their potential."[19] His published work was characterized by an attention to the role that ordinary Americans, black as well as white, had played in the nation's history.

17. The Society of American Historians, Inc., "Prospectus for the History Agency," March 1953, folder 1, box 72, Allan Nevins Papers, Rare Book and Manuscript Library, Columbia University. The SAH was founded in 1939.

18. For biographical details on Wiley, see *The Bell Irvin Wiley Reader,* ed. Hill Jordan, James I. Robertson Jr., and J. H. Segars (Baton Rouge: Louisiana State University Press, 2001), 1–16.

19. Ibid., 5.

Rivaling the CWCA as a source of centennial planning, the District of Columbia round table made up in energy what it lacked in academic prestige. One of the most successful discussion groups of its kind, with a membership composed largely of metropolitan businessmen and federal employees, the 500-member Washington organization owed much of its dynamism to Karl Sawtelle Betts. A leading figure in centennial affairs, Betts was born in small-town Kansas in April 1892. Having attended high school in Abilene and St. Louis and received an A.B. degree from the University of Michigan in 1914, he briefly taught journalism back home in Kansas and, after being wounded while serving in the American Expeditionary Force during World War I, forged a career in public relations. In 1933 he moved to suburban Maryland as an employee of the National Association of Dyers and Cleaners and from 1936 onward was a freelance writer engaged in publicity and advertising as well as the representative of investment firms in Baltimore and New York. His relocation to the Upper South appears to have spurred his interest in the Civil War, for he was a founding member of Washington's round table in January 1951. He quickly established himself as one of the most prominent and effective leaders of the drive for a government body that would take charge of centennial proceedings—his efforts aided by the fact that he was a boyhood friend of President Eisenhower and a conservative Republican with a proven record of corporate fundraising. He regarded himself as a "can-do" businessman capable of marketing the centennial to the American people in the service of cold war nationalism. "His idealism was simply indigenous patriotism," remarked one sympathetic observer after his death, "—patriotism not for a State, not for a section, but for the concept of America as a whole."[20]

Betts was no less eager to mark the hundredth anniversary of the Civil War than the historians belonging to the CWCA. On August 17, 1956, he was present with several other District of Columbia round table members, including Ulysses S. Grant III, at a meeting to create a special committee to press for the establishment of a federal centennial agency. Betts then invited representatives from other interested parties to gather at the Army and Navy Club on October 9. There he revealed plans for a nineteen-member federal commission responsible for planning the centennial in cooperation with assorted state organizations, civic bodies, and historical groups. To be endowed with

20. Victor Gondos Jr., "Karl S. Betts and the Civil War Centennial Commission," *Military Affairs* 27 (1963): 60. For extensive biographical details, in all likelihood prepared by Betts himself, see "Karl S. Betts" in folder on "Commission Staff—Commission Members," box 184, Wiley Papers.

an initial appropriation of $100,000, this agency was described as "a clearing house and information center for all programs, meetings, exercises, and projects whether instituted by members of its staff or by other groups and organizations." That this particular centennial project grew partly out of concerns over national security was apparent in a claim that one of the main purposes of the commemoration was "[t]o create and strengthen the patriotic feeling in the people of all ages in the United States."[21]

If the District of Columbia round table and the CWCA had the same fundamental objective—an adequate commemoration of the Civil War centennial—they were not in complete agreement over what form the event should take. Whereas Betts and his allies envisaged a democratic and commercialized observance that would entertain as well as educate, the CWCA favored a more sober, scholarly approach to the proceedings. Here lay not only one of the main fault-lines within what can loosely be described as the centennial coalition but also the germ of future division between the event's main supporters. Differences of emphasis were evident in the CWCA's recommendation that the centennial should be planned by a grand "seminar" attended by representatives from a range of interested public and private parties, notably state universities, state historical societies and state archives, historians, editors, and round tables. In the view of Bell Wiley this seminar should be sponsored by a respectable college such as the University of Virginia. While recognizing that participants should represent a number of different constituencies, he believed "strongly that in the interest of avoiding commercialism, commanding respect and keeping the meeting on a high level of quality and dignity, participation should be limited to those who have achieved eminence for solid contributions to the history of the period. If the doors are opened to publicity seekers, popularizers, and 'quickie' artists anxious to capitalize on current interest in the conflict, the meeting will fall short of the objectives desired."[22] Although it would be wrong to explain the tensions between the CWCA and the District of Columbia round table solely in terms of a difference of perspective between professionals and amateurs, there is no doubt that historians like Wiley anticipated a rather narrower and more dignified commemoration of the Civil War than that planned by media-savvy businessmen like Karl Betts.

21. District of Columbia Committee on Organization, "The Civil War Centennial," typewritten agenda, Oct. 9, 1956, frames 64–7, reel 2, Horn Papers.

22. Bell I. Wiley to Richard B. Harwell, April 19, 1956, folder on "General Correspondence, 1955–1957," box 184, Wiley Papers.

During late 1956 Betts sustained the momentum of the centennial drive. First, he secured broad support for the District proposal from patriotic organizations such as the SUV (which boasted nearly 6,900 members) and other round tables across the country.[23] Second, he began lobbying influential politicians in Washington in an effort to win congressional agreement for a centennial commission. At a meeting in New York City in November, the CWCA leadership backed the proposal for a federal agency, but in a move later endorsed by ordinary members, it rejected Betts's contention that an appropriation of $100,000 was an essential precondition for the preparation of a preliminary report.[24] Revealingly, Carl Haverlin noted that he looked on the Washington program as "a scheme to provide jobs for some people who are now out of work."[25] The CWCA's objections were raised at another organizational meeting that took place in the *Washington Post* auditorium on December 18. This gathering adopted a draft congressional resolution providing for the creation of a twenty-five-member national Civil War centennial commission.[26]

Those lobbying hard for an official commemoration of the Civil War were fortunate that their objectives coincided fairly closely with those of the National Park Service in the mid-1950s. Determined to respond effectively to the growth of mass tourism in the United States after World War II, Conrad Wirth and his staff pinned their hopes on securing congressional backing for their Mission 66 program, an ambitious (not to say expensive) scheme intended to improve and expand facilities in wilderness areas and at the nation's historic sites. The advent of the Civil War centennial offered the NPS useful leverage in its campaign to gain federal funding for Mission 66, and Wirth himself proposed that a government commission should be created in order to supervise commemorative activities.[27] At a staff meeting in Washington on June 11, 1956, there was general agreement that such a bill "might provide a good publicity front for the Park Service in carrying out the MISSION 66 work and that

23. Fred E. Howe to Karl S. Betts, Nov. 5, 1956, House Judiciary Subcommittee Number 4, Hearing on H.J. Res. 233 etc., May 20, 1957, folder 2, box 350, Committee on the Judiciary HR85A-D10, 85 Congress, Records of the U.S. House of Representatives, National Archives, Washington, DC (hereafter Hearing). See also Hambleton Tapp to Betts, Nov. 8, 1956, ibid.

24. Haverlin to CWCA Board of Directors, Nov. 8, Dec. 14, 1956, frame 70, reel 2, Horn Papers.

25. Haverlin to Christopher Crittenden, memo of telephone conversation, Jan. 18, 1957, frame 83, reel 2, Horn Papers.

26. Gondos, "Karl S. Betts," 53–54.

27. On Mission 66, see Alfred Runte, *National Parks: The American Experience* (Lincoln: University of Nebraska Press, 1979), 171–73.

it would provide the basis for official collaboration with the numerous State agencies which are expected to be established."[28] While the staffers decided not to introduce legislation until Congress had funded Mission 66 and were reluctant to surrender control of the centennial to private parties, it is clear that they supported Wirth's idea of setting up a government agency ("headed up within the [Interior] Department lest it take a political turn") in order to coordinate centennial events.[29]

By the spring of 1957 Congress had approved substantial funding for Mission 66, and the time was ripe for centennial promoters to make their move. Five separate proposals were introduced into the House of Representatives in the early months of the new year—four by southern members and one by Congressman Wint Smith of Kansas, a modern-day doughface.[30] The most important of these was modeled directly on the District of Columbia round table plan but also incorporated the main wishes of the NPS. It was introduced by the former Democratic governor of Virginia, Representative William M. Tuck.[31] A leading member of his state's segregationist regime, Tuck managed to have his joint resolution referred to subcommittee number four of the House Judiciary Committee headed by a Democrat, James B. Frazier of Tennessee. Frazier's five-man body then scheduled a formal hearing on all of the measures plus a joint resolution embodying the concerns of the CWCA introduced by Iowa Republican Fred Schwengel at the last minute.

When proceedings began in the Old House Office Building on May 20, discussion centered primarily on Tuck's Joint Resolution 253, which provided for the establishment of a federal commission, most of whose twenty members were to be appointed by the president, House, and Senate. This body was authorized "to prepare an overall program to include specific plans" for commemorating the Civil War centennial giving "due consideration to any similar and related plans advanced by State, civic, patriotic, hereditary, and historical bodies." The Park Service was named "general administrative agent" for the commission, and its chairman was required to call the first meeting. To ensure effective coordination of centennial events the NPS was also "authorized to

28. Roy E. Appleman to Chief Historian of the National Park Service, memorandum, June 12, 1956, in folder on "Commission Legislation," box 69, subject files 1957–66, CWCCR.

29. W. G. Carnes to Conrad L. Wirth, memorandum, June 12, 1956, folder on "Commission Legislation," box 69, subject files 1957–66, CWCCR.

30. In the antebellum period, northern Democratic politicians with southern principles were regularly referred to as "doughfaces."

31. For a biography of Tuck, see William Bryan Crawley, *Bill Tuck: A Political Life in Harry Byrd's Virginia* (Charlottesville: University Press of Virginia, 1978).

undertake as part of the Mission 66 program, the further preservation and development of such battlefields and sites, at such time and in such manner as will insure that a fitting observance may be held at each such battlefield or site as its centennial occurs during the period 1961–1965."[32] The commission was provided with an appropriation of $100,000 to allow for preparation of a preliminary report by January 1, 1958. The only other discussion concerned Schwengel's less ambitious proposal, which called for a National Conference of Historians to meet at a place selected by the CWCA no later than April 12, 1958. The delegates attending this seminar would be selected by state governors and local historical groups (including the CWCA and "several Civil War Round Tables"). Serving without pay, the historians were empowered to formulate policies for the centennial which would be delivered to the president of the United States in the form of a report prepared by the CWCA. The assembly was asked specifically to "propose and recommend to the American people standards to be observed in the conduct of such commemorative exercises, including standards of emphasis, taste and tone; as well as standards of historical evidence, its interpretation and presentation."[33]

Congressman Tuck introduced his measure as a symbol of intersectional reconciliation. It was, he said, "a powerfully important piece of legislation" that represented America "at its best." Participants and their descendants on both sides, he continued, were proud of the part each side had played in what he pointedly called "the War Between the States."[34] Representative Schwengel, an ardent admirer of Abraham Lincoln, agreed that the Civil War had to be commemorated, being "the most significant war in the history of mankind in many respects." However, he concurred with the CWCA that the centennial should not be staged at taxpayers' expense and injected a note of caution into the debate by asserting "that as we commemorate this war and matters concerned with it we should do it pretty much on reason. I see the possibility of some ugly things creeping up as a result of this, and that should be avoided."[35] Manifestly, the suggestion that professional historians should be put in charge of the planning stage was designed to reduce the possibility that, in the words of Schwengel's resolution, "angry passions, or reckless utterance, or erroneous

32. H.J. Res. 253, Feb. 27, 1957, in folder on "Commission Legislation," box 69, subject files 1957–66, CWCCR.

33. Fred Schwengel, draft of "Joint Resolution to Establish Civil War Centennial Com[m]ission," folder 1, Hearing.

34. Typewritten transcript, 5, folder 1, Hearing.

35. Ibid., 12.

assumption, or biased chronicle, or pride in partisanship (actual or vicarious), or outgrown jealousy could obscure an understanding of the nobility of motive, or the purity of purpose, or the sublimity of heroism, or the tragedy of personal sacrifice, which characterized both opposing forces on and off the field."[36]

Although Schwengel's language exhibited an awareness that the centennial might exacerbate existing North-South divisions (now reopened by the ongoing crisis over public school integration), the oral testimony threw up remarkably few hints of concern about the potential for sectional antagonism. Having requested views from interested parties, the hearing's chairman, James Frazier, did seek assurances that support for the proposal under discussion came from all parts of the country. Congressman Tuck's allies assuaged whatever fears Frazier might have had by assuring him that the centennial would be a truly national occasion. Karl Betts proclaimed that Tuck's resolution had the support of a large number of civil and patriotic groups across the United States. "[A] very wide and growing interest in the history of the Civil War" existed, he said: "It is our firm belief that the centennial recreation of the great drama of the Sixties will point up forcefully and dramatically the aspirations, the enthusiasms and the achievements of our forebears in a rededication of our will to achieve a greater American union."[37] The southern historian Robert Henry concurred. "This is a matter of national interest," he told the congressman. "After all, it was an American war. It was a war in which we are entitled to glory in the valor and achievements of the men on both sides . . . [I]t was probably the greatest event and the greatest crisis in the history of our Nation" and "the one thing which achieved national unity."[38]

Southern representatives at the hearing were vocal in their support for a national commission. All matters relating to the centennial, said Col. H. C. Harrison of the SCV, should be "strictly removed from the hands of private and/or commercial interests, parties, or individuals."[39] Implicit here was a feeling on the part of southerners that a privately financed centennial would benefit well-connected Yankees and, likely as not, result in an arrogant celebration of Union victory. The strength of patriotic sentiment (and southern influence) in Congress would ensure that any federal centennial agency would have to coordinate affairs in the national interest—which, by definition, meant

36. Schwengel, draft of "Joint Resolution," folder 1, Hearing.
37. Typewritten transcript, 17, folder 1, Hearing.
38. Ibid., 19.
39. Ibid., 21.

granting full recognition to southern historical memory. This point was made more explicitly by Virgil Carrington ("Pat") Jones, a Virginia segregationist and amateur historian who worked as manager of the Washington bureau of the giant Curtis Publishing Company. The impending "pageant," he stated, would be "the greatest America has ever had." While local planning could be left to ordinary people, Congress must exercise overall control in order to ensure "a national celebration." He had, he continued pointedly, only recently heard of the CWCA and understood that it was based in the North.[40]

While Tuck, Betts, and their predominantly southern allies spoke of the need for a federally funded commemoration, the CWCA representatives at the hearing pressed their case for a centennial run by professional organizations such as the American Historical Association and the Southern Historical Association. Allan Nevins, the highly respected president of the SAH, was unable to be present in Washington, but he had already notified the subcommittee that he aligned himself with the CWCA position on Tuck's measure. "We wish a dignified and effective observance of the centenary of the Civil War," he wrote, "free from any taint of unnecessary expense or any reproach of duplication of activity." CWCA president Carl Haverlin, who did attend the hearing, reiterated his organization's view that holding a national assembly of historians would allow "experts" to prepare a preliminary plan of action without the need for a hefty congressional appropriation.[41] Support for this position came from Clyde Walton, the Illinois state historian, and another CWCA member, Ralph Newman of Chicago's Civil War Book Club. Like Walton and Haverlin, Newman agreed that the centennial could be privately financed—indeed, he alluded to the successful Lincoln centennial of 1909 to show that this was entirely possible. However, he added to his argument the belief that "there is some danger of a partisan feeling developing from trying to do too many of these things nationally. I think that some states might resent too active participation by a federal body in their own observation. It might become a matter of state's rights."[42]

Although Newman declined to articulate any concerns he might have had about civil rights issues, it is clear that such worries lay behind his comments at the hearing. Away from the gaze of white supremacists like Tuck and Jones, he was prepared to be more specific. "I wonder," he wrote to Emanuel Celler, the Brooklyn Democrat who chaired the House Judiciary Committee,

40. Ibid., 52–53.

41. Allan Nevins to [James B. Frazier], May 17, 1957, folder 2, Hearing; typewritten transcript, 45–46, folder 1, Hearing.

42. Ibid., 43.

on June 5, "... if there is a realization of the problems that might confront a federal commission. The same people who might be enthusiastic over a commemoration of the 100th anniversary of the battle of Gettysburg might frown on a similar commemoration of the 100th anniversary of the issuance of the Emancipation Proclamation and vice versa."[43] Newman's prescience, however, appears to have had little impact on the politicians who now decided the fate of the various proposals.

Tuck's measure received the assent of the Judiciary Committee with a number of significant amendments and was read to the House on August 19. As amended it still provided for the creation of a federal centennial commission authorized to coordinate observances under the auspices of the NPS. The membership, however, was reduced to eighteen, two of whom were to come from the Department of Defense, and the $100,000 appropriation was limited to "both the planning and the execution" of the entire program.[44] The main amendment in the committee of the whole reflected a desire to incorporate the concerns of the CWCA. This was Fred Schwengel's motion that a national assembly of "civic, patriotic, and historical groups" was to meet no later than mid-January 1958 to make recommendations to the commission "for the most fitting and appropriate way to commemorate" the Civil War centennial. The House concurred in Tuck's amended joint resolution and passed the measure without a recorded vote.[45]

Two days later Joseph O'Mahoney reported the joint resolution from the Senate Judiciary Committee with only minor changes. The Wyoming Democrat described the initiative as "very meritorious" and emphasized both its national scope and its educative function in the bipolar world of the cold war. "The purpose of the observance of this great schism between our people," he stated reassuringly, "is not to stress that which divides us but rather to reaffirm that which unites us—the basic desire for unity, liberty, freedom, and self-government." In case anyone was in danger of missing the point, he added that a commission should be created in order to remind Americans how the nation passed through the crisis of 1861–65 "and how out of that crisis was forged the unity of this country which is so much the envy and, it is hoped,

43. Newman to Emanuel Celler, June 5, 1957, folder 2, Hearing.

44. 85th Congress, 1st Session, House of Representatives Report 650, "Commemorating the 100th Anniversary of the Civil War," June 27, 1957, in folder on "Commission Legislation," box 69, subject files 1957–66, CWCCR.

45. *Congressional Record*, 85th Congress, 1st Session, 15185–15186. Support for the centennial measure was bipartisan and non-sectional, *New York Times*, June 9, 1957, sec. 10, 13.

the ideal of the rest of the world." [46] Once the House had agreed to changes made by the Senate (the main alteration was an increase in the size of the federal commission from eighteen to twenty-five), Tuck's joint resolution creating the Civil War Centennial Commission was signed into law by President Eisenhower on September 7. [47]

Two weeks later Arkansas governor Orval E. Faubus moved to obstruct court-ordered school desegregation in Little Rock, thereby inducing Eisenhower to dispatch the 101st Airborne Division to the city in order to protect black schoolchildren from angry crowds of segregationists. Like most hard-liners, William Tuck—perhaps the chief proponent of the centennial in Congress—was appalled by the president's action. It could, he wrote, only "serve to solidify our people in opposition to the Court decision [Brown] and the tyranny to which we are now being subjected." [48] For a commemoration that was intended to bring Americans together, this was hardly an auspicious beginning.

THE COMMISSION TAKES CHARGE

The passage of Public Law 85-305 represented a victory for the amateur enthusiasts of the District of Columbia round table and southern supporters of a national bureau that would take proper account of their Confederate heritage. However, neither grouping wielded significant influence over the appointing process that took place in late 1957. Karl Betts's organization submitted a list of desirable appointees to the federal commission. It included several leading southern senators who had been supportive of the centennial project, notably Richard Russell of Georgia and James O. Eastland of Mississippi. Not one of these conservative politicians was given a place on the agency. "All of our group," Betts informed Congressman Tuck angrily, "were greatly disappointed and chagrined" at this snub. "It is a damn shame that after doing all of the work, that our recommendations should not be followed and that we now find ourselves at the mercy of a political gang who see nothing in this tremendous program." [49] Rumors later circulated that the White House chief of staff, ex-

---

46. 85th Congress, 1st Session, Senate Report 1076, "Civil War Centennial Commission," Aug. 21, 1957, folder on "Commission Legislation," box 69, subject files 1957–66, CWCCR.

47. *New York Times*, Sept. 8, 1957, 46; 85th Congress, 1st Session, Public Law 85-305 (H.J. Res. 253), Sept. 7, 1957, in folder on "Commission Legislation," box 69, subject files 1957–66, CWCCR.

48. William M. Tuck to E. L. Forrester, Dec. 25, 1957, folder 5263, William M. Tuck Papers, Special Collections, Earl Gregg Swem Library, College of William and Mary.

49. Betts to Tuck, Dec. 2, 1957, folder 5263, Tuck Papers.

New Hampshire governor Sherman Adams, had vetoed the recommendations of the Betts group.[50]

The appointees (announced from Eisenhower's home at Gettysburg in early December) were a motley collection of businessmen, professional historians, round table representatives, and politicians. The president's ten members were the retired super-patriot General Grant; Consuelo N. Bailey, a former Republican lieutenant governor of Vermont; Alvin L. Aubinoe, a Bethesda builder; W. Norman Fitzgerald, a Milwaukee ink manufacturer and prominent round table member; William S. Paley, the chairman of CBS television in New York; Aksel Nielsen, a Denver businessman; and four Civil War scholars—Bruce Catton, Bell Wiley, Avery Craven, and John A. Krout. Senators Clinton P. Anderson (D-NM), Joseph O'Mahoney (D-WY), John W. Bricker (R-OH), and Edward Martin (R-PA) received their appointment from Vice President Richard Nixon, while Congressmen William Tuck (D-VA), Wint Smith (R-KA), Fred Schwengel (R-IA), and Frank M. Coffin (D-ME) made up the House contingent. Two Department of Defense representatives, Assistant Secretary of the Army Dewey Short and Vice Admiral Stuart H. Ingersoll of the Naval War College in Newport, Rhode Island, and two statutory members, Conrad Wirth of the NPS and David C. Mearns, representing the librarian of Congress, made up the rest of the acting committee. Eisenhower, Nixon, and the speaker of the House were named as ex officio members.[51] While only a handful of the appointees—notably Wiley, Tuck, and Craven—were southerners, the apparent sectional imbalance was misleading. The northerners on the commission were cold war patriots broadly sympathetic to southern concerns and, in some cases, just as fearful as any segregationist that the centennial might fall into the hands of dangerous radicals. The commission, right-wing congressman Wint Smith of Kansas told Bill Tuck, "could do a lot of damage to the cause you and I so firmly support—namely States Rights. I am determined that no left wing group is going to run off with this 'show.'"[52] (Among those Smith probably had in mind as undesirable was Bell Wiley, a Georgia liberal known to be opposed to bitter-end segregationists.) The conservatives, moreover, won an important victory at the first meeting of the centennial commission, which took place on December 20, 1957.

Hosted by Conrad Wirth, the meeting's first major business was to elect a chairman. Congressman Tuck nominated General Grant for the position—a

50. Tuck to Virgil C. Jones, June 4, 1959, folder 5268, Tuck Papers.

51. *Civil War History* 4 (1958): 197–98.

52. Wint Smith to Tuck, Dec. 12, 1957, folder 5263, Tuck Papers.

move that was seconded by Bruce Catton and passed unanimously. A veteran U.S. Army officer who had served his country with distinction in Cuba, Mexico, and two world wars, Grant would head the CWCC for the next three and a half years. Described by Michael Kammen as "a well-meaning yet insensitive and not very energetic traditionalist," the elderly patrician had already completed two terms as head of the SUV and had only just acceded to the position of commander-in-chief of the Loyal Legion. Such patriotic credentials combined with his impressive lineage to make him an obvious choice to head the commission.[53] As well as being a fierce defender of his grandfather's reputation, he was married to the daughter of Elihu Root, the well-known and phenomenally wealthy Progressive-era politician, and correctly reputed to be a staunch defender of American values.[54] Notwithstanding his Yankee roots, the general's right-wing political views made him a natural ally for southern conservatives like William Tuck. An inveterate opponent of communism, Grant shared the late senator Joseph McCarthy's belief that the republic was under perpetual threat from subversives and seldom hesitated to make known his views. Determined to "have no infiltration of Communists," he counseled against the appointment of labor leader Walter Reuther to the CWCC's advisory council. "So many of us think him subversive and having a bad influence against the best interests of our country," he warned Karl Betts in July 1958, "that his appointment would leave a very bad taste in the mouths of many good citizens."[55] In a draft forward to a book by Edwin C. Bearss on his grandfather's Vicksburg campaign, he gratuitously advised readers that "[a] more thorough study of American history will make you proud to be an American even though we know there are bad and criminal Americans about us today."[56]

53. Michael Kammen, *Mystic Chords of Memory: The Transformation of Tradition in American Culture* (New York: Alfred A. Knopf, 1991), 592.

54. For a characteristically stalwart defense of the Union commander, see Ulysses S. Grant III, "Civil War: Fact and Fiction," *Civil War History* 2 (June 1956): 29–40. A capsule biography of General Grant can be found in *Who's Who in America*, vol. 31, 1960–61 (Chicago, 1961), 1130.

55. Ulysses S. Grant III to Betts, July 31, 1958, in folder on "Grant, General U.S., Office Memos 1958," box 133, subject files 1957–66, CWCCR.

56. Grant, draft foreword to Edwin C. Bearss, *Decision in Mississippi: Mississippi's Important Role in the War Between the States* (Jackson: University Press of Mississippi, 1962), in folder on "U.S. Grant III," box 712, Records of the Mississippi Commission on the War Between the States, Record Group 19, Mississippi Department of Archives and History (hereafter MCWBTSR). The published version omitted the reference to "bad and criminal Americans" on the advice of Sidney T. Roebuck, head of the Mississippi commission. Bearss, *Decision*, vii; Roebuck to Grant, Feb. 13, 1961, folder on "U.S. Grant III," box 712, MCWBTSR.

One of the main reasons he so strongly favored an official commemoration of the Civil War was his conviction that it would serve the ongoing struggle against totalitarianism. Writing to the House subcommittee in support of Tuck's joint resolution in May 1957, Grant had asked, "[W]hat better lesson in patriotism and self-sacrifice for a cause can be given to our children of today and future generations than to teach them what Americans did in those days of crisis and greatness? We today cannot do better than to emulate the patriotism and ready self-sacrifice of the men and women who fought that war."[57]

If General Grant was an obvious choice to head the commission, he was also a poor one—not so much because of his age (he labored rather more vigorously for the commission than Kammen implies) but because his inflexible right-wing views rendered him incapable of presiding over a genuinely inclusive national pageant at a time when the country was undergoing rapid social change. Of course this process was barely discernible at the end of 1957: the civil rights movement had not yet taken to the streets in earnest; American women were still constrained by the effects of domestic containment; and significant numbers of white students had not yet embraced a culture of protest. Judged by the ideological climate of his age, Grant's views were by no means unrepresentative—indeed, what is striking about them today is how uncontroversial they appear to have been even to intelligent historians like Bruce Catton and Bell Wiley. But there was in his past at least one incident that might have given some people cause for concern. In 1949 the radical journalist I. F. Stone had publicly criticized Grant, then chairman of the National Park and Planning Commission, for helping Washington real estate interests perpetuate segregation laws in the capital at a time when even the U.S. government, long a bulwark of Jim Crow, had begun to recognize that the institution was becoming a national embarrassment.[58] Along with his predilection toward anti-Semitism, Grant's lack of interest in, and understanding of, the condition of African Americans would eventually help derail the centennial in which he so firmly believed.

Having elected Grant as its chairman, the CWCC sought to impart momentum to the centennial project. With only three years to plan the inaugural events there was no time to waste. The agency's immediate focus was the statutory national convention scheduled to be held in Washington on January 14–15, 1958. Concerns that this event should set the proper tone for the centennial were very much in evidence at the inaugural meeting of the commission in

---

57. Grant to James B. Frazier, May 15, 1957, folder 1, Hearing.
58. Kammen, *Mystic Chords*, 592.

December and were explicit in Senator Joseph O'Mahoney's statement that the new agency should "impart to the Centennial a tone that would emphasize the great goals of peace and freedom that underlay the Civil War, rather than its divisive aspects."[59] A total of 131 delegates attended the national assembly, which convened at short notice in the Interior Department auditorium in Washington. They represented a wide range of civic organizations, including the SCV, SUV, UDC, Jewish War Veterans, the American Legion, assorted Civil War round tables, and various national, state, and local historical groups. Even if it was not quite the grand scholarly seminar that the CWCA had once envisaged, the assembly nonetheless served O'Mahoney's purpose by emphasizing the patriotic, consensual nature of the coming commemoration.

Bell Wiley delivered the keynote address on January 14. The energetic southern historian propounded the official line on the centennial (heavily rooted in the orthodox interpretation of the Civil War) and in doing so powerfully recommended the event to the doubters in his own region. The CWCC, he told the delegates, hoped "earnestly to avoid any sort of activity that will tend to revive the bitterness and hatred engendered by the conflict of a century ago." The Civil War, he said, "was a time of supreme greatness for both the North and South—and for the American nation." Thus there would be no attempt to hold a sectional or partisan pageant: "The war was America's greatest experience and the centennial commemoration of it should be an American activity, an American ceremonial, recognizing the sincerity of both contestants and glorifying in the greatness that they demonstrated in support of their respective causes."

Wiley contended that the most appropriate way to commemorate the conflict was to determine what he called "the true facts" about it, chiefly by collecting and disseminating original documents and compiling new bibliographies. He told the assembly that the CWCC saw its role in terms of "stimulation and help": "We could not mastermind this vast and important program if we wished to do so. But it is not our desire, in any exclusive or arbitrary fashion, to tell the people or their agencies what they shall do. Rather it is our aim and hope to help them do what they think needs to be done and coordinate their desires and efforts to the best interest of all."[60] The centennial then was to be a largely decentralized event (it could hardly be otherwise in view

59. CWCC, minutes of the meeting held Dec. 20, 1957, folder on "Minutes—Commission Meetings Agenda, etc," box 184, Wiley Papers.

60. Wiley, CWCC first national assembly, introductory remarks, Jan. 14, 1958, folder on "Wiley—Speeches at National Assembly and Elsewhere," box 184, Wiley Papers. Significantly this speech was later reprinted in the *United Daughters of the Confederacy Magazine* 23 (1960): 13–14, 30.

of the limited federal funding granted to the commission) and one that would lay stress on the Civil War as the supreme national experience that had given birth to the modern United States.

In line with Wiley's comments the Washington assembly passed a number of resolutions for the federal commission to consider.[61] They provided a blueprint for the centennial which was transmitted in the form of a report by General Grant to Congress in late February 1958. The agency prefaced the recommendations with the unashamedly presentist statement that the Civil War had preserved "the American Union as an instrumentality of freedom for all the peoples of the world." The centennial, it read, must be based on "a broad knowledge of the underlying facts," constituting "a new study of American patriotism—a study which should give us a deeper understanding of the immense resources of bravery, of sacrifice and of idealism which lie in the American character." The recommendations spoke to the need for a genuinely grassroots commemoration. The CWCC was directed, first, to "[e]ncourage States and localities to organize for themselves observances of the anniversaries of Civil War events with which they were especially concerned. Such observances should not be directed from Washington; they should spring into being in response to the wish of the people in each political subdivision." The commission was also mandated to assist local plans when requested, establish a historical section "to make correct replies" to any questions, prepare a chronological list of events as an aid for local bodies, support the NPS's Mission 66 program of battlefield improvements, encourage the collection of Civil War materials, and disseminate historical information to schools, colleges, museums, libraries, historical societies, and federal government offices. For evidence that the experts were not in full control of affairs, professional historians needed to look no further than the suggestion that the commission would consistently "strive for Centennial activities that are varied, informative and interesting, for it believes that artistry and entertainment will serve along with scholarship to enhance the inspirational values associated with the Civil War." [62]

Once these broad policy decisions had been sent to Capitol Hill, it was left for the commission itself to implement the several recommendations. While

61. For a transcript of the assembly's meetings, see "Digest of Action taken by the Civil War Commission[,] January 14–15[,] 1958 [i]n the Interior Department Auditorium[,] Washington, DC," folder on "National Assembly Booklet," box 48, subject files 1957–66, CWCCR.

62. Grant to the Speaker of the House of Representatives and the Vice President, Feb. 28, 1958, frames 18–20, reel 2, Horn Papers.

the CWCC hosted a national assembly during each year of its existence, basic policy was set by the full commission or, more often, its smaller executive committee. Day-to-day control was exercised by a salaried executive director in conjunction with his small staff quartered in offices at 700 Jackson Place in Washington, DC. The individual appointed to this strategically vital post was Karl Betts, chairman of the District's round table. In October 1957 Betts had written to Conrad Wirth advising him that the next six months should be devoted "to selling" the centennial across the country. It would be wise, he urged, to develop contacts with leading business organizations, especially those involved in the travel industry. Above all else, the man appointed as executive director "should be a super-salesman, first of all."[63] At the start of this communication Betts took care to note his substantial experience in publicity and advertising. It would have been difficult for the NPS director to avoid the conclusion that his correspondent had himself in mind for the vacant post.

In fact, while Karl Betts was a strong candidate for executive director because of his business expertise and formative role in the creation of the CWCC, his name was not considered by an ad hoc search committee set up by the commission in the winter of 1957–58. Chaired by Professor T. Harry Williams of Louisiana State University, the committee initially came up with the names of three possible appointees: historians Bell Wiley, Holman Hamilton, and Edwin B. Coddington. After taking advice from Frank Vandiver at Rice, however, Williams told Grant that it was unlikely that any of these eminent scholars would want to spend more than a year away from their research to serve as executive director. He recommended the appointment of Georgian Richard B. Harwell, a Civil War specialist working in Chicago. "As you may or may not know," he informed Grant, "there has been quite an undercurrent of criticism in the South of the lack of Southern representation on the Commission." Giving the job to Harwell "would go far to stall this criticism and please groups in the South the Commission will want to work with."[64]

Williams's advice was ignored. Grant, Tuck, and Wint Smith convened as the agency's executive committee in March 1958 and handed the post of executive director to Karl Betts. This would prove to be a critical decision. It was another blow to the notion (held mainly by historians) that the centennial should be first and foremost a solemn, educational event. Betts was no

63. Betts to Wirth, Oct. 31, 1957, folder on "Suggestions on Organization of Civil War Centennial Commission," box 138, subject files 1957–66, CWCCR.

64. T. Harry Williams to Grant, Feb. 25, 1958, folder on "Commission Staff—Commission Members," box 184, Wiley Papers.

scholar and conceived of the centennial as a grand pageant that would genuinely excite Americans of all ages and in all parts of the country. As David Glassberg has shown, the United States possessed a solid tradition of historical pageantry. Seeking "the illusion of consensus through mass participation," Progressive-era civic elites had sought to promote and legitimize change by involving ordinary people in a compelling array of colorful, scripted dramas.[65] Pageantry was in retreat by 1960, but showman Betts was keen to translate this community-level tradition onto a national stage. It would not do, he thought, for his commission to purvey stuffy academic history that no one would read. Instead it must attempt to mobilize patriotic Americans with an irresistible range of properly marketed entertainments.

Once appointed to his new post, Betts joined Grant in the immediate task of making the CWCC function effectively as a coordinating body for the upcoming centennial. As well as procuring appointments to the large advisory committee that would contribute toward planning, they worked to secure the creation of separate state commissions that would guarantee a broadly based pageant. Their continuing organizational efforts highlighted not only the cold war underpinnings of the entire centennial project but also the restricted nature of their "national" vision.

MOBILIZING THE PEOPLE

Starting in the spring of 1958, the newly organized CWCC labored with some success to turn the dream of a popular centennial observance into a reality. As Terence Bell has suggested, the cold war was, certainly from an American perspective, "above all a war of ideas and ideologies, of psychology and propaganda."[66] From the late 1940s onward, American political, professional, and managerial elites recognized culture as a significant weapon in the crusade against communism, not least because of its capacity, both potential and actual, to mobilize ordinary citizens in the fight for freedom. Even though red-blooded patriots assumed that American values were superior to those of the eastern bloc, they could not take it for granted that civilians at home were steeled for the urgent task at hand, particularly in the new era of material plenty. At the national and local levels, elites—liberal and conservative—

---

65. David Glassberg, *American Historical Pageantry: The Uses of Tradition in the Early Twentieth Century* (Chapel Hill: University of North Carolina Press, 1990), 2.

66. Terence Bell, "The Politics of Social Science in Postwar America," in Lary May, ed., *Recasting America: Culture and Politics in the Age of Cold War* (Chicago: University of Chicago Press, 1989), 82.

turned to history as an antidote to what Richard Fried calls "flaccid citizenship."[67] Projects like the Freedom Train, a collection of original documents including the Declaration of Independence and the Constitution which crisscrossed the country to great acclaim between 1947 and 1949, were designed to arouse the people by strengthening their attachment to national values that were putatively shared by all Americans. Herein lay the principal flaw in the strategy. The dominant conformist culture of the 1950s was hegemonic in the sense that it connected most Americans (who were consumers as well as citizens) to elites whose power, influence, and status were rooted in the corporate-capitalist system. However, because culture is always a pliable product of innumerable daily struggles and negotiations between institutions, social groups, and individuals, it could never be wholly uniform. Governing elites at every level of America's plural society were not unaware of this problem and strove hard to suppress, marginalize, or ignore the awkward views of certain subgroups (particularly those who lacked power) in the pursuit of domestic consensus. The Civil War centennial, envisaged by many of its supporters as a subtle contribution to civil defense, revealed the strengths and weaknesses of culture, specifically historical memory, as a weapon of war.

Having scotched the historians' vision of a predominantly scholarly event, Betts and Grant embarked on the difficult task of enthusing large numbers of their compatriots about the Civil War. Although interest in the conflict had certainly been building since the 1930s, Americans were notoriously present-minded. Thus the agency could not assume complacently that the arrival of the hundredth anniversary of secession or the attack on Fort Sumter would automatically bring the men, women, and children of the modern republic out onto the streets in celebration or commemoration of their forebears. From the very beginning, it was clear the CWCC would find it difficult to convince everyone that this was an anniversary worthy of formal acknowledgment.

Opposition to the centennial had diverse roots and emerged even before Congress finally sanctioned a federal commission. On June 8, 1957, Virginia Livingston-Hunt, a wealthy Washingtonian, wrote to Congressman Emanuel Celler introducing herself as a direct descendant of a Union war hero and protesting approval of the centennial measure by Celler's House Judiciary Committee. "We are denying ourselves needed defense," she wrote, "and also needed aid abroad for the sake of economy yet you undertake to tax us for something that is best forgotten. I have no desire to help celebrate a tragic war

---

67. Richard M. Fried, *The Russians Are Coming! The Russians Are Coming! Pageantry and Patriotism in Cold-War America* (New York: Oxford University Press, 1998), 28.

in which my grandfather Philip Kearny of New Jersey lost his life when my mother was just six months old. The South is only just recovering from northern devastation after ninety years. Congress is struggling with the problem of States Rights. That was exactly the same in 1861. The negro will just be further inflamed. What is the purpose; what is to be gained?"[68]

Many other Americans who read about the planned centennial in the national press during the late 1950s shared Livingston-Hunt's concerns that commemoration of the country's bloodiest single conflict portended only ill at a time when domestic unity was essential if the cold war were to be fought successfully and when that unity was already threatened by strife over racial integration. In March 1958, for example, a Dallas couple sent a telegram to Senator Lyndon Baines Johnson of Texas strongly opposing the centennial. "Please try," they wrote, "to stop this effort to cause further internal hate and disruption between sections and races."[69] A newspaper proprietor in Macon, Georgia, concurred. The Civil War, Peyton Anderson told General Grant, had unified the country "as it should be." He continued, "I find myself, therefore, in a frame of mind that gets to the feeling that too much Centennial celebration might again bring back a strife and build up even stronger sectional feelings than would exist if we let the historians handle the whole matter."[70] Further dissent was registered by a Delaware woman who told Grant that it seemed to her "that at this most crucial time we should be united in our beliefs and that to hold such a celebration and over a five-year period, could cause nothing but harm and hard feelings."[71] For patriotic American conservatives resident primarily, though not exclusively, in the South, news of the centennial was manifestly a cause of great concern.

Buoyed by Congress's decision in September 1958 to appropriate a maximum of $100,000 for each year of the centennial, the CWCC responded to criticism from anxious conservatives by insisting, as its supporters had done before the agency's creation, that the centennial would render the coun-

68. Virginia Livingston-Hunt to Celler, June 8, 1957, folder 2, Hearing. A distinguished division commander in the Army of the Potomac, Major General Phil Kearny was killed at Chantilly in September 1862.

69. Mr. and Mrs. W.B. Woolley to Lyndon B. Johnson, March 1, 1958, folder on "Complaints re Commission," box 69, subject files 1957–66, CWCCR.

70. Peyton Anderson to Grant, Aug. 4, 1958, box 6, folder on "Advisory Council: Georgia," subject files 1957–66, CWCCR.

71. Mrs. Pierre S. (Jane Holcomb) DuPont to Grant, Sept. 16, 1959, folder on "Complaints re Commission," box 69, subject files 1957–66, CWCCR.

try better, not less, equipped to win the ongoing ideological struggle against communism.[72] It disseminated this message in a variety of forms, principally official policy statements and public speeches and media appearances by members of the commission. The agency passed up few opportunities to emphasize its relevance in the cultural cold war by linking the events of the past directly to the exigencies of the present.

On April 16, 1959, delegates to the second national assembly of the CWCC in Richmond heard Assistant Secretary of the Army Dewey Short, an Eisenhower appointee to the commission, expound on the reasons for marking the one hundredth anniversary of what he called America's greatest "tragedy." Stressing that it was important not to romanticize "this most terrible of fratricidal strifes," Short chose to emphasize the positive, that "out of the holocaust, heartbreak, misery, terror and tragedy" had come "unity." And yet, he contended, notwithstanding the passage of nearly a century, America's problems were little changed and the "mosaic of events" much the same: "Today, we do not have Bleeding Kansas or John Brown's raids, but . . . we do have Berlin, Korea, Indochina, Lebanon, Matsu and Quemoy, and Hungary." The issue then as now, he said, was "freedom." Drawing on the entrenched consensual interpretation of the Civil War, Short argued that Unionists and Confederates had, in their own ways, fought "sincerely, deeply, and emotionally" for that great cause: "The South was convinced that it should be allowed to secede from a union it no longer understood and whose laws and attitudes were working to disrupt a system long held honorable and viable. The North, just as determined, believed that a nation deemed for leadership should not be divided at a time when history was preparing the dawn of greatness."[73]

He pulled no punches. Communists were attempting "to destroy the concept of freedom," he said. There was "no act however vile, no risk however great, no course however repulsive that they are not willing to take in order to carry out their avowed intention to bury us." However, by honoring the great deeds and spiritual values of the fighting men on both sides of the Civil War, modern Americans would better understand how the nation had been forged "through a great common sacrifice" and thereby intensify their commitment

72. 85th Congress, 2nd Session, Public Law 85-918 (H.J. Res. 557), Sept. 2, 1958, folder on "Commission Legislation," box 69, subject files 1957–66, CWCCR.

73. Dewey Short, address at first national assembly of CWCC, April 24, 1959, attached to Betts to All Members of the Civil War Centennial Advisory Council and State Civil War Centennial Commissions," April 24, 1959, envelope containing speeches by Bruce Catton et al., box 100, subject files 1957–66, CWCCR.

to defeating the current enemy: "With conviction weak nations have wrecked mighty empires; without conviction great states have fallen."[74] So impressed was Karl Betts by Short's justification of the commemoration that he quickly circulated it to as many centennial planners as possible. "We wish every American could read this inspiring message," he wrote, "as it contains so much of the idealism behind the Centennial program and so admirably expresses the desire of all of us to commemorate the true lessons of the war."[75]

Here, then, was the central message that the CWCC wished to purvey. Twentieth-century Americans could not ignore the Civil War because it contained valuable lessons for their own lives. Fears that the centennial would reopen old wounds were unfounded because the Civil War had been a collective, national experience. As Karl Betts put it in April 1960, "there was glory and honor for all who fought in the war . . . THEY WERE ALL GOOD AMERICANS."[76] This unsubtle contribution to consensus ideology, it should be stressed, was not restricted to the conservatives on the CWCC. Bruce Catton and Bell Wiley, both receptive to social change, repeatedly gave speeches that echoed the cold war rhetoric of Dewey Short. Speaking to the District of Columbia round table in late 1958, for example, Catton admitted that the Civil War was a singularly tragic event in American history but insisted that its course "also shows us that man has something magnificent in him." It was wrong, he urged, to say that the war divided the United States—partly because the country was already sundered in 1861, partly because "in a strange and mystic way, the Civil War united us . . . by the sharing of a great and unique experience."[77]

Of course, to insist that the centennial could only serve to bring Americans closer together, to rededicate themselves to the noble purposes articulated by the likes of Lincoln and Lee, was to accept without question the orthodox narrative of the Civil War era, which had remained largely unchanged since its emplotment in the late nineteenth century. Among other things this clearly required the black counter-memory of the war to remain marginalized, for any effort to showcase the Emancipation Proclamation or the Union military service of African-American troops was bound to alienate southern whites. There was nothing in Karl Betts's background (still less those of other leading figures associated with the CWCC such as Bill Tuck, Ulysses S. Grant III, or

74. Ibid.
75. Ibid.
76. Betts to Tuck, April 26, 1960, box 7, reading file 1958–66, CWCCR.
77. Bruce Catton, "Why a Civil War Observance?" speech to Civil War Round Table of the District of Columbia, [Nov. 1958], folder on "Catton, Bruce," box 131, subject files 1957–66, CWCCR.

Pat Jones) to suggest that they regarded the centennial as an interracial affair. As far as they and the vast majority of white Americans were concerned, blacks had played an essentially passive role in the Civil War—their only noteworthy contribution to the conflict being the continued loyalty that they allegedly showed to their masters in the Confederacy.

In an interview with Dan Wakefield of *The Nation* in January 1959, Betts made it clear that the centennial was dependent for success on the exclusion of awkward facts. Asked if any commemoration of emancipation was being planned, he replied, "We're not emphasizing Emancipation. You see there's a bigger theme—the beginning of a new America. There was an entire regiment of Negroes about to be formed to serve in the Confederate Army just before the war ended. The story of the devotion and loyalty of Southern Negroes is one of the outstanding things of the Civil War. A lot of fine Negro people loved life as it was in the old South."[78]

In the context of the dominant historical orthodoxy this was not a contentious statement. Indeed, it was true that (after a bitter and prolonged debate among Rebel leaders) a few companies of southern blacks were being recruited into the Confederate armed forces at the close of the Civil War.[79] As a Civil War buff, however, it is inconceivable that Betts did not know that much larger numbers of blacks had fought for the Union or that he was unaware of the political significance of the Emancipation Proclamation. While the CWCC's executive director may well have discounted the military effectiveness of black troops (contemporary scholars were hardly united on the subject) and, like most round table members, was probably uninterested in the political events of the war, his primary motive for making this statement was organizational necessity. This was clear, for example, from his defensive line on the issue of black appointments to the advisory council. While the twenty-five-member full commission was made up entirely of whites (and just one of them female), a handful of African-American academics were named to the advisory body. When a prominent Georgia segregationist wrote to complain about the appointment of one "Negro" to this group, Betts replied that if there were no black representa-

78. Dan Wakefield, "Civil War Centennial: Bull Run with Popcorn," *The Nation*, Jan. 30, 1959, 97.

79. Bruce Levine, *Confederate Emancipation: Southern Plans to Free and Arm Slaves During the Civil War* (Oxford: Oxford University Press, 2006), 125. Levine argues convincingly that Confederate efforts to recruit slaves as soldiers were a product solely of military necessity, that the policy remained fiercely contested throughout the latter stages of the war, and that its proponents did not regard it as a death-blow to the established racial order at home.

tion "we might come under criticism for discrimination." He added, "I devoutly hope that this realistic appraisal of a troublesome problem will not cause us undue embarrassment in the South."[80] The director's expectation was that as long as blacks and their counter-memory were sidelined during the centennial, white southerners would be among the most enthusiastic supporters of the event.

Although initially there was mixed support for the centennial below the Mason-Dixon line, the CWCC's efforts to prepare the groundwork for a successful four-year commemoration of the Civil War had begun to bear fruit by the start of 1961. Crucial to the success of the project was the creation of state centennial commissions throughout the country. A press release in June 1958 noted that the actual planning of centennial observances was to be "carried out at the grass-roots level."[81] Each state, county, and community would devise its own program while maintaining contact with the national commission and keeping in mind Civil War events of local importance.

Betts, Grant, and other leading members of the agency worked closely with interested parties to set up state bodies that would popularize the centennial. In trying to persuade politicians at all levels of the federal system that the centennial was worthy of their support, they found a willing ally in the Democratic governor of Virginia, J. Lindsay Almond. An apparently staunch segregationist, Almond secured unanimous support for the CWCC agenda at the national governors' conference in Miami in May 1958. This meeting passed a resolution requesting members to work for the creation of state commissions and to plan and conduct appropriate ceremonies to mark "this significant event in the building of an enduring nation."[82] Revealingly, Almond used General Grant's tell-tale rhetoric to secure approbation for the measure. By properly marking the hundredth anniversary of the Civil War, Americans would "appreciate more keenly the greatness that has come to our reunited country" and promote renewed civic efforts "to keep America American, and to resist the so specious and plausible efforts of its enemies, whether avowed or hidden, to subvert the basic tenets and principles of our Constitution and the institutions we inherited from those great men of 1861 to 1865."[83]

80. Betts to Allen P. Julian, July 18, 1958, folder on "Advisory Council: Georgia," box 6, subject files 1957–66, CWCCR.

81. CWCC press release, June 24, 1958, ibid.

82. *100 Years After,* 1 (June 1958). This was the CWCC's official monthly newsletter.

83. J. Lindsay Almond, remarks at Miami national governors' conference, May 1958, folder on "Maps—Mayors' Conference," box 86, subject files 1957–66, CWCCR. Almond quoted directly from Grant's statement on accepting chairmanship of the CWCC.

While not every governor who signed up to the centennial resolution ex- ecuted it enthusiastically when he got home, the CWCC reported a steady growth in the number of state commissions: twenty-nine by May 1959, forty- one by May 1960, and forty-four a year later.[84] Idaho, Nevada, and North Dakota joined Hawaii and Alaska in ignoring the centennial, but commissions were established throughout the South, the Midwest, New England, and the Mid-Atlantic states.[85] With differing degrees of vigor, these bodies began to or- ganize statewide programs in conjunction with local committees. The CWCC proffered a range of advice to cooperating groups. It did so by way of direct correspondence, invited talks by members of the full commission, and the dis- tribution of published materials. During its short existence the CWCC issued a number of booklets. These included a *Guide for the Observance of the Centen- nial of the Civil War* (1959), which outlined the main purpose of the event ("to bring home to the citizens of our country the great lessons in Americanism learned from the Civil War") and suggested ways of generating popular inter- est.[86] This publication admitted that a centralized commemoration was imprac- tical owing to the limited extent of congressional funding. It therefore urged state commissions to encourage local people to undertake local commemo- rations, ideally with the aid of historical societies and patriotic groups. Such activities might include memorial services, the sponsorship of educational ac- tivities and publications, systematic efforts to locate and preserve valuable doc- uments, and the staging of pageants and battle reenactments. Strenuous efforts were to be made to enlist media coverage of these activities "to call the public's attention to them," and the booklet advised state commissions to send notice of major events to Washington in order that the CWCC could give them national publicity through its regular press releases.[87] As an additional aid to planning, the CWCC also prepared and distributed an extensive chronology of Civil War events that, Karl Betts proudly noted, had been generated by computer cards.[88]

84. *100 Years After*, 2 (May 1959); 3 (May 1960); CWCC, "Centennial Observance Unfolds," folder on "Washington Trip—Oct. 25–26, 1961," box 184, Wiley Papers.

85. CWCC, *The Civil War Centennial: A Report to the Congress* (Washington, DC: Govern- ment Printing Office, 1968), 51.

86. CWCC, *Guide for the Observance of the Centennial of the Civil War* (Washington, DC: Government Printing Office, 1959), unnumbered page.

87. Ibid., 11.

88. Betts to John A. May, April 27, 1959, Confederate War Centennial Commission Folders, box 1 (1955–65), Office of the Director, Agencies, Commissions and Organizations file (S108163), Records of South Carolina Department of Archives and History, South Carolina Department of Archives and History.

As the geographical distribution of state agencies revealed, greatest enthusiasm for the centennial was evident in those regions of the country that had been most affected by the Civil War. The western states therefore evinced only limited interest in the planning process, whereas Americans east of the Mississippi proved to be more involved. There were exceptions. California had an active commission, but General Grant found New Englanders disappointingly apathetic.[89] Several southern states, as we shall see, were slow to set up commissions.[90] Everywhere, round table members, battle reenactors, patriotic societies, archivists, librarians, and historians (both amateur and professional) provided the main nucleus of support for planners. These were mostly white, male, and middle-class Americans with a unique interest in commemorating the Civil War, though the participation of organizations such as the Daughters of the American Revolution and eventually the UDC (as well as the appointment of some women to state and local centennial groups) ensured that planning was not entirely a male preserve. Karl Betts's insight was to recognize that unless the CWCC broadened support for the centennial beyond this, its natural constituency, the prospects for a genuinely popular pageant would be slim. Politicians like Lindsay Almond provided part of the solution to the problem of how to disseminate the commission's uplifting patriotic messages about the Civil War, but no group proved more central to the executive director's ambitious plans than American businessmen.

With his own background in public relations and investment brokerage, Betts knew instinctively that business elites would only embrace the centennial if they reckoned they could make money out of it. As a conservative Republican, he saw nothing untoward in this. A commercial approach would hardly conflict with the ideological tenor of the project and more importantly would surely serve to make it a more democratic one. It was for this reason that he regarded "promotional work" in the field of tourism as his agency's principal contribution to the centennial.[91] He worked vigorously to interest the American Automobile Association, oil companies, and hotel chains in the work of the commission, bombarding them with statistics showing the

89. Grant to Betts, Oct. 9, 1960, folder on "Grant, General U.S., Office Memos 1958," box 133, subject files 1957–66, CWCCR. New Englanders, commented Grant in an acid reference to John F. Kennedy, "are not prone to enthusiasm, except when running for President."

90. See pp. 65–66 herein.

91. Confederate States Centennial Conference, minutes of meeting held Oct. 27, 1960, folder on "Confederate States Centennial Conference 1960–62," box 2, Records of the Georgia Civil War Centennial Commission, Record Group 079-01-001, Georgia State Archives.

expected increase in visitors to Civil War sites and urging state tourist offices to do the same. As the centennial approached, many businesses involved in the travel industry recognized the enormous commercial potential of the event and made it a prime feature of their marketing strategy for 1961. Souvenir road maps directed travelers to NPS battlefield sites, and full-page color spreads in *Time, Newsweek,* and *National Geographic* informed the public about forthcoming centennial events. Those paid for by the Sinclair Oil Company represented an investment of $250,000.[92] One such advertisement heralded a grand reenactment of the battle of First Bull Run in Virginia on July 22–23, 1961. "You'll hear music of massed bands, and stirring addresses by national and state leaders," it read, "but you'll know that freedom is not won nor liberty bought with words alone. The price was patriots' blood, paid for you by men you'll never know, but to whom you stand in debt for all you have. At Bull Run, you'll feel determination to match their valor, to live up to the task of keeping America's heritage alive *in a world when all free men face challenge.*" Another spread, one that flagged Civil War sites in the Shenandoah Valley, informed tourists that a visit to this area would enable them to understand America's reverence for the Confederate general, Thomas "Stonewall" Jackson: "His heroic deeds are reassurance to a free world that, in times of crisis, America always produces such great leaders . . . men of the hour who can rally this nation's manhood in defense of its ideals."[93] There could have been no clearer evidence of the close correlation between the centennial, cold war ideology, and the lure of commercial gain.

Karl Betts's preoccupation with the material aspects of the centennial would eventually come to haunt him. However, it cannot be denied that his unabashed commercial instincts were part and parcel of his broader design to interest as many white Americans in the observance as possible. Critical here was his deep-rooted conviction that the centennial must be entertaining. Americans, he told Grant in March 1959, "will have pageants." Thus, he thought, the worst possible error the commission could make would be to "discourage the enthusiasm and the mounting interest" of northerners and southerners in commemorating the Civil War as they wished.[94] Although historians on the CWCC understood that popular entertainments might be useful as a mobilizing tool, they were concerned about the consequences of

92. Betts to Campbell H. Brown, Aug. 24, 1960, frame 1332, reel 3, Horn Papers.

93. Sinclair Oil advertisements in folder on "S—Misc. [Sept. 1961–Feb. 1962]," box 720, MCWBTSR.

94. Betts to Grant, March 19, 1959, box 2, reading file 1958–66, CWCCR.

commercial excess and emphasized other activities such as document collection and the dissemination of factual knowledge. Betts feared that this dry-as-dust approach would doom the centennial from the start. He therefore urged the newly appointed head of New Jersey's Civil War commission to appoint a public relations specialist rather than an academic as his deputy and confidently told a reporter from the *Washington Post* that the centennial would be "the greatest pageant in the history of the Nation."[95]

Giving interviews to the press was part of Betts's intelligent strategy to imprint the event on the public consciousness well before the inaugural ceremonies in January 1961. So were his efforts, positively supported by Grant, to trumpet the commission's backing for a grand reenactment of First Bull Run. The private First Manassas Corporation, incorporated for this purpose in 1960, received rhetorical and material aid from the CWCC in anticipation of a deluge of positive national publicity before, during, and after the event. Even though some people frowned upon sham battles attended by paying spectators, there was no denying that many Americans enjoyed them. When a U.S. senator told Betts about his fears that battle reenactments would "serve to re-open rather than to heal the wounds" caused by the Civil War, the executive director told him (misleadingly in view of the Bull Run project) that the commission would not initiate plans for any reenactment and had tried to discourage such events because of the amount of preparation required. But there was, he added, little chance that sham battles could create any serious disturbance. Americans, he wrote, "have always loved pageants and the Civil War apparently provides the background for carrying out these very sincere desires of the people at historic battle sites."[96]

The CWCC's strenuous efforts to publicize the centennial—particularly in the South, where there was much initial suspicion of federal efforts to commemorate the Civil War—were aided by the timely death of Walter Williams of Houston in December 1959. Claiming to have fought for the Confederacy as a boy, Williams had been hailed by the commission as the last surviving veteran of the Civil War. In April 1958, Fred Schwengel journeyed to Texas to present the agency's first honorary membership at a carefully staged ceremony (the bedridden Williams was clad in a Rebel uniform) in the home of the old man's daughter. Reading from a five-page script, Schwengel gave thanks that out of the bloodshed of the war had been "distilled a cement which has

95. *Washington Post*, Aug. 30, 1959, B6.

96. A. Willis Robertson to Betts, Oct. 6, 1959, Betts to Robertson, Oct. 12, 1959, folder on "Congressional Mail," box 70, subject files 1957–66, CWCCR.

finally and surely bound this, Our Union, into one fabric which shall never again, please God, be shattered." "To you, Mr. Williams," concluded the Iowa congressman, "valiant upholder still of the honor and spirit of a most gallant, most American, army, we offer our hearty congratulations."[97] Even though the ancient Texan's claim was probably fraudulent, his demise the following year presented the CWCC with an unmissable opportunity to publicize the centennial.[98] The commission asked President Eisenhower to issue a statement marking this apparently significant passing. Eisenhower, keenly aware that Americans should consider both the "historic and present meanings" of the Civil War, was happy to oblige.[99] In doing so he underlined the consensual motif of the impending centennial. Referring pointedly to "the War Between the States," he observed that "[t]he wounds of the deep and bitter dispute which once divided our nation have long since healed, and a united America in a divided world now holds up on a larger canvas the cherished traditions of liberty and justice for all." With Williams's death, "the hosts of Blue and Gray who were the chief actors in that great and tragic drama a century ago have all passed from the world stage. No longer are they the Blue and the Gray. All rest together as Americans in honored glory."[100] With the president's help, this miraculous event received significant media attention. Americans could have had no better signal that their civil war was worth commemorating.

By January 1961 the United States was as ready as it was ever going to be for the Civil War centennial. The CWCC had survived a number of blows, including moves in Congress to cut its funding and General Grant's endorsement of a spurious claim that Jewish financiers in Europe had tried to break up the United States in the 1860s.[101] Its achievements were modest but con-

---

97. Schwengel, speech delivered at Houston, Texas, April 26, 1958, and clipping from *Houston Post*, April 27, 1958, sec. 1, 11, folder on "Veterans of the Civil War—Remaining," box 105, subject files 1957–66, CWCCR. Williams claimed to have arrived in Texas at the age of fourteen and joined Company C of Hood's Brigade near Corinth, Mississippi, when he was twenty-two. The man regarded as the last Union veteran, Albert Woolson of Duluth, had died in August 1956. *Washington Daily News*, Aug. 11, 1959, 7, ibid.

98. Allen C. Guelzo, *The Crisis of the American Republic: A History of the Civil War and Reconstruction Era* (New York: St. Martin's, 1995), xiii.

99. Dwight D. Eisenhower to Grant, April 15, 1959, folder on "National Assembly," box 184, Wiley Papers.

100. *Public Papers of the Presidents of the United States: Dwight D. Eisenhower, 1959* (Washington, DC: Government Printing Office, 1960), 864–65.

101. Grant endorsed an article entitled, "Abraham Lincoln and the Rothschilds," which appeared in the *Loyal League Bulletin* in June 1959. The essay was condemned immediately by lead-

crete enough. Most states had set up a centennial commission; several of them were already very active planning events in line with the chronology of the Civil War. Those most frustrated with the agency's work were probably historians. Bell Wiley, head of the CWCC's committee on historical activities, reported that achievements in the field of scholarship and document collection had been "disappointing," yet even he noted that some progress had been made. A Guide-Index to the valuable *Official Records* was in preparation, for example, and Virginia had begun a systematic program of microfilming Civil War–era newspapers.[102] Beyond the centennial agencies and their supporting organizations, positive work was also being undertaken by the NPS, which was concerned about the effects of economic development on putatively sacred military sites. By June 1960 the Park Service had purchased around 600 acres of additional battlefield land (mostly at Manassas) and, with the help of Mission 66 appropriations, spent nearly $5 million upgrading existing Civil War parks.[103] National and local press coverage of the centennial was limited in quantity (not to say mixed in tone), but at the commencement of festivities it is unlikely that large numbers of Americans were unaware of what was about to hit them.

The centennial proper began on Sunday, January 8, 1961. President Eisenhower made a short public address on television and radio calling on all Americans to participate in the commemoration. Highlighting the central message of sectional reconciliation, special services were held in both New York City and Lexington, Virginia. At Grant's tomb on Manhattan's Upper West Side,

---

ing Jewish Americans, including Congressman Emanuel Celler, who denounced it to President Eisenhower as "a collection of vicious anti-Semitic nonsense." In spite of the fact that it was used as propaganda by the white citizens' councils, Karl Betts defended the piece as "an expression of academic freedom." See Celler to Eisenhower, July 10, 1959, folder 5268, Tuck Papers; and H. Edelsberg to Wiley, June 24, 1959, folder on "General Grant—Jewry Controversy," box 184, Wiley Papers. Allan Nevins, who replaced Grant as head of the CWCC in 1961, described it as "from several points of view decidedly sickening." It was, he added, "a travesty on the name of history" and "a vicious piece of anti-Semitism," which "at several points . . . seems to have a Communist bias." Nevins to Justin G. Turner, July 19, 1959, folder on "California State Commission," box 108, subject files 1957–66, CWCCR. The general's grandfather had angered Jews by trying to exclude them from trade with the Union Army during the Civil War. See William S. McFeely, *Grant: A Biography* (New York: W. W. Norton, 1981), 123–24.

102. Wiley, speech at CWCC national assembly, May 5, 1960, folder on "Wiley—Speeches at National Assemblies and Elsewhere," box 184, Wiley Papers.

103. CWCC, minutes of the meeting held Jan. 5, 1960, folder on "Minutes—Commission Meetings, Agendas, etc," box 184, Wiley Papers.

flurries of snow whipped across the faces of attendant soldiers as they watched dignitaries lay wreaths, listened to consensus-oriented speeches from, among others, the chairman of the centennial commission, and heard a West Point band play patriotic airs. At the last resting place of Robert E. Lee in the chapel of Washington and Lee University, college chancellor Dr. Francis Pendleton Gaines praised the magnanimity of Grant at Appomattox and reminded the audience of how the "beautiful dream of reconciliation" had flowered first in the capacious soul of General Lee.[104] These official ceremonies (which received front-page coverage in the national press) were complemented by the ringing of church bells in many communities across the United States. Done at the behest of the CWCC to increase awareness of the centennial, this was another sign that large numbers of Americans stood ready to join Karl Betts in his cold war pageant. Interest was particularly evident in the Deep South. Governor John Patterson of Alabama, for example, had proclaimed the day as the official start of the centennial in his state. In Montgomery the church bells rang clear to announce the beginning of what one prominent local clergyman called "this big event."[105] White southerners would take the centennial to their hearts in the early months of 1961—with baleful consequences for all those who believed that the planned commemoration would bring Americans closer together.

104. *New York Times*, Jan. 9, 1961, 23. Lee's chapel benefited from an extensive refurbishment program funded by a $376,000 grant from the Ford Motor Company Fund in 1960. Pamela H. Simpson, "The Great Lee Chapel Controversy and the 'Little Group of Willful Women' Who Saved the Shrine of the South," in Cynthia Mills and Simpson, eds., *Monuments of the Lost Cause: Women, Art, and the Landscapes of Southern Memory* (Knoxville: University of Tennessee Press, 2004), 96.

105. Montgomery Advertiser, Jan. 8, 1961, B1.

·2·

The White South Commemorates the Civil War

EMERGING INTO THE southern sunlight after a rewarding day's work in the archives, the renowned liberal historian Comer Vann Woodward wandered over to a nearby newsstand and bought a paper. It was a hot day in the mid-1950s when opposition to school desegregation was at its height. Blinking in the glare, Woodward experienced a bewildering sense of déjà vu. The headlines denouncing federal usurpation of states' rights were virtually the same as those he had just been perusing in Reconstruction-era newspapers. For a moment it seemed to him that he was caught in a time warp.[1]

If the South in the middle of the twentieth century was a very different place from the South of 1861, this was not always obvious in the late 1950s and early 1960s. The Civil War centennial coincided with the period of fierce southern resistance to integration sparked primarily by the U.S. Supreme Court's decision in *Brown v. Board of Education.* In the words of one local observer, Chief Justice Warren's controversial ruling "revived, as nothing else could have, the South's 'historic consciousness,' its consciousness of its own identity—which ... was, by 1954, sagging pretty badly."[2] The centennial looked to be a godsend for segregationists seeking to mobilize popular opposition to *Brown* by deploying what historian George Lewis terms "a broad arsenal of possible resistance weapons" that included Civil War memory as well as red-baiting, racism, and narrow construction of the U.S. Constitution.[3] White southerners had risen up courageously in defiance of federal authority

---

1. J. R. Pole to the author, July 10, 2004.

2. Marion H. Sass to John Temple Graves, April 4, 1960, folder on "General Papers, 1960," box 1, William D. Workman Jr., Papers, Modern Political Collections, South Caroliniana Library, University of South Carolina.

3. George Lewis, *The White South and the Red Menace: Segregationists, Anticommunism, and Massive Resistance, 1945–1965* (Gainesville: University Press of Florida, 2004), 2.

a hundred years previously. What was to stop their heirs doing something similar in the modern age?

In truth, there were many barriers to such a development—not least the region's twentieth-century allegiance to the American nation-state. Segregationists who seized on the centennial as a means of bolstering their cause had to reckon with the fact that the vast majority of local whites considered themselves patriotic Americans. The cold war strengthened this allegiance: no other region of the country was as staunchly opposed to communism. Notwithstanding the obstacles, however, the defenders of Jim Crow understood that "massive resistance" to the *Brown* decision had begun to erode the existing consensual orthodoxy on the Civil War and Reconstruction. As fears of federal intervention and civil rights activism grew, parallels between the Confederate past and the uncertain present became increasingly persuasive. After an initial phase when many of them regarded the centennial with some suspicion, white southerners came to embrace the Civil War pageant with greater enthusiasm than any other group. Successful and genuinely popular commemorations of secession in Alabama and Mississippi revealed the raw power of historical memory as a tool of political and cultural warfare.

SUSPICIOUS MINDS

There was nothing inevitable about what many commentators began to see as the white South's co-option of centennial proceedings by the spring of 1961. The region was undergoing profound economic and social changes in the aftermath of World War II. Industrialization occurred at a dramatic rate, primarily as a result of military Keynesianism (which induced the massive intraregional growth of defense-related businesses and installations) and federal support for agribusiness, which, along with mechanization of the cotton sector, hastened the collapse of the sharecropping system that had bolstered Jim Crow for more than a generation. The resulting movement of whites and blacks from the land to the cities placed huge strains on segregation. For growing numbers of southerners, particularly urban, middle-class whites, Jim Crow was now a serious incubus to a region that was at last starting to share in the nation's material success. Progressive business elites did not always concur with neo-populist politicians who appealed to blacks as well as poorer whites, but they shared a conviction that racial segregation threatened the healthy development of a region widely stigmatized as dysfunctional for many decades.[4]

4. Numan V. Bartley, *The Rise of Massive Resistance: Race and Politics in the South During the 1950s* (Baton Rouge: Louisiana State University Press, 1969), 3–27.

After 1940 Jim Crow came under increasing pressure from African Americans. Military service and urban living produced more assertive and better-educated individuals—southern black men and women who were aware, often for the first time, of the possibilities for change at the community level. Frustrated with the persistence of discrimination and poverty, many exhibited their dissatisfaction with southern life by challenging petty apartheid restrictions on public transportation, by participating in voter registration drives, and by trying to negotiate improvements in public services with white elites. Their influence enhanced to a degree by the federal courts, as well as their own actions, southern blacks were no longer regarded as entirely insignificant political players—hence the willingness of some southern politicians to accede to African-American calls for change. Even though these calls were generally couched in terms of reforming, rather than overturning, Jim Crow, they represented a strong signal to die-hard segregationists that local blacks were no longer willing to accept the status quo.[5]

It was the resulting awareness of impending change that helped to energize the defenders of southern conservatism because, as the momentum for reform began to gather pace, so too did countervailing pressures. The first major indication that bitter-enders were preparing to mobilize in defense of Jim Crow was the refusal of many southern Democrats to support the regular ticket in the general election of 1948. President Truman's limited actions on behalf of civil rights alienated some influential members of his party below the Mason-Dixon line. When, at the behest of northern liberals, the national convention adopted a relatively strong civil rights plank, southern "Dixiecrats" staged a secessionist-style walkout and then proceeded to form their own states' rights organization. They chose the Confederate battle flag as the symbol for their political rebellion and made opposition to federal power their principal rallying cry. Although the Dixiecrats secured less than 2.5 percent of the popular vote in the November election, they performed well in several Deep South states. It was evidence not only of the depth of many white southerners' commitment to the existing racial order but also of the extent to which that attachment was bolstered by a particular variant of historical memory.[6]

5. On growing black assertiveness in the Jim Crow South, see J. Mills Thornton III, *Dividing Lines: Municipal Politics and the Struggle for Civil Rights in Montgomery, Birmingham, and Selma* (Tuscaloosa: University of Alabama Press, 2002); Robin D. G. Kelley, "'We Are Not What We Seem': Rethinking Black Working-Class Opposition in the Jim Crow South," *Journal of American History* 80 (1993): 75–112.

6. Bartley, *Rise*, 32–36.

In spite of this harbinger of resistance, most liberal commentators in the early 1950s adhered to their belief that economic progress would bring about a peaceful transition from Jim Crow to New South. When Carl Rowan, a young black reporter for the *Minneapolis Daily Tribune,* made a tour of his native South in 1951, he discovered a region on the cusp of real change. Although he encountered signs of persistent racial discrimination, he found that in the wake of recent Supreme Court decisions segregation was no longer rigidly enforced in public accommodations or in the higher education systems of certain states of the Upper South.[7] When the same tribunal unanimously declared segregated public schools to be unlawful under the Constitution, the justices had reason to suppose that after some initial opposition, white southerners would bow to the inevitable and dispense with their embarrassing modern-day peculiar institution. And so it might have been had southern liberals, those people who recognized the need to abandon Jim Crow, embraced the new world awaiting them on the other side of the *Brown* decision. Instead, a fatal combination of inertia on their part and inaction by the Eisenhower administration allowed segregationists to seize the initiative and convince large numbers of southern whites that their best interests lay in maintaining the status quo. Citizens' councils and terrorist groups like the revived Ku Klux Klan quickly gained a stranglehold over public opinion in the Deep South and the old plantation areas of the Upper South. Their intimidatory activities marginalized liberal sentiment in these areas, providing the impetus for a concerted state-supported campaign of massive resistance to school desegregation. While this campaign was knocked back by federal military intervention during the Little Rock crisis and a series of unpopular school closures in the late 1950s, the demise of Jim Crow was far from guaranteed by the time centennial planners began their work. Those segregationist politicians who gorged on the ensuing racial and sectional tensions recognized the power of historical memory. No one was surprised when the Georgia legislature announced its support for massive resistance by incorporating the Confederate battle flag into the state's official ensign in 1956 or when Governor Orval Faubus used the arrival of U.S. paratroops at Central High School to denounce the consequences of federal tyranny to the voters of Arkansas.[8]

7. Carl T. Rowan, *South of Freedom* (1952; reprint, Baton Rouge: Louisiana State University Press, 1997).

8. Numan V. Bartley, *The New South, 1945–1980* (Baton Rouge: Louisiana State University Press, 1995), 187–222; Neil R. McMillen, *The Citizens' Council: Organized Resistance to the Second Reconstruction, 1954–64* (Urbana: University of Illinois Press, 1971).

In spite of these developments, it was by no means certain that the centennial would be of much help to bitter-end segregationists. James J. Kilpatrick, the editor of the *Richmond News Leader* who masterminded the Byrd machine's campaign of massive resistance in Virginia, found ideological justification for opposing the *Brown* decision not in secession but in nullification.[9] While there were sound tactical reasons for this, Kilpatrick's decision hinted at the Civil War's ambiguous legacy at a time when many white southerners were looking to the past for guidance and support.

As the Richmond journalist knew very well, tens of thousands of his fellow white southerners had been reared on stories of the Civil War, many of them handed down directly by elderly kinfolk who had witnessed the conflict at first hand. These stories were legion and as diverse as the South's Civil War experience. In some instances, as in that of the progressive Atlanta journalist Ralph McGill (whose Tennessee forebears included Unionists and Confederates), they fostered a relatively inclusive view of the region's history—one that did not regard an attachment to segregation as a critical determinant of southern identity.[10] Tales of wartime devastation, moreover, were often used to justify not continued resistance to federal authority, but a forward-looking commitment to socioeconomic progress within the wider nation.

For many southern whites in the 1950s, however, particularly those in the black belt, the region's Civil War tribulations were a source of lingering sectional grievance. UDC-approved historical education early in the century often combined with hidebound political rhetoric and youthful encounters with embittered Confederates (male and female) to feed a tangible hostility to Yankees that was barely concealed by the mainstream nationalist consensus. Insofar as northerners were willing to accept significant elements of Lost Cause ideology, the latter may not have been entirely incompatible with the consensual interpretation of the Civil War. But differences in emphasis (for example, the South's black legend of Sherman and his vandal hordes) did exist, and these were easily exposed whenever sectional tensions increased.

Shortly after President Eisenhower had reluctantly dispatched troops to preserve law and order in Little Rock, the prominent Virginia novelist and

9. Joseph J. Thorndike, "'The Sometimes Sordid Level of Race and Segregation': James J. Kilpatrick and the Virginia Campaign against *Brown*," in Matthew D. Lassiter and Andrew B. Lewis, eds., *The Moderates' Dilemma: Massive Resistance to School Desegregation in Virginia* (Charlottesville: University Press of Virginia, 1998), 51–71.

10. For a biography of McGill, see Leonard R. Teel, *Ralph Emerson McGill: Voice of the Southern Conscience* (Knoxville: University of Tennessee Press, 2001).

historian Clifford Dowdey responded testily to a suggestion from Allan Nevins that a draft essay written by him appeared excessively partisan. Nevins, a
northern historian who wrote in the dominant nationalist mode, had objected
to Dowdey's failure to emphasize southern respect for northern courage on
the battlefield and to his suggestion that ordinary Confederate soldiers had
not fought to preserve slavery. The Virginian retorted that northerners should
make more strenuous efforts to understand the Civil War from the viewpoint
of southern whites. This, he argued, was embedded in the searing experience
of wartime defeat and destruction. "In the people of my generation," wrote
Dowdey, "all stories of our past began, 'Before the Yankees came.' On our first
trips in the country we were shown the ruins of some house, 'Where your
Aunt Sarah lived,' and the ruins of a mill, 'where your Uncle Elmo ground
meal,' and so on. This was not pointed out in bitterness, but in simple explanation of a passing of property that caused our poverty. I have heard it said
1,000 times in complete casualness about persons in my parent's [sic] generation, 'That was after the war and, of course, they couldn't go to college.'" It
was, insisted Dowdey, imperative for northerners to understand that progressives like himself (he claimed to be a supporter of gradual integration) could
only be harmed by the kind of harsh antisouthern criticism that had accompanied the Little Rock crisis. "Not only for the centennial observance, but for
the gravity of the situation today," he wrote, "it is a vital necessity that the
sections work together in a compassionate and appreciative understanding of
their fundamental differences."[11]

If avowed opponents of massive resistance like Clifford Dowdey were
sensitive enough about their Confederate heritage, die-hard segregationists
placed even greater stress on the southern past to advance their political goals
in the stormy present. As C. Vann Woodward observed, the legitimacy of the
South's racial order in the 1950s "rested upon historical assumptions that constituted a veritable credo of the region."[12] Segregationist politicians, moderates and hardliners alike, seldom missed an opportunity to depict themselves
as heirs to, and defenders of, a glorious legacy. Speaking in the summer of
1956 at a ceremony to mark the opening of a park dedicated to the memory
of Jefferson Davis, Democratic senator Lister Hill of Alabama told his audience that the Confederate president exemplified the character that had in-

11. Clifford Dowdey to Allan Nevins, Oct. 12, 1957, folder 2, box 72, Allan Nevins Papers, Rare
Book and Manuscript Library, Columbia University.

12. C. Vann Woodward, *Thinking Back: The Perils of Writing History* (Baton Rouge: Louisiana
State University Press, 1986), 61.

spired southerners through the years "to defend those institutions we hold sacred—institutions built on the Founding Fathers' constitutional concept of self-government and States' Rights." The South, he said, had now "entered into a new day of progress and prosperity," but its people must still "be vigorous to reject any encroachments on our constitutionally ordained freedoms and the freedoms they guarantee, lest they slip from our grasp and be lost forever."[13] The annual ceremony at Rivers Bridge, South Carolina (the site of a Confederate rearguard action against Sherman's hated bluecoats), afforded bitter-enders an ideal stage on which to draw out the parallels between past and present struggles. Around two thousand people—adults and youngsters—attended the eighty-third ritual gathering in May 1959. They heard the president of the Rivers Bridge Confederate Memorial Association declaim that he was "convinced that God is with the Confederacy." When he asked, "if God be with us, who can be against us?" a boy cried out, "Chief Justice Warren!" causing great mirth among the crowd. Ex-governor James F. Byrnes then paid tribute to the association "for maintaining the ideals of State Rights and the Confederate cause." Southerners' belief in "divine inspiration" and the loyalty of the region's women, he said, had played a crucial role in preserving "the integrity of the white race and our own way of living in the South."[14]

Yet, notwithstanding the emotional power of present-minded appeals to the southern past, segregationists like James Kilpatrick recognized the dangers of anchoring massive resistance to the South's experience in the Civil War. The main problem, of course, was that the rebellion was not called the Lost Cause for nothing. Ultimately the war had ended in defeat. It had confirmed U.S. sovereignty over the region and permanently blasted local dreams of independence. This unavoidable fact, combined with the steady growth of federal power during the twentieth century, meant that even if many southern whites in the 1950s did share the desire of one Tennessean "to secede and fight the Civil War all over again," they had no option but to discount such thoughts as impractical.[15]

There can be little doubt that southern supporters of the centennial—men like Congressman William Tuck and the author Pat Jones (both of whom shared Kilpatrick's allegiance to the Byrd organization in Virginia)—regarded

13. *United Daughters of the Confederacy Magazine* 19 (1956): 5, 32.

14. *Charleston News and Courier,* May 9, 1959, clipping in folder on "General Correspondence, 1959," box 184, Bell I. Wiley Papers, Manuscript, Archives, and Rare Book Library, Emory University.

15. Pete Daniel, *Lost Revolutions: The South in the 1950s* (Chapel Hill: University of North Carolina Press, 2000), 38.

Civil War memory as a useful vehicle, one among several, for promoting white unity at another critical juncture in the history of the American South. However, we should not blithely assume that the idea won immediate support from like-minded individuals any more than we should think that every Jim Crow defender was an advocate of tactical red-baiting or rabble-rousing racism. Not only did the reality of defeat limit the war's utility to segregationists in the ongoing fight against federal intrusion, but any heritage project overseen by a federal commission chaired by a descendant of Ulysses S. Grant was bound to be regarded with suspicion by white southerners. Even the use of the term "Civil War" (which, as a reference to an internal domestic dispute, appeared to be an explicit denial of Confederate nationhood) was anathema to venerable guardians of the Lost Cause such as the UDC and SCV. Thus, in spite of evident enthusiasm for the centennial in certain circles, early responses to the initial organizing drive were frequently cool and occasionally hostile.

Struggling to generate legislative support for a state centennial commission in Tennessee, historian Stanley Horn told Karl Betts that many local people believed the impending commemoration was "somehow designed to be a celebration of the defeat of the South by the North, without regard to the feelings and sentiments of the defeated."[16] Although CWCC officials were careful to stress the consensual aims of their work, even the prospect of a bland love-fest outraged proud southerners like Clifford Dowdey, who launched a blistering attack on the centennial in the *Virginia Record* in May 1959. Southerners, he claimed, were being asked to downplay their Confederate heritage because the stated purpose of the exercise was to build a national consensus. "This unacceptable Blue-and-Gray attitude," he wrote, "has at last come out into the open, and Southerners are not going for it."[17] Backing for this view came from an Atlanta correspondent of Bell Wiley who told the Emory historian that "[i]t is not becoming in any American to sit idly by and let a moronic horde dance through the American scene with a 'Sweet, Sweet, Sweet' song of Conformity about nothing!!! If the whole subject is nothing why put on the show at all?"[18] Local observers were not slow to point out the paucity of southerners on the federal commission. One SCV official in Alabama complained that

16. Stanley F. Horn to Karl S. Betts, April 22, 1959, microfilm 1115, frame 986, reel 1, Stanley F. Horn Papers, Tennessee Historical Society Collections, Tennessee State Library and Archives.

17. Clifford Dowdey, "The South in the Nation, I: What Does 'National' Mean?" *Virginia Record* 81 (1959): 67.

18. May Frank Duffey to Bell I. Wiley, Nov. 17, 1959, folder on "General Correspondence, 1959," box 184, Wiley Papers.

this "unequal distribution" represented "a breach of trust . . . The most frequent comment heard regarding the Commemoration is that it will be 'Merely
a glorification of Lincoln.'"[19] A few out-and-out racists sensed a conspiracy
in the offing. One Atlanta woman told General Grant that the Civil War had
been "a War of Suicide for the Great Nordic Race" and that the centennial
was "suspected of being an international plot for takeover via Integration, of
Nordic and Negro races in order to give World Domination to the Jews."[20] If
one adds to this catalogue of criticism mainstream fears of internal division
in the midst of the cold war and complaints about the commercialization of
sacred Confederate symbols, it is evident that centennial planners faced an
uphill task in convincing local people that it was worth spending taxpayers'
money on the event.

The task of overcoming southern opposition and apathy fell initially to
the CWCC. During late 1957 segregationists and their allies on the agency
worried that President Eisenhower and Congress would fail to appoint de-
pendable right-wingers to the commission and thereby thwart their plans
for a centennial that would bolster white opinion in the context of both the
cold war and the fight against integration. As noted, however, the shortage of
southerners on the full commission was no guide to the latter's position on
civil rights. There were no radical allies of the black freedom struggle on the
CWCC. The chairman, General Grant, and his deputy, Karl Betts, justifiably
saw themselves as friends of the white South and were relaxed in the company
of segregationists like Bill Tuck who occupied the strategically important roles
of vice chairman and head of the executive committee.[21] Pat Jones, a leading
member of the agency's Washington staff, was delighted to find Grant such
a reliable friend of the South.[22] But what was soon obvious to the segregationists connected with the CWCC was not—in the wake of the Little Rock
crisis—immediately apparent to others who held similar values. Curry Carter,
a southside Virginia legislator, informed Tuck that he was unimpressed with
the congressman's public assertion in December 1957 that the wounds of
the conflict had now been healed. A chastened Tuck insisted that while he

19. Ira L. West Jr. to Ulysses S. Grant III, April 19, 1959, folder on "Complaints—re Commission," box 69, subject files 1957–66, Records of the Civil War Centennial Commission, Records of
the National Park Service, Record Group 79, National Archives (hereafter CWCCR).

20. Mrs. Elton M. Chapman to Grant, Jan. 7, 1960, folder on "Complaints—re Commission,"
box 69, CWCCR.

21. See, for example, Betts to William M. Tuck, Oct. 6, 1958, box 4, reading file 1958–66,
CWCCR.

22. Virgil C. Jones to Tuck, June 2, 1959, box 4, reading file 1958–66, CWCCR.

had indeed made the statement attributed to him, he had also made it clear "that we cherish the principles for which our forefathers fought during the War Between the States, and that we continue to embrace the principles of States rights, and that we have a strong adherence to the view that the country must return to these principles to be saved."[23] "I am frank to concede," replied Carter, "that you have a magnanimous heart toward the Yankees that I do not have." He had, he contended, "always despised Lincoln, Sherman, Sheridan and others that I could mention that wore . . . the 'blue.'"[24]

Intersectional amity was no more evident in South Carolina where, during the spring of 1958, the legislature debated proposals to set up a state centennial agency. The preamble of a bill to establish the "South Carolina War Between the States Centennial Commission" began by observing that the state had "participated with the Confederate States of America, South, against the Federal Union of the United States, North, with steadfast devotion to duty, and supreme loyalty to the divine principle of the unalienable right of a free people to govern themselves." It continued with a forthright assertion of the classic Lost Cause position on the Civil War that was hardly compatible with the consensual message of the CWCC: "Whereas, the terrible hardships borne by the people of the South, and the awful sacrifice of our people, and the indignities thrust upon and suffered by the helpless people of our ravaged and plundered State, ground into the dust under the ruthless heel and relentless heels of overpowering military might, spurred by a bestial ferocity unmatched by savagery, that laid waste our land and homes by death, destruction, fire, pillage, plunder, pestilence, famine, loot, poverty, and vandalism, invoking upon the defenseless women and little children of Columbia and of South Carolina a holocaust of horrors."[25] Manifestly, at a time when southern whites were genuinely fearful of social change and when they could still peruse first-hand recollections of Reconstruction in their newspapers, Tuck and his allies on the national commission were not going to find it easy balancing cold war imperatives with local concerns.[26]

23. Tuck to Curry Carter, Dec. 27, 1957, folder 5263, William M. Tuck Papers, Special Collections, Earl Gregg Swem Library, College of William and Mary.

24. Carter to Tuck, Dec. 31, 1957, folder 5263, Tuck Papers.

25. South Carolina, Senate, Joint Resolution S685, March 5, 1958, Confederate War Centennial Commission Folders, box 1 (1955–65), Office of the Director, Agencies, Commissions and Organizations file (S108163), Records of South Carolina Department of Archives and History, South Carolina Department of Archives and History (hereafter SCDAHR).

26. Civil War–era memories surfacing in the early 1960s included those of Mrs. C. B. Turner. On the occasion of her one hundredth birthday she recalled how she had watched "helplessly" in

TURNING THE TIDE

During the late 1950s the CWCC's attempts to interest southern whites in its organizing efforts began to pay off—to the extent that by the time the centennial opened, widespread grassroots interest in the commemoration was clearly evident. Several factors explain why the commission was able to overcome the initial skepticism: not only its own emphasis on consensus and decentralization but also, and perhaps even more crucially, a dawning awareness on the part of many leading southern whites that the centennial could bring positive economic, cultural, and political gains to their region.

Although CWCC leaders, sympathetic to southern whites' concerns about race and cognizant that their cold war pageant could not succeed without southern support, were eager to involve the white inhabitants of Dixie in their plans, they were not helped by the reluctance of some northern politicians to bestow formal recognition on the Confederacy. In May 1958, for example, an appropriations subcommittee of the U.S. House of Representatives rejected a request from the National Archives and Record Service that funding be made available to microfilm the service records of Confederate soldiers.[27] While this was no more than a temporary setback (Lister Hill had the appropriation restored in the Senate), the House's action did nothing to assuage the fears of those southerners who regarded the centennial as a Yankee trick, particularly when it came only months after the appointment of a predominantly northern commission.[28] However, the CWCC bent over backward to assure southern whites that it was not a threat to their interests. In speech after speech, agency members hammered home the message that they intended the centennial to unite, not divide, Americans. In doing so they explicitly recognized the legitimacy of the Confederate war effort (without, of course, implying any dissent from the orthodox view that Union victory had been a good thing). In his introductory remarks to the commission's first national assembly in January 1958, Bell Wiley, a proud southerner himself, stressed that his agency was determined to avoid any activity that might revive intersectional bitterness.

---

the final weeks of the Civil War "while a Yankee soldier ripped a gold watch and chain from her mother's neck after he had ransacked their home." *Birmingham News,* March 13, 1961, clipping in folder 2, Alabama Department of Archives and History Public Information Subject File, SG6949, Alabama Department of Archives and History (hereafter AlaPIF).

27. Robert H. Bahmer to Wiley, May 15, 1958, folder on "General Correspondence, 1958," box 184, Wiley Papers.

28. Wiley to Tuck, May 28, 1958, folder on "General Correspondence, 1958," box 184, Wiley Papers.

"Rather," he announced, "we want to commemorate the greatness demonstrated by both sides in that momentous struggle. The Civil War was a time of supreme greatness for both North and South—and for the American nation."[29] Bruce Catton, like Wiley one of the CWCC's busiest speakers, told the District of Columbia round table the following November that all Americans had learned from the shared tragedy of internecine strife. Robert E. Lee's home, he noted, was now a national shrine, and a memorial bridge across the Potomac served to connect two great *American* heroes, Lee and Abraham Lincoln.[30] As Clifford Dowdey's objections clearly revealed, efforts like these to promote the agency's cold war agenda did not win over all southern whites. But when combined with gestures such as the honoring of the man reputed to be the last Confederate veteran, they did help to demonstrate that the CWCC was by no means hostile to the South. They thus confirmed the wisdom of those southerners who had argued from the outset that a federal commission would actually protect southern interests by accepting the validity of the region's dominant memory of the Civil War.

The CWCC's stress on a decentralized commemoration, as Michael Kammen has noted, also proved critical in attracting southern white support for the centennial. Karl Betts and his fellow staff members were aware that their vision of a genuinely popular event would be stillborn without the assistance of the individual states. The agency did not have sufficient funds to organize grassroots events. The latter, it was agreed from the very beginning, must be the responsibility of state centennial commissions that could galvanize interested parties at the local level. The logical result of this policy decision was that the CWCC would have to allow the states a good deal of leeway in centennial planning. As long as southern organizers understood that the commemoration was conceived primarily as a weapon in the cultural cold war, they were free to celebrate their nineteenth-century past as they saw fit.

The task of forming southern commissions received an enormous fillip when J. Lindsay Almond of Virginia recommended the centennial to his fellow governors in May 1958. At this stage of his career Almond was regarded as a reliable member of the segregationist Byrd regime.[31] His appeal, couched

29. Wiley, introductory remarks, CWCC first national assembly, Jan. 14, 1958, folder on "Wiley—Speeches at National Assembly and Elsewhere," box 184, Wiley Papers.

30. Bruce Catton, "Why a Civil War Observance[?]," [Nov. 1958], folder on "Catton, Bruce," box 131, subject files 1957–66, CWCCR.

31. James W. Ely Jr., *The Crisis of Conservative Virginia: The Byrd Organization and the Politics of Massive Resistance* (Knoxville: University of Tennessee Press, 1976), 30–107.

though it was in the terms of cold war nationalism, seemed to provide evidence that the centennial was regarded by the Byrd organization as a potentially useful weapon in the fight against integration. This was certainly how the CWCC's executive chairman, ex-Virginia governor William Tuck, viewed matters, and the backing advanced for the centennial project by several of Harry Byrd's fellow southern senators probably stemmed in part from similar motives. Richard Russell of Georgia, Lister Hill of Alabama, and J. Strom Thurmond of South Carolina possessed not only great personal pride in the southern past but also a canny awareness of the emotional power of southern historical memory. The neo-populist governor of Alabama, James Folsom, had a clear understanding that the Confederate past was a potent weapon in the hands of the region's conservatives. Significantly, perhaps, he resisted the advances of the CWCC and declined to send an official delegate to the agency's first national assembly in Washington.[32]

Although some segregationists recognized the value of connecting past and present struggles for states' rights, we should resist the conclusion, first, that all segregationists immediately supported the centennial, and, second, that a racially motivated impulse to celebrate the Confederacy was the sole or even the paramount reason why southern states opted to set up their own commissions. On the first of these points, we have already noted that there were several good reasons for die-hards not to embrace the centennial. The war had ended in defeat for the South. Southerners were outnumbered on the national commission. Any extended observance of the conflict might intensify intersectional friction and play into the hands of communists. While some Virginia segregationists did embrace the Civil War centennial from the outset, their peers in many other Jim Crow states failed to do so. Ruling Democratic politicians in Texas, Louisiana, Georgia, Arkansas, Tennessee, and South Carolina exhibited little enthusiasm for using the centennial as a means of generating popular support for massive resistance. At the root of this apathy was money. At a time when the U.S. economy was in recession and retrenchment was the order of the day, cash-strapped southern states needed convincing reasons to spend taxpayers' dollars on a grandiose national heritage project. The All-South Centennial Conference, a small "travel promotion planning group" based in Montgomery, Alabama, had been arguing since the mid-1950s that a full-scale commemoration of the Civil War would boost the

32. Grant to James E. Folsom, Feb. 20, 1958, folder 6, Administration Files, Alabama, Governor (1959–1963: Patterson), SG14004, Alabama Department of Archives and History (hereafter AlaG).

contribution of tourism to the region's diversifying economy.[33] Unsurprisingly, this contention carried the greatest weight in Virginia, the state possessing the lion's share of major Civil War sites.

One of the wealthiest southern states, Virginia was in the vanguard of preparing for 1961. The scene of fierce fighting between Union and Confederate forces throughout the war, it could boast more battlefields and memorials than any of its rivals. The state was diverse. Committed segregationists like Byrd and Tuck depended heavily for votes on agricultural districts like the southside where Jim Crow mores were still entrenched. The commonwealth, however, was developing rapidly, particularly in the north (where communities like Arlington and Falls Church were prosperous suburbs of Washington) and in other metropolitan areas like Richmond and Norfolk. Hostility to the Byrd organization's policy of closing the public schools to thwart desegregation was particularly intense among the burgeoning urban, white middle class. Mindful of this influential constituency and aware of the damage that massive resistance was doing to the state's reputation, Governor Almond parted company with the regime when he announced his opposition to school closures in January 1959. Much better, he reasoned, to accept a modicum of token and gradual school desegregation than hinder economic growth by remaining wedded to outmoded social practices that had been deemed unlawful by the federal courts.[34]

For the Almond administration (as distinct from the Byrd machine) the centennial represented less an opportunity to revel in the past for reasons directly related to the political campaign against integration than a chance to benefit economically from the marked increase in battlefield tourism after World War II. The Virginia Travel Council noted that in fiscal 1956–57 a daily average of 48,000 cars licensed by other states entered the Old Dominion. They carried 113,400 passengers, who stayed an average of 2.4 days each. This added up to a total of 40 million visitors occupying nearly 29 million spaces in the state's growing list of segregated hotels and motels.[35] No matter how encouraging these statistics, the council's main conclusion was that a quarter of

33. Thomas L. Blake to John M. Patterson, Sept. 25, 1959, folder 6, AlaG. By the time the centennial began, tourism ranked as "the second or third largest employer and generator of wealth in the South." W. Fitzhugh Brundage, *The Southern Past: A Clash of Race and Memory* (Cambridge, MA: Belknap Press of Harvard University Press, 2005), 221.

34. Matthew D. Lassiter and Andrew B. Lewis, "Massive Resistance Revisited: Virginia's White Moderates and the Byrd Organization," in Lassiter and Lewis, eds., *Moderates' Dilemma*, 1–21; Ely, *Crisis*, 122–43.

35. Virginia Travel Council, "Fact Sheet on Virginia's Travel Economy," folder on "Travel—Virginia Travel Council," box 104, subject files 1957–66, CWCCR.

all public accommodation capacity remained unused. What better way to fill these empty beds than to capitalize on growing popular interest in the Civil War and make Virginia the mecca of the forthcoming observance? This was the reason why the state legislature appropriated a massive $1.75 million for the centennial (a significant proportion of this to be spent on building a visitors' center in Richmond) and why Virginia was the first southern state to set up its own centennial commission.[36]

Notwithstanding considerable support for the centennial at the Miami governors' conference in May 1958, southern state backing for the commemoration outside Virginia was less forthcoming. The task of procuring support from executive departments and legislators was left primarily to brittle coalitions made up largely of historians, state archivists, politicians, businessmen involved in the travel industry, round tables, and patriotic groups. Acting in collaboration with each other and with the CWCC and its advisory council members, these groups sought to convince the Democrats in control of regional politics that the Civil War was worth commemorating in some meaningful way. They often found penny-pinching and present-minded politicians reluctant either to consider the idea of setting up a state commission or to commit significant sums of public money to such an agency. In Tennessee, Governor Frank Clement, "a nationally minded man" as Bell Wiley described him, exhibited little interest in setting up a centennial agency before stepping down in January 1959.[37] Against a background of straitened economic circumstances Nashville's Confederate historian Stanley F. Horn, Gilbert E. Govan (librarian at the University of Tennessee at Chattanooga), and Dan M. Robison (the state archivist) therefore struggled to interest legislators in the project. "There is a feeling that Tennessee should take part in this observance," Robison told Govan in October 1958, "but a person well versed in the financial affairs of the state and with the problems facing the incoming administration suggested that we go slowly in planning things that would require very much money. What with the expanding costs of state government and the determination not to increase taxes, I am told that appropriations for new projects such as this might be hard to come by."[38]

36. Dan Wakefield, "Civil War Centennial: Bull Run with Popcorn," *The Nation*, Jan. 30, 1959, 95; James J. Geary to Betts, March 17, 1960, folder on "National CWCC," box 2, Records of the Virginia Civil War Centennial Commission, Library of Virginia (hereafter VaCWCCR).

37. Wiley to Edmund Gass, Aug. 12, 1958, folder on "General Correspondence, 1958," box 184, Wiley Papers.

38. Dan M. Robison to Gilbert E. Govan, Oct. 30, 1958, microfilm, frame 1244, reel 3, Records of the Tennessee Civil War Centennial Commission, Tennessee State Library and Archives.

Although a commission bill was introduced the following winter with the backing of a more conservative governor, Buford Ellington, Horn reported only limited progress. "[S]o far as I can learn," he wrote in March 1959, "there is no particular opposition to it. On the other hand, nobody seems particularly interested in it, and I have some fears that it may fall by the wayside while the legislators are debating some of the more controversial subjects."[39] A centennial enthusiast in Florida found her efforts to promote enabling legislation equally frustrating. Sounding out a number of potential lobbyists, she "found only the old resentment over the War and Reconstruction and expression of the view that the South might have joined in the celebr[a]tion if the desegregation issue had not been raised."[40]

Progress was not much greater elsewhere in 1958. In Texas the efforts of centennial organizers were stymied by Governor Price Daniel's concerns about the opposition emanating from patriotic organizations like the UDC, SCV, and the Daughters of the American Revolution, all of which had expressed fears that the centennial would be a Yankee celebration.[41] In South Carolina a bill to create a state commission was lost because of inaction in the lower chamber.[42] In Georgia the campaign to secure enabling legislation was hampered by a general preoccupation with the political fight to sustain Jim Crow. Colonel Allen P. ("Ned") Julian, director of the Atlanta Historical Society, reported in the spring of 1959 that those close to Governor S. Ernest Vandiver had declined to press the matter of a state commission upon him. "This past session [of the legislature] was a tense one," he told Karl Betts, "taken up with settling local issues and in seeking some means to protect Georgia's school children from the ruthless political manipulations of Senators [Paul] Douglas and [Jacob] Javits and their sycophants."[43] Support for a state agency was greater in Mississippi, but while Governor James P. Coleman, a moderate segregationist and keen student of the Civil War, did create an unofficial volunteer body during the winter of 1958–59, legislators declined to vote it any funds.[44]

39. Horn to Govan, March 4, 1959, frame 620, reel 5, Horn Papers.

40. Ella Lonn to Betts, Feb. 10, 1959, folder on "Florida State Commission," box 111, subject files 1957–66, CWCCR.

41. Betts to Grant, Oct. 30, 1958, box 2, reading file 1958–66, CWCCR.

42. J. H. Easterby to Betts, Nov. 11, 1958, folder 5, SCDAHR.

43. Allen P. Julian to Betts, March 5, 1959, folder on "Advisory Council: Georgia," box 6, subject files 1957–66, CWCCR. Douglas (D-IL) and Javits (D-NY) numbered among the most vocal supporters of black civil rights in Congress.

44. Charlotte Capers to J. Lindsay Almond, Feb. 12, 1959, folder on "Mississippi CWCC," box 3, VaCWCCR.

Resistance and apathy were overcome, at least to some extent, in every southern state during the course of 1959 and 1960. Lindsay Almond played his part, writing to recalcitrant fellow governors in an effort to persuade them to set up commissions. His circular appeal (which may have been prompted by the CWCC) remained couched in the same language of cold war nationalism that he had used in Miami. In recommending "a dignified observance" of the Civil War to southern governors like Orval Faubus of Arkansas in January 1959, he contended that it was well for every state "to pay tribute on the highest plane to the valiant men of a hundred years ago who gave themselves for the high principles in which they believed. This American spirit of devotion and self-sacrifice must endure in our own people today if this nation is to successfully resist the perils of these times." [45] One Democratic politician apparently influenced by the Virginian was John Patterson, newly installed in the Alabama governor's mansion in Montgomery. A rabid segregationist who owed his election in part to the worst kind of racist demagoguery, Patterson responded as positively as his correspondent could have hoped. "I am certainly interested in this project," he replied, "and I will work with you every way possible to see that we have such a commission here in Alabama." [46] The governor was as good as his word. An Alabama centennial agency was created by the state legislature in September 1959. [47] Lindsay Almond's intervention went beyond gubernatorial contacts. Even though Price Daniel was allegedly doing "approximately nothing" to foster the centennial in Texas, Karl Betts reported in August 1959 that Almond's message to a hundred leading cities had resulted in the formation of sixty-six local commissions in the Lone Star State. [48]

The Virginia governor could not take all the credit for the drift toward compliance with the centennial project, for pressure told from below as well as above. As befitted a diverse collection of interest groups, local centennial promoters used a range of debating points to persuade governors to support their

45. Almond to Orval E. Faubus, Jan. 26, 1959, folder on "Mississippi CWCC," box 3, VaCWCCR.

46. Patterson to Almond, Jan. 30, 1959, folder 6, AlaG.

47. *Atlanta Constitution,* Sept. 27, 1959, clipping encl. in Wiley to Betts, Sept. 29, 1959, folder on "Alabama State Commission," box 107, subject files, 1957–66, CWCCR. A press release issued by the Alabama governor's office (Oct. 29, [1959], folder 6, AlaG) noted that the legislature had created a state centennial agency "as a means of promoting a better understanding of the heroic and valorous sacrifices of the people of Alabama in this great war for principles which they believed to be true and eternal."

48. Frank E. Vandiver to Wiley, Aug. 13, 1959; Betts to Wiley, Aug. 20, 1959, folder in "General Correspondence, 1959," box 184, Wiley Papers.

case for a commission. Rather than stressing cold war exigencies as Almond had, they tended to emphasize the local historical significance of the impending observance or the material benefits likely to accrue. Embarrassment and flattery were also useful weapons. Charles L. Anger, head of the department of history at The Citadel in Charleston, reminded Governor Ernest F. Hollings that the one hundredth anniversary of secession was approaching. "At no time in American history," he wrote, "did South Carolina play a more important, a more vital part than at that period." Many states had already made provision for official recognition of the centennial, he continued, and it would be "most unfortunate" if South Carolina, "the leader and center of the [secession] movement," failed to participate. "It is too important an undertaking," he went on, "to be handled by a private organization or even by a city; it is something the entire state glories in and should also share in."[49] Albert B. Moore, a Civil War historian at the University of Alabama, added his voice to that of Lindsay Almond, telling Governor Patterson in April 1959 that he had been asked by Karl Betts to devise a centennial program for the state in collaboration with his more liberal predecessor, James Folsom. "I did not do so," wrote Moore (an outspoken defender of segregation), "because I knew we could do a better job with you, and I wanted you to have credit for the enterprise."[50] The implication of Moore's letter was clearly that he believed the centennial could be used as an effective weapon in the fight to preserve Jim Crow. Racial considerations were seldom far from the surface of southern centennial negotiations and occasionally were made explicit. Mary Givens Bryan, the veteran director of the Georgia State Archives, urged Governor Vandiver to follow Mississippi's example and create a centennial agency by executive order. "We have a rich heritage and a glorious history to tell the nation," she contended: "Never in the history of our country have people been so interested in history and records as they are today. It is NECESSARY TO PRESERVE OUR PERMANENTLY VALUABLE RECORDS TO PROVE WE ARE WHITE! Our GOLDEN HOUR has arrived as we approach the event of commemorating the great sacrifices made by Georgians during the Civil War."[51]

---

49. Charles L. Anger to Ernest F. Hollings, Jan. 13, 1959, folder 5, SCDAHR.

50. Albert B. Moore to Patterson, April 6, 1959, folder 6, AlaG.

51. Mary Givens Bryan to S. Ernest Vandiver, Jan. 26, 1959, Records of the Georgia Civil War Centennial Commission, Record Group 079-02-004, Georgia State Archives (GaCWCCR hereafter). The archiving of southern history had been closely linked to white supremacism since the beginning of the twentieth century. See Brundage, *Southern Past*, 105–37.

The persistent lobbying paid off. By January 1960 every southern state could boast some kind of centennial commission, set up either by executive order or by legislative action.[52] Even though most received at best only modest funding compared with Virginia, it was plain that the region's political elite had overcome its most serious reservations about the commemoration.[53] Cajoled externally by the CWCC and Lindsay Almond and pressed from below by a range of interested parties, southern governors ultimately concluded that it was safer to embrace the centennial than to ignore it. Respected (not to mention highly vocal) guardians of the Lost Cause such as the UDC and SCV were determined, as ever, to pay tribute to the heroism and sacrifice of their Confederate forebears. Local scholars, librarians, and archivists regarded it as an ideal opportunity to broaden their own influence and at the same time educate a southern public thirsting for knowledge about the region's past. Businessmen and state travel officials insisted that the centennial would help to promote economic development—a goal shared by most segregationists and liberals alike. When combined with the enticing prospect that this grand event might strengthen popular resolve in the interrelated struggles against communism and civil rights, these arguments proved sufficient to generate the degree of state backing without which the centennial could not succeed.

The CWCC had no doubt that active state commissions held the key to realizing its main goal of a popular, patriotic commemoration of the Civil War.

52. *100 Years After*, 3 (Jan. 1960).

53. State funding for southern centennial agencies outside of Virginia ranged from a relatively generous $200,000 for the first biennium in Mississippi to more miserly initial appropriations of $10,000 in Tennessee and $25,000 in Georgia. Frank E. Everett to Betts, May 30, 1960, folder on "Betts, Karl S.," box 708, Records of the Mississippi Commission on the War Between the States, Record Group 19, Mississippi Department of Archives and History (hereafter MCWBTSR); Horn to Govan, March 23, 1959, frame 623, reel 5, Horn Papers; *Atlanta Journal*, Jan. 2, 1961, 18. The Florida, Louisiana, and Texas commissions were particularly weak and starved of funds. See, for example, Charlton W. Tebeau to Betts, March 16, 1960, and Adam G. Adams to Betts, Aug. 26, 1960, folder on "Florida State Commission," box 111, subject files 1957–66, CWCCR; Betts to Charles Dufour, June 8, 1960, folder on "Louisiana State Commission," box 114, subject files 1957–66, CWCCR; Cooper K. Ragan to Betts, Dec. 31, 1959, June 2, 1960, folder on "Texas State Commission," box 126, subject files 1957–66, CWCCR. Staff sizes were small. Mississippi director Sidney T. Roebuck reported that he had only five employees, some of them temporary. Roebuck to Ross R. Barnett, Dec. 5, 1960, folder on "Correspondence: B—Misc., July–Dec. 1960," box 707, MCWBTSR.

Jackson Place would provide the basic framework for observances, but for ideological, political, and financial reasons it was determined that local people should take the lead in running most of the events. To a large extent (Virginia's richly endowed agency was something of an exception) the work of the state commissions mirrored that of the parent body. Blessed with limited resources, their task was to stimulate centennial organizing in local communities. "Our general idea," wrote Stanley Horn after the first meeting of the Tennessee commission, "is to encourage the local and community groups to formulate their own plans for such commemorative activities as they deem advisable with our state Commission acting in an advisory capacity, giving the fullest possible cooperation, but not undertaking to supervise any decisions."[54]

Although CWCC officials were determined to devolve ultimate responsibility for organizing events to the states, they were not averse to intervening directly in local plans if they ran counter to those of the national commission. In December 1959 Karl Betts questioned the Virginia commission's proposed commemoration of the abortive 1861 Washington Peace Conference. "[W]e must be very careful not to over-emphasize secondary events," he remarked. "We are concentrating our energies in bringing to the attention of the American people the significance of the Centennial years through a nationwide and carefully organized program."[55] In this particular instance, Betts's tactless behavior failed to dissuade the state commission from pursuing its course of action. Indeed, it served to illustrate the almost inevitable friction that existed between the chronically underfunded CWCC and the well-resourced Virginia agency.

The southern state commissions (like their northern counterparts) comprised broad public-private coalitions that reflected the principal motives for local participation in the centennial. Mississippi's pointedly titled Commission on the War Between the States included representatives of the UDC, the SCV, the Jackson Civil War Round Table, the Mississippi Park Commission, the Mississippi Automobile Club, the Garden Clubs of Mississippi, the Mississippi Manufacturers' Association, the Mississippi Agricultural and Industrial Board, the Mississippi Historical Society, and the state's Department of Archives and History.[56] Alabama's centennial agency, belatedly established by

54. Horn to Betts, May 18, 1959, frame 998, reel 1, Horn Papers.

55. Betts to Lyon G. Tyler, Dec. 28, 1959, folder on "General Correspondence, 1959," box 184, Wiley Papers.

56. Charlotte Capers to Almond, Feb. 12, 1959, folder on "Mississippi Civil War Centennial Commission," box 3, VaCWCCR.

legislative action in the late summer of 1959, was made up of the governor, the lieutenant governor, the speaker of the House of Representatives, the director of the State Archives, chairs of the history departments at Auburn and Tuscaloosa, the state presidents of the UDC and the SCV, the president of the Alabama Historical Association, one member from each of the state's nine congressional districts, and five at-large members.[57]

Each state commission was run primarily by its chairman and/or executive director who was assisted in a minority of cases by a handful of staff and who consulted from time to time over policy with the full members of the agency. The leading figures on the southern commissions were a diverse collection of individuals, though most had some tie to the Democratic administration that controlled the politics of their respective state. John Amasa May, chairman of the South Carolina agency, was a maverick member of the state legislature from Aiken who was known familiarly as "Mr. Confederate" because of his enthusiastic attachment to the Lost Cause. Peter Zack Geer, the ambitious career politician who initially took charge of affairs in Georgia, was an ally of Governor Vandiver. Sam Dickinson, voice of the Arkansas commission, was a hard-drinking, pro-Faubus journalist on the *Little Rock Gazette.* Alabama's Albert B. Moore was a historian who, as we have seen, regarded himself as a close ally of Governor Patterson. Sidney T. Roebuck, the Mississippi commission's executive director, was president of the state's Motel Association and strongly committed to the values propagated by the state's new governor, Ross R. Barnett. Staunch segregationists, all five men bore the unmistakable stamp of the Jim Crow regime that employed them. It was no accident that Virginia and North Carolina, two states with relatively pragmatic executive officers by 1961, possessed politically moderate commission chairmen: James J. Geary and Norman Larson, respectively.

Once established, the southern commissions began making preparations within the broad framework laid down by the CWCC. Among their most important tasks was to generate support from businessmen, particularly those working in the South's developing tourist industry. Lyon G. Tyler, an official of the Virginia commission and direct descendant of former U.S. president John Tyler, met with a range of interested parties to stress the significance of forthcoming events. "The Centennial," he told the Virginia Broadcasters' Association in June 1960, "is an opportunity for profit . . . for this will be the biggest tourist attraction in our history. The Centennial will cover the whole State and it will last almost five years. We can expect reams of free publicity because

57. *Montgomery Advertiser,* Sept. 29, 1959, clipping, folder 2, AlaPIF.

60% of the Civil War happened in this State."[58] Interesting the local media in the centennial was a critical precondition for getting ordinary southerners involved. Other stages in the process of grassroots mobilization included the appointment of local commissions to organize community events, the devising of educational programs for schools, and the dissemination of reading materials. The southern commissions produced their own literature—leaflets and pamphlets that outlined the centennial's relevance to the inhabitants of their states and offered guidance on how to orchestrate commemorative events. Virginians were encouraged to rededicate Confederate monuments with appropriate ceremonies, to collect Civil War documents such as soldiers' letters and diaries for preservation, to sponsor essay contests in local schools, and to set up Civil War museums in their home towns.[59]

Most of these promotional efforts comported with the federal agenda grounded in the cultural cold war. Georgia's centennial manual, for example, outspokenly characterized the Civil War as the wellspring of American hegemony in the twentieth century. "This nation started from scratch," boasted the booklet, "and now is the most successful in the history of the world. The Centennial gives us an opportunity to discern from our history what made us the most powerful and united on the face of the earth."[60] Some anxious conservatives in the same mold as General Grant were attracted by the prospect of using a consensual memory of the Civil War experience to instill quintessential American values into the southern people. Alluding to the recent demise of the U.S.-backed Kishi administration in Japan, Lyon Tyler articulated his conviction that Americans could only wage the cold war effectively if they renewed their faith in democracy. There could be no better way to promote this renewal, he told the Virginia Broadcasters' Association, than to educate people about the elevated character of Civil War heroes like Robert E. Lee, "a man largely without hate, without fear and without pride, greed or selfish ambition." Continued Tyler, "The enemy is working while we are still groping for our National Purpose[,] . . . for the faith to sustain us."[61]

58. Tyler, "Remarks to the Virginia Broadcasters' Association," June 30, 1960, folder on "Virginia Association of Broadcasters," box 1, VaCWCCR.

59. Virginia Civil War Centennial Commission, "Suggestions for Local Committees: The Civil War Centennial, 1961–1965," folder on "Grassroots Organization," box 1, VaCWCCR.

60. Georgia Civil War Centennial Commission, *Civil War Centennial: Manual for Georgians* [Atlanta, 1960], 13, in folder on "Georgia Civil War Centennial Committee," box 3, VaCWCCR.

61. Tyler, "Remarks to the Virginia Broadcasters' Association."

If these comments suggested a relatively close match between the political objectives of the CWCC on the one hand and the southern commissions on the other, so too did the racially exclusive nature of the southerners' organizing efforts. All of the southern commissions took it for granted that the Confederate experience had impinged primarily on whites and that therefore whites would be the only southerners involved in commemorating the Civil War. When setting up a centennial body in Savannah, Peter Zack Geer, chairman of the Georgia commission, advised municipal and county officers to secure representation from "all existing *white* PTAs."[62] The national commission did nothing to discourage this trend. Indeed, its patronizing pronouncements on the role of blacks in the Civil War can only have served to calm the fears of local whites that the centennial was a stalking-horse for civil rights. When the CWCC did make an occasional token gesture toward African Americans, it soon uncovered the acute racial sensitivity of some southerners. In July 1958 Ned Julian, a member of the Georgia commission's pageants and reenactments committee, expressed outrage that one of Atlanta's black college presidents had been appointed to the national agency's advisory council. The colonel told Karl Betts sarcastically that "if the integrationists and the Negrophiles have already seized so dominant a place in the Commission that we are faced with a centennial observance of Reconstruction, too, let us, at least, keep it in its proper chronological sequence; to do otherwise will damage irreparably the whole, splendidly-conceived program."[63]

Julian's fears that the CWCC would promote black civil rights were entirely groundless. As well as being ideologically predisposed toward white southern concerns over race, Grant and Betts believed they were indebted to the powerful southern Democrats in Congress who played an important role in securing the commission's $100,000 annual appropriation in 1958.[64] Even if they had considered questioning the white supremacist policies of the southern commissions, they would have had to deal with the fact that the decentralized format of the centennial necessarily devolved most of the decision-making on those commissions and their white-dominated local committees. Charged

---

62. Peter Zack Geer to H. Lee Fulton Jr., June 8, 1960, folder on "Chatham County, Savannah CWCC," box 2, GaCWCCR, RG 079-01-001. Emphasis added.

63. Julian to Betts, July 10, 1958, folder on "Advisory Council: Georgia," box 6, subject file 1957–66, CWCCR.

64. Betts to Wiley, Aug. 22, 1958, folder on "General Correspondence, 1958," box 184, Wiley Papers; Betts to Tuck, Aug. 22, 1958, folder 5266, Tuck Papers.

with promoting consensus at a time when the civil rights movement appeared to have stalled, the CWCC went out of its way not to alienate southern whites. It made little effort to involve blacks in its programs and poured cold water on the idea of any event to mark the anniversary of John Brown's abolitionist raid on Harpers Ferry.[65] By the beginning of 1959 Karl Betts was confident that his efforts had begun to pay dividends. "I sense a very strong undercurrent of mounting interest in the Centennial," he told Bill Tuck, "and I confidently believe that any possible complications resulting from the integration problem will soon disappear. At least that is the reaction we get from all our correspondence from all over the country and particularly in the South."[66]

SECESSION FEVER

Karl Betts was right about growing popular interest in the centennial in the South during the late 1950s, for the organizing drive was well underway. Lyon Tyler reported that twenty-five out of thirty-one cities and fifty out of ninety-eight counties in Virginia possessed centennial committees by November 1959.[67] Over half the counties in Alabama had set up similar bodies by the end of the following year.[68] Even Georgia, which was late to embrace the centennial project, had twenty-four county committees by December 1960.[69] Support for the centennial was certainly patchy. Robert E. Covington, an organizer in Quitman, Mississippi, commented that although he had approached several people about forming a committee, he had "had no luck whatsoever." In observing that older communities in the vicinity were probably more interested in "this sort of thing than we are," Covington put his finger on an

65. Despite the CWCC's lack of interest in John Brown, the town of Harpers Ferry staged "a very successful four-day observance" of the raid's centennial on October 15–18, 1959. An estimated 65,000 visitors tested local facilities to breaking point. Highlights included a reenactment of the storming of the engine house, a sham battle, a daily performance of a play entitled "The Prophet," and a historical seminar at which professional scholars discussed the raid "in a thoroughly objective and dispassionate manner." To mark the event Maryland officials announced that the state was deeding 625 acres of land on Maryland Heights to the NPS. The commemoration was organized by a committee of interested local citizens and NPS staff based at the Harpers Ferry National Monument. Boyd B. Stutler, ed., "Notes and Queries," *Civil War History* 6 (1960): 89–90.

66. Betts to Tuck, Feb. 5, 1959, folder 5267, Tuck Papers.

67. Tyler, "Report on Grass Roots Program," Nov. 11, 1959, folder on "Operations, Grass Roots Organization," box 1, VaCWCCR.

68. Albert B. Moore to Betts, Dec. 21, 1960, folder on "Alabama State Commission," box 107, subject files 1957–66, CWCCR.

69. *Atlanta Constitution,* Dec. 7, 1960, 47.

obvious but important truth about the centennial.[70] Grassroots interest was concentrated heavily in those parts of the South that had physical links to the Civil War. Commemorating that conflict made most sense to local people if a community possessed a veterans' cemetery, well-preserved antebellum buildings, or, best of all, a battlefield—tangible places that could be made the focal point for civic observances. It was also the case that areas with a strong attachment to the Confederacy tended to exhibit more interest than those that had favored the Union. There were at least two reasons for this discrepancy. One was that the old Unionist areas of the South were often poor and mountainous. Even in the mid-twentieth century they lacked the clusters of wealthy elites that formed centennial committees in less remote parts of the region. But another major explanation was that the southern commissions themselves were committed primarily to a celebration of the Confederacy. "We have no centennial committee in Greenville," remarked the executive director of the Tennessee commission, "and I have found no interest in the formation of one since they apparently have the idea that they have no part in the centennial."[71]

If Betts was right about the growth of southern interest in the centennial, he was wrong to conclude that "the integration problem" would cease to be a problem for his commission. While there was a good fit between the commission's position on race and that of the southern agencies, maintaining it depended on the willingness of outside parties to indulge southern whites' determination to commemorate the Confederate experience. In the late 1950s relatively few white northerners wanted to endanger national unity by imposing wholesale integration on their unwilling peers in the South. Little Rock aside, the Eisenhower administration had minimal interest in enforcing the *Brown* decision. Indeed, the federal courts and the FBI were complicit in the effort of southern state governments to obstruct the pace of public school desegregation. It was little wonder, therefore, that the CWCC—a federal body created in the image of a conservative regime—was content to cooperate with segregationists and allow them to plan a racially exclusive centennial that had an obvious bearing on contemporary political issues. Had the southern commissions resisted the temptation to link a celebration of Confederate valor with contemporary racial issues all might have been well. But this was not to be. For while the Eisenhower administration did not pose an immediate threat

70. Robert E. Covington Jr., to Roebuck, Dec. 10, 1960, folder on "Correspondence—Miscellaneous [1960]," box 708, MCWBTSR.

71. Campbell H. Brown to Mrs. James R. Stokely Jr., Aug. 1, 1960, frame 127, reel 5, Horn Papers.

to Jim Crow, southern racists knew that their traditional way of life was under attack from worryingly assertive blacks and their supposedly manipulative leftist and liberal allies. Many southern commission members recognized that the centennial presented them with an opportunity to use Civil War memory as a means of steeling ordinary whites in the fight to defend the crumbling racial order. Patriotic groups such as the UDC and the SCV did not always agree with radical segregationists on the proper use of Confederate symbols like the battle flag, but they all believed that diffusing their particular version of the southern past was essential if the region's institutions and customs—indeed, its very identity—were to survive the interconnected threats of federal power, modernity, and what they regarded as creeping socialism.

A position paper drawn up, in all likelihood, by Sidney T. Roebuck, head of Mississippi's centennial agency, noted "a real present danger to this Southern heritage"—one that stemmed as much from popular apathy and ignorance as from the ongoing school crisis. Ordinary white southerners, claimed the document, were "not aware of the cycle of history in which we find ourselves. We have grown complacent and *fat* in more than one sense of the word." Too often southerners were made to feel guilty about their past. Yet, it continued, "We have a great heritage. On it has been built the greatest civilization and economy the world has ever known. We should let our pride in our achievements overcome our fears and self-pity." To lose the battle to preserve this heritage meant "disaster and chaos." To win it required the full support of "men steeped in our Southern Heritage": "We must go on the offensive. We have been on the defensive too long."[72] While the centennial offered substantial material benefits to the South (and in this respect appealed both to liberals working in the business-progressive tradition of the region and to die-hard segregationists), it was clearly much more than a matter of dollars and cents to men like Sidney Roebuck.

Segregationists had good reason to suppose that their way of life was under imminent threat. During the course of 1960 well-dressed, disciplined black students across the South engaged in a campaign of sit-ins to end segregated eating facilities in public places. Although the protests were successful primarily in the rim South, that they happened at all placed Jim Crow under renewed pressure, for they made it plain to the watching world that African Americans were not content living unequal lives and were now willing to fight actively

---

72. [Roebuck?], "Vehicles for Preserving Our Southern Heritage," folder on "Mississippi—State Director," box 717, MCWBTSR. This undated draft document contains emendations in Roebuck's hand.

and collectively for justice. One entirely unforeseen result of the sit-ins was to further politicize the upcoming centennial. Segregationists simply did not regard the demonstrations as legitimate expressions of protest, nor were they impressed by indications of support for the students emanating from northern Democrats and liberal Republicans. One SCV member in Meridian, Mississippi, admitted (not entirely convincingly) that the centennial should not be an excuse for refighting the Civil War. However, he added, "if the iron heel of tyranny of the impatient radicals of both National Political Parties are successful in putting across the Civil Rights planks in their platforms, there will again be bloodshed in the South before the end of 1965."[73] As the pressure on them increased, segregationists looked even more to the past for succor. With sectional tensions on the rise again, there was, for some, no better place to look than the example of southern secession.

On May 27, 1960, state senator John D. Long, right-wing Democrat, staunch Baptist, and member of the South Carolina centennial commission, delivered a prolix address on the approaching anniversary of secession to the upper chamber in Columbia. The speech testified to the fragility of the nationalist orthodoxy on the Civil War and the limited appeal of the CWCC's consensual agenda below the Mason-Dixon line even at the height of the cold war. Long began by casting suspicion on the notion of a centennial commemoration initiated by Washington. Northerners, he claimed, had always tried to blame southerners for starting the Civil War. Now, "[w]hile South Carolina and the other Confederate States are being lured to prepare for a 'Love feast' the signs point to all out preparations on the part of the federal government to blacken and damn our good name forever beyond repair." After an extensive historical account of Yankee wrongs and southern sufferings, Long turned his attention to contemporary matters by using Ulysses S. Grant's alleged anti-Semitism and William T. Sherman's racism to illustrate northern hypocrisy on civil rights. "Now isn't that attitude in the Yankees back there," he asked, "consistent with Vice-President Nixon and Chief Justice Warren avoiding racial integration in their own families by sending their children to private white schools, while those who cannot afford to do otherwise because of financial inability are compelled to send their children to racially mixed public schools regardless of how offensive or detrimental it may be to them?"

Considering himself a patriotic southerner and American, Long made it clear that he had no truck with the country's foreign enemies. Indeed, one of

73. Jim B. Collier to Roebuck, July 18, 1960, folder on "Correspondence—Miscellaneous [1960]," box 789, MCWBTSR.

his main objectives in making this speech was to criticize President Eisenhower for reducing the United States to the level of "a second rate power." Communists, he insisted, were the "enemies of God" and of "all mankind": "If Red China should devour Red Russia or Red Russia should gobble up Red China it would suit me just fine, provided, of course, that the survivor was so weakened in the process that the free world would have no difficulty exterminating that one, too, thus ridding the world of both pests." The remainder of Long's address was a justification for southern secession. South Carolinians, he proclaimed, had fought for the right of local self-government—"the only guarantee of personal liberty and human freedom as we know and enjoy them under republican forms of government of the democracies of the free world." It was time for an end to humbug-ridden talk about the mistreatment of slaves: in 1860 the U.S. government had been engaged in exterminating the Indians. The laws of nature had now been overturned by "a sociologized Supreme Court" on the authority of one "Gunnel Myrdar [sic]." Lincoln had attacked Fort Sumter to make the Confederates fire the first shot. And so on, and so on. A long list of southern grievances in which those of the past merged seamlessly with those of the present.[74]

Long's self-indulgent speech accurately reflected the confused state of the segregationist mindset at a critical juncture in southern history. By turn angry, bitter, patriotic, and disloyal, the rhetoric highlighted the segregationists' search for a usable past. Positing a direct connection between 1860 and 1960 enabled them to locate the meaning of current events. As Governor James P. Coleman of Mississippi phrased it in a televised address to the Jackson Civil War Round Table, the Civil War had "catapulted" the Negro "into the forefront of all political controversies. There he remains today because of a United States Supreme Court decision rendered in 1954 which good lawyers consider legally unsound and which Mississippi is wholly unwilling to accept because of its unsoundness. Of course, the 1954 decision itself is one of the long line of direct consequences of the Civil War. One step led to the next, and one thing brought on another."[75]

74. *Address by the Honorable John D. Long on the South Carolina Secession Ordinance Delivered before the Senate of the Ninety-Third General Assembly of the State of South Carolina, May 27, 1960* (n.p., n.d.), quotations on 7, 30, 37, 45, 48. Gunnar Myrdal's progressive analysis of racism and segregation in the United States, *An American Dilemma* (1944), was cited as an authority by Earl Warren in the *Brown* decision.

75. James P. Coleman, *The Effect of the Civil War on Mississippi, 1865–1958: An Address Delivered by Governor J. P. Coleman Before the Jackson Civil War Round Table, November 21, 1958. Repeated on WLBT-Television, November 25, 1958* (n.p., n.d.), 1.

Efforts to connect federal wrongs in the past and the present proved especially convincing in the winter of 1960–61 as some district judges brought pressure to bear on urban school systems in the region that were continuing to resist even token integration. Against a background of mob action in New Orleans and Atlanta, Senator Harry Byrd of Virginia told the annual meeting of the National Cotton Council in January that "federal centralization" was sapping American freedoms.[76] The secession observances of early 1961 gave ordinary southern whites the chance not only to enjoy themselves but also to show their determination to preserve their liberties as they perceived them.

Fervent grassroots participation in these festivities indicated widespread popular support among southern whites for the Civil War centennial during its early months. Montgomery, Alabama, the first capital of the Confederacy, was one of several communities to plan an extensive set of activities that winter. Local and state-level elites were heavily involved in the project to mark the genesis of the aspirant southern nation. The Alabama commission chairman, Albert Moore, cooperated closely with civic leaders in the city who saw the potential for moneymaking and political gain. These notables included not only Paul Fuller, who committed the support of the chamber of commerce, but also Mayor Earl D. James. James, a staunch segregationist whose power base lay in the white, lower-middle-class wards of east Montgomery, had been elected in 1958 as a vociferous defender of Jim Crow. His chief opponent was William A. "Tacky" Gayle, mayor at the time of the 1955–56 bus boycott. Gayle, claimed James, had allowed "racial agitators" to torment the city: "Strong leadership is needed to resist these forces that are bent on destroying our Southern way of life."[77] What better way to defend that way of life and promote greater solidarity among Montgomery whites than by organizing a grand celebration of the Confederacy?

The principal vehicle for mobilizing the populace was to be a spectacular week-long historical pageant, "The Man and the Hour," to mark both the founding of the Confederate government in Montgomery and the inauguration of Jefferson Davis as the new nation's provisional president. As Bruce Baker has pointed out, southern pageants in the early decades of the twentieth century were designed with a specific objective in mind. Whereas northern reformers normally used pageants inclusively to generate solidarity between classes and ethnic groups, southern civic elites regarded them as a means of

76. *Montgomery Advertiser,* Jan. 11, 1961, A6.
77. Thornton, *Dividing Lines,* 111.

promoting an exclusive white racial unity.[78] In line with this tradition, Montgomery segregationists set up a nonprofit organization that employed George H. Elias and the John B. Rogers Company of Ohio to produce the event.[79] Looking to generate a large hometown cast and guarantee packed houses at the municipal coliseum, the pageant's organizers and supporters enthusiastically promoted the centennial to white residents. Encouraged by right-wing governor John Patterson, the chamber of commerce, downtown businesses, and the local press and churches, Montgomerians rushed to enlist in the southern cause almost as keenly as they had done a hundred years earlier.[80] Local men, reveling in patriarchal display at a time when their control of Jim Crow society was under threat, joined "Confederate Colonel" chapters, donned gray uniforms, and grew beards and mustaches. Most were recruited at the workplace: as early as the second week of January, chapters had been formed in several offices of the state government, as well as at the Alabama Power Company.[81] White children learned about the "War Between the States" from teachers who came to school dressed in nineteenth-century clothing.[82] Girls and boys in grades one to six were granted permission by school authorities to wear Civil War–era costumes each Thursday.[83] Local white women seemed especially willing to embrace the centennial. They welcomed the opportunity to form "Confederate Belle" chapters, centered in the workplace and in their own civic groups; they collected period items for an Old South exhibition at the city's Museum of Fine Arts; they participated in a "Belle of the Confederacy" beauty contest, which was won by Mrs. Bobbie Garman, a "pretty secretary for the State of Alabama"; and they enthusiastically dressed up in *Gone with*

78. Bruce E. Baker, "Devastated by Passion and Belief: Remembering Reconstruction in the Twentieth-Century South" (Ph.D. thesis, University of North Carolina, 2003), 256–57. Northern pageants, it should be stressed, were hardly models of interracial participation, but African Americans did play a role in some community-wide events. Blacks, for example, danced and marched in Manhattan's Hudson-Fulton festival in 1909. Alessandra Lorini, *Rituals of Race: American Public Culture and the Search for Racial Democracy* (Charlottesville: University Press of Virginia, 1999), 215–17.

79. The John B. Rogers Company had been producing historical pageants on a commercial basis since 1919. David Glassberg, *American Historical Pageantry: The Uses of Tradition in the Early Twentieth Century* (Chapel Hill: University of North Carolina Press, 1990), 257.

80. *Montgomery Advertiser*, Jan. 8, 1961, B1.

81. Ibid., B4.

82. *Montgomery Advertiser*, Jan. 15, 1961, D4.

83. *Montgomery Advertiser*, Jan. 18, 1961, A6.

the Wind finery in anticipation of the forthcoming centennial ball.[84] White
women were also instrumental in drumming up wider interest in the Montgomery festivities by taking part in full-costume Confederate motorcades that
toured outlying towns such as Wetumpka and Dadeville.[85]

The pageant took place during the week of February 12, 1961. Attended
by an estimated 50,000 people, it was a colorful affair complete with voodoo
dancers and minstrels.[86] The accompanying brochure bore witness to the business community's support. One advertisement—for Montgomery Fair, former employer of the bus boycott heroine Rosa Parks—featured drawings of
Civil War regalia and a southern belle and boasted that it had been central
Alabama's "leading department store" since 1868. Another, carrying a Rebel
flag, proclaimed "Winn Dixie and Kwik-Chek Show Phenomenal Growth
During a Century of Progress in Dixieland." Spectators who paid up to five
dollars for a ticket watched a sixteen-segment performance by a home-grown
cast numbering over a thousand.[87] The two-hour pageant, a combination of
the spoken word, music, and dancing, began with a salute to the Belle of the
Confederacy and then took viewers through the major events of the secession crisis. In a section entitled "General Davis Speaks," the audience heard an
almost verbatim staging of the Confederate president's inaugural in which he
trumpeted the cause of states' rights and the legitimacy of secession. On leaving the coliseum, spectators were greeted with a crashing fireworks display to
mark the founding of the southern nation. A watching journalist pronounced
the whole performance a genuine "spectacular," though he did complain that
in the inauguration scene Jefferson Davis had been portrayed "as a corn-pone
politician at a Black Belt party rally."[88]

On the night of February 17, hundreds of Montgomerians waited in the
rain at Union station to greet the arrival of a local attorney playing the part

84. *Montgomery Advertiser*, Jan. 11, 1961, A6; Jan. 22, 1961, B5; Jan. 29, 1961, B1. Garman, the
blonde, twenty-two-year-old wife of a local student, worked as a secretary in the state's Alcoholic
Beverage Control Office. "I'm so happy," she said after being told of her success, "I don't know
what to do." Around 39,000 people bought tickets to vote in the beauty contest. *Montgomery Advertiser*, Feb. 8, 1961, A1.

85. *Montgomery Advertiser*, Jan. 29, 1961, A1.

86. *Montgomery Advertiser*, Feb. 20, 1961, A2.

87. *Montgomery Centennial Commemoration of the Civil War*, official program, Feb. 12–18,
1961, folder 22A, Records of the Alabama Department of Archives and History, SG11137, Alabama
Department of Archives and History.

88. *Alabama Journal*, Feb. 15, 1961, clipping in folder 2, AlaPIF.

of Jefferson Davis. Equipped with torches approved by the fire department, they escorted Davis to the Exchange where the new president was met by the serving chief justice of the Alabama Supreme Court, J. Ed. Livingston, an outspoken white supremacist who was playing the part of his antebellum predecessor, E. C. Bullock.[89] The highlight of Montgomery's centennial proceedings came the next day. Large crowds braved more wet weather to watch a long parade move slowly up Dexter Avenue past the modest brick church only recently vacated by Martin Luther King to the white-domed statehouse that had been the site of President Davis's inauguration a hundred years previously. Among the parade were several militia units, a minstrel band, and carriages containing the real-life governors of Alabama, Virginia, and Mississippi (all clad in wartime garb supplied by the Rogers Company). There followed a careful reenactment of the inauguration ceremony in which John Patterson played secessionist governor A. B. Moore, city commissioners Lester B. Sullivan and Frank Parks acted the parts of the original reception committee, and state circuit judge Walter B. Jones assumed the role of Georgian Howell Cobb to administer the oath of office. (In a careful act of symbolism, Jones used the same Bible that had been employed in 1861.)[90] That night 5,000 people attended the centennial ball, and the following day, Sunday, thousands more purchased copies of the *Montgomery Advertiser*'s best-selling "Confederate Centennial Edition."[91] Commentators marveled at the class and racial unity evinced by these events. A delighted Governor Patterson told Karl Betts that "the Centennial observance here was most outstanding. The entire city really got in on the act, and I do not believe that I can recall more community spirit and interest in any other event."[92] Paul Fuller, from the chamber of commerce, said that he had "never seen the people of Montgomery join in anything so wholeheartedly."[93]

Of course, evidence that a broad cross-section of Alabama whites was excited about taking part in festivities to mark the birth of the Confederacy tells us very little about what such involvement actually meant to participants— beyond the obvious fact that it afforded individuals a welcome change from

89. *Montgomery Advertiser,* Feb. 18, 1961, A1.

90. *Montgomery Advertiser,* Feb. 19, 1961, A1, A2.

91. *Montgomery Advertiser,* Feb. 20, 1961, A2. The paper's Centennial Edition appeared on Feb. 19.

92. Patterson to Betts, Feb. 27, 1961, folder on "Alabama Civil War Centennial Commission 1961," box 107, subject files 1957–66, CWCCR.

93. *Montgomery Advertiser,* Feb. 20, 1961, A2.

their daily work routine. Certainly it cannot be assumed that the rush to dress up like Robert E. Lee or Scarlett O'Hara indicated a general desire on the part of white Montgomerians to refight the Civil War. At least one speaker during the observances to mark secession emphasized the need for national unity at a time of acute international tension over Laos and the Congo—a message that one presumes was not lost on the city's red-blooded patriots.[94]

This said, it would have been difficult for anyone living in one of the remaining hubs of massive resistance to overlook the contemporary threat to segregation. Several high-profile events that winter, not least the mob efforts to prevent court-ordered school desegregation in New Orleans and Atlanta, demonstrated that the fight to save Jim Crow was intensifying. Of particular concern to bitter-enders was that recently Governor Vandiver of Georgia had bowed to the federal judiciary over the admission of black students to the state university in Athens.[95] It did not therefore take a great leap of imagination for Montgomery whites to connect their own embattled situation to that of their ancestors. As one contributor to the main local newspaper wrote during the centennial festivities:

Today the South is facing many of the same problems it faced in 1861. Federal dictatorship is literally being stuffed down our throats. Integration is now a major issue, not just a rumor. The battle is not solely one of segregation versus integration, any more than the Civil War was one of slavery versus freedom of slaves.

Then, it was the right of the people to withdraw from a partnership which had become unsatisfactory because one faction sought to impose beliefs upon the other. Today it is a matter of democracy versus autocracy, the majority versus nine Supreme Court Justices.

The South as a whole has been politically blacklisted. We the people of a democracy should stand up and fight as our forefathers did so we can lick this ever present battle with the federal government as it continues to usurp rights delegated to the states.[96]

Judge Walter Jones, a leading figure in his state's campaign to suppress the NAACP, made a similar point while reflecting approvingly on the recent centennial events. Elated by his own role in the inauguration pageant, Jones

---

94. *Montgomery Advertiser,* Feb. 13, 1961, A1.
95. *Montgomery Advertiser,* Jan. 29, 1961, A1, A2.
96. *Montgomery Advertiser,* Feb. 3, 1961, C3.

argued that Montgomery's centennial program had given whites in the state "a deeper appreciation of the things the Confederacy fought for, and helped them to realize that unrestrained federal power is destroying this nation."[97]

The capacity of the centennial to generate and reflect a distinctively southern memory at odds with the consensual aims of the CWCC was evident throughout the South in the spring of 1961. In Mississippi, a Jackson newspaper editor greeted his city's commemoration of secession with the observation that Jefferson Davis had forecast that the cause of states' rights would not die with the Confederacy: "His prophecy has come true. Local self-government in the form of national independence for the South is, of course, no longer an issue, but local self-government in the form of States' Rights definitely is a burning issue today."[98] Mississippi's governor, Ross Barnett, an enthusiastic exponent of the centennial, made his views plain at a business conference in Florida by first extolling the separation of the races and then insisting, "If the rights of a sovereign state are taken away, they will be replaced by a totalitarian government—a police state."[99] Shortly after this speech, Barnett led Jackson's secession-day parade, riding in a horse-drawn carriage. Hundreds of white Mississippians (some of them citizens' council members), organized under the auspices of the state centennial commission into militia-style units of "Mississippi Greys" and clad in Confederate uniforms, followed in procession behind a huge Rebel flag owned by the state university. These efforts to recapture the spirit of the Confederacy coincided with the stirrings of an indigenous civil

97. *Montgomery Advertiser,* Feb. 27, 1961, A4. On Jones's role as a persecutor of the Alabama NAACP, see Dan T. Carter, *The Politics of Rage: George Wallace, the Origins of the New Conservatism, and the Transformation of American Politics* (New York: Simon and Schuster, 1995), 92–93. At the time of the Montgomery pageant, Jones was presiding in the case of *Sullivan v. New York Times* in which the city's police commissioner was suing local civil rights activists and the *Times* for libel. According to one historian, "At the trial five members of the all-white jury were wearing beards grown for the centennial celebrations. The defense objected that these obvious Confederate symbols created a prejudicial atmosphere. But Judge Jones overruled the objection and went on to enforce strict segregation in the courtroom." Jon Wiener, "Civil War, Cold War, Civil Rights: The Civil War Centennial in Context, 1960–1965," in Alice Fahs and Joan Waugh, eds., *The Memory of the Civil War in American Culture* (Chapel Hill: University of North Carolina Press, 2004), 238.

98. *Jackson Clarion-Ledger and Daily News,* March 26, 1961, E2.

99. *Jackson Clarion-Ledger,* March 27, 1961, 2. Barnett had intervened directly in preparations for the Jackson parade by prompting the city's mayor to set up a local organizing committee. See Ross R. Barnett to Allen C. Thompson, July 7, 1960, folder on "Barnett, Ross. R. [June 1960–June 1962]," box 708, MCWBTSR.

rights movement in Jackson. Black students protesting the incarceration of nine sit-in demonstrators were harried by police dogs and tear-gassed on the same day as the secession parade.[100]

Smaller-scale centennial events occurred in many other southern communities in the early months of 1961 including Atlanta, Charleston, Raleigh, and Savannah, as well as Milledgeville, Georgia, and Winchester, Tennessee. They may not have been as politically charged as the observances in Montgomery and Jackson, but several of them attracted support from influential politicians. In avowedly progressive Atlanta, where Rich's famous department store (a focal point for recent student sit-ins) was decked out in Civil War memorabilia, the major event was a gala-studded centennial ball held in March to coincide with a recreation of the premiere of *Gone with the Wind*.[101] At the airport Mayor William B. Hartsfield greeted the English actress Vivien Leigh (the original Scarlett O'Hara) with an armful of red roses.[102] Governor Ernest Vandiver and his wife attended the ball dressed in Civil War clothing.[103] Also backing the centennial was North Carolina governor Terry Sanford, an enthusiastic booster for Raleigh's "Confederate Festival" staged during the following month.[104] Hartsfield and Sanford were both racially moderate business-progressives. Their backing for centennial events revealed that support for the heritage project was not necessarily symptomatic of an unyielding attachment to Jim Crow. The same could be said for Governor Lindsay Almond's endorsement of the Virginia commission's plans to commemorate the 1861 Washington Peace Conference. Indeed, Almond appears to have viewed this observance of a gathering originally intended to mediate between the sections as a means of publicizing the advantages of his own middle course between massive resistance and full integration.[105]

100. *Jackson Clarion-Ledger*, March 29, 1961, 1, 12. On the Jackson sit-ins, see John R. Salter Jr., *Jackson, Mississippi: An American Chronicle of Struggle and Schism* (1979; reprint, Malabar, FL: R.E. Krieger, 1987), 7–8. Ed Bearss, former NPS regional research historian duty stationed at Vicksburg National Military Park, confirmed that a number of Mississippi Greys were active in local citizens' councils in taped comments to the author, Jan. 2004.

101. *Atlanta Constitution*, Jan. 7, 1961, 1.

102. *Atlanta Constitution*, March 10, 1961, 1.

103. Ibid., 23.

104. Terry Sanford to Stanley R. Smith, April 22, 1961, folder on "Confederate States CWCCs: Mississippi CWCC, 1960–64," box 1, RCB 7548, GaCWCCR, RG 079-01-001.

105. Speaking in Richmond on February 4, 1961, at the centenary commemoration of Virginia's call for a sectional peace conference, Almond drew explicit parallels between past and present conflicts. "Now as then, peaceful adjustment of issues that divide the nation must be sought,"

For many patriotic observers, however, the dominant message emanating from these popular centennial events was one of resistance to federal authority on the basis of a redundant Confederate past. At a time when the cold war was entering one of its most dangerous phases, this was intensely disturbing. One U.S. soldier was so concerned about the explosion of Rebel pageantry in South Carolina that he wrote to the newly inaugurated president, John F. Kennedy, to tell him that southerners were using the centennial to fight the Civil War all over again. He had, he reported, "seen confederate flags flying from school flag poles" as well as "small children carr[y]ing confederate pennants dressed in full confederate uniforms and using the term yankee as if it was taking the lord himself in vain." Southerners, insisted the bemused soldier, "are always looking behind insted [*sic*] of ahead and at this rate it could endanger our country so great it might cause the fall of our great nation."[106]

Some southern progressives were hardly less worried than this serviceman about the negative impact of the centennial on their efforts to promote ordered change in the region. Ralph McGill, the prominent Atlanta journalist, shared the view of the CWCC's Bell Wiley that many whites were behaving "as if they had not come back into the Union."[107] In common with most anticommunist liberals in the South, McGill was deeply alarmed by the escalation of quasi-Confederate activity during the early weeks of the centennial. In an impassioned outburst in the *Atlanta Constitution* on April 8, he expressed his support for a dignified commemoration of the Civil War as the conflict that had ended slavery and confirmed America's existence as "a union in fact beyond the power of legalistic, hair-splitting sophistry to destroy." Yet, he wrote, "what we have now are increasing numbers of persons wandering about the South wearing sleazy imitations of Confederate uniforms, growing beards, stirring up old hatreds, making ancient wounds bleed again, reviving Ku Klux Klans, working themselves into immature fits of emotionalism, recreating old battles, and otherwise doing a great disservice to the memory of those who fought and died in the war of 1861–65." Unconsciously revealing the malleability of southern historical memory, McGill explained that the war had not been

---

declared the governor. In a coded attack on bitter-end segregationists and civil rights activists (as well as a defense of his own *via media*), he went on, "It has unfortunately been the course of our history that men have raised false issues which could influence the minds and stir the emotions instead of exercising constructive leadership in the effort to mold common opinion in support of that which is best for the nation and the world." *New York Times*, Feb. 5, 1961, sec. 1, 45.

106. Bill Wallace to John F. Kennedy, Feb. 7, 1961, box 69, subject files 1957–66, CWCCR.

107. Wiley to John Harrison, April 10, 1961, box 62, Wiley Papers.

"an all-white affair"—that black regiments had fought on both sides and that the South "acknowledges the debt of gratitude to the thousands of slaves who, during the four years of war, behaved with such understanding and good will that they left legends yet handed down in some families." [108]

Of course, for some centennial planners the extent of white southerners' participation in commemorative events in Montgomery, Jackson, and other communities was simply an indication that their hard work had begun to pay off. These included not only those segregationists on the southern commissions who had a vested political interest in fostering a Confederate heritage boom but also CWCC officials like Karl Betts who viewed pageants and parades as essential conduits for popular involvement in the centennial. But while in one sense the crowds who participated in the secession observances in Montgomery and Jackson vindicated the efforts of organizers like Betts, the criticism that these events elicited from some commentators also cast doubt on the wisdom of the centennial. The corrosive racial fault-line at the heart of the project was nowhere more evident than in Charleston, South Carolina, in the damp spring of 1961.

108. *Atlanta Constitution,* April 8, 1961, 1.

3

Let's Call the Whole Thing Off

The Charleston Crises of 1961

WHILE SEGREGATIONISTS LABORED to turn the Civil War centennial into a bulwark against integration, countervailing pressures continued to build. The student sit-ins of 1960 announced the onset of the decisive direct-action phase of the civil rights movement and alerted many Americans to the inhumanity of Jim Crow. Growing numbers of cold war liberals were beginning to see segregation not, as the majority of southern whites regarded it, as a legitimate institution with deep roots in the region's history but, rather, as a hindrance in the nation's ongoing struggle against communism. "The problem of the American Negro is no more local than the rockets that will descend upon us if we fail him in his human cause," insisted one commentator. "Jim Crow is treason." [1]

It was in this increasingly polarized context that the CWCC accepted an invitation from the South Carolina Commission on the War Between the States to hold its fourth national assembly in Charleston, a southern tourist mecca since the 1920s. This plenary meeting was designed to coincide with a reenactment of the Confederate attack on Fort Sumter, the event that had unleashed domestic strife in April 1861. The South Carolinians were preparing a spectacular pageant and fireworks display to mark the occasion, and it seemed good sense (as well as good manners) for the federal agency to give the local plan its stamp of approval. Valuable media attention was bound to be targeted on the fort at this moment in history. Patently the centennial as a whole could only benefit from the happy conjuncture of the two events.

It was not to be. What happened during March and April 1961 paled into insignificance compared with the fateful happenings a hundred years previously. However, the political imbroglio that developed over the issue of whether a black woman, Madaline Williams, would be accommodated equally at the na-

---

1. John Ciardi, "Jim Crow Is Treason," *Saturday Review,* Feb. 4, 1961, 23.

tional assembly proved to be a defining moment for the centennial, one that almost derailed the observance before it had started. The events in Charleston attracted enormous publicity but not for the right reasons. Although the new Kennedy administration eventually brokered a compromise solution to its first civil rights crisis, a subsequent row at the assembly compounded the problems facing the CWCC. Observers pointed to the racial tensions evident during the Fort Sumter affair to support claims that the centennial was morally flawed in conception and hideously bungled in execution. Although Karl Betts's hopes for a popular pageant were not entirely ruined, any idea that the centennial could be a positive weapon in the cultural cold war was gone for good.

THE IMPENDING CRISIS

When the CWCC decided that Charleston should be the venue for its assembly in April 1961, no one considered the possibility that racial issues might wreck not only the meeting but also the long-term health of the centennial itself. While this lack of foresight spoke volumes for the planners' restricted vision in the sphere of race relations, it was hardly surprising in view of both the complete absence of black representation on the full commission and the prominence at Jackson Place of racial conservatives like Ulysses S. Grant III, Karl Betts, and William Tuck. The CWCC leadership's failure to rethink its policies in the wake of the student sit-ins that rocked America during 1960, however, proved to be its undoing.

The seeds of disaster were sown on February 4, 1961, when Everett Landers, executive director of the New Jersey Civil War Centennial Commission, informed Karl Betts that all of his members were likely to travel to Charleston for the national assembly. "As you may know," he wrote, "one of our members, Mrs. Williams, is a Negro. She has expressed concern over her reception by hotel people in South Carolina. Naturally we do not want to be separated from one of our members. Please advise me what we can expect." If necessary, Landers added, Betts should communicate with South Carolina's governor, Ernest F. Hollings: "Here will be the proof of the pudding, a chance to prove to the nation that the lofty thoughts behind the Centennial are really what we say they are."[2] On the same day Landers also wrote to Joseph N. Dempsey, a prominent lawyer and liberal Democrat who served as the New Jersey agency's vice chairman. "This is the perfect opportunity," he said, "for the National

2. Everett J. Landers to Karl S. Betts, Feb. 4, 1961, folder on "National Civil War Centennial Commission (Correspondence)," box 8, Records of the New Jersey Civil War Centennial Commission, New Jersey State Archives (hereafter NJCWCCR).

Commission, and if necessary, higher authority, to prove that these lofty ideas behind the Centennial really mean what they say."[3] It was plain from the content, as well as the forceful tone, of Landers's messages that individuals on the New Jersey commission set out from the beginning to spark a crisis that would challenge the bland, consensual message disseminated by the CWCC.

Madaline A. Williams was one of a handful of African Americans appointed to a state centennial commission. Unlike John Hope Franklin and Charles H. Wesley, notable black historians who served respectively on the New York and Ohio agencies, Williams was an experienced politician—a former Democratic assemblywoman who had originally been chosen to represent the New Jersey legislature on the commission but who was now serving as the register of deeds in Newark. A sixty-five-year-old, silver-haired Georgia native, she had moved north in 1917 and was married to the president of the local branch of the NAACP.[4] There is no evidence that she was either the prime mover in an African-American conspiracy to use the Charleston gathering as a platform to promote civil rights or that she was placed intentionally on the New Jersey commission to create problems for the CWCC. However, it is clear that some of her white colleagues on the Garden State's agency decided to use her appointment both to demonstrate New Jersey's commitment to civil rights and to expose the racism of the national commission. Joseph Dempsey had conferred with Everett Landers in January about "our proposal to Charleston" and now intimated that the issue should be pressed if, as he presumed, Mrs. Williams were not made welcome at the conference hotel.[5]

Although Dempsey and Landers probably shared a genuine commitment to civil rights, the state commission's policy must be seen in broader political context. Hardly one of the most radical northern states during the Civil War, New Jersey had encountered subsequently large-scale black migration to its main industrial cities (Newark included). By 1961 a population of over half a million African Americans exerted a significant influence in local politics particularly, though not exclusively, inside the state's relatively progressive Demo-

3. Landers to Joseph N. Dempsey, Feb. 4, 1961, folder on "Dempsey, Joseph N.," box 6, NJCWCCR.

4. For biographical details on Madaline Williams, see L. Ethan Ellis, *Steps in a Journey Toward Understanding: Activities of the New Jersey Civil War Centennial Commission in 1961 at Trenton, Charleston and Salem Church* (Trenton, 1963), 7; *The State* (Columbia), April 12, 1961, B1.

5. Joseph N. Dempsey to Landers, Feb. 24, 1961, folder on "Dempsey, Joseph N.," box 6, NJCWCCR.

cratic party.[6] Madaline Williams's appointment to the commission was but a small reflection of this influence.

Whereas the southern commissions made virtually no attempt to include blacks within their remit, northern centennial agencies in states such as New Jersey, New York, Ohio, and Illinois, where blacks did have limited political clout, made some effort to develop racially inclusive commemorative programs. One early example of this was a formal reenactment of the appearance that President-elect Abraham Lincoln had made in Trenton on the way to Washington for his inauguration. The movie star Anthony Quinn was hired to read Lincoln's address to a specially convened joint session of the New Jersey legislature on February 21, 1961. African Americans played a prominent part in this occasion. Overseeing affairs was a Republican assemblyman, Herbert H. Tate, the first black politician ever to preside over a joint session of the state legislature. Tate took the chance to note not only the progress that had been made on civil rights issues in New Jersey but also the work that was still to be done. In the audience was John Harris, a 103-year-old black man who had been born a slave in North Carolina.[7] Although the presence of the two African Americans on this occasion was little more than symbolic, it emphasized the readiness of the New Jersey centennial commission to make race a centerpiece of its plans.

If Karl Betts understood the full implications of Everett Landers's dynamite-laden inquiry, he did not show it. Instead he waited four days before writing to Julian Metz, the head of Charleston's chamber of commerce, to determine what kind of reception a northern black woman could expect to receive at the Francis Marion Hotel, the venue chosen for the assembly. Metz told him on the telephone "some days later that he had taken the matter up with the hotel people and they would attempt to work it out." Betts let the matter rest here while the South Carolinian went on a business trip to Spain. He saw no reason to do otherwise. Previous practice suggested that Mrs. Williams would be allowed to attend the discussion sessions, but he believed that he had no legal authority to press the state authorities to accommodate her on an integrated basis.[8]

---

6. Landers to John F. Kennedy (hereafter JFK), folder on "Fourth National Assembly," box 3, NJCWCCR.

7. Ellis, *Steps*, 7.

8. Betts to Carl Haverlin, April 28, 1961, folder on "National Assembly—1961—General Correspondence," box 52, subject files 1957–66, CWCCR. Betts omitted to mention Metz's phone call in

By the third week of February 1961 Betts had no excuse for supposing that the segregation issue lacked the power to destabilize the centennial. In the wake of the sit-ins, evidence was mounting that African Americans and their liberal white allies were preparing to contest what they saw as conservative domination of the observances. An article in the *New York Post Magazine* criticized centennial planners like Betts (tellingly, though erroneously, described as "a bluff, hearty Virginian") for overlooking the critical role that slavery had played in causing the Civil War. "The official celebrants are so unified . . . ," asserted the writer, "that they keep forgetting to mention what the war was about." Dr. Charles H. Wesley, president of the venerable Association for the Study of Negro Life and History, was quoted as saying that the only way Betts had tried to include blacks in commemorative planning was on a separate-but-equal basis. However, Wesley sensed better days ahead: "Now that we've got a new administration in Washington changing officials in various agencies, perhaps, before this centennial becomes a complete glorification of the Southern point of view, there should be some new appointments to the National commission."[9]

A similar message was being disseminated by New York's liberal Republican administration. Governor Nelson A. Rockefeller publicly praised student civil rights protesters when he designated February 12–18 Negro History Week and called for statewide recognition to be given to the contributions that black people had made to New York and the nation as a whole.[10] The state's education commissioner criticized centennial programs for their attention to "inconsequential matters." He added, "I feel that these things will rekindle old interests in issues that are long since outmoded. They will hinder the acceptance of more basic democratic principals [*sic*] guaranteeing justice and equality and full educational opportunities for all minorities."[11]

In spite of, or possibly because of, this changing political climate, Karl Betts opted to stall rather than to act. Instead of keeping the New Jerseyans

a subsequent memorandum to Ulysses S. Grant III, "A Statement of Facts Regarding the Charleston Assembly as related to the Action of the New Jersey State Centennial Commission," May 5, 1961, box 9, reading file 1958–66, Records of the Civil War Centennial Commission, Records of the National Park Service, Record Group 79, National Archives (hereafter CWCCR).

9. *New York Post Magazine*, Feb. 7, 1961, 6.

10. *New York Amsterdam News*, Feb. 18, 1961, 7. Rockefeller had supported a strong civil rights plank at the Republican national convention in 1960. James Desmond, *Nelson Rockefeller: A Political Biography* (New York: Macmillan, 1964), 272–74, 279.

11. *New York Times*, Feb. 19, 1961, clipping in folder on "Newspaper and Magazine Stories About," box 184, Bell I. Wiley Papers, Manuscript, Archives, and Rare Book Library, Emory University.

informed, he stayed silent. Toward the end of February, Joseph Dempsey revealed his hand, telling Landers that he had discussed the situation with his fellow commission member, the historian Earl Schenck Miers. "[W]e feel," he wrote, "that if a satisfactory response is not received from Betts by the time of our next meeting, that we should notify the other Centennial Commissions of our disability to attend and suggest that it would be inappropriate for them. I hope that by the time of the next meeting we will have some definite response from Betts, and I suggest that you insist on some kind of an answer from him immediately."[12]

On March 3, Landers dispatched a sharp letter to Betts urging him to respond to communications and blaming him for the volume of "useless [commercial] brochures and other trash" received daily by his commission. "Your continued emphasis on the 'fast buck' aspect of the Centennial is causing growing public discontent and considerable adverse press attention which is getting more difficult to cope with every day."[13] Betts met Landers the next day in Washington at a well-attended ceremony to commemorate Lincoln's first inaugural. However, it is unlikely that he had received the letter by this time. He later claimed that he used the occasion to inform Landers about Julian Metz's absence but had found that the New Jerseyan did not regard the problem as urgent.[14]

By March 8, the national commission had formulated a public policy (of sorts) without contacting Metz again. Betts wrote twice to Landers that day. One of his missives denied that the CWCC was engaging in commercial excess. The agency dealt only, he wrote, with "responsible businessmen," and it was entirely up to individual state agencies whether they wished to respond to overtures from companies trying to promote their wares. Something more than irritation was evident in his statement that some aspects of Landers's letter of March 3 were "decidedly offensive and odious. Naturally I resent them."[15] Betts's second communication was brief. After consulting with members of the national commission (most likely Grant and Tuck), it had been determined that nothing could be done for Madaline Williams. The matter, he contended,

12. Dempsey to Landers, Feb. 24, 1961, folder on "Dempsey, Joseph N.," box 6, NJCWCCR.

13. Landers to Betts, March 3, 1961, folder on "National CWCC (Correspondence)," box 8, NJCWCCR. I have corrected a typo in "difficult."

14. Betts to Grant, memorandum, "A Statement of Facts Regarding the Charleston Assembly as related to the Action of the New Jersey State Centennial Commission," May 5, 1961, reading file 1958–66, box 9, CWCCR.

15. Betts to Landers, March 8, 1961, encl. in Landers to Harris Wofford, April 14, 1961, folder on "General Correspondence, 1961," box 184, Wiley Papers.

"is entirely outside our jurisdiction and we, therefore, cannot concern ourselves with it."[16] This was the reply the New Jerseyans had been expecting. The
following day they met in Trenton and resolved not to attend the fourth national assembly. Other state centennial commissions were urged to follow suit.
The resolution made it clear that segregation was the target and that the federal
government had a responsibility to act against it. "The Civil War," it insisted,
had been fought at great sacrifice "to preserve and to amplify the fundamental
law of our land, as set forth originally in the Bill of Rights." The perpetuation of
the Union had been guaranteed by the result of the conflict and a segregated assembly would abrogate "the fundamental concepts of human decency" as well
as New Jersey law.[17] "We don't feel . . . ," stated chairman Donald Flamm, a the-
atrical and business entrepreneur, "that the Federal Government should sponsor any activity which doesn't respect the fundamental laws of this nation."[18]
Given coverage by the *New York Times* and other papers, the dispute between
Landers and Betts was now in the public domain. Suddenly, the centennial had
become a test of America's commitment to progress on civil rights.

In view of the growing internal and external pressure on Jim Crow, the
southern response to the threatened boycott of the Charleston meeting was
entirely predictable. John A. May, the unreconstructed Democrat who headed
South Carolina's centennial agency, said his group had no control over state
law and that it was the New Jerseyans' business if they did not want to ven-
ture south.[19] A Charleston editor expressed surprise that a "colored" woman
"should refuse to stay at a hotel for colored people" but agreed with May that
people were entitled to stay away from the national assembly if they did not
concur with its objectives. "We can think of many individuals and organizations whose absence we shall applaud," he added gratuitously.[20] Indifference
turned to anger as the issue was politicized in the North. The New Jersey resolution received immediate backing from the state's legislature, U.S. Senator
Clifford Case (a Republican), Walter H. Jones (an assemblyman standing in
the forthcoming gubernatorial election), and local branches of the NAACP.[21]

16. Ibid.

17. New Jersey Civil War Centennial Commission, resolutions passed March 9, 1961, in folder
on "Fourth National Assembly," box 3, NJCWCCR.

18. *New York Times*, March 10, 1961, 29.

19. *Charleston News and Courier*, March 10, 1961, A1, A2.

20. *Charleston News and Courier*, March 11, 1961, A6.

21. *New York Times*, March 14, 1961, 32, March 15, 1961, 1, 33; Clifford Case to Landers,
March 14, 1961, folder on "Fourth National Assembly," box 3, NJCWCCR; *Charleston News and
Courier*, March 14, 1961, A8.

These developments convinced South Carolinians that the boycott issue was just a political football for unscrupulous northern politicians. Governor Hollings told a crowded press conference in Columbia on March 14 that the New Jerseyans were trying to make "political capital" out of the affair. "We mean to maintain local control of our public affairs," he added pointedly.[22] The *Charleston News and Courier* singled out Representative Jones for criticism: "We smell an old political trick. When politicians have little else to talk about, they invent an issue, preferably concerning something a long way off. Mr. Jones is running against Southern customs."[23]

Whatever the truth of such charges, there was no doubt that the injection of the segregation issue had plunged the centennial into crisis. In part this was because African Americans themselves were galvanized by New Jersey's action. NAACP involvement was particularly significant but so was support offered by John Hope Franklin of Brooklyn College. One of the country's most prominent black historians, Franklin said he was "delighted" by the boycott resolve and would raise the matter at the next meeting of the New York agency.[24] In fact as early as March 9, Bruce Catton, a racial moderate caught between a rock and a hard place in his dual role as chairman of the New York agency and a member of the CWCC, announced that his state would not be represented officially in Charleston.[25] In the altered political climate created by the sit-ins, black representation on official centennial groups, no matter how small, made it difficult for nonsouthern whites to ignore the segregation issue after it was brought into the open by the New Jerseyans.

Once Jim Crow had become entangled with a national commemoration supported by federal funds, the recently installed Democratic administration of John F. Kennedy had little option but to get involved. The new president was an enthusiastic student of American history. In 1955, recuperating from a

22. *The State* (Columbia), March 15, 1961, B1. Hollings's views were not dissimilar to those of the incumbent Democratic governor of New Jersey. In the course of criticizing opponents for using the centennial as a political football, Robert B. Meyner observed that the Republican-controlled state senate in Trenton had passed a resolution condemning racial discrimination in Charleston but had taken no action on a pending bill to outlaw housing discrimination at home. *Paterson News*, March 15, 1961, clipping in Scrapbooks . . . Fourth National Assembly, March 1961, box 20, NJCWCCR.

23. *Charleston News and Courier,* March 14, 1961, A8.

24. *Jersey City Jersey Journal,* March 10, 1961, clipping in Scrapbooks . . . Fourth National Assembly, March 1961, box 20, NJCWCCR; John Hope Franklin to Landers, March 13, 1961, folder on "Fourth National Assembly," box 3, NJCWCCR.

25. *New York Times,* March 10, 1961, 29.

serious operation on his back, he had written a Pulitzer Prize–winning study of political leadership in the U.S. Senate, *Profiles in Courage*.[26] Hardly a masterpiece but rendered respectable by the assistance of detailed comments from renowned historians like Allan Nevins and Arthur M. Schlesinger Jr., it revealed a man heavily influenced by the orthodox interpretation of the Civil War era.[27] One telling chapter lauded the role of Edmund Ross of Kansas and six other Republican senators whose votes had saved conservative president Andrew Johnson from impeachment in May 1868. Although his negative depiction of radical Reconstruction was not unusual for its time, it had attracted the wrath of Blanche Ames Ames, daughter of Mississippi's carpetbag governor, Adelbert Ames. Kennedy, she insisted, had been excessively influenced by racist historians like Claude G. Bowers writing in the 1930s. Unlike her father, modern-day politicians had failed to stand up for justice: "Congress has closed its eyes to the unjust treatment of colored people in the Southern states; politicians have winked at the travesty on 'sound democracy' existing there."[28] In 1957 (as if to prove her point) the Massachusetts senator cast his vote for the emasculation of the first civil rights bill to be passed by Congress since Reconstruction.[29]

John F. Kennedy's lukewarm record on civil rights was not necessarily a good guide to how he would react to the crisis the New Jerseyans engineered. It is true that he owed his nomination for president in part to support from segregationist southern governors like J. Lindsay Almond, John Patterson, Ernest Hollings, and Ernest Vandiver. However, he headed a party that contained large numbers of liberals sympathetic to the cause of black civil rights and which could not afford to sit complacently on the fence at a time when many Americans, white as well as black, were coming to see the destruction of Jim Crow as either a moral imperative or an essential step in the propaganda war against communism. Besides, in what promised to be a close presidential race, he needed African-American backing to sustain his bid for political

26. John F. Kennedy, *Profiles in Courage* (New York: Harper, 1956).

27. JFK to Allan Nevins, July 6, July 20, 1955, Feb. 21, June 26, 1956, box 24, Allan Nevins Papers, Rare Book and Manuscript Library, Columbia University; Arthur M. Schlesinger Jr., to JFK, July 4, 1955, JFK to Schlesinger, July 20, 1956, folder on "Correspondence: Item 1," box 31, JFK Personal Papers, John F. Kennedy Presidential Library. Kennedy biographer Robert Dallek rightly describes the book as "more the work of a 'committee' than of any one person," in *John F. Kennedy: An Unfinished Life, 1917–1963* (2003; London: Penguin, 2004), 199.

28. Blanche Ames Ames to JFK, June 6, 1956, folder 2, box 71, Nevins Papers.

29. Mark Stern, *Calculating Visions: Kennedy, Johnson, and Civil Rights* (New Brunswick, NJ: Rutgers University Press, 1992), 15–17.

power. In May 1960, shortly before the Democratic national convention, he had telephoned Harris Wofford, an aspiring young white lawyer with an interest in civil rights issues, to find out how he could improve his image among blacks. Later, the senator's brother, Robert, also called and told Wofford that the Kennedys "had concluded that they were in trouble with the Negro vote."[30] Wofford later agreed to set up a civil rights section for the presidential nominating campaign. With his help Senator Kennedy not only secured the vast majority of black delegates at the convention but also developed important contacts with prominent African-American leaders like Roy Wilkins, head of the NAACP, and Martin Luther King, president of the Southern Christian Leadership Conference (SCLC). Even though Wofford correctly concluded that Kennedy did not have a strong personal interest in civil rights, some members of his campaign team were so desperate for black votes that they advised the candidate to make a supportive telephone call to Coretta Scott King after her husband was incarcerated in Georgia in November. Gestures like this undoubtedly helped to increase Kennedy's support among blacks. Indeed, this one contributed to his narrow victory over Richard Nixon in the election.

During the winter of 1960–61 the president-elect named Harris Wofford as his civil rights adviser and appeared to sanction more vigorous executive action in the field of civil rights. Recognizing that conservative influence in Congress would not only make it difficult to pass civil rights legislation but also endanger the implementation of White House initiatives in what he regarded as more important areas, Kennedy charged his brother Robert with the politically delicate task of promoting black equality under the law. The young attorney general was no more committed to black rights than the president, but he recognized the need for ordered progress in this sphere. Persistent mob opposition to southern school desegregation in major cities like New Orleans and Atlanta was embarrassing for the administration and the country. So was street disorder triggered by the sit-ins and the continued disfranchisement of southern blacks. Shortly after assuming office, Robert Kennedy announced publicly that the White House was determined to exhibit leadership on civil rights issues and that his department would move strongly in this field. He immediately initiated behind-the-scenes contact with southern governors on the assumption that state leaders would be amenable to the slow but steady erosion of Jim Crow.

The Charleston crisis provided early evidence that this belief was wishful thinking. Segregationist sentiment remained firmly entrenched in the Deep

---

30. Wofford, oral interview, Nov. 29, 1965, 8, JFK Library.

South. Relatively pragmatic politicians like Governor Hollings of South Carolina were eager to promote economic development at home (even at the expense of a certain amount of social change), but politically they could not
afford to be seen to favor integration. Similarly the Kennedys were aware that,
in the wake of the *Brown* decision and the sit-ins, they could hardly pose as
the guardians of liberal democracy (at home or abroad) if they ignored completely black calls for equality. While the action of the New Jersey commission
gave the president an opportunity to prove his commitment to social justice, it
also threatened to damage his warm relations with powerful southern Democrats who had supported his election.

During the second week of March 1961, press coverage of the New Jerseyans' revolt alerted the White House to the looming controversy over the
CWCC's Charleston gathering. Staff member Kenneth O'Donnell told Harris
Wofford to call Everett Landers and find out what was going on. Wofford did
so and was informed that Landers's commission had made several attempts
to contact Karl Betts. Madaline Williams would not be accommodated at the
Francis Marion Hotel, nor would she be allowed to attend official luncheons
and banquets. Wofford then outlined the situation to O'Donnell, explaining,
first, that the New Jersey legislature had already called for a change of venue;
second, that two federal officials wanted to know whether they should now
decline their invitations to Charleston; third, that White House staffer Richard
Goodwin had contacted the Bureau of the Budget to ascertain the extent of
the president's powers in this situation; and fourth, that steps were being taken
to appoint an African American to the CWCC. Wofford thought the latter
"might be a good next move now." He added that the assembly might yet be
salvaged if CWCC officials agreed to follow the procedure of the U.S. Civil
Rights Commission and hold the meeting at a desegregated federal military
installation. Failing this, he concluded, "if it appears we have the power, as
I think we do, the Assembly should, I think, be called off, or at least all Federal funds to be spent in connection with the Assembly should be cut off, and
no representative of the Executive Branch should participate."[31] Wofford also
paid a visit to CWCC headquarters in Washington. Karl Betts promised to
raise the matter with Grant and Tuck but came back with the reply "that it
was not within their responsibility to assure equal treatment to their officially
invited guests from state commissions."[32]

---

31. Wofford, undated memo to Kenneth O'Donnell re "The New Civil War" [March 1961],
folder FG633, box 198, White House Central Files, JFK Library (hereafter WHCF).

32. Wofford to JFK, memorandum, March, 14, 1961, folder FG633, box 198, WHCF.

On March 14 the young civil rights adviser outlined the situation to President Kennedy, already preoccupied with foreign policy crises in Laos and the Congo. He iterated the CWCC's reluctance to cooperate as well as the agency's constitutional position as "a U.S. Government body under your responsibility." Added Wofford, "In principle and on political grounds I think you should take action."[33] After apparently discussing the issue with his closest aide, Theodore Sorensen, Kennedy concurred with Wofford's implicit view that the new administration could not afford morally or politically to go on record in support of segregation.[34] The same day he signed a letter to General Grant drafted by Wofford. The message was unambiguous. The commission, observed Kennedy, was "an official body of the United States Government"; thus "the Constitutional rule of equal treatment of all Americans, regardless of race or color, should of course apply to all of its operations." "It is my understanding," he added, "that a delegate to this Conference has been denied lodging at the headquarters hotel. While it is my understanding that this delegate would be allowed to participate in all meetings planned for this Assembly, it seems to me that the Commission has the responsibility to see that all of its members and guests are treated on a basis of equality at all the facilities arranged by the Commission. I would appreciate it if you and the other members of the Commission would take action assuring that the arrangements for the Fourth National Assembly meet this standard set forth by our Constitution and by our national conscience."[35]

The receipt of this communication caused an immediate rift among CWCC members. The self-proclaimed "Southern liberal," Bell Wiley, urged Grant to allow him to seek the good offices of a White House staffer and to telephone the manager of the Francis Marion Hotel where the National Assembly was due to meet.[36] The manager, an Ohio native, precluded the possibility of an easy answer to the crisis by saying that recent publicity made it impossible for him quietly to accommodate Madaline Williams.[37] General Grant, Karl Betts, and William Tuck, however, were unwilling to accept this information

33. Ibid.

34. Wofford, handwritten note clipped to the letter he had drafted from JFK to Grant, March 14, 1961, in folder FG633, box 198, WHCF.

35. JFK to Grant, March 14, 1961, folder on "General Correspondence, 1961," box 184, Wiley Papers.

36. Bell I. Wiley to Anne Freedgood, March 29, 1961, folder on "General Correspondence, 1961, March 25–31," box 62, Wiley Papers.

37. Wiley to Charles O'Neill, March 30, 1961, folder on "General Correspondence, 1961, March 25–31," box 62, Wiley Papers.

as sufficient reason to comply with the president's request. On March 17, the three men accepted the challenge laid down by the troublesome New Jerseyans. Responding to a note from Landers accompanying the state commission's boycott resolution, Grant announced that the CWCC had no legal authority to change its plans and lamely ventured his hope that the New Jersey group would change its mind and send representatives to Charleston.[38] He also dispatched what must have been a similarly unacceptable reply to President Kennedy's letter of March 14. In it he defended his agency's actions to date and reported unconvincingly that "[c]onsiderable progress" had been made in the search for a solution to the crisis. Specifically, he said that he had called an emergency meeting of the commission's executive committee for March 21. "I feel confident," he concluded, "that we can make sure no such embarrassing issues will be raised about any future assembly, and that we all desire to comply with your wishes."[39]

Grant was mistaken if he expected these responses to end discussion of the segregation issue. Media coverage of the crisis was intensified by the White House's decision to make public the president's request to the CWCC even before Grant's reply had been received. While this move was embraced by Everett Landers as a "skirmish" on behalf of New Jersey, "the whole nation and all humanity," it caused consternation in South Carolina.[40] President Kennedy's intervention may have stopped well short of demanding an end to segregation, observed the *Charleston News and Courier,* but it "has cast a new and to us a most unwholesome light on observance of the Civil War centennial." The South, added this editorial (against a cold war backdrop of killings in the Congo and Angola), asked nothing more than to be left alone: "Instead of peaceful commemoration of a war long past, the U.S. government, egged on by radical organizations, seems bent on fanning the flames of hatred into new and possibly disastrous flames. Headlines of atrocities out of Africa signal even grimmer warning of race troubles. Will U.S. leaders never learn?"[41]

For the wiser heads among the CWCC, public revelation of the president's wishes made current policy untenable. Leading the campaign for a change of

38. Grant to Landers, March 17, 1961, folder on "National Civil War Centennial Commission (Correspondence)," box 8, NJCWCCR.

39. Grant to JFK, March 12, 1961, folder FG633, box 198, WHCF. This letter appears to be misdated.

40. Landers to JFK, March 18, 1961, folder on "Fourth National Assembly . . . ," box 3, NJCWCCR.

41. *Charleston News and Courier,* March 19, 1961, A12.

direction was Bell Wiley. Determined to find a compromise that would save the centennial from complete disaster, the Emory professor floated the idea that the national commission could switch its assembly from the Francis Marion Hotel in segregated Charleston to an integrated federal military facility just outside the city.[42] This proposal, which mirrored Wofford's thinking in the White House, received immediate backing inside the agency from Edmund Gass, a fellow white southerner. Seconded to the national commission from the NPS, Gass shared Wiley's view that the leadership's foolhardy recalcitrance threatened to destroy the centennial. In a memorandum dated March 20, he reminded Grant and Betts that they worked for a federal agency; that the national assembly was "a statutory adjunct" of the commission; and that therefore this meeting was covered by the same federal laws as the commission itself. More pointedly, he advanced his conviction that "we face . . . the fact of a policy that has already been decided and not an arguable question of legal exegesis." "Quite aside," he concluded, "from the vast domain of the President's legal powers, from the eminence of his office, and from any question of justiciability, I cite realities. Among the latter are political realities that are both vocal and powerful in Congress and among many leaders of both political parties."[43]

The following morning the CWCC's executive committee met with a handful of full commission members and key staffers in Washington. The atmosphere was tense. Wiley could not be present, but his suggestion, backed by Congressman Fred Schwengel of Iowa, that the assembly be held at a desegregated military base was conveyed to the meeting by General Grant. Bill Tuck was appalled. The whole affair, he said, represented an attempt to involve the commission in what he called "a political question." This he adjudged "was really outside of the Commission's mandate" because the agency lacked the legal machinery to force any state commission to attend or to "require the hotel management to administer its private property in violation of local laws and customs." This articulation of the familiar southern defense of segregation was followed by prolonged discussion in which the diametrically opposed views of Betts and Gass were prominent. Around midday the issue was decided in Tuck's favor. It was agreed that, as chairman of the executive committee, the Virginian should prepare a formal rebuttal to the president explaining the

42. CWCC executive committee, minutes of the meeting held March 21, 1961, folder on "Executive Committee Meetings—Minutes," box 184, Wiley Papers.

43. Edmund G. Gass to Grant and Betts, memorandum, March 20, 1961, box 9, reading file 1958–66, CWCCR.

decision. One member, Norman Fitzgerald, recorded that "he was not too happy over the conclusion reached."[44]

THE COMPROMISE OF 1961

In the course of the next few days the CWCC leadership flirted irresponsibly with disaster and then, belatedly, stepped back from the brink. Initially, however, matters went from bad to worse. On March 21 Congressman Tuck dispatched his explanatory letter to President Kennedy. The work of an angry, bitter-end segregationist, it was a masterpiece of sophistry. From the outset, Tuck contended, the CWCC had asked delegates to the fourth national assembly to make their own arrangements for accommodation. Madaline Williams had never tried to make a reservation at the Francis Marion Hotel, which, it so happened, was now fully booked. The commission, he claimed, had held no segregated meetings "for the Centennial belongs to all Americans." However, the executive committee had concluded that in this instance its parent body had "no authority or jurisdiction" over a private business and therefore could not "undertake to dictate to hotelkeepers as to the management of their property."[45] It was, of course, true that Williams had not applied personally to the Francis Marion Hotel. Everett Landers (and others) had made inquiries on her behalf, but no formal room booking had been attempted. Tuck's claim that the CWCC had never held segregated gatherings was also accurate. What he neglected to mention was that when Bell Wiley telephoned the hotel manager, the latter had made it clear that under the current gaze of publicity he could not admit Williams under any circumstances. Wedded as they were to the southern position on segregation, the conservatives on the CWCC had over-reached themselves. As Edmund Gass made clear, the new administration had already laid down its policy on Jim Crow and the commission was a creature of the executive branch. The result was foreordained.

While the South Carolina press precipitately welcomed the executive committee's decision as a victory for sanity and the South, the opposition was swift to mobilize.[46] The following day New Jersey's centennial commission adopted a formal statement condemning the national commission for its blinkered re-

44. CWCC executive committee, minutes of the meeting held March 21, 1961, folder on "Executive Committee Meetings—Minutes," box 184, Wiley Papers.

45. William M. Tuck to JFK, March 21, 1961, folder 5272, William M. Tuck Papers, Special Collections, Earl Gregg Swem Library, College of William and Mary. Tuck released a similar statement to the press on the same day. See *New York Times*, March 22, 1961, 34.

46. *The State* (Columbia), March 22, 1961, A1.

fusal "to recognize its responsibility as a Federal agency" and its spineless attempt to shift the blame onto "the discriminatory law and customs of the State of South Carolina." It also lambasted Karl Betts for failing to answer repeated inquiries about Williams's accommodation but expressed the hope "that the wisdom of President Kennedy and other responsible statesmen" would eventually prevail.[47]

Tuck's views having been widely reported by the national media, cries of protest came from well beyond the core constituency of the centennial. Significantly, those cries emanated from northern liberals who rejected the racist consensus narrative of the Civil War era in favor of a dormant emancipationist version that was being rendered increasingly relevant by the ongoing efforts of the civil rights movement. Roy Wilkins, head of the NAACP, dispatched a public telegram to Betts attacking the commission's "abysmal mishandling of this affair." As a federal body with complete jurisdiction over its own meeting places, it could simply decline South Carolina's request to host the national assembly on the grounds that an acceptance of Jim Crow laws would exclude "the overwhelming majority of Americans who do not subscribe to the racial policy which they thought was destroyed as a tenable American precept at Appomattox." Any gathering in Charleston, averred Wilkins (unworried about the complexities of the past), would signal the commission's subscription "to the racial theories which brought on the Civil War."[48] Evidence that civil rights activity had begun to alert growing numbers of whites to the contemporary importance of the black counter-memory could be found in the similar responses of several northern politicians. For example, Richard Hughes, the Democratic candidate in New Jersey's gubernatorial election, cavalierly described the CWCC's stand as "an unfortunate travesty on history."[49]

For southern segregationists, the furor over Madaline Williams's attendance in Charleston was another disturbing sign that the country was being destabilized by its enemies. One outraged North Carolinian told Bill Tuck that communist agents had infiltrated the New Jersey commission and that the incident was "another flagrant example of the continuous efforts to stir up trouble in our country and turn one section of the nation against another."[50]

47. New Jersey Civil War Centennial Commission, statement, March 22, 1961, folder on "National Civil War Centennial Commission (Correspondence)," box 8, NJCWCCR.

48. Roy Wilkins to Betts, March 22, 1961, folder 5272, Tuck Papers; *New York Times*, March 23, 1961, 26.

49. *New York Times*, March 23, 1961, 26.

50. Paul A. Rockwell to Tuck, March 22, 1961, folder 5272, Tuck Papers.

Any attempt to make an issue of segregation, insisted one of Tuck's constituents from southside Virginia, "only serves to stiffen the people of the South to the social revolution that some elements in the North are attempting to force on us."[51]

With the country's attention focused momentarily on the ongoing crisis, progressives on the national commission labored to find a workable solution with the help of the Kennedy administration. While Harris Wofford privately asked the CWCC to reconsider its decision, sensible members of the agency tried to drive a wedge between Grant and Betts on the one hand and Tuck on the other by underlining the urgency of the situation. In recommending Wiley's previously discounted suggestion that the assembly should be moved to a desegregated military base, Fred Schwengel urged "that unless we find a constructive solution to this problem, the work of the Commission and its wonderful plan will be jeopardized."[52] Bruce Catton warned Grant and Betts that Tuck's statement had put the commission "in the light of endorsing a policy of racial discrimination." "I am sure," he continued diplomatically, "that that was not intended, but that is the way the statement is being received; and as a result our commission's ability to perform the kind of service we all have in mind is apt to be very gravely handicapped."[53]

Important developments in the controversy occurred on Thursday, March 23. Responding to the CWCC's announcement that it had no intention of changing its plans, the influential state centennial commissions of New York and Illinois announced definitively that they would join New Jersey in a boycott of the national assembly. While Bruce Catton (wearing his Empire State hat) hoped the national commission might still defuse the crisis by moving the gathering to a federal facility, he admitted that as things stood the effective closure of the observance to "Negro citizens" made it impossible for his group to be represented officially in South Carolina.[54] Governor Otto Kerner of Illinois said simply, "We cannot ignore the fundamental precept of equality for all people and still represent Illinois, the state of Abraham Lincoln."[55] The decisive intervention came from the White House. At a televised evening news conference in Washington, President Kennedy announced that executive authority would be used continuously to promote equality of opportunity

51. *Charleston News and Courier,* March 22, 1961, A8.

52. Fred Schwengel to Grant, March 22, 1961, folder 5272, Tuck Papers.

53. Bruce Catton to Grant and Betts, March 22, 1961, folder 5272, Tuck Papers.

54. *New York Times,* March 24, 1961, 18.

55. Ibid.

in all areas. To demonstrate the point, he added that because the CWCC was a government body using federal funds it was his "strong belief" that such an agency had a responsibility to provide facilities that did "not discriminate on the grounds of race or color."[56] Front-page news in the *New York Times* and the *Washington Post*, Kennedy's latest intervention left no one in any doubt that the administration would set its face against Jim Crow in those areas where it had clear authority to do so.

The cost of this action was soon evident. The next day South Carolina's political elite lined up in Columbia to criticize the president for his comments. Governor Hollings, doubtless sensitive about the fact that he had given Kennedy's election campaign qualified support, measured his words carefully, but he had no compunction in questioning the White House's authority to "dictate" racial integration in Charleston. "Neither the President nor the governor," he said, "can dictate to a hotel who it may or may not receive as guests." Others by his side adopted a more defiant tone. Senator Strom Thurmond, a keen student of the Civil War as well as a longstanding opponent of civil rights, disputed Kennedy's authority to compel the commission, a creation of Congress, "to bring about integration in Charleston." The centennial's purpose, he added, was to "commemorate the observance of the War Between the States. It is not for the purpose of starting another war." Two state representatives contributed their views. William Jennings Bryan Dorn expressed mock bewilderment at how the president could tell South Carolinians what to do, and L. Mendel Rivers blamed the renegade southerner, Bell Wiley, for "leading the fight to embarrass Charleston."[57]

Fortunately for those who had the welfare of the centennial at heart, the immediate crisis was about to pass. As Mendel Rivers unwittingly intimated, Bell Wiley was continuing to play a constructive role behind the scenes. Having failed initially to persuade Grant and Betts to change direction (largely because of their own conservative views and closeness to Tuck), Wiley recognized at once that the president's public criticism of the commission gave him the ammunition he needed. The next morning he telephoned one of Kennedy's White House aides, Arthur Schlesinger, a fellow historian and liberal anticommunist. Together they discussed the evolving plan to relocate the national assembly to the U.S. naval station in Charleston. Schlesinger (who later admitted

56. JFK, remarks at news conference, March 23, 1961, *Public Papers of the Presidents: John F. Kennedy, 1961* (Washington, DC: Government Printing Office, 1962), 217; *New York Times*, March 24, 1961, 1, 18.

57. *The State* (Columbia), March 25, 1961, A1, A3.

that "the call was responsible for breaking the . . . stalemate") was apparently taken by the southerner's helpful suggestion that the Navy should offer the use of its facilities to the commission. "He was very nice," Wiley reported later; "said he would see that the matter was pushed."[58]

It is not difficult to see why the White House found the proposed compromise the optimal solution to the Charleston controversy. Moving the site of the CWCC's national assembly gave the administration a chance to prove its bona fides in the ongoing fight against segregation. Indeed, it was an early indication of the importance that the Kennedys attached to symbolic actions in the civil rights sphere—morally resonant gestures intended to demonstrate to African Americans and liberal whites that the new administration had their interests at heart. Of course, the White House had not actively encouraged the crisis, and a cynical reading of executive policy might stress that symbols had little or no practical effect. Transferring the assembly to an integrated military base signaled federal distaste for Jim Crow, but the move had no concrete impact on the existence of segregation laws in the southern states. However, even symbolic gestures had costs. In tandem with early civil rights pronouncements by the attorney general, President Kennedy's decision to require a change of policy from the centennial commission heralded an end to the close relationship that had existed between himself and some powerful southern Democrats. Besides, as Bell Wiley himself was at pains to point out, *indirectly* the transfer was a major blow to segregation. Southern hotels would now "see the point. If they continue to insist on segregated service, we can take meetings of other organizations to places like Ft. McPherson here in Atlanta, Ft. Gordon in Savannah, the Air Base in Montgomery—and this will mean loss of money to the hotels. It will, in my opinion, help to break down the barriers of segregation."[59] Even if Wiley's judgment might have seemed complacent in the eyes of some observers, he was neither alone nor incorrect in supposing that the financial cost of maintaining segregation would prove to be the institution's Achilles' heel.

Confronted with a torrent of bad publicity and pressured vigorously behind the scenes by Harris Wofford and several members of his own commission, Grant was forced to shift his ground. On March 25, having the previous day "tentatively agreed" to a solution with Wofford and talked matters over

58. Schlesinger to Wiley, March 31, 1961, Wiley to O'Neill, March 30, 1961, folder on "General Correspondence, 1961, March 25–31," box 62, Wiley Papers.

59. Wiley to O'Neill, March 30, 1961, folder on "General Correspondence, 1961, March 25–31," box 62, Wiley Papers.

with Congressman Tuck, he announced that the forthcoming national assembly would be held at Charleston's desegregated U.S. naval station "in compliance with the President's policy."[60] Bell Wiley was overjoyed with the result of his covert efforts. It was to be hoped, he mused privately, that everyone would accept "this sensible arrangement and that we can go ahead and commemorate the war as *Americans.* I was afraid that if the National Assembly was called off altogether, or taken away from Charleston, Southern states might pull out of the commemorative program—that would be the end, in my opinion."[61] As for the hosts, mused Wiley, they "ought to be glad they got off as lightly as they did. I don't think the South Carolinians yet realize that the North won the Civil War; certainly, many act as if they have not come back into the Union."[62]

Although reaction to the commission's shift in policy was decidedly mixed, Wiley must have been heartened by the constructive responses emanating from the New Jersey commission. On being informed of the CWCC's change of heart, chairman Donald Flamm stated that he was "delighted" by the news and that his agency would now send representatives to Charleston. Madaline Williams professed to be equally satisfied by the decision, telling reporters that "it is a victory for the democratic process in America."[63] While she personally had no great desire to travel south, she felt that her group would be letting down both the state and the president if it did not attend the assembly.

Other views were less positive and revealed the polarizing effects of the Charleston crisis. Bridling at the reversal of his executive committee's decision, William Tuck announced publicly from his home in South Boston, Virginia, that he was opposed to the naval base compromise. Privately he struggled to conceal his bitterness. "I had a most difficult time with the Executive Committee," he wrote, "but finally prevailed on them, only to have General Grant and the other members of the Commission capitulate to the President and the NAACP. I am terribly worried about the future of the Centennial Commission."[64] Segregationists praised what they saw as his principled efforts to

60. Wofford to Kenneth O'Donnell, memorandum, March 24, 1961, folder FG633, box 198, WHCF. The president had reason to remember the Charleston naval base. He was assigned there against his will in early 1942 after the Office of Naval Intelligence became concerned that his girlfriend, Inga Arvad, was a Nazi spy. Dallek, *Kennedy,* 84.

61. Wiley to Seale Johnson, March 26, 1961, folder on "General Correspondence, 1961, March 25–31," box 62, Wiley Papers.

62. Wiley to John Harrison, April 10, 1961, folder on "General Correspondence, 1961, April 8–15," box 62, Wiley Papers.

63. *New York Times,* March 26, 1961, sec. 1, 72.

64. Tuck to Wint Smith, April 4, 1961, folder 5272, Tuck Papers.

protect the rights of individuals against outside interference. One Charlottesville correspondent (who expressed relief that he hailed from a state that had
not helped to elect John F. Kennedy) insisted that hotels could not be coerced
into accommodating blacks: "If this was granted the next step would be to
ask the Supreme Court to enforce their rights into our homes."[65] Several supporters revealed the extent to which recent developments had soured their
perception of the centennial project. "The whole idea of this celebration is re-
pugnant to me," wrote a southside banker. He knew of no reason whatsoever
"to celebrate a war which we lost, and which wiped out our rights as a free
State and reduced us to a province dominated entirely by the North."[66] Anger was not confined solely to residents of the South. One Ohio woman told
Tuck that "these northern trouble-makers have turned my stomach against
any celebration of the Civil War Centennial. More than that: they have made
an 'unreconstructed rebel' of me and a lot of northerners I know." Surely, she
ventured, it was time for another war on domestic tyrants: only Congress
stood "between us and a complete take-over by Communists—internally."[67]
Tuck's fellow congressman, Wint Smith of Kansas, commented that he was
"furious" with developments. "I felt from the start," he wrote apoplectically,
"that the 'funks' and liberal 'nit wits' would be using the 'nigger' question to
parade their new social theories to the forefront."[68]

Opposition to the compromise from conservative whites was matched by
the frustration of those African Americans who realized that it left Jim Crow
untouched. The president of one NAACP branch in New Jersey described it
as "most offensive" and an entirely unsatisfactory solution to the "discriminatory practice" perpetrated in South Carolina.[69] He urged New Jersey's centennial commission to insist that unless the local facilities were opened up to
delegates on a nondiscriminatory basis, the national assembly should be held
in a city where equal accommodations were available to everyone. While this
position reflected the NAACP's longstanding policy of attacking segregation
directly, it did not take account of political realities. In the early spring of 1961
few people outside the incipient civil rights movement (certainly not those in-

65. John C. Heidenreich to Tuck, March 27, 1961, folder 5272, Tuck Papers.

66. B. F. Jarratt to Tuck, March 30, 1961, folder 5272, Tuck Papers.

67. Mrs. Rex L. Tomb to Tuck, March 28, 1961, folder 5272, Tuck Papers.

68. Smith to Tuck, March 31, 1961, folder 5272, Tuck Papers.

69. Everett B. Simmons to Donald Flamm, March 26, 1961, folder on "Fourth National Assembly . . . ," box 3, NJCWCCR.

side the federal government) were ready for an immediate head-on confrontation with Jim Crow.

This said, many of the pseudohistorical reflections that accompanied resolution of the crisis betokened little domestic sympathy for Jim Crow's defenders. The *Boston Globe* welcomed the educative effect of Kennedy's intervention, proclaiming that there was "no room for the humiliation of anybody" during centennial observances intended to commemorate the courage of both sides in the Civil War. When all was said and done, however, the South *had* been defeated because slavery was outmoded: "Southern slavery made governments abroad stop short of giving the Confederacy effective support. A century later, the doctrine of white supremacy has also become obsolete. It is something the United States, above all other nations, can no longer afford."[70] A *New York Times* editorial on March 27 evinced rather less enthusiasm for the compromise because Charleston hotels had not been compelled to recognize that in the 1860s "this nation under God [had] a new birth of freedom." "The Civil War," contended the *Times*, "was a grim, bitter and deadly contest. It decided once and for all that no slave system should exist on this continent. It made ultimate equality inevitable. It destroyed a civilization, in blood and tears, in order to build a better one. Major Anderson at Sumter, Lincoln at Gettysburg, the Supreme Court in May, 1954—all have been actors in a great pageant."[71] While some black readers might have been struck by the complacent teleology of this liberal commentary, it clearly offered little comfort to bitter-end segregationists.

Although most observers assumed that the immediate issue had been settled by the naval base compromise, one final piece of the jigsaw remained out of place. The positive noises made initially by Donald Flamm and Madaline Williams were somewhat deceptive in that they represented the personal views of two individuals and not the collective wish of the New Jersey commission. At a meeting to discuss the group's formal response to the compromise, divergent views were apparent. While Williams was understandably concerned about the possibility of segregationist violence in Charleston, Joseph Dempsey, one of the main orchestrators of the crisis, confessed that the proffered solution was against his better judgment because it did not provide for equal facilities in Charleston itself. Dempsey, however, did volunteer that he did not want to exhibit a "higher sense of virtue than JFK" and expressed

70. *Boston Globe*, March 27, 1961, 8.
71. *New York Times*, March 27, 1961, 30.

his reluctance to embarrass "that great man" after all his hard work on the agency's behalf. Donald Flamm stated that any rejection of the compromise would surrender all the goodwill built up by his commission over the previous few days.[72]

The New Jerseyans' efforts to determine their likely reception in Charleston resulted in a "steaming telephone conversation" between Everett Landers and Nat Cabell, head of Charleston's delegation in the South Carolina legislature, on March 28. Cabell took the call in the lobby of the Columbia statehouse and was quickly surrounded by reporters who, by this time, were eager for any new copy on centennial matters. What transpired was not, evidently, a meeting of minds. "We would prefer you did not come," Cabell was heard to say. "We welcome visitors but when they visit with us we think they should observe our laws and customs." When Landers asked if Williams would be allowed to accompany the other members of his group to segregated restaurants in Charleston, Cabell inquired acidly, "What's the matter . . . Doesn't she like to associate with members of her own race?" Continuing to spout orthodox segregationist dogma, he added: "We believe we are more genuine in our respect for the colored people as people in South Carolina than you in fact, are. We can and do have a warm and fine regard for these people without intermingling with them." There would be no overt hostility, Cabell promised, but "there would be a lot of ignoring of those who prefer to associate with people of other races." He also told Landers that stirring up racial conflict fitted "right into the intentions of Communism to create strife throughout the world"— something that was "most peculiar even if it is not intentional."[73]

This conversation did nothing to convince the members of New Jersey's centennial commission that they would be safe in Charleston. However, after a two-hour meeting in Trenton, Landers's group formally announced that it would attend the upcoming assembly. A statement released to the press bemoaned the inaction of the CWCC, lauded the role played by President Kennedy, and noted "with deep regret" that its members would "probably be denied freedom of movement" in Charleston.[74] Within days the New York commission had withdrawn its own boycott threat, and the Massachusetts

72. Landers, pencil notes on undated meeting to discuss Charleston compromise, folder on "Fourth National Assembly . . . ," box 3, NJCWCCR.

73. Al Lanier, AP Report of Landers-Cabell telephone conversation (typed copy), March 28, 1961, folder on "Fourth National Assembly . . . ," box 3, NJCWCCR; *The State* (Columbia), March 29, 1961, A1, A9.

74. *New York Times*, March 29, 1961, 5.

LET'S CALL THE WHOLE THING OFF

commission, which had been urged to stay away by the state's attorney general, announced that it too planned to attend the national gathering.[75]

Eager to make the White House–engineered compromise stick in order to prevent further political embarrassment, Kennedy aide Harris Wofford worked strenuously to ensure that the New Jerseyans did go to Charleston by calming their lingering concerns about segregationist violence. Several members were reluctant to make the trip, but the group's chairman, Donald Flamm, felt strongly that they could not betray the president in view of Kennedy's conviction (conveyed by Wofford in a telephone conversation) that he would feel "unequivocally" let down if they decided to stay at home.[76] On April 4, Wofford conferred with Landers and Flamm in Washington. The visitors told him that they had no desire to attract more attention. "[W]e have made our point," they said, "thanks to a generous and statesmanlike assist from the Administration."[77] Wofford in return left them in no doubt "that both he and the president were in complete sympathy" with their views and agreed that he would relay any FBI warnings about likely trouble.[78] He also telephoned Karl Betts in their presence to request that the national commission ensure safe conduct for the New Jerseyans between the Charleston railroad station and the U.S. naval base.[79] So worried were some of the New Jerseyans (Joseph Dempsey, for example, apparently feared that he might be arrested on arrival in Charleston) that Wofford later spoke to CWCC staff member Edmund Gass. The latter agreed to provide further reassurances that the group would be transported safely to the base. In the course of doing this, Gass asked if it was true (as reported in the press) that the New Jersey delegates were likely to attend a meeting of the Charleston branch of the NAACP. Dempsey responded evasively that he would not be doing so and that he did not know anyone else in the group who planned to attend. Exasperated by the possibility that the New Jerseyans might still want to score points on the segregation issue, Gass later told Bell Wiley that "[i]f this wasn't potentially so explosive it would be funny." Dempsey, he hoped, would be sensible: "But if he wants to

75. *The State* (Columbia), March 30, 1961, A7; April 1, 1961, A1.

76. Flamm to Robert B. Meyner, April 9, 1961, folder on "Donald Flamm, Chairman, NJCWCC," box 7, NJCWCCR.

77. Landers to Wofford, April 5, 1961, folder on "Fourth National Assembly . . . ," box 3, NJCWCCR.

78. Flamm to Meyner, April 9, 1961, folder on "Donald Flamm, Chairman, NJCWCC," box 7, NJCWCCR.

79. Landers to Wofford, April 5, 1961, folder on "Fourth National Assembly . . . ," box 3, NJCWCCR.

prowl the streets of Charleston daring the KKK to come out and fight, I hope
he'll wait until the gavel has fallen & the Base has hauled everybody back to
the gate—to a line of waiting taxis."[80]

Notwithstanding the hard work of Wofford, Gass, and others, the naval
base compromise failed to disguise the damage done to the centennial by
the rift over Madaline Williams's accommodation. Intersectional peace was
hardly confirmed by news that the Confederate States Centennial Conference,
a loose coordinating body of the southern state commissions formed in July
1960, would hold a concurrent meeting with that of the CWCC in Charleston
or by the reports, observed by Gass, that the New Jerseyans would attend an
NAACP meeting on their visit to South Carolina.[81] Most worrying for centennial organizers, however, was the fact that press focus on the Williams issue
during March 1961 had begun to spur not only criticism but also mockery of
the entire project.

Typifying the negative publicity arising out of the Williams affair was a
semihumorous commentary written by Cleveland Amory in the *Saturday Review* on April 1. "Just where in the first place the idea of the Civil War Centennial came from we honestly don't know," mused Amory, "but we suspect the
Russians."[82] An article by Murray Kempton in the *New York Post* was couched
in a similarly derogatory vein and displayed further evidence that the black
counter-memory was undergoing a renaissance. According to Kempton, President Kennedy had missed a splendid opportunity when the CWCC decided in
its wisdom to meet in Charleston: "He could have announced that the United
States would have nothing to do with the whole Centennial. This would save
a certain amount of money and lessen our exposure to what is, by all odds,
the emptiest and most tedious event ever inflicted upon a free people." Denouncing the Civil War as the obsession of men too young for World War I
and too old for World War II, the article observed that Americans were being
asked to believe that the founding of the Confederacy and the Emancipation
Proclamation were "acts of equal moral force." Northerners specifically were
being required "not to remember history but to forget it" (otherwise why were
they not commemorating Lincoln's repeal of habeas corpus or the bloody New

80. Gass to Wiley, April 5, 1961, folder on "Charleston—National Assembly," box 184, Wiley
Papers.

81. For the deliberations of the first meeting of the Confederate States Conference, see the
two-volume transcript in frames 1617–1741, 1743–1930, reel 3, Records of the Tennessee Civil War
Centennial Commission, Tennessee State Library and Archives.

82. Cleveland Amory, "First of the Month," *Saturday Review,* April 1, 1961, 5.

York draft riots of 1863?). Perhaps, concluded Kempton, the war should be refought properly: "Then we can proceed to re-enact the Fourteenth Amendment. This time, we might even enforce it!"[83]

This astute commentary was clipped by Arthur Schlesinger and sent to Bell Wiley, but whether the southerner was as "entertained" as the White House aide surmised is open to doubt.[84] Certainly, Wiley and all those closely involved with the centennial can only have been alarmed by renewed calls for the observance to be abandoned and growing evidence, reflected in the letter columns of the local and national press, that many Americans had already had enough. One communication to the *New York Times* from Frank G. Dawson, chairman of the Inter-American Legal Studies Group at Yale, was particularly searing. Prompted to write by coverage of the Charleston fiasco, Dawson argued that the centennial's problems were caused by his countrymen's warped conception of the Civil War as a gentlemanly conflict fought by "good guys" on both sides. In fact, he wrote, the Civil War was "as morally reprehensible as any conflict fought upon principles of mass destruction." It was sad, therefore, "to contemplate the money, energy and talent expended on the resurrection of national shame and agony when the United Nations is desperately in need of funds and when the under-developed nations of Asia, Africa and Latin America require our aid for economic and political viability."[85] As well as providing further proof of the Civil War's continuing relevance to Americans at the height of the cold war, the Charleston controversy underlined the urgent need for a complete overhaul of policy by the CWCC. Manifestly, any major reconceptualization of the centennial would require a change of leadership at the top. "I'd think Betts should be levered out," mused one of Wiley's correspondents on April 8, "but how can it in fact be done?"[86]

BATTLE RESUMED: THE FOURTH NATIONAL ASSEMBLY

Any hopes that the CWCC might regain its credibility in the immediate wake of the naval base compromise were quickly dashed by an unseemly spat that dominated the ill-fated fourth national assembly. On April 10, Major General

83. *New York Post,* March 30, 1961, encl. in Schlesinger to Wiley, April 3, 1961, folder on "General Correspondence, 1961, April 1–7," box 62, Wiley Papers.

84. Schlesinger to Wiley, April 3, 1961, folder on "General Correspondence, 1961, April 1–7," box 62, Wiley Papers.

85. *New York Times,* April 9, 1961, sec. 4, 12.

86. O'Neill to Wiley, April 8, 1961, folder on "General Correspondence, 1961," box 184, Wiley Papers.

Ulysses S. Grant III arrived in Charleston to attend his commission's gathering. A welcome committee inadvertently went to the wrong terminal of the municipal airport, but, after scurrying around Charleston for an hour, it finally met up with Grant at the U.S. navy yard. The old soldier was the grateful recipient of a Confederate battle flag presented to him by the reigning Miss Confederacy. Asked if recent events would cause lasting scars, Grant responded firmly in the negative. "I don't see why it should," he said. "It's all adjusted now and everybody should be satisfied."[87] At first, his optimism seemed well placed. The New Jersey delegates, Madaline Williams among them, arrived by train the same day and were driven safely to the base. But it was just the calm before the storm.

With the Rebel battle flag now flying proudly atop the South Carolina capitol in Columbia, Confederate States delegates convened in downtown Charleston while the national commission's assembly opened at the naval base with only around 100 out of an expected 300 people in attendance.[88] At lunchtime the Confederates listened to two speeches. Ostensibly the most important of these was delivered by former U.S. secretary of state and South Carolina governor James F. Byrnes. Fittingly, the elder statesman's words had a bearing on the related issues of domestic unity and race. He began with a surprisingly pessimistic appraisal of the centennial. Congress's stated purpose in establishing the CWCC, said Byrnes, had been to encourage public knowledge of the Civil War, "but in my humble opinion it was a mistake." For the war, he continued, was "the greatest tragedy" in American history: "After two centuries its battles might be commemorated but one century is a short period in the history of a country and I fear it is quite impossible to re-live the four years of the Civil War without recalling experiences that will be unpleasant to the people of the North and the South."

Having advanced from the trenches, Byrnes then fell back. He knew, he said, that General Grant would oversee the centennial in a sensitive manner, presumably taking full account of the southern view of the war, which Byrnes proceeded to review. As befitted a respectable segregationist politician who

87. *The State* (Columbia), April 11, 1961, A1.

88. *The State* (Columbia), April 12, 1961, A5. The Confederate battle flag was raised over the South Carolina capitol on April 11, 1961, at the behest of John A. May. While the Fort Sumter celebrations served as the pretext for this act, the legislature voted in March 1962 to keep it there. It was not removed to the statehouse grounds until July 2000. Brett Bursey, "The Day the Flag Went Up," *Point* 10 (fall 1999), available online at http://www.scpronet.com/point/9909/p04.html (accessed Aug. 27, 2002). A hard copy is located in Folder on "Flag, Confederate, Controversy," Vertical File, Modern Political Collections, South Caroliniana Library, University of South Carolina.

once had labored to increase state spending on black schools (largely to stave off an integration decision by the U.S. Supreme Court), the ex-governor was keen to demonstrate the extent to which southern blacks had prospered under Jim Crow.[89] After "that nightmare" of Reconstruction, he claimed, "Negro men worked by the side of white men; Negro women worked in the homes of white women. Without a Marshall plan or aid of any kind from the federal government, they brought the South from poverty to prosperity." He added: "In the years that have passed, the Negro has made greater progress in the South than in any other place on earth. One has but to read of the Negroes in Africa today to realize the fabulous progress of the Southern Negroes. They are being educated and, certainly in this state, their schools are as good and in many instances, are superior to the schools for white children. They have gone into the professions and into business. Thousands own their farms and their homes. I am proud of their progress."[90] Here before an admiring collection of southern centennial commission members, James Byrnes thus delivered not only a defense of his own gubernatorial record but also a thinly disguised slap to ill-informed northern liberals who equated segregation with injustice.

As far as the future of the centennial was concerned, however, the second lunchtime speech proved to be more significant. It was given by Ashley Halsey Jr., a Charleston-born journalist well known as the author of a series of mildly entertaining articles on the Civil War in the popular *Saturday Evening Post* of Philadelphia. Resentful of the way segregation had been made the object of attack in recent weeks, Halsey delivered an inflammatory address that reignited sectional passions within and beyond the centennial's immediate constituency. Although most of the speech was no more newsworthy than any of his published writings on the war, his claims that current racial problems should be settled by referenda rather than Supreme Court decisions and federal bayonets were hardly designed to promote good relations between the various centennial commissions. The same was true of his jibes directed against the state of New Jersey's civil rights record. Racial discrimination was so extensive in the Garden State, he said, that it took "amazing effrontery for its politicians to rebuke any other state or community upon any circumstance or pretext."

89. Dewey W. Grantham, *The Life and Death of the Solid South: A Political History* (Lexington: University of Kentucky Press, 1988), 126.

90. James F. Byrnes, Address at "Charleston Confederate Centennial," April 11, 1961, folder on South Carolina State Commission [Jan. 1963–April 1964 and undated]," box 721, Records of the Mississippi Commission on the War Between the States, Record Group 19, Mississippi Department of Archives and History (hereafter MCWBTSR).

African Americans, he claimed, had been excluded from New Jersey hotels and only admitted to the state's largest housing development with the assistance of the federal judiciary.[91] Had Karl Betts not invited Halsey to give the main address at the national assembly's banquet that evening, it is possible that the damage caused by the journalist's remarks might have been contained.[92] As it was, news of Halsey's lunchtime comments quickly spread to the naval base where the CWCC assembly was meeting for its first day's business.

In fact, Halsey's dinner speech was surprisingly tame. One right-wing Oklahoma Republican who had been attending the Confederate States conference in Charleston hurried over to the naval base to witness what he expected would be "an exciting time." Unbeknown to him, Grant and Betts had prevailed on Halsey to delete any offensive passages with the result that Halsey "pulled his punches on this occasion and made about as flat and uninteresting talk as I ever heard."[93] This was not, however, enough for the New Jerseyans, whose chairman, Donald Flamm, demanded an opportunity to rebut the earlier charges against his state. Grant refused on the grounds that the following day's business meeting would be a more opportune venue for this purpose than the banquet. Frustrated, the New Jersey delegates proceeded to give an impromptu press conference outside the dining hall. As well as denouncing Halsey, they apparently called for Grant's resignation.[94] That evening, in what looked like a fit of pique but may well have been a prior arrangement, Everett Landers, Joseph Dempsey, and Madaline Williams drove to a local NAACP meeting, where their group was fêted for its stand on segregation.[95] Halsey's attack and the New Jerseyans' angry response provided more front-page copy for the national press (the controversy received equal billing with Yuri Gagarin's historic orbit of the earth), and the centennial was dragged through the mire once again.[96]

Shortly before dawn the next day, April 12, five members of the old Civil War Centennial Association—Carl Haverlin, Ralph Newman, Fred Schwengel,

91. Ellis, *Steps,* 22.

92. Betts to Ashley Halsey Jr., Feb. 14, 1961, box 9, reading file 1958–66, CWCCR.

93. Henry B. Bass, "Report on Charleston Meeting," folder on "Oklahoma—State Chairman," box 718, MCWBTSR.

94. *New York Times,* April 12, 1961, 1, 36. Although the New Jerseyans subsequently denied that they had asked for Grant's resignation, Joseph Dempsey was reported as saying in a private interview on April 11 that Grant and Betts should both step down because "they were doing a pretty pathetic job" and were "guilty of gross incompetence." *Atlanta Constitution,* April 12, 1961, 17.

95. *The State* (Columbia), April 12, 1961, A2.

96. See, for example, *Boston Globe,* April 12, 1961, 1.

Bell Wiley, and Clyde Walton—gathered in the Charleston gloom. In a ritual act they cracked open a bottle of French brandy (1861 vintage) to mark the precise moment when, a hundred years earlier, Confederate guns had opened up on Fort Sumter.[97] Each of them could have been forgiven for wondering what might have been had their scholarly plans for the centennial not been subsumed by the bloated public history enterprise now teetering on the brink of disaster.

Later that morning, the second day of the national assembly, the New Jersey delegation denied it had ever called for Grant's resignation but repeated its criticism of Ashley Halsey. Donald Flamm announced disingenuously that his colleagues would leave Charleston "saddened and disillusioned because this noble effort, the memorializing of the Civil War, has been sabotaged in large measure by the bad manners and the bad judgment of last night's principal speaker from the City of Brotherly Love." He also described Halsey's lunch-time remarks as a "pattern of character assassination, not only on members of our commission but also on the state of New Jersey and on our Legislature, that would have made experts in the field of endeavor green with envy." They were, he said, "calculated to incite bitterness, to open old wounds, and for good measure, to rub salt into the tortured flesh."[98] These stinging comments drew something of an apology from the Philadelphia journalist, but it was hardly one to paper over the gaping cracks now evident in the ranks of centennial participants. Denying any intention to cause personal harm to individuals, Halsey insisted that his lunchtime speech had been "hopefully intended to emphasize the awful error made in using force and coercion to settle a national issue 100 years ago and to suggest a peaceful, constructive solution to current problems which still concern us all as Americans as a result of that century old mistake." Pointedly, he declined to withdraw his combustible assertion that racial discrimination was still practiced in the state of New Jersey.[99]

The spat occasioned by what Carl Haverlin described as Ashley Halsey's "intemperate and reprehensible speech" had several consequences.[100] Inevitably it brought the centennial into further disrepute. The national press used it

97. *Charleston News and Courier,* April 13, 1961, clipping, microfilm 1115, frames 118–19, reel 2, Stanley F. Horn Papers, Tennessee Historical Society Collections, Tennessee State Library and Archives.

98. Ellis, *Steps,* 25; *New York Times,* April 13, 1961, 1, 25.

99. *Boston Globe,* April 13, 1961, 45.

100. New York Civil War Centennial Commission, minutes of the first assembly, April 17, 1961, box 1, office files, A1444-78, Records of the New York Civil War Centennial Commission, New York State Archives.

to cast more doubt on the wisdom of the commemoration. An editorial in the *Atlanta Constitution* contended that the recent furor was "a warning that the centennial could well degenerate into just the sort of useless brooding over the past that so many of its critics said it would." While debate on the Civil War could help Americans understand their nation, "nostalgia is not study, celebration is not commemoration, and haggling is not debate." [101] The *New York Times* meanwhile seized the occasion to reprint James Byrnes's warnings about a revival of sectionalism. Widespread coverage like this made an impression on ordinary Americans who had followed the events of March and April with growing interest. When three members of the New Jersey delegation appeared on a local NBC television program on April 16, they were greeted with a battery of probing questions from viewers in the New York metropolitan area. Wasn't the centennial just a tourist gimmick? Wasn't it stirring up sectional tensions over the segregation issue? How could the United States compete with Russia in the space race if segregation persisted? Why did "the Negro" try to obtain a reservation in Charleston "while she knew they would not accept her?" [102]

Consistently negative coverage of events from Charleston also had an impact on Congress, where the House appropriations committee began moves to cut the CWCC funding for fiscal 1962 from $100,000 to $75,000. To have any chance of restoring the cut, Edmund Gass told Bell Wiley, "our Commission has to get religion and take a large dose of castor oil—confession, conversion & purge." [103] Wiley, whose intervention had helped save the national assembly, was personally furious at the recent turn of events. Halsey, he claimed, had "destroyed at one stroke all of the work we had done to allay sectional animosity and get through this difficult meeting in a manner that would not do irreparable harm to the commemorative program." [104] He blamed the unrepentant Karl Betts for having "mismanaged the affair terribly all the way through" and was not optimistic that the "recurrence of such bungling" could be prevented by the commission as it was currently constituted. Confederates were now "squared off against the Yankees," he told his friend James Silver, a like-minded liberal who worked (under constant pressure from

<hr>

101. *Atlanta Constitution,* April 13, 1961, 4.

102. Brunswick, NJ, *Sunday Home News,* April 16, 1961, clipping and related file in folder on "Direct Line–NBC TV," box 6, NJCWCCR.

103. Gass to Wiley, April 15, 1961, folder on "General Correspondence, 1961," box 184, Wiley Papers.

104. Wiley to Ira M. Koger, May 1, 1961, folder on "General Correspondence, 1961, May 1–3," box 62, Wiley Papers.

segregationists) in the history department at Ole Miss, "and Bill Tuck, Congressman from Virginia, rank segregationist and follower of Byrd, is both Vice-Chairman of the Commission and chairman of the executive committee. He will side with the Executive Director and I am not sure that we can accomplish any reform. Unfortunately, most of the members of the Commission are not really interested in the program or how it is conducted."[105] The obvious conclusion, already reached by Wiley and his allies on the commission, was that the only way to stave off further disasters was to jettison the conservatives who, in their view, were threatening to ruin the entire centennial commemoration. The same Charleston crises that wrought such damage to the agency impelled a process of reorganization that would culminate in the departure of Grant, Betts, and Tuck by mid-summer.

On the night of April 12, 1961, crowds congregated in Charleston to watch the much-anticipated ceremonies planned by the South Carolina Commission on the War Between the States and the local chamber of commerce to mark the hundredth anniversary of the Confederate attack on Fort Sumter. It had been a difficult day. Driving rain had forced the organizers to abandon their dawn observances, but a spring sun and brisk wind dried the streets in time for a grand parade witnessed enthusiastically by small boys perched in trees and cheering adults who, taking a break from centennial cocktail parties, crowded the windows and balconies of the city's genteel antebellum homes. Large numbers of people then watched a full-dress pageant depicting the final, fateful negotiations between Major Robert Anderson and the Confederate authorities. After dusk came the dramatic climax—a colorful fireworks display over Fort Sumter, now the property of the NPS, to mimic the assault that had begun the Civil War. A reporter for the *New York Times* described the rockets flashing over the ramparts and thousands of spectators, many of them seated precariously on authentic cannon in South Battery Park, whooping and yelling every time a geyser of flame rose up from the fort to indicate a direct hit.[106] Most of those who watched in wonder had no idea that the days of grand centennial pageantry were already numbered.

105. Wiley to James W. Silver, May 2, 1961, folder on "General Correspondence, 1961, May 1–3," box 62, Wiley Papers.

106. *New York Times*, April 13, 1961, 1, 25.

4

The Historians Take Control

THE TWIN CRISES at Charleston in the spring of 1961 cast a pall over the centennial, raising serious questions about whether it was really possible to make Civil War memory a vehicle for forced consensus in the cultural cold war. The unexpected racial controversy sparked by the New Jerseyans had impinged upon the consciousness of many people who, under normal circumstances, would not have paid attention to any kind of public history jamboree. Against a backdrop of mounting tension over civil rights (May 1961 witnessed shocking assaults on black and white "freedom riders" in Alabama), the centennial seemed at best a national embarrassment and at worst a sinister excuse for segregationists to mobilize southern whites on the basis of the Lost Cause. The resulting media criticism of the heritage project seriously divided the organizing coalition. The rift was particularly evident within the CWCC. Racial liberals committed to the original cold war agenda were convinced that Karl Betts was insensitive to the changing political context in which commemorative events were taking place. During the summer of 1961 their covert efforts to oust the executive director were given additional momentum by a fresh wave of media criticism directed at a controversial reenactment of the First Battle of Bull Run. Although conservatives on the national commission sought to stall the opposition, Bell Wiley and his allies finally succeeded in procuring Betts's dismissal in August—a move that had the unanticipated consequence of prompting the resignation of the agency's venerable chairman, Ulysses S. Grant III. The resulting power vacuum presented liberals with the opportunity to take control of the CWCC in order to fashion a centennial consonant with both the times and the policy considerations of the new Kennedy administration. Under Grant's successor, the eminent historian Allan Nevins, the commission embarked on a more self-consciously inclusive observance of the Civil War, one that would serve as a genuinely useful tool in the struggle against communism. Inevitably, the passing of the old guard was a cause of consternation among the segregationists who dominated many of the southern state commissions. Their fears were accentuated especially by the prospect of a formal ceremony to mark the one hundredth anniversary of Abraham Lincoln's preliminary Emancipation Proclamation. By the spring of 1962, however, those fears appeared to have been assuaged. The centennial had been rescued from oblivion, but it would proceed in a more subdued manner than the high-profile people's festival Betts and his supporters envisaged.

THE SOUND AND THE FURY: THIRD BULL RUN

The centennial did not grind to a halt after the CWCC's disastrous fourth national assembly. Numerous events took place at the state and local levels across the United States during the late spring and early summer of 1961. Many of these observances continued to develop the consensual agenda of the national commission and to reflect genuine popular enthusiasm for the project. Mississippi, for example, won praise for its ambitious program of intersectional amity and tourist development at Vicksburg. Between March 26 and July 8, a week of ceremonial activities was devoted to every northern state that had built a monument to its soldiers in the now serene National Military Park. During "Indiana Week" in June, the chairman of the Indiana centennial commission used the commonplace language of sectional reconciliation to give thanks that the Union had been preserved, for had it been broken up into fragments, "[n]one of these smaller countries would be strong enough to cope with the world problems of today." The Hoosiers who died at Vicksburg, he said, had deplored fighting against other Americans and in their "free time" had actually made friends with the brave southerners against whom they struggled. Twentieth-century Americans owed much to their predecessors, who endeavored "to see that differences within would not break the unity and the bonds which holds [sic] these states together and which enables us to be the strongest power in the world today."[1]

It is likely that many people who participated in the host of community-level events that occurred during the early stages of the centennial took home a similarly morale-boosting message. This was particularly the case in the North. The absence of battlefields may have rendered the centennial less of a financial inducement to northerners than southerners, but it did not prevent significant

1. Indiana Civil War Centennial Commission, news release, June 24, 1961, folder on "Indiana—State Chairman [July 1960–November 1961]," box 713, Records of the Mississippi Commission on the War Between the States, Record Group 19, Mississippi Department of Archives and History (hereafter MCWBTSR).

numbers of them taking part in formal and informal observances. In Ohio, for example, the vice chairman of the state commission reported "literally scores, even hundreds, of commemorative events . . . at the local level. These affairs seem to run themselves and we offer nothing except encouragement."[2] A similar situation prevailed in New York, where a network of public historians cooperated closely with an active state agency to promote grassroots interest in the Civil War. As in the South, politicians, businessmen, and civic groups played a central role in setting up northern centennial bodies. In Brookhaven on Long Island, the inaugural meeting of the town's commission was attended by the local historian, Laura Ebell, along with two councilmen and representatives from the Masonic War Veterans, AmVets, the NAACP, the American Legion, and the Veterans of Foreign Wars.[3] Coalitions like this planned a wide range of activities. Penn Yan, a small community near Ithaca, organized a "Union Days" retail program sponsored by the chamber of commerce and "Keuka Rifles Day" to commemorate the first organized company to leave rural Yates County for the front. The Rifles Day began with a lunch at the village hall as well as a display of nineteenth-century farm equipment and muskets. It ended with a parade of seventy-eight uniformed Riflemen along Main Street toward the Pennsylvania Railroad station whence the original company had departed a hundred years previously. Accompanying the soldiers were school bands playing Civil War tunes, costumed officials in horse-drawn carriages, area firemen, and members of local riding clubs in historical dress.[4] Other New York communities hosted beard-growing contests, musical events, museum displays, shooting contests and, as in the case of Rochester, the occasional full-blown pageant. These events were often well attended. Around 3,000 people, for example, watched the Lake George Skirmish in August in which 700 men and women from nine eastern states and Washington, DC, participated in authentic garb.[5]

Notwithstanding the national media's conviction that the South was winning the centennial hands down, northerners' enthusiasm for the Civil War in the middle of 1961 sometimes exceeded that of white southerners. Although

2. Erwin C. Zepp to Karl S. Betts, Aug. 30, 1961, folder on "Washington Trip—Oct. 25–26, 1961," box 184, Bell I. Wiley Papers, Manuscript, Archives, and Rare Book Library, Emory University.

3. *Long Island Advance,* May 18, 1961, clipping in box 1, scrapbooks and clippings 1961–62, A0208-78, Records of the New York Civil War Centennial Commission, New York State Archives (hereafter NYCWCCR).

4. *Geneva Times,* May 9, 1961, clipping in book 3, scrapbooks and clippings 1961–62, A0208-78, NYCWCCR.

5. *Troy Morning Record,* Aug. 14, 1961, clipping in box 1, scrapbooks and clippings 1961–62, A0208-78, NYCWCCR.

well-planned events such as the Confederate Festival in Raleigh, secession-day celebrations in Nashville, and the Battle of Philippi pageant in West Virginia proved to be popular, apathy toward the centennial continued to pervade many southern communities. This said, northern observances were not as overtly politicized as those in the South. Certainly nothing above the Mason-Dixon line compared with the secession-day celebrations in Montgomery and Jackson. The main reason for this was that the Civil War meant less to northerners in the mid-twentieth century than it did to white southerners. Their forebears had won the victory, sacralized it through the construction of cemeteries, statues, and war memorials, and, in the main, embraced the cloying spirit of reconciliation. High levels of immigration at the turn of the century, moreover, meant that many Americans living outside the South had no tangible memory of the Civil War at all. Those northerners who participated in the burgeoning Civil War subculture after 1945 did so primarily as consumers who sought to experience the war vicariously as an adjunct, perhaps even an antidote, to life in the most successful industrial society on earth.

In contrast, the impact of neo-Confederate education in the Jim Crow South and the continuing imperative to protect white supremacy from external assault ensured that the Lost Cause remained an important part of the fabric of modern southern culture—its salience accentuated by the rear-guard action against integration in the 1950s. Whereas white southerners could hardly attend centennial events without being aware of the connection between the defense of racial privilege and states' rights in the 1860s and the 1960s, most northerners at the start of the commemoration "remembered" the Civil War in a less sectional manner. If they did draw a lesson from their centennial activities in 1961, it was not that they were still fighting the battles of the nineteenth century—after all, no one doubted that the Union had been preserved—but, rather, that the courage of their ancestors constituted a source of patriotic inspiration in the cold war. As one woman reflected after watching the Keuka Rifles parade through Penn Yan: "Today, when news is concerned with the struggle between freedom and enslavement through communism, it is worthwhile to stop and think of our American Heritage and our own struggle for freedom within our own boundaries." This, she added, "might be a good time to re-evaluate the problems of today and to fight more firmly for the ideals and goals of a free world."[6] There could have been no clearer evidence that the message propounded by the CWCC was getting through to the grassroots.

6. *Penn Yan Chronicle Express*, May 25, 1961, clipping in box 2, scrapbooks and clippings 1961–62, A0208-78, NYCWCCR.

While large numbers of Americans continued to mark the centennial well into the summer of 1961, there were, too, telling signs of the damage wrought by controversies surrounding the fourth national assembly in South Carolina. In 1907 the New Jersey legislature had made a grand gesture of sectional amity by erecting a monument to celebrate the valor of the 23rd New Jersey Volunteers and the 9th Alabama Infantry, two regiments engaged in a ferocious action at the Battle of Chancellorsville. On May 6, 1961, around 200 people attended a rededication ceremony hosted by Virginia's Civil War agency at Salem Church.[7] They included two black women—Mrs. Eola J. Jett, a director of the New Jersey NAACP, and Madaline Williams, almost a household name in the wake of the Charleston fiasco—but not a single representative from Alabama. Some members of the Trenton commission had regarded Salem Church as a chance to mend fences with their southern peers. However, the Alabama commission announced that it would not be sending representatives, ostensibly because the legislature would be in session and because of its own preference for a full-scale commemoration of the battle in 1963.[8] This rebuff prompted a fierce blast from Joseph Dempsey, the liberal Democratic lawyer whose contempt for the centennial establishment had grown after the racial controversy at Charleston. He told fellow members of the New Jersey centennial agency that he opposed a conciliatory approach to the Alabamans. Instead he favored dispatching the following letter to Governor John Patterson and the head of the state's Civil War commission, Albert Moore: "In the event we have failed to demonstrate the purpose of this Centennial, which is to unify the people of the country behind a common memorial, we shall be forced to assume that there has arisen a hostile alignment behind Karl Betts which has caused the Centennial to become a national embarrassment. And we shall be disposed to take whatever action necessary in the light of our failure, and in the failure of our good intentions, to see that the Centennial observance is concluded forthwith."[9] While the Trenton commission declined to follow Dempsey's uncompromising advice by seeking to curtail the centennial, the decision to send Madaline Williams as its representative to Salem Church was unlikely to persuade the Alabamans that they had been wrong to boycott the ceremony.

7. *New York Times*, May 7, 1961, sec. 1, 61.

8. Albert B. Moore to Everett J. Landers, April 18, 1961, folder on "Salem Church Rededication, May 6, 1961," box 3, Records of the New Jersey Civil War Centennial Commission, New Jersey State Archives (hereafter NJCWCCR).

9. Landers, undated memorandum on Salem Church rededication, May 1961, folder on "Salem Church Rededication, May 6, 1961," box 3, NJCWCCR.

Sectional ire was as evident among centennial planners below the Mason-Dixon line as it was above it. Sidney T. Roebuck, chairman of the Mississippi commission, told Governor Terry Sanford of North Carolina that the southern states had to cooperate with one another "in all Centennial matters since New Jersey has tried to throw a stumbling block in the Centennial path."[10] Refusing, like some antebellum slaveholder, to credit Yankees with any moral conscience, he insisted that northerners were envious of the tourist dollars likely to flow south as a result of Civil War–related events and thus were hell-bent on ruining the commemoration. Roebuck's confidence that these efforts would not succeed was sorely tested by the appearance of an editorial on the centennial in *Holiday* magazine in July 1961. Influenced by the recent negative coverage of Confederate theatrics, this mouthpiece of the domestic tourist industry warned that over the next few years anyone traveling in the South was "likely to encounter certain other sights and sounds and excitements, of a very special nature, which may give him cause for wonder and alarm." It went on to point out that a sanguinary civil war had been fought over slavery, finally culminating in the demise of that institution. Now the country was preparing to commemorate the conflict in "holiday mood . . . cheered on by gleeful commercial interests, and blessed by sentimentalists who prefer to forget . . . that some of us even now are being brutally denied certain personal freedoms."[11]

Adverse publicity like this boded ill for southern states that regarded the centennial as a cash cow. Organizers in the South were outraged, not least because their states had invested substantial sums of money in promotional ads. From Mississippi (which had spent $23,620 on ads in *Holiday* alone) Roebuck denounced the offending editorial as "unfair, unwarranted and highly damaging" to the centennial.[12] It was, he told the president of the magazine's publishing company, particularly unwarranted in view of the efforts that southern states were making to promote good intersectional relations and play a stronger role in fostering national economic growth.[13] Alabama's Albert Moore complained that the article was "motivated by a desire to disparage the South"

10. Sidney T. Roebuck to Terry Sanford, May 10, 1961, folder on "North Carolina—State Chairman [July 1960–November 1962]," box 718, MCWBTSR.

11. *Holiday*, July 1961, clipping in folder on "Newspaper Stories," box 184, Wiley Papers.

12. Roebuck to Betts, June 30, 1961, folder on "Betts, Karl S.," box 708, MCWBTSR; Roebuck to Moore, June 28, 1961, folder on "Alabama—State Director [July 1960–Dec. 1962]," box 707, MCWBTSR.

13. Roebuck to Robert E. MacNeal, June 28, 1961, folder on "Curtis Publishing Company," box 70, subject files 1957–66, Records of the Civil War Centennial Commission, Records of the National Park Service, Record Group 79, National Archives (hereafter CWCCR).

as well as "a fear that the Centennial commemoration of the Civil War will give the South much publicity and add tourist dollars to its economy." He went on to disparage the implication that the Union had fought to free the slaves and derided the idea that race relations were perfect in the North. "Before we sit in critical judgment over each other . . . ," he concluded, "we would do well to follow Christ's admonition to remove the beam from our own eyes . . . What is needed in our dealings with each other, particularly in this critical time, is good manners, good fellowship, and a deep regard for harmony between the sections as a means of national unity." [14]

The growth of sectional friction within the centennial establishment and persistent criticism of the entire project from outside placed growing pressure on the CWCC's embattled executive director, Karl Betts. In early June, Betts confided to General Grant that "we have our hands full selling the American public on keeping them united in the aims and purposes of the Centennial." [15] Efforts to maintain his position by refusing to hold a meeting of the commission to review the problems at Charleston did little to increase his popularity; nor did the surprise resignation of his conservative ally, Congressman William Tuck, from the agency in the second week of July. [16] Betts's fate, however, was finally sealed by adverse publicity arising out of a spectacular reenactment of the Confederate victory at First Bull Run.

For some Americans, sham battles—commercial reenactments of historic military engagements staged by reenactors clothed in authentic uniforms— were controversial events, especially when they were fought on ground stained with the blood of patriots. Critics attacked them as vulgar entertainments that mocked the sacrifices of the dead, and several of the northern centennial commissions openly declared their opposition to them. Yet there was little doubt that large numbers of Americans, adults and children, found them a compelling form of pageantry. They enabled the public to relive the nation's past (or at least to think it was doing so) and to witness the drama of war without actually seeing its hideous consequences. Karl Betts considered sham battles to be

14. Moore to editors of *Holiday,* July 13, 1961, encl. in Moore to Roebuck, July 14, 1961, folder on "Alabama—State Director [July 1960–Dec. 1962]," box 707, MCWBTSR.

15. Betts to Ulysses S. Grant III, June 5, 1961, box 9, reading file 1958–66, CWCCR.

16. Tuck told Speaker of the House Sam Rayburn that he was resigning from the CWCC because of his extensive political duties. William M. Tuck to Sam Rayburn, July 13, 1961, folder 5273, William M. Tuck Papers, Special Collections, Earl Gregg Swem Library, College of William and Mary. However, Bell Wiley's conjecture that the Virginian's decision was influenced by rumors of an impending black appointee has a ring of truth about it. Wiley to Norman Fitzgerald, July 26, 1961, folder on "General Correspondence, 1961, July 16–31," box 63, Wiley Papers.

effective vehicles for guaranteeing popular participation in the centennial—in marked contrast to most historians, who viewed them in an entirely negative light. While he and Grant consistently made it clear that the CWCC did not have the resources or the desire to stage its own battle reenactments, they did nothing to discourage state commissions from organizing such events. From a very early stage they regarded Bull Run as an ideal opportunity to get ordinary Americans interested in the Civil War centennial. "This first major land battle of the war *must* be restaged," they urged in March 1960, "—and restaged successfully and impressively—to set the pattern for the four years of commemorative programs which will follow."[17] To this end they encouraged the formation of the First Manassas Corporation, a makeshift company (under the direction of retired U.S. Army general James C. Fry) sponsored jointly by the CWCC, the Virginia commission, the Department of Defense, and the NPS.[18] The battle was to be refought on July 22–23, 1961, in the Manassas National Military Park by National Guardsmen and professional reenactors belonging to groups like the North-South Skirmish Association. Betts's opponents on the commission were appalled as the CWCC's public enthusiasm for the event increased by the day. A press release in late June boasted that Bull Run "is expected to be the outstanding event of the entire Centennial period and will be staged through the cooperation of the National Centennial Commission." "This," Bell Wiley told Representative Fred Schwengel, "comes at a time when the Commission is under heavy attack throughout the country for devoting too much attention to reenactments, on the score that they tend to romanticize and glorify war, and reactivate the passions of war."[19]

To some extent, Third Bull Run justified the description of one observer as "an outstanding success."[20] Large crowds attended the reenactment staged opposite Henry Hill, scene of some of the fiercest fighting in 1861. Although the majority of the spectators were southerners, large numbers of northern

17. Grant and Betts to R. Jackson Ratcliffe, March 24, 1960, microfilm 1115, frame 72, reel 7, Stanley F. Horn Papers, Tennessee Historical Society Collections, Tennessee State Library and Archives.

18. Set up in mid-1960, the 41-member board of directors of the First Manassas Corporation included representatives from northern Virginia cities and counties. Businessman Herbert Goodman and CWCC staffer Pat Jones served as co-chairmen, with General Fry as executive director. Francis F. Wilshin to Horn, July 7, 1960, frame 30, reel 7, Horn Papers.

19. Wiley to Fred Schwengel, July 1, 1961, folder on "General Correspondence, 1961," box 184, Wiley Papers.

20. Wilshin to Lyon G. Tyler, Aug. 31, 1961, folder on "Manassas Reenactment," box 1, Records of the Virginia Civil War Centennial Commission, Library of Virginia (hereafter VaCWCCR).

tourists journeyed into the Virginia countryside to view the heavily publicized spectacle. Among them was Millard E. Crane, who drove to Manassas with his family from their hometown of Fonda, New York. Stopping at Baltimore and Alexandria on the way, the Cranes equipped themselves with thermoses of coffee and ice water and set off for the battlefield shortly after 8 A.M. on Saturday, July 22. By the time they arrived the crowds were already gathering and the temperature was soaring toward the 100-degree mark. They paid four dollars each for seats at the top of the grandstand and invested in a commemorative program costing twenty-five cents. In it they read an explanation of the "living spectacle" they were about to witness: "There was a curious thing about the men who came against each other here a hundred years ago. Whether they wore the blue or the gray they were all deeply in love with their country. *And the country they loved was America,* though they saw America in segments then. Now it is wonderful to know that out of the misery of their differences came the magic and miracle of Union, Union cemented and accepted and cherished. When the smoke cleared away and the passions withered in the heat of war the America they all loved spread out before them, and before us, their children, as one wide, majestic land of infinite opportunity for all." The program also contained a pertinent message from ex-president Dwight D. Eisenhower: "Out of the Civil War came a Nation tempered in liberty and destined for leadership in the free world." [21]

Looking up from their program the Cranes, perspiring heavily, stared from their lofty vantage point at the colorful scenes below. Honor Guards practiced for review; a New England Yankee playing the part of Stonewall Jackson rode backward and forward brandishing his sword; wives and children of the 2,000 or so participants wandered around the field in homemade period clothing. Cameras clicked everywhere. The Cranes ate their lunch and then, at 1 P.M. precisely, witnessed the arrival of Governor Lindsay Almond and other guests. After the playing of the national anthem a U.S. army captain delivered a stirring prologue. This was followed by a parade of units and a "Pageant of American Unity." Then came the battle itself—a carefully coordinated medley of movement, color, and noise narrated by Pat Jones of the CWCC staff. Millard Crane was impressed. "We have never witnessed anything like it," he wrote later: "It had been so well rehearsed . . . that one had a distinct sense of immediacy. The pop-pop of musketry; the booming of cannon belching fire

21. *Centennial Commemoration July 22–23, 1961: The First Battle of Manassas (Bull Run)*, official commemorative program, folder on "Reenactments—Manassas," box 97, subject files 1957–66, CWCCR.

and smoke; the sound of a bugle faintly heard in a lull in the sound and fury; the falling bodies; the flags unfurled in the breeze; all seemed to catch one up into a sense of living history and one could almost feel it was 1861." A thunderous artillery duel proved especially thought-provoking. "Truly," mused Crane, "our forebears were dedicated men with a cause, no matter which color uniform they wore." At the end of the day, as the participants returned to the field and the band played Civil War tunes, the southern family in the row in front turned round to say their farewells. "See you at Gettysburg," the father called out. Driving away from the setting sun, the Cranes encountered a highway scarcely less clogged than the crowded roads of a century before. Dusk was falling by the time they crossed the Potomac into Washington. Finding the nation's capital almost deserted, they gazed upon imposing white monuments to the presidents, deep in thought about what they had learned from the day's experience. "The great Union was preserved," Millard Crane told readers of his hometown newspaper, "and reunited by stronger bonds than ever. We have suffered together through four great wars and today present a united front to the foes of our way of life. With God's help, let's be about it." [22]

The Cranes' visit to Manassas appeared to vindicate the attempts of Karl Betts and his allies on the federal commission to encourage the widest possible participation in the centennial. They were ordinary Americans entertained and awed by their encounter with the Civil War. Their patriotic experience was far from unique. A total of 70,000 spectators attended the event (Friday's dress rehearsal included). It was costly to produce ($170,000) but yielded a profit which, according to General Fry, would be invested in a Civil War Hall of Fame. (No musty museum, according to one unnamed official; rather "something as alive and modern as Disneyland.") [23] Yet notwithstanding these pluses, media accounts of the sham battle were decidedly negative. So negative, in fact, that they cast further doubt on the wisdom of turning the Civil War into an exercise in mass public history and furnished Betts's critics with additional ammunition in what was fast becoming a coordinated campaign to secure his dismissal.

An editorial in the *New York Herald-Tribune* on July 22 set the tone for newspaper coverage of the event. Three and a half thousand grown men, it was observed, were about to reenact the First Battle of Bull Run—this in spite of the fact that the Civil War was one of the most tragic events in American

---

22. *Fonda Democrat*, Aug. 17, 1961, clipping in box 1, scrapbooks and clippings 1961–62, A0208-78, NYCWCCR.

23. *New York Times*, July 24, 1961, 8.

history: "If that were not enough to condemn this puerile show, we can point out that it is not over yet, that the issues it was fought for are still scars across our body as a nation."[24] The sham battle itself was described in the *New York Times* the next day as "almost ninety minutes of profuse feigned violence in scorching heat." The watching reporter observed that the predominantly southern crowd "came to their feet and cheered as the shouting Confederates chased the Union troops back into the woods in a panic."[25] Also noted was the plethora of tents behind the grandstand selling literature, souvenirs, ice cream, beverages, and hot dogs.

While some of the criticism targeted the perceived overcommercialization of the event alluded to by this *Times* report, rather more of it picked up on the disparity between play and reality—the theme underlined by the *Herald-Tribune*. An op-ed piece in the *Buffalo News*, for example, mockingly listed the casualties from bee stings and heat stroke, comparing them with those of both the real Civil War and modern troubles. War's "terrible dimensions," the author contended, "are less suggested these days by tourist mobs and bright uniforms than by the dead in Bizerte's streets, or the grim weapons under the lock of the powers now intent on Berlin."[26] Other commentators, frustrated by the damaging impact of segregationist violence on internal peace and the country's image abroad, chose a more blatantly sectional line of criticism by berating white southerners for their apparent preference for silly games over racial equality. One northern editor typically assailed "the ludicrous restaging" of First Bull Run, accusing southerners of trying to obscure their proslavery cause "with pageantry and chivalric legend."[27] Referring to the reenactment as "a grisly pantomime" and "a grotesque evasion of the more challenging task before us at this juncture in history," an irate New Englander wrote to the *New York Times* in similar vein. Such trivialization of violence, he contended, caused Americans "to overlook those grievous imbalances and necessities in our body politic which, one hundred years ago, made the outbreak of violence a tragic but necessary preliminary to the arduous reconstitution of our

24. *New York Herald-Tribune*, July 22, 1961, clipping in box 1, scrapbooks and clippings 1961–62, A0208-78, NYCWCCR.

25. *New York Times*, July 23, 1961, sec. 1, 1.

26. *Buffalo News*, July 26, 1961, clipping in box 1, scrapbooks and clippings 1961–62, A0208-78, NYCWCCR. Earlier that month 700 Tunisians had died in the successful French effort to recapture the naval base of Bizerta. Alistair Horne, *A Savage War of Peace: Algeria, 1954–1962* (London and Basingstoke, UK: Macmillan, 1977), 474–75.

27. *Jamestown Sun*, July 29, 1961, clipping in box 1, scrapbooks and clippings 1961–62, A0208-78, NYCWCCR.

society."[28] Betts and Grant had tried to build support for the centennial on the basis of the orthodox interpretation of the Civil War. With the civil rights movement becoming more assertive—the Freedom Rides were intended to coerce federal intervention against Jim Crow—that interpretation was becoming increasingly contested. It seemed to many that the edifice erected by CWCC leaders was in danger of crumbling away.

A CHANGE AT THE HELM

More than any other individual, Karl Betts had placed his stamp on the centennial. It seemed obvious, then, to some concerned members of the CWCC that his removal was the only thing that could prevent their centennial dream from turning into a nightmare. In fact, a clandestine campaign to unseat Karl Betts as executive director was well advanced even before newspapers sank their teeth into Third Bull Run. It was led by the southern historian Bell Wiley, Iowa congressman Fred Schwengel, and the head of the manuscript division of the Library of Congress, David C. Mearns.[29] The bill of indictment against the executive director was long and growing. Progressives inside the CWCC and liberals outside it blamed him for the appalling mess at Charleston—not only his egregious failure to deal with the issue of Madaline Williams's accommodation but also his decision to invite an unreconstructed southerner, Ashley Halsey, to speak at the national assembly. The New Jerseyans blamed him personally for virtually every perceived blemish on the centennial's record. Still fuming at the mistreatment of Williams and Halsey's verbal assaults on their state, they also suspected him of having masterminded the dispatch of an anonymous note to the Trenton commission telling its members to stop causing trouble. Equally seriously, they contended that he was responsible for what they saw as the crass overcommercialization of the centennial.[30]

Had criticism of the executive director been confined to New Jersey, he would have survived. However, there were other charges. Virginia's centennial agency fell out with him over the national commission's lack of support for their commemoration of the Washington Peace Conference, as well as Betts's

---

28. *New York Times,* July 29, 1961, 18.

29. None of these men, it must be emphasized, wished to replace Grant. While the chairman's illustrious pedigree and kindly, patrician manner were probably enough in themselves to guarantee the continued loyalty of fellow commission members, it was by no means clear, even to insiders, how closely his views were aligned with those of Betts.

30. Wiley to Schwengel, July 1, 1961, folder on "General Correspondence, 1961," box 184, Wiley Papers.

claims that the Virginians were not putting enough money into the Manassas project that was so close to his heart.[31] Historians on the CWCC moaned that he gave insufficient attention to their own concerns, particularly scholarship and education. Opposition was also generated by the leadership's refusal to hold a postmortem on the damaging events at Charleston—something that General Grant had promised the New Jerseyans in the midst of the controversy over Halsey's speech. By far the gravest indictment leveled against Betts, however, was that he was no longer in step with the times. America's political climate had changed since 1957 when he had played a crucial role in the effort to create a federal commission to oversee the Civil War centennial. What was required, argued critics like Wiley, was a reform of the commission that would render it more responsive to shifts in national public opinion, especially given the inauguration of a new president and the quickening pace of the African-American freedom struggle.[32]

How fair were these charges? In some cases, they were far from justified. The New Jersey police carried out a laboratory test on the offensive missive to the Trenton commission and reported that the typewriter on which it had been written was not the same brand as those used in the CWCC's Washington office.[33] As for overcommercialization, there is no doubt that many U.S. companies regarded the centennial as a perfect opportunity to make money and, in many cases, paid no attention to questions of taste in order to maximize their profits. News of a set of girls' underpants sporting a Confederate motif was received with particular alarm by Campbell Brown, director of the Tennessee commission, and all of the state agencies—not just New Jersey's—were deluged with junk mail from firms manufacturing other items keyed in to the centennial.[34] But Karl Betts was entirely comfortable with the fact that commerce went hand in hand with the centennial. He had been appointed in large measure because of, not in spite of, his business expertise. His task, as he saw it, was to market the centennial to the American people and in the process help to generate economic growth. Since the majority of the state commissions, certainly those in the South, agreed with him that tourist

31. Wiley to Schwengel, July 5, 1961, ibid.

32. Wiley to Schwengel, July 22, 1961, ibid.

33. State Bureau of Identification, Division of State Police, New Jersey Department of Public Safety, laboratory report in folder on "National CWCC (Correspondence)," box 8, NJCWCCR.

34. Campbell H. Brown to Betty S. Forio, Dec. 9, 1960, folder on "Confederate States CWCC: Tennessee CWCC, 1960–65," box 2, RCB 7547, Records of the Georgia Civil War Centennial Commission, Record Group, 079-01-001, Georgia State Archives (hereafter GaCWCCR).

development should be a central feature of the ambitious heritage project, it seems unreasonable to chastise Betts for fostering close relations with business. Besides, if the centennial was to reach the widest possible audience, then advertising and marketing clearly had a legitimate role to play in the CWCC's overall strategy. It is doubtful if manifestly popular events such as Third Bull Run would have attracted large crowds without the expensive promotional campaigns undertaken by companies like Sinclair Oil and the American Automobile Association.

The historians' case against Betts had more merit but was hardly an open-and-shut one. In the spring of 1959, the CWCC's historical activities committee chaired by Bell Wiley sponsored a series of meetings to fashion a coherent policy on the scholarly and pedagogical aims of the centennial. Attended by historians, archivists, and buffs, these gatherings provided Wiley with the material for a report which was published in *Civil War History* the following December. Recommendations included encouraging people to seek out soldiers' diaries and letters, the soliciting of funds to microfilm these and other documents, and the compilation of a comprehensive bibliography of scholarship on the Civil War.[35] By early 1960 Wiley was fretting that the CWCC was not doing enough to further these aims. Betts tried to deflect such concerns, writing in February that the commission simply did not have enough money to accomplish every objective.[36] In truth the executive director had little sympathy for the ideas of scholars like Wiley. While he was right about the limitations on spending, he probably would not have devoted large sums of money to scholarly activities even if they had been available. As had been clear from the start of the project, professional historians and amateur buffs differed subtly in their conception of the centennial. Whereas the former stressed the importance of promoting high-quality Civil War scholarship and diffusing the "facts" (as professionals understood them) to a needy citizenry, the buffs placed far greater emphasis on entertainment and grassroots involvement in a range of activities. Both groups wanted a popular commemoration, but each had its own understanding of what such an observance should entail. As a leading member of the District of Columbia round table, Betts belonged in the enthusiasts' camp. It was hardly surprising, then, that privately (and perhaps with a measure of justification) he suspected that a centennial dominated

35. Wiley, "Report of the Activities Committee to the Civil War Centennial Commission," *Civil War History* 5 (1959), 374–81.

36. Betts to Wiley, Feb. 1, 1960, folder on "General Correspondence, 1960," box 184, Wiley Papers.

by academics would be the kiss of death for a truly compelling observance of the Civil War.

If Karl Betts did much to pave the way for a grassroots commemoration, there were clearly costs. A great deal of tacky commercialization was one of them. So was a sometimes heavy-handed attitude toward the activities of the state commissions. (The Virginians were surely justified in resenting the CWCC's lack of enthusiasm for their Peace Conference observance.) But his Achilles' heel was his inability to recognize the increasing salience of civil rights issues and to understand that the federal commission could not continue its cozy association with southern agencies dominated by white supremacists. His own conservative racial views not only prevented him from empathizing with the unfolding black liberation struggle but also rendered him blind to the po-litical content of southern centennial exercises. As he told Ulysses S. Grant on July 5, 1961, the commission ran into trouble every time it got "involved in the reaffirmation of the rights of man and the cause of freedom." Business would proceed much more smoothly "if some of our over-serious-minded friends would seek to recapture the good humor, the enthusiasm which dominated the Centennial during the first three years of preparation. I think everyone up North could take a lesson from the folks down South who are happily and busily engaged in commemorating the Civil War *just as it happened.*"[37]

Bell Wiley and Fred Schwengel, the chief plotters against Betts, were not civil rights radicals. However, they knew that segregation had become a na-tional embarrassment and that unless the CWCC worked harder to promote a more inclusive program, the centennial would be discredited completely. Their plan was a simple one: to generate so much support among the other members of the commission for Betts's dismissal that Grant would have no op-tion but to request his resignation. During the early summer of 1961, with the connivance of Kennedy's civil rights lieutenant, Harris Wofford, they strove to convince the agency's presidential and congressional members that Betts had to go for the good of the centennial.[38] Although the resignation of Bill Tuck, Betts's chief ally on the commission, helped their cause, few CWCC members

37. Betts to Grant, July 5, 1961, memorandum, box 9, reading file 1958–66, CWCCR.

38. Wiley told Schwengel that he had promised to keep Wofford "apprised of developments." Wiley to Schwengel, July 22, 1961, folder on "General Correspondence, 1961," box 184, Wiley Pa-pers. The Emory scholar shrewdly cultivated good relations with Wofford by plying him with in-formation about his great-grandfather, Jefferson Llewellyn Wofford, who had been a Confederate officer. See Wiley to Robert Bahmer, July 21, 1961; Harris Wofford to Wiley, July 31, 1961, folder on "General Correspondence, 1961, July 16–31," box 63, Wiley Papers.

with any political common sense required much persuading after the Charleston crises' publicity fiasco. The response of Vermonter Consuelo Bailey was typical. "I have a strong feeling," she told Wiley, "that the effectiveness of [the] Commission will be a minus by 1965 if the present direction is followed."[39] The real problem confronting the conspirators was that the agency's veteran chairman, General Grant, stubbornly refused to cooperate with the plan.

On July 7, Congressman Schwengel told Wiley that they could already count on the backing of over half the commission, including the influential (and relatively liberal) Texas Democrat Ralph Yarborough. "I hope earnestly that what we want done can be accomplished by informal *persuasion*," replied the Emory historian, a reluctant revolutionary if ever there was one: "If we have to resort to discussion of this thing in a meeting of the full Commission it will be embarrassing and damaging and it might result in some backing down that would defeat the effort."[40] Two weeks later, the day before the Manassas reenactment, Schwengel visited General Grant in Washington accompanied by Yarborough and Mearns. The three men told the general that Karl Betts had lost the confidence of the commission and that he should be asked to resign. Somewhat to their consternation, Grant refused to believe them. He told them he wanted to mull things over at home in Clinton, New York, and later in the day spoke in "closed session" with the executive director.[41] Wiley responded to this curiously unanticipated news by telling Schwengel that if Betts opted to resist, there was plenty of ammunition to level against him: "From my tours in the office, I know that he has loafed on the job, has failed to give the staff specific instructions as to their responsibilities and in general conducted himself in such a way as to forfeit their respect and depress morale." What was essential, Wiley stressed in a reference to the Williams controversy, was "to avoid letting this thing become a racial issue. The basic issue is not race, but how Karl handled an explosive matter, and particularly how he let things drift along until they reached a point that imperilled our program, embarrassed the President and did untold damage all around."[42] By early August, Wiley was telling fellow southerner Avery Craven that Betts had decided not to resign

39. Consuelo N. Bailey to Wiley, Aug. 11, 1961, folder on "General Correspondence, 1961," box 184, Wiley Papers.

40. Wiley to Schwengel, July 7, 1961, folder on "General Correspondence, 1961," box 184, Wiley Papers.

41. Wiley to W. Norman Fitzgerald Jr., July 22, 1961, folder on "General Correspondence, 1961," box 184, Wiley Papers.

42. Wiley to Schwengel, July 22, 1961, folder on "General Correspondence, 1961," box 184, Wiley Papers.

and that Grant had no intention of asking him to do so.[43] Staunchly loyal to his junior official (partly because he shared his right-wing political views and suspicion of professional historians like Wiley), Grant had opted to follow the example set by his grandfather and fight it out all along the line.

Once apprised of this fact, the anti-Betts forces successfully petitioned the reluctant chairman for a meeting of the full commission.[44] All eight congressional members signed including Representative Frank Smith, a liberal, pro-Kennedy Mississippi Democrat who had replaced Bill Tuck.[45] Along with Wiley's covert operations, Smith's support for Betts's dismissal provided further evidence that several southern whites in the centennial establishment recognized the dangers posed to the commemoration and to national unity by the agency's existing leadership. The same could be said for the useful tactical advice provided by Ed Gass, the Tennessean who was the closest ally of Wiley and Schwengel on the CWCC staff.[46] A full commission meeting in Washington was scheduled for August 30. In the meantime the plotters redoubled their efforts to ensure that they had a majority if the matter came to a vote, while Grant and Betts sought to rally their own supporters in the Confederate States Conference. Fears that racial liberals were attempting to take over the national agency were uppermost in the minds of the latter. Presumably tipped off by Betts, Sam Dickinson of the Arkansas commission urged his fellow Confederates to write letters of support for the CWCC's current leadership and policies. "I understand," he wrote, "that the groups which are trying to convert the

43. Wiley to Avery O. Craven, Aug. 8, 1961, folder on "General Correspondence, 1961," box 184, Wiley Papers.

44. Wiley and his friends knew that their best hope of getting rid of Betts was via a meeting of the full commission (as opposed to the small executive committee). Although Grant and Betts were opposed to calling such a gathering, a statutory provision obligated the chairman to call a full meeting on request from five or more members of the agency. See Wiley to John Harrison, Aug. 21, 1961, folder on "General Correspondence, 1961," box 184, Wiley Papers.

45. Wiley to Frank E. Smith, Aug. 21, 1961, folder on "General Correspondence, 1961," box 184, Wiley Papers. Smith had been a graduate assistant to Wiley at the University of Mississippi before the United States entered World War II. Dennis J. Mitchell, *Mississippi Liberal: A Biography of Frank E. Smith* (Jackson: University Press of Mississippi, 2001), 38. Although he signed the Southern Manifesto in 1956 to avoid political destruction, Smith backed JFK for the Democratic nomination four years later, hoping the Bostonian "would be the leader to begin the end of segregation" (138).

46. Edmund Gass to Wiley, Aug. 22, 1961, folder on "General Correspondence, 1961," box 184, Wiley Papers.

National Civil War Centennial Commission into a civil rights pressure agency are still harassing our friends." [47]

On August 28 Bell Wiley journeyed to Washington to discuss tactics the following evening with David Mearns, Fred Schwengel, and the other congressional members. He went equipped with a discussion document listing the grievances against Betts. Drawn up by Wiley in July, the original draft listed a series of specific charges: allegations that the executive director had offended the Virginia commission, botched the handling of Madaline Williams's accommodation at Charleston, and done little to promote the historical aspects of the CWCC's program. It also cited a number of general criticisms of Betts that encapsulated the mainstream "national" case against him. Prominent among them was his "[l]ack of wisdom and statesmanship in a position that required much of both," particularly insofar as his inexcusable lack of attention to the black counter-memory and its contemporary relevance was concerned:

By their very nature, many of the fundamental problems with which he has to deal are sensitive and delicate. Sectional feeling still remains strong in certain areas, particularly in the South, yet the Centennial program to be what it set out to be, has to be one in which the whole nation can actively participate. Then, the ever-sensitive problem of race enters in. The Civil War was the greatest experience in the history of the Negro race in America; it cut the bonds of slavery and set the Negro on the road to full citizenship. But most of the Negroes live in the South, and the Confederate flag which symbolizes gallantry and heroism to Southern whites represents to many Negroes an effort to perpetuate their enslavement . . . One of the essential ingredients of statesmanship is to detect controversies in their incipiency and to take the necessary steps to prevent them from developing into major crises. This has not been done, as witness the experience of the recent National Assembly.[48]

Although these observations reflected his longstanding empathy for blacks, Wiley was under no illusions that this feeling was shared by the more

47. Sam Dickinson to Stanley R. Smith, Aug. 28, 1961, folder on Confederate States Civil War Centennial Commissions: Arkansas CWCC 1959–63," box 1, RCB 7548, GaCWCCR, RG 079-01-001.

48. Wiley, "Case Against Executive Director, CWCC," July 22, 1961, folder on "Aug. 30, 1961 Meeting of Commission and Preliminaries and Following," box 184, Wiley Papers.

conservative members of the CWCC. Sensing shrewdly that the case against Betts was best made on grounds of incompetence rather than racial prejudice, he therefore omitted the comments on African Americans from a second draft of his statement, which was, in all likelihood, the document submitted to the meeting of the conspirators in Washington.[49] At that conference Wiley, Mearns, and the congressmen worked up a statement along the lines suggested by the Atlanta college professor. However, they agreed not to present it unless they were forced to do so.

The gathering of the full commission on Wednesday, August 30, was a tense affair. Bruce Catton saw the writing on the wall and chose not to attend. Wiley thought he was "dodging the issue" along with two other absentees, William S. Paley of CBS and Alvin L. Aubinoe, the Maryland businessman who, Wiley reckoned, did not even "know when the war started."[50] Karl Betts himself was not present, being on a tour of the West (where, among other duties, he was scheduled to present a centennial medal to Governor Orval Faubus of Arkansas).[51] Wiley was profoundly worried about hurting Grant, but he mustered sufficient courage to charge Betts with a grievous lack of "understanding, foresight, tolerance, and tact." This was not enough for the opponents of dismissal. Vice Admiral Stuart H. Ingersoll from the Naval War College at Newport, Rhode Island, demanded to know what Betts had actually done wrong. To which Wiley responded, "We think there is danger in bringing these things up and spelling them out in detail, of getting into the newspapers and of creating intersectional misunderstanding and disharmony and doing further damage to the Commission."[52] Although Grant sought to defend his ally by contending, not without justification, that the Williams crisis had been planned months beforehand, he did not have the votes to save him. The commission voted 10–3 to remove Betts. Insisting that this maneuver would ruin the agency, Grant quickly announced his resignation from the CWCC.[53] Pub-

49. Wiley, second draft of statement against Betts, ibid.

50. Wiley to Charles O'Neill, Sept. 6, 1961, folder on "Aug. 30, 1961 Meeting of Commission and Preliminaries and Following," box 184, Wiley Papers.

51. Betts presented a CWCC medallion to Governor Faubus in Little Rock on Sept. 12, 1961. See his speech in folder on "Speeches by Karl Betts—Souvenirs—Speeches," box 100, subject files 1957–66, CWCCR.

52. CWCC, meeting of Aug. 30, 1961, transcript of proceedings, folder on "Full Commission Meetings, August 30, 1961—Agenda and Minutes (full)," box 57, subject files 1957–66, CWCCR.

53. Wiley to O'Neill, Sept. 6, 1961, folder on "Aug. 30, 1961 Meeting of Commission and Preliminaries and Following," box 184, Wiley Papers. Karl Betts formally resigned his $17,600-per-year post as executive director on September 15. See New York Times, Sept. 16, 1961, 44.

licly, he claimed that he needed more time to spend caring for his sick wife in New York. Privately, he was deeply hurt and angered by the sudden turn of events.[54]

Bell Wiley was not only saddened by Grant's departure but also bruised by the confrontation in Washington. "I wish I had more of Lincoln's ability to disagree with folk without incurring their personal hostility," he reflected wistfully.[55] Yet he did not regret his actions and could scarcely conceal his delight that the executive director's influence had been removed. "Betts was busted for ineptness, maladroitness, clumsiness and general incompetency," he wrote. "If he had had half vision in one eye, he could have seen many months ago what was going to happen. But, as is often the case with little people suddenly put on a big stage, he soon began to think that he was the show."[56] Avery Craven was just as pleased and no less supercilious. Betts, he contended, had taken over the centennial "as a personal project and ran it as he wished. His values were all one-sided,—one show after another, with no real understanding of what the whole business was about. Here we are only a few months into the war period and he has beaten the drums to the point where the intelligent people of the country are disgusted. I've heard dozens of people say they are sick of the Civil War—editorials point the same way and even the cartoons reflect it. We had to move to save our self-respect."[57]

The daunting task facing the CWCC in the next six months was not only to restore the validity of the centennial in the eyes of a skeptical media but also to accomplish this task without alienating those southern whites who hitherto (and sometimes to their great surprise) had found little reason to quarrel with the Grant regime. There was no doubt that things would have to change. The centennial could not survive more embarrassment, and the Kennedy administration itself seemed determined to see the commemoration more attuned to White House policy objectives in the domestic and foreign policy spheres. The president made this clear on September 5 when he named a black civil servant, Roy Davenport, to a vacancy on the commission. Bell Wiley pronounced

54. Grant to Bruce Catton, Sept. 8, 1961, box 8, reading file 1958–66, CWCCR; Grant to Wiley, Sept. 14, 1961, folder on "Aug. 30, 1961 Meeting of Commission and Preliminaries and Following," box 184, Wiley Papers; *New York Times,* Sept. 7, 1961, 31.

55. Wiley to O'Neill, Sept. 6, 1961, folder on "Aug. 30, 1961 Meeting of Commission and Preliminaries and Following," box 184, Wiley Papers.

56. Wiley to John Harrison, Sept. 11, 1961, folder on "General Correspondence, 1961 Sept. 1–3," box 64, Wiley Papers.

57. Craven to Wiley, Sept. 6, 1961, folder on "Washington Trip—Oct. 25–26, 1961," box 184, Wiley Papers.

this "a splendid move" and one for which Harris Wofford was "primarily responsible."[58] However, the key personnel decisions to be made concerned the
vacancies for chairman and executive director. Aware of the need to conciliate
southern whites while pressing ahead with a more inclusive strategy, Wiley's
own preference for director was for "a Southerner who is also an American
and who believes that being an American, and doing such things as voting,
riding on the front seat of a bus and eating in public places is not a privilege
and a responsibility restricted to folk with white skins."[59]

On September 2 Wiley also set down his thoughts about centennial policy
in a memorandum to Fred Schwengel. He suggested that the reformed federal agency should call a two-day conference in December at which historians would join representatives from the media, the drama world, libraries,
archives, museums, and the state commissions to compile a report on how
to proceed with the official commemoration of the Civil War. The CWCC,
he argued, should transfer its support from "ephemeral, sensational activities
like battle reenactments to programs which will educate, inform and lead to
enduring benefits." The resulting program had to be (1) "broad in its scope
so as to include all aspects of the conflict and all elements of the population,"
(2) "dignified and in keeping with the fact that the war was a great tragedy,"
(3) informative, (4) one that would "unify North and South and make us all
better Americans."[60]

Bell Wiley's influential suggestions accurately reflected the views of the
patriotic liberals who, as Schwengel's appointment as interim chairman revealed, were now in control of the CWCC. They also meshed neatly with the
policy requirements of the Kennedy administration. This happy conjunction
found concrete form during the late summer of 1961 in a concerted effort to
secure the appointment of Professor Allan Nevins as the new chairman of
the CWCC. Nevins was an obvious choice for centennial organizers. He had
written many books on the Civil War era. As well as being works of impeccable scholarship, they were accessible to the general public—a fact exemplified by his two Pulitzer Prizes and one that reflected both the author's early
training as a journalist and his laudable commitment to high-quality popu-

58. Wiley to O'Neill, Sept. 6, 1961, folder on "Aug. 30, 1961 Meeting of Commission and Preliminaries and Following," box 184, Wiley Papers.

59. Wiley to Harrison, Sept. 11, 1961, folder on "General Correspondence, 1961, Sept. 1–3," box
64, Wiley Papers.

60. Wiley to Schwengel, Sept. 2, 1961, folder on "Washington Trip—Oct. 25–26, 1961," box 184,
Wiley Papers.

lar history. He wrote nineteenth-century history in the grand narrative—and nationalist—tradition. He readily embraced the survival of the Union in 1865 without denigrating the bravery of Confederate soldiers or unduly stressing the role of African Americans in the war. He defended the actions of the great capitalists, the so-called robber barons, as critical contributions to the emergence of the United States as a major power. Approachable, personable, and famously energetic, Nevins was the doyen of consensus historians. However, he was no friend of the centennial as it was currently constituted.

On September 2 the *Saturday Review* printed a timely attack by Nevins on what he regarded as the mindless frivolity of recent centennial exercises. Reminding readers that the Civil War was a murderous conflict that had to be fought in order to save the Union, he called for renewed "attention to its darker aspects" and a more critical examination of the romantic brothers' war trope.[61] While this intervention in the centennial debate confirmed Nevins's stature in the eyes of his scholarly peers, his political allegiances gave him added luster. As well as being a skilled historian, he was also a committed Democrat—a close acquaintance of the powerful Illinois politician Adlai Stevenson and an active participant in Kennedy's 1960 election campaign.[62] Thus, when Bell Wiley, seeking to head off a potentially divisive candidate from the New Jersey commission, telephoned the White House on September 8 and told Harris Wofford that Nevins would be the ideal man to take charge of the centennial, he was speaking to the converted.[63] President Kennedy quickly made known his own support for Nevins's appointment and by September 14 Wofford was

61. Allan Nevins, "The Glorious and the Terrible," *Saturday Review,* Sept. 2, 1961, 48. The Chicago-based historian Paul Angle described the article as "superb," "a credit not only to you but to the whole historical profession." Angle to Nevins, Sept. 8, 1961, folder 1, box 76, Allan Nevins Papers, Rare Book and Manuscript Library, Columbia University. Fellow scholar Avery Craven of the CWCC called it "a magnificent job" and denounced the centennial's prevailing "carnival atmosphere." Craven to Nevins, Oct. 16, 1961, folder 1, box 76, Nevins Papers.

62. Having previously contributed a laudatory foreword to Kennedy's book on senatorial courage, Nevins edited a collection of the Massachusetts senator's speeches that was released in time for the presidential campaign of 1960. Kennedy, *Profiles in Courage* (New York: Harper, 1956), ix–xvi, and JFK to Allan Nevins, July 26, 1959, box 24, Nevins Papers. In addition, Nevins was asked to write a draft of Kennedy's acceptance speech at the Democratic National Convention and received $800 for writing a campaign piece in *Life.* Theodore Sorensen to Nevins, June 22, 1960, box 29, Nevins Papers, and Thomas J. Walsh to Nevins, Sept. 8, 1960, box 24, Nevins Papers.

63. Wiley to Schwengel, Sept. 8, 1961, folder on "Aug. 30, 1961 Meetings of Commission and Preliminaries and Following," box 184, Wiley Papers. See also Wiley, "Memo for Record," Sept. 8, 1961, ibid.

asking Arthur Schlesinger to instigate an approach. Professor Nevins's services, advised Wofford, "would be a real contribution to this administration."[64]

Having retired from Columbia, Nevins was now working intensively at the Huntington Library in California to complete his multivolume history of the Civil War era. However, he was not one to shirk civic responsibility, especially when the request emanated from the White House. Accordingly he made it known that he would accept the job of chairman but not that of executive director—a stance that Bell Wiley, a former U.S. Army historian, described as perfectly reasonable for such an eminent and talented scholar. Nevins, he told the young Princeton historian David Donald, would not be happy dealing with red tape. "I think," he wrote, "that people who are accustomed to the freedom of coming and going enjoyed by academicians often chafe at the rigid schedule to which the Government adheres. I know I did myself when I was with the Army, and I should not be willing to put myself in a government strait jacket again unless by compulsion."[65] On October 13 President Kennedy duly appointed Allan Nevins to the troubled centennial agency as a successor to General Grant.[66]

The triumph of academic expertise over salesmanship was cemented by the appointment of James I. ("Bud") Robertson Jr. as executive director at the end of October. Robertson was only thirty-one, the stocky, clean-cut editor of *Civil War History* and a former doctoral student of Bell Wiley. In spite of his youth and lack of administrative experience, Robertson was a sound choice for Karl Betts's replacement—the official who would oversee the day-to-day work of the CWCC in Washington while Nevins, for the most part, continued his scholarly labors in San Marino. As well as being a committed patriot who had spent two and a half years as a navigator and radar man in the U.S. Air Force, he was a proud southerner and "traditional conservative Democrat" who "wanted to see Jim Crow abolished in the most orderly manner possible."[67] He was therefore

64. Wofford to Arthur M. Schlesinger Jr., Sept. 14, 1961, folder on "Civil War Centennial Commission," box WH3B, Arthur M. Schlesinger Jr. Papers, White House Files, JFK Library.

65. Wiley to David Donald, Sept. 21, 1961, folder on "Aug. 30, 1961 Meetings of Commission and Preliminaries and Following," box 184, Wiley Papers.

66. *New York Times,* Oct. 14, 1961, 10.

67. There is a brief biographical sketch of the new executive director in *Danville Register,* Dec. 5, 1961, clipping in folder 5274, Tuck Papers. James I. Robertson Jr.'s description of his partisan affiliation and views on segregation are voiced in a communication to the author, Dec. 1, 2005. He recalls that he was initially reluctant to leave his teaching post at the University of Iowa "to take on duties in a federal agency beset with problems," but that "[c]lose friends eventually convinced me that I might be able to bring some order out of chaos for the national good." He adds that the

someone who might be able to accomplish the difficult goal of keeping the seg-regationists on board while promoting more progressive modes of Civil War remembrance. Bill Tuck expressed every confidence that his fellow Virginian's services would be "worthy and meritorious in every way"—a comment that led a grateful Robertson to assert revealingly that he had "never felt that war, especially so brutal a conflict as a civil war, should be remembered with gaudy pictures and a carnival-type atmosphere."[68] By late 1961 historians were at the helm in Washington. Their immediate task that winter was to salvage what they could from the disastrous year that lay behind them.

SAVING THE CENTENNIAL

Nevins and Robertson had a tough job on their hands if they were going to resurrect the centennial as a successful exercise in public history. Certainly no one could doubt that it had fallen into serious disrepute by late 1961. Writing in the *South Atlantic Quarterly,* historian Paul Angle labeled the commemora-tion "an irresponsible and commercialized flop" and suggested that southern-ers had been unable to resist the chance of licking the Yankees a second time around. His comments were reprinted by the *Chicago Daily News* in an article headed "Open Fire on the Civil War Centennial" and corroborated by Ralph Newman of the Illinois centennial commission. Newman, present at the cre-ation of the CWCC, mused that Chicago's local commission had not indulged in commercial excess, having limited itself to a respectful observance of the hundredth anniversary of the death of Stephen A. Douglas. There was, he thought, little else to do. "Perhaps we'll print a brochure describing the few Civil War-connected places that can be seen in the city and let it go at that," he was quoted as saying.[69]

While the northern press sank its teeth into the centennial, members of the southern state commissions continued to worry that the new CWCC leaders

---

local Iowa congressman and interim CWCC chief, Fred Schwengel, and his former adviser, Bell Wiley, "took the lead in pushing me to be [the] new Executive Director of CWCC." Initially Wiley had been reluctant to press Robertson's appointment. "I have to go slow with reference to him," he wrote in the fall, "as he was my Ph.D. student here [Emory]." Added Wiley, "He is might[y] young and inexperienced to throw into such a difficult spot and he is inclined to seem to agree with everyone whom he talks with, and this can get an administrator, walking a tightrope between two extreme groups, into trouble." Wiley to Seale Johnson, Sept. 14, 1961, folder on "Aug. 30, 1961, Meetings of Commission and Preliminaries and Following," box 184, Wiley Papers.

68. Tuck to Robertson, Dec. 5, 1961, Robertson to Tuck, Nov. 24, 1961, folder 5274, Tuck Papers.

69. *Chicago Daily News,* Jan. 13, 1962, 40.

would try to turn the centennial into a vehicle for civil rights. Their concerns were exacerbated by the Kennedy administration's developing assault on segregation. In November 1961, in what segregationists regarded as federal capitulation to meddlesome freedom riders, the Interstate Commerce Commission complied with a request from the attorney general to ban segregation in interstate transportation facilities.

Southern fears about a radical change in policy by the CWCC originated with the surprise departure of Grant and Betts. Determined to retain his position as executive director, Betts had done nothing before the August coup to discourage rumors that he was being targeted by liberals and blacks as a result of the events in Charleston. At one point, seeking to shore up his support, he warned the head of the Virginia commission that he was the victim of a "political conspiracy" waged by "Yankees and 'nigger lovers.'"[70] William Tuck was of a similar mind. He told Grant that his own resignation in July had been prompted by the discovery that a bipartisan "cabal" was "intending to subvert the high purposes of the Commission."[71] Segregationists outside the commission therefore could hardly be blamed for thinking the worst. "This," commented Congressman Wint Smith of Kansas shortly after Betts's resignation, "simply shows how the NAACP–Brooklyn Indians thru the liberal press are all hell bent for destroying America."[72] The former executive director retained his contacts with southern conservatives in the wake of his departure from the commission. He was especially eager to have them cooperate closely with NPS officials when they came to plan special events such as battle reenactments. At the end of November he wrote to John A. May, head of the Confederate States Conference, about the appointment of Nevins and Robertson. "I wouldn't count very much on either one of them for any particular aid," he said snidely.[73]

As well as worrying about negative media coverage and the possibility that an embittered Karl Betts might push the southern commissions into open warfare with the CWCC, the new leadership team had reason to be concerned about the loyalty of their Washington-based staff. As the popular history magazine *Civil War Times* reported, the summer's events had caused "turmoil"

70. Wiley to Frank Smith, Sept. 8, 1961, folder on "Aug. 30, 1961 Meeting of Commission and Preliminaries and Following," box 184, Wiley Papers.

71. Tuck to Grant, Oct. 16, 1961, folder 5274, Tuck Papers.

72. Wint Smith to Tuck, Sept. 23, 1961, folder 5274, Tuck Papers.

73. Betts to John A. May, Nov. 28, 1961, folder on "South Carolina State Chairman [July 1960– Nov. 1962]," box 721, MCWBTSR.

inside the commission.[74] Apart from Ed Gass, there were few at the Jackson Place headquarters whose loyalty could be trusted. Pat Jones and a secretary, Nancy Lee Callender, posed the biggest problem because of their open attachment to Betts and Grant. Neither made any secret of their reactionary views. Indeed, it is likely that Gass had both of them in mind when he told Wiley in October of "the outspoken advocacy [in the office] of extreme reaction and almost venomous dislike of Jews, 'liberals' and a number of Com. Members."[75] Jones, a prolific writer on the Civil War, had worked closely with Betts to stave off the latter's departure, at one point calling a member of the Louisiana commission to tell him that "[t]he NAACP are out to get us."[76] But the problems went beyond even this serious indictment of a federal agency. There was no clear chain of authority, and the staffers themselves were poorly qualified: only one was a college graduate. "Too few can compose correspondence," wrote Gass, "except for the brief, routine type of letters of acknowledgment or thanks. Too few can take hold of a run-of-the-mill problem and manage it."[77]

The most daunting task confronting Nevins and Robertson was the urgent need to devise a new, workable policy before the centennial lost what remained of its rapidly diminishing credibility. Commemorative events had not come to a halt. Kentucky hosted a successful commemoration of the Battle of Perryville on October 7, and Carl Sandburg opened a centennial exhibition at the Library of Congress two weeks later.[78] However, the absence of strong direction from the top during the fall left the CWCC's planning activities well behind schedule. Again it was Ed Gass, better placed than anyone, who sounded the alarm. "Valuable time is being lost," he told Wiley in mid-October. "Organizationally we're in a mess and the longer the shadowy, uncertain situation lasts the more time we'll lose and the worse the mess will become."[79]

74. *Civil War Times* 6 (Oct. 1961): 11.

75. Gass to Wiley, Oct. 8, 1961, folder on "Washington Trip—Oct. 25–26, 1961," box 184, Wiley Papers.

76. Wiley to Schwengel, Nov. 13, 1961, folder on "Washington Trip—Oct. 25–26, 1961," box 184, Wiley Papers.

77. Robertson to Nevins, Dec. 17, 1961, folder 1, box 76, Nevins Papers; Gass to Wiley, Oct. 8, 1961, folder on "Washington Trip—Oct. 25–26, 1961," box 184, Wiley Papers.

78. *Lexington Herald Leader,* Oct. 8, 1961, clipping in folder on "General Correspondence, 1961, Oct. 1–12," box 64, Wiley Papers; Library of Congress press release no. 62-14, Oct. 23, 1961, box 23, subject files 1957–66, CWCCR.

79. Gass to Wiley, Oct. 16, 1961, folder on "Washington Trip—Oct. 25–26, 1961," box 184, Wiley Papers.

Happily for the future of both the CWCC and the centennial, Nevins and Robertson were in accord over what had to be done. The two men favored not only a more sober observance of the Civil War (which is to say a less overtly commercialized one as well as one that was as free as possible of sham battles) but also a commemoration that paid some attention to the black counter-memory of the conflict. While Nevins's age, reputation, northern upbringing, and preoccupation with political and institutional history distinguished him from his hard-working southern assistant, whose interests lay primarily in military events of the Civil War, both men were intelligent scholars who understood that contemporary racial issues could not be divorced entirely from discussion of that conflict. Crucially, in marked contrast to Betts and Grant, they were also attuned to contemporary political developments, in particular to the domestic and foreign policy agenda of the Kennedy administration. As a political ally of the president, Nevins did not have to remain in constant touch with the Kennedys to know what was required of him. Besides, he and Robertson could always ask their fellow historian, Arthur Schlesinger, for help if they needed direct access to the White House. The Civil War centennial did not feature significantly on the presidential radar after the spring of 1961, but as what Wiley called "the Charleston stink" had proved, it was important for the administration that the event did not become a national embarrassment.[80] As Schlesinger, Wofford, and the president himself well knew, Allan Nevins could be depended on to ensure that this negative goal was achieved and perhaps even to transform Civil War memory into a genuinely useful tool of federal policy.

Both of these objectives were uppermost in the minds of those CWCC members who formally elected Nevins as chairman at a full meeting of the commission on December 4. In setting out the reasons for the recent personnel changes, Fred Schwengel explained that the agency had been "missing a great opportunity to develop that interest in and understanding of history so necessary as we prepare ourselves and those who must serve posterity—our young people—so that we will be better prepared for an intelligent and adequate patriotism to meet the challenge to freedom in this, the most dangerous time in the history of the human family."[81] If these words did not appear far removed from the cold war agenda of the Eisenhower years, this was no

---

80. Wiley to Johnson, March 26, 1961, folder on "General Correspondence, 1961, March 25–31," box 62, Wiley Papers.

81. CWCC, minutes of the meeting held Dec. 4, 1961, folder on "Minutes—Commission Meetings, Agenda etc," box 184, Wiley Papers.

accident. The demise of the old guard presaged changes in tone and style at Jackson Place but not an abandonment of the CWCC's consensual mission. The key phrase in Schwengel's statement was his reference to the need for "*an intelligent and adequate patriotism.*" Patently, neither General Grant nor Karl Betts had been up to this task. Allan Nevins, however, took no more than a couple of minutes to show that he was up to the job. In a crisp policy statement that amounted to thinly veiled criticism of his predecessors, he said that under his guidance the CWCC would work to make the centennial "both instructive and constructive":

> To this end we shall discourage observances that are cheap and tawdry, or that are divisive in temper, or that in any other respect fall short of expressing the magnanimity of spirit shown by Lincoln and Lee, that fall short of honoring the heroism of the 600,000 men who gave their lives. We shall encourage observances that will assist the American people to understand the mingled tragedy and exaltation of the war, and to draw from it lessons both practical and moral commensurate with its importance.
>
> Above all our centennial theme will be unity, not division, for out of the brothers' war slowly emerged the basis of a firm union of hearts instead of an uncertain union of jarring political elements. So far as we can, we shall allow the just pride of no national group to be belittled or besmirched. A host of white Southerners died for what they believed a just cause; a host of white Northerners died for what they held a sacred duty; a host of Negroes died, many in the uniforms of the United States, for the achievement of freedom and human equality. We must honor them all. When we finally reach the commemoration of Appomattox, we shall treat it not as victory or defeat, but as a beginning—the beginning of a century of increasing concord, mutual understanding, and fraternal affection among all the sections and social groups of the republic.[82]

This formal statement, which received widespread publicity in the national press, was carefully drafted to bring official centennial policy into line with the Kennedy administration's position on civil rights—the gradual but steady dismantling of Jim Crow (ideally obtained with the backing of southerners themselves) as a necessary adjunct to the achievement of domestic peace and the winning of the propaganda war against the communists. National unity would remain the watchword of the centennial, but, said Nevins, that unity required

82. Ibid. I have corrected a typo in "jarring."

an awareness of what the Civil War had meant for African Americans as well as whites—precisely the point that Wiley had made in his initial indictment of Karl Betts. The crucial question now was whether this iterated shift in policy would rejuvenate, or further divide, the troubled centennial coalition.

Under the leadership of its new chairman, the CWCC launched three major initiatives during the winter of 1961–62 to signal the adoption of a more scholarly and inclusive centennial program. The first of these was the "Impact" series of historical monographs, the brainchild of Nevins himself. Commissioned and funded by the agency, each book in the series was intended to be a scholarly examination of the Civil War's effect on a specific aspect of nineteenth-century American life. Alfred A. Knopf of New York agreed to publish the studies, five of which had already been commissioned by the first week of February 1962.[83]

The second initiative, modeled on the idea that Wiley had proposed in the summer, was for a joint meeting between the full commission and representatives from the state commissions in Washington at the end of January. The main purpose of the gathering was not only to allow the various parties to learn about one another's future plans but also to clear the air after the recent leadership changes within the CWCC. The utility of this meeting would depend largely on how effectively the new-look federal agency handled the thorny subject of race.

During the previous summer several proposals had been advanced for an official commemoration of President Abraham Lincoln's Emancipation Proclamation, first introduced as a preliminary measure in the wake of the strategic Union victory at Antietam in September 1862 and then promulgated officially on January 1, 1863.[84] These proposals originated with blacks and their northern white allies and were clearly designed with the contemporary civil rights struggle in mind. A bipartisan resolution to set up a special commission to mark the anniversary of the famous edict was introduced into the U.S. Senate on September 15, 1961, and was only lost in the rush to adjourn. The New York state centennial commission evinced particular enthusiasm for marking the proclamation, partly because one of the surviving copies of the document was housed in Albany, partly because the liberal Republican administration

83. Nevins to Gass, Jan. 7, 1962, folder on "Nevins, Allan—October 13, 1961," box 134, subject files 1957–66, CWCCR.

84. On the battle and its wider political significance, see James M. McPherson, *Crossroads of Freedom: Antietam* (Oxford: Oxford University Press, 2002).

of Governor Nelson Rockefeller wanted to publicize its support for black civil rights for reasons that were both altruistic and politically expedient—as in New Jersey, New York's African-American voters could not be ignored by either of the main parties. Thoughtful individuals on the CWCC, particularly Fred Schwengel, recognized that formal commemoration of the Emancipation Proclamation offered an ideal means of restoring the centennial's credibility in the eyes of nonsoutherners.[85] Allan Nevins was in full agreement with this view and, with what appeared to be enthusiastic backing from the White House, rapidly instigated plans to make the one hundredth anniversary of the preliminary Emancipation Proclamation the focal point of his commission's activities in 1962.[86] By mid-December 1961 moves were already underway for the CWCC's third new initiative: the staging of a dignified ceremony at the Lincoln Memorial on Saturday, September 22, attended by President Kennedy along with other American and foreign dignitaries.[87]

Although the southern commissions were alarmed by these plans, they were hardly surprised by them. In the fall of 1961, shortly before Karl Betts announced his resignation from the CWCC, southern centennial representatives had convened in Little Rock to adopt a "Reaffirmation of Policy." In this terse statement that typically obscured their own deeply political motives, they expressed their conviction that the national commission should "continue to be non-political, non-partisan, non-sectional, non-sectarian and non-profit." Declining to mention civil rights specifically, they also protested "any attempt to dilute, distort, or deviate from the law [of September 1957] as it now stands."[88] Word of an emancipation ceremony, therefore, merely confirmed that their fears were well founded. John A. May demanded to know immediately if it was true that the CWCC was "going to use the Emancipation Proclamation as a vehicle to promote so called Civil Rights?" If so, he warned, "we in the South will vigorously oppose any effort to turn the Commemoration of the Civil War

85. Schwengel to Wiley, Oct. 11, 1961, folder on "Washington Trip—Oct. 25–26, 1961," box 184, Wiley Papers.

86. At a meeting in early December, Nevins apparently conferred with President Kennedy about displaying New York's copy of the preliminary Emancipation Proclamation. See Thomas Mulligan to Charles H. Palmer, memorandum, Dec. 18, 1961, box 2, office files 1961–64, A1444-78, NYCWCCR.

87. Nevins to Schlesinger, Dec. 13, 1961, folder on "Civil War Centennial Commission," box WH3B, Schlesinger Papers.

88. "Reaffirmation of Policy," Sept. 12, 1961, folder on "Georgia—State Director [July 1960–Nov. 1961]," box 712, MCWBTSR.

into a political issue of any kind." [89] Karl Betts, still smarting over his dismissal, urged May to be "extremely cautious about any commitments to the new Centennial regime which would involve the Southern States." Attendance at the conference in Washington would be especially problematic for they might "discover it is just another one of the Schwengel traps to secure endorsement of their program." Added Betts (who was probably getting inside information from Pat Jones or Nancy Callender), "I can assure you that the only events receiving any attention are the promotion of the civil rights–emancipation proclamation." [90] Reluctant to sabotage the entire centennial without finding out exactly what was being planned, most of the southern commissions did send representatives to Washington in late January. [91] As Mississippi's Sidney T. Roebuck explained matters to Betts, "[W]e are a little afraid not to go. If the going gets too rough, we might be able to secede again and proceed with our Southern Conference." [92]

While a sectional split was clearly visible within the ranks of the centennial establishment, the situation was not entirely polarized along regional lines—certainly no more than it had been during the real Civil War. The good old boys who dominated the majority of southern commissions found their unreconstructed views contested by relatively liberal whites possessing less parochial views on how the centennial should be commemorated in the light of economic change, the civil rights movement, and the battle against communism. These included not only Bell Wiley, James Robertson, and Edmund Gass, but also James J. Geary and Norman Larson who headed the Virginia and North Carolina commissions respectively, Congressman Frank Smith of

89. May to Nevins, Dec. 13, 1961, folder on "South Carolina State Chairman [July 1960–Nov. 1962]," box 721, MCWBTSR.

90. Betts to May, Dec. 20, 1961, folder on "Betts, Karl S.," box 708, MCWBTSR.

91. May to Dickinson, Jan. 2, 1962, folder on "Confederate States Civil War Centennial Commissions: South Carolina Confederate Centennial Commission," box 2, RCB 7547, GaCWCCR, RG 079-01-001. Fifty-nine delegates representing thirty state commissions attended the joint meeting with the CWCC held in Washington on January 31 and February 1, 1962. Most leading members of the South's centennial establishment were present. See "Minutes of the First Joint Meeting of the State Civil War Centennial Commission Representatives and the National Civil War Centennial Commission Held at the Interior Department Auditorium in Washington, DC[,] January 31, and February 1, 1962," in folder on "State Commissions—Meeting—January 31, 1962," box 106, subject files 1957–66, CWCCR.

92. Roebuck to Betts, Jan. 22, 1962, folder on "Betts, Karl S.," box 708, MCWBTSR. Roebuck's reference to another secession was to the decision to hold a meeting of the Confederate States Centennial Conference at the same time as the CWCC's fourth national assembly.

Mississippi, and Daniel Hollis, a historian at the University of South Carolina whom Avery Craven described as "the only sane person" on the centennial agency in Columbia.[93] Predisposed to accept the inevitability of social change in their region, they were also keenly aware of political realities and in some cases did their best to transmit this understanding to those harboring more conservative views. "I do not know of any way in which the observance of . the Emancipation Proclamation can be avoided," Frank Smith told Sidney Roebuck bluntly on January 15. "The Emancipation Proclamation was a major event in the War between the States . . . The chances are that there will be some type of additional commission which will assume the major responsibilities in regard to the Emancipation Proclamation observance. Senator [Everett] Dirkson [sic] and other Members of Congress offered this proposal late last year, and I am sure that they will push it again this year."[94]

A damaging southern secession from the national centennial coalition was a very real possibility in the winter of 1961–62, but in the early months of the new year an uneasy compromise over the emancipation ceremony began to take shape. The southerners did not exactly give in. On February 1, the second day of the joint meeting of the CWCC and state commissions held in the Department of the Interior auditorium, John May presented a resolution passed by the Confederate States Centennial Conference. Noting first that the lesson of intersectional reconciliation in the United States was "a lesson that the peoples of the world sorely need to know today," it went on to make clear the Confederate bloc's conviction that "it would be a mistake for the National Civil War Commission to engage in any activity, or to promote in any way any program that could, or would, be considered by any section of our nation as propaganda for any cause that would tend to reopen the wounds of war."[95]

This thinly veiled threat to break up the centennial coalition if the emancipation program became a weapon to attack segregation greatly alarmed the CWCC's new executive director, James Robertson—and with good reason. As a southerner himself, Robertson understood the segregationists' residual power at home and, more specifically, their capacity to destroy the positive results (in terms of organization and planning) arising from the Washington plenary. Convinced, as he later recalled, that "CWCC severing its ties with

93. Craven to Nevins, Feb. 2, 1962, folder 1, box 76, Nevins Papers.

94. Smith to Roebuck, Jan 15, 1962, folder on "South—Mississippi [Sept. 1961–Feb. 1962]," box 720, MCWBTSR.

95. "Resolution of the Confederate States Centennial Conference," Feb. 1, 1961, folder on "Confederate States Centennial Conference (11 States)," box 107, subject files 1957–66, CWCCR.

Southern states would have killed the basic intent of the Centennial—to bring all Americans closer together," he suggested to Nevins after the meeting that he should go south and meet personally with May in an attempt to secure his support for the emancipation ceremony.[96] By playing down the civil rights aspects of the event and having the national commission act only as a co-sponsor (along with the Lincoln Group of Washington, DC, and the District of Columbia round table), Robertson believed he could win over the South Carolinian. "I think," he told Nevins, "this is the only strategy that we can pursue safely and with any hope of success."[97] Convinced that this was "the wise course," the chairman gave Robertson's trip his blessing, adding only (in an effort to strengthen the Virginian's backbone) that Robertson should avoid "any impression that we are simply saying 'me, too,' and holding the robe of a local body. There is no reason why all fifty of the States should not recognize the importance of the Proclamation; no reason, that is, why we should not represent all the States in commemorating it."[98] Bell Wiley held a similar view. Co-sponsorship was the least the CWCC should offer, he told Nevins. "I am opposed to our tucking tail and running just because a few deep South extremists, who have not yet recognized the equality of Negroes before the law, register a protest."[99]

On February 26, James Robertson conferred with John May at the latter's Mayfields home in Aiken. He made a strong plea for southern toleration, contending that the proposal for co-sponsoring the event at the Lincoln Memorial represented a genuine effort on the part of the national commission to seek compromise.[100] His soothing words did enough to convince "Mr. Confederate" that the CWCC was not in the business of promoting civil rights. Perhaps swayed also by his visitor's protestations of loyalty to the South, May informed his fellow southern chairmen that Robertson was "in accord with our thinking in that he strongly believes that the Centennial should be a commemoration of the true events of history and no political issues should be brought into it in any way."[101] (By "true events," of course, May was referring to the Lost Cause

96. Robertson to the author, Dec. 1, 2005.

97. Robertson to Nevins, Feb. 15, 1962, box 11, reading file 1958–66, CWCCR.

98. Nevins to Robertson, Feb. 20, 1962, folder on "Nevins, Allan—Oct. 13, 1961," box 134, subject files 1957–66, CWCCR.

99. Wiley to Nevins, Feb. 21, 1962, folder 2, box 76, Nevins Papers.

100. Robertson to Nevins, Feb. 28, 1962, box 11, reading file 1958–66, CWCCR.

101. May to James J. Geary, Feb. 26, 1962, folder on "Confederate States Centennial Conference—Administration," box 2, VaCWCCR.

account of the southern past on which he and other segregationists had been reared since birth.) His conclusion—that the emancipation ceremony did not pose a major threat to the segregationists' dubious conception of a "nonpolitical" centennial—was enough to keep the ramshackle centennial coalition together. James Robertson, tired after sipping cocktails with May into the early morning and a long journey on the overnight sleeper back to Washington, was pleased with his endeavors. If all went according to plan, he told Nevins, "we will have a more united front than at any time in at least the last twelve months."[102]

Perhaps Robertson did not have a monopoly on credit for saving the centennial. The southern commissions were predisposed toward compromise. Notwithstanding the troubles of 1961, they had profited significantly from the events of the first year. Mississippi, for example, had enjoyed "a banner tourist year" according to the manager of the state's travel department. With more than a hundred communities hosting centennial events, inquiries generated by official tourist advertisements were nearly double the number for 1960 with over a quarter of the new total (97,699) relating specifically to Civil War commemorations.[103] Breaking ties with the national commission would only have threatened this travel boom by making visitors even more nervous about driving into a state that was already becoming an arena for civil rights activism. More surprisingly perhaps, a strong sense of political realism added to the financial inducements to stay onside. Colonel May and his allies were not entirely oblivious to the CWCC's problems, especially its need to satisfy a national constituency. As long as the Federals were prepared to downplay the racial aspects of the Civil War (as Robertson intimated), the southerners were willing to remain guardedly cooperative.

One man less than pleased with this outcome was Karl Betts. The former executive director never recovered from his sacking and spent the final months of his life (he died of a heart attack in June 1962) bemoaning his lost power and prestige. "It will always be a sad thing," he told Sidney Roebuck in late February 1962, "to contemplate that our original Centennial program should have been so messed up by political schemes. It is quite apparent that any bu[d]get allowed the National Commission will be spent by Schwengel, Wiley, Nevins and others in traveling to and from Washington and in paying fees to historians to write more about the Civil War. In other words, a

---

102. Robertson to Nevins, Feb. 28, 1962, box 11, reading file 1958–66, CWCCR.

103. Ned O'Brien to Roebuck, Jan. 17, 1962, folder on "O—Miscellaneous [Jan. 1962—April 1964 and Undated]," box 718, MCWBTSR.

fraction of 1% of the American people will have any active part in the Centennial which is contrary to the nationwide approach which we had organized." [104] Notwithstanding his evident bitterness, Betts had a point. The historians had emerged victorious from the schisms of 1961, and the kind of scholarship now accorded priority over pageantry was no guarantor of a grassroots commemoration. The next few years would reveal whether a dignified and socially useful program of Civil War remembrance was compatible with the development of an ambitious public history exercise that had been intended to reach as many people as possible. Some of the answers to this question would be evident in the way that African Americans were touched by the centennial.

104. Betts to Roebuck, March 15, 1962, folder on "Betts, Karl S.," box 708, MCWBTSR.

5

African Americans and the Civil War Centennial

JAMES ROBERTSON'S DEAL with the Confederate States Conference over an official commemoration of the Emancipation Proclamation was symptomatic of the national agency's determination not to lose the support of the white South. However, the CWCC's determination to mark the hundredth anniversary of Lincoln's celebrated state paper looked to be a clear signal that centennial affairs were at last being brought into line with the Kennedy administration's policy on civil rights. It also appeared to highlight the fact that the basic chronology of the Civil War—early southern successes on the battlefield followed by Federal utilization of black manpower, the destruction of slavery, and eventual northern military victory—might actually help to further the cause of black equality in the mid-twentieth century. For, if segregation was widely regarded as treason at the height of the cold war, surely its discredited pseudo-Confederate defenders could be labeled unpatriotic in marked comparison with those true patriots, black and white, who yearned for the belated triumph of racial equality in America.

Black leaders were slow to grasp the political significance of the centennial insofar as their own struggle was concerned. This was hardly surprising. Historical memory was not at first a major weapon of the civil rights movement—certainly not compared to direct-action forms of protest such as sit-ins and demonstrations—and, besides, the centennial establishment did not exactly go out of its way to encourage black involvement in the Civil War obsequies. Only when newspaper reports began to suggest that the centennial had become a tool for segregationists did black leaders recognize the dangers inherent in ignoring the event. Although, as the emancipation ceremony at the Lincoln Memorial in September 1962 revealed, federal efforts to commemorate the death of slavery did not betoken an unqualified commitment to racial justice, civil rights leaders and organizations had already begun to see the value of the black counter-memory as a weapon of struggle. African

Americans never engaged in Civil War activities to the extent that whites did in the early 1960s, but the advent of the centennial furnished them with powerful leverage in their intensifying efforts to close the gap between the promise and the reality of American life.

WHEN SHERMAN MARCHES TO THE SEA: HOW AFRICAN AMERICANS CAME TO ENGAGE WITH THE CENTENNIAL

If the black counter-memory of the Civil War exercised little purchase on mainstream American opinion in the Jim Crow era, many African Americans worked tirelessly to sustain it. Black veterans constructed their own narrative of wartime service by participating as Grand Army of the Republic members in Decoration (Memorial) Day services to honor the local Union dead and testifying on behalf of federal pensions applicants.[1] They also featured prominently in well-attended parades, especially in the South, which had supplied the majority of Union "colored troops." As many as 8,000 people commemorated Decoration Day in Beaufort, South Carolina, in its heyday at the turn of the century. Although intensifying white efforts to control public space in the region made inroads into events like this (the Beaufort crowds dwindled with the passing of the veterans and in the face of white moves to co-opt the rites after World War I), African-American memories of the Civil War era endured in part because of the autonomy provided by racial separation.[2]

Even as the veterans were dying off, lambent images of rebellious slaves, sable liberators, and assertive Reconstruction-era politicians were kept alive by an activist generation of African-American historians in the 1920s and 1930s. Critical to the survival of a coherent oppositional narrative during this period was the work of the Association for the Study of Negro Life and History (ASNLH), founded by Carter G. Woodson in 1915.[3] Born of slave parentage in Virginia, Woodson spent his youth working as a farm laborer and coal

1. Donald R. Shaffer, *After the Glory: The Struggles of Black Civil War Veterans* (Lawrence: University Press of Kansas, 2004), 60–62, 121–37, 171–72.

2. Bruce E. Baker, "Devastated by Passion and Belief: Remembering Reconstruction in the Twentieth-Century South" (Ph.D. thesis, University of North Carolina, 2003), 212–13. For an insightful assessment of black historical memory in the postbellum South, one that stresses its remarkable durability, see W. Fitzhugh Brundage, *The Southern Past: A Clash of Race and Memory* (Cambridge, MA: Belknap Press of Harvard University Press, 2005), 55–104.

3. On the founding of the ASNLH and Woodson's pioneering contribution to the modern black history movement, see Jacqueline Goggin, *Carter G. Woodson: A Life in Black History* (Baton Rouge: Louisiana State University Press, 1993).

miner in the Upper South. He enrolled at Berea, a one-time abolitionist college in the Appalachians, and then, after a period teaching school, undertook graduate work in history at the University of Chicago. He received his doctorate from Harvard in 1912.

While attending the Exposition of Negro Progress in Chicago three years later (an event intended to mark the fiftieth anniversary of constitutional emancipation), Woodson was importuned by fellow boarders at the city's black YMCA to set up a group specifically to promote black history. Initially enjoying significant financial support from white philanthropic foundations interested in black education, the Washington-based ASNLH quickly emerged as the primary vehicle for black historical scholarship. A small coterie of black historians including Charles H. Wesley, the scion of a middle-class family in Louisville, and the younger Fisk graduate Lawrence D. Reddick clustered around Woodson in the interwar years, producing revisionist accounts of topics such as Reconstruction, which, had they been taken seriously by white academics, would have posed a serious challenge to the white supremacist orthodoxy on the Civil War. Most of them shared their mentor's "searing awareness of the contradiction between the democratic creed and American racial practices," as well as his conviction that promoting a more accurate understanding of the Negro's past would further the cause of equal rights, first, by fostering a greater sense of race pride and self-worth and, second, by convincing whites that blacks had participated fully in the national experience.[4] Although Woodson could be overbearing at times, there was no denying his commitment not only to scholarship but also to its diffusion to ordinary blacks. When white philanthropic funding dried up in the early 1930s, he tapped the only alternative source of money by intensifying efforts to bring African-American history to the masses through innovations such as Negro History Week and the ASNLH's popular magazine, the *Negro History Bulletin*. One of the more positive products of segregation, the ASNLH may have been the black community's main defense against historical amnesia.

It is difficult to judge precisely how successful the organization was as a vehicle for sustaining the counter-memory among the black masses. Eighty percent of African Americans resided in the Jim Crow South in 1940. Many of them, especially those in rural areas, lived in poverty and were poorly educated. Depression-era radicals did attempt on occasions to revive the tradition of interracial working-class political participation evident during

---

4. August Meier and Elliott Rudwick, *Black History and the Historical Profession, 1915–1980* (Urbana: University of Illinois Press, 1986), 93.

Reconstruction. However, their efforts at mobilization met with only limited success because NAACP and left-wing activity ran into stiff resistance from segregationists, who harbored a very different and extremely potent memory of the 1870s. In Greenville, South Carolina, NAACP president James A. Briar, a black teacher and federal employee whose father had been an active Republican after the Civil War, tried to organize a voter registration drive among African Americans ahead of municipal elections in 1939. His campaign sparked a fierce response from Ku Klux Klansmen who assaulted local blacks and vandalized black businesses. A press release from the state's Grand Dragon defended these activities on the grounds that "almost the same influences which caused the trouble seventy years ago are at work in this country" and that only his organization could save South Carolina "from negro rule and northern political domination" as it had done "during Reconstruction days."[5]

Despite the problems encountered in trying to perpetuate subversive memories of the Civil War era in the repressive climate of Jim Crow, southern blacks managed to sustain a remarkably durable resistance narrative during the first half of the century. Although the oral tradition of family storytelling helped to keep the torch of Frederick Douglass alive, the ASNLH-assisted efforts of black history teachers, predominantly women, probably did more in this respect. The teachers, particularly those in the somewhat better funded urban schools, functioned as "insurgent scholars" during the interwar years, taking advantage of the white neglect of black schools to disseminate a history of the race that "highlighted the record of black perseverance in the face of white oppression and the fundamental perversity of white supremacy."[6] Emancipation celebrations, held on several different days in the Lower and Upper South, also played a critical role in fostering the counter-memory. Normally hosted by schools or churches, these events—especially those held under the auspices of the NAACP—served a political, as well as a social, function. Not only did they give African Americans a chance to recall the liberation of their slave forebears, but they also enabled black citizens to reassert their rights under the federal Constitution. A large emancipation-day celebration in Atlanta on January 1, 1945, for example, passed a resolution to recruit 10,000 new voters.[7] Blacks who attended an emancipation program at the segregated training school in Ridgeland, South Carolina, six years later listened to a reading of the

5. Baker, "Devastated by Passion," 287.

6. Brundage, Southern Past, 178.

7. William H. Wiggins Jr., O Freedom! Afro-American Emancipation Celebrations (Knoxville: University of Tennessee Press, 1987), 112.

Gettysburg Address and a speech (probably devoted to voter registration) by the president of the local NAACP.[8]

Notwithstanding the determination of many African Americans to convey a usable past for the benefit of the race, the first cracks in the entrenched white supremacist account of the Civil War era were primarily the result of structural changes taking place in U.S. society as a whole. The potent combination of a prolonged economic depression, an activist government response in the form of the New Deal, and the ultimately successful struggle against militarism and fascism in World War II produced a new generation of white scholars more receptive to the work of black historians and keen to overturn what they regarded as stale interpretations of the American past.[9] Carter Woodson and individuals outside his immediate circle such as W. E. B. Du Bois played their part in making liberal and radical whites more aware of black history, yet so too did the growth of interracial class struggle in the 1930s and the jarring persistence of segregation and discrimination in a war that largely discredited Nazi racial ideology. Politically conscious white historians such as Howard K. Beale, C. Vann Woodward, Kenneth M. Stampp, and Herbert Aptheker began to sketch the outlines of a more inclusive interpretation of the Civil War era, one that highlighted the active role played by blacks in the American past and challenged myths about slavery and Reconstruction. They also sought to make connections with their African-American peers and helped to ease their admission into professional groups such as the Mississippi Valley Historical Association and the Southern Historical Association (SHA). Notwithstanding the impediments to such access (principally white racism and the heavy burden of teaching at black colleges), a handful of young African-American scholars began to make names for themselves by publishing books with mainstream presses and writing articles in refereed journals. Prominent among them were John Hope Franklin, the son of an Oklahoma lawyer who was educated at Fisk and Harvard, and Benjamin Quarles, a Bostonian who received his doctorate from the University of Wisconsin. Franklin's bestselling black history text, *From Slavery to Freedom* (1947), established African-American history as a viable field for study. Two years later, at the behest of program committee chairman C. Vann Woodward, he was the first black historian to deliver a paper at the SHA.[10]

8. "The [Ridgeland, SC] Great Emancipation Day Program," Jan. 1, 1951, John H. McCray Papers, South Caroliniana Library, University of South Carolina.

9. Meier and Rudwick, *Black History*, 107–15.

10. Ibid., 115–21.

Although, as we shall see, the insights of these historians, white and black, eventually helped to demolish the moonlight-and-magnolias interpretation of the southern past, the consensus-dominated 1950s represented a transitional phase between the progressive scholarship of the Truman years and the more radical history of the later twentieth century that was clearly influenced by the social movements of the 1960s.[11] Kenneth Stampp's *The Peculiar Institution* (1956)—a devastating critique of antebellum slavery published in the wake of the *Brown* decision—was generally well received within the academy. However, it did not convince everyone. David Donald, for example, called it "long on morality and short on historical understanding."[12] Still less did the findings of this groundbreaking work trickle down quickly to the American public.

The transitional state of historical writing on topics such as slavery, abolition, and Reconstruction left consensus orthodoxy untouched outside the academy, thereby helping national politicians to sanction a centennial commemoration of the Civil War that incorporated the constructed memory of southern whites while largely ignoring that of African Americans. Ulysses S. Grant III and Karl Betts were steeped in the reigning narrative of the Civil War. They were also paternalistic racists charged with organizing an intersectional observance at a time of acute international tension. Predictably, therefore, when black historians evinced an interest in participating in the centennial, they received little support from the CWCC. In the fall of 1959 Albert N. D. Brooks, a Washington, DC, high school principal who served as secretary-treasurer of the ASNLH, conferred with Betts about the possibility of funding for black centennial projects. The venerable association was struggling at this juncture of its history, for it was ridden with factionalism in the wake of Carter Woodson's sudden death in 1950 and in poor financial health because of waning grassroots interest in black history over the previous decade. Betts, however, made it clear that his agency had no money to distribute to any participating organizations.[13]

The national commission did sanction the ASNLH's modest centennial plans, but no financial support was involved. The official line, articulated by Betts at an executive committee meeting in early January 1960, was that "responsible Negro groups" like the ASNLH were welcome to organize and fund their own events in the same way as similar organizations in other minor-

11. See pp. 249–60 herein.
12. Meier and Rudwick, *Black History,* 140.

13. Charles H. Wesley, "The Civil War and the Negro-American," *Journal of Negro History* 47 (1962): 83.

ity communities. The most ardent segregationist at this gathering, an agitated William Tuck, expressed his guarded willingness to accept the involvement of blacks in the centennial "providing their activities were confined to true history and not to propaganda." "I think," he added in order to clarify his attachment to Lost Cause mythology, "the greatest contribution the Negroes made during the Civil War was their outstanding characteristic of loyalty, and they are only bad when they come under the influence of some low-down white man." General Grant moved quickly to offer further reassurance. Charles Wesley (head of the ASNLH) and Albert Brooks, he said, "would do a first-class job and would not, in any way, be influenced by the NAACP."[14]

Although the CWCC's very modest appropriation would have made it difficult for the commission to offer any subsidy to black organizations, it is clear that Jackson Place was profoundly unsympathetic to the unique financial difficulties faced by black centennial organizers and that it had no intention of highlighting the central role that racial issues had played in the origins and outcome of the Civil War. Grant, Betts, and other conservative members of the CWCC in the late 1950s were willing to hive off limited observances of black military efforts and emancipation to African Americans (on a "separate-but-equal basis" as Wesley put it) but, deeming anything that smacked of civil rights to be "political," they were not prepared to grant official recognition to the persistent counter-memory that was now beginning to gain sanction in academic circles.[15]

14. CWCC, executive committee, minutes of the meeting held Jan. 4, 1960, folder on "Executive Committee Meetings—Minutes," box 184, Bell I. Wiley Papers, Manuscript, Archives, and Rare Book Library, Emory University.

15. Wesley, "Civil War and the Negro-American," 85. In late 1958 Betts reported that he had received several requests urging the CWCC to participate and endorse an exposition to mark black progress over the previous century. "We are side-stepping it as gracefully as possible," he said, "as it is impossible for us to go into this sort of thing." The influential CWCC member Fred Schwengel concurred with this approach though he did add, "Hope it isn't misunderstood." Karl S. Betts to Fred Schwengel, Dec. 10, 1958; Schwengel to Betts, Dec. 16, 1958, folder on "Schwengel, Fred (Hon.)," box 136, subject files 1957–66, Records of the Civil War Centennial Commission, Records of the National Park Service, Record Group 79, National Archives (hereafter CWCCR). When a constituent of Congressman Harold C. Ostertag (R-NY) suggested that the centennial "could be used constructively and very profitably to emphasize the remarkable strides the Negro has made since the Emancipation Proclamation," Ostertag sent the missive to CWCC headquarters for comments. In his reply Betts simply ignored the idea. Katherine B. King to Ostertag, March 15, 1959; Betts to Ostertag, March 25, 1959, folder on "Congressional Mail," box 70, subject files 1957–66, CWCCR.

What little pressure emanated from inside the CWCC to involve blacks in the centennial stemmed mainly from Bell Wiley. By the 1950s the Atlanta-based historian was best known for his writings on Civil War soldiers (a refreshing alternative to the traditional focus on politicians and generals), but his first book, *Southern Negroes, 1861–1865* (1938), was actually an unconscious contribution to the growth of the nascent black history movement.[16] Despite the book's frequent use of various racial epithets and its pronounced reluctance to challenge the accepted wisdom that most slaves had remained loyal to their masters in wartime, African-American critics generally welcomed *Southern Negroes* because it granted agency to blacks and acknowledged black history as a legitimate object of study. Over time—especially at Yale and as the author of an official study of the training of African-American troops in World War II—Wiley overcame some of his ingrained prejudices to the point at which, in the mid-1950s, he was a vocal supporter of black involvement in SHA proceedings. As president of the association in 1955, he delivered an address on the role of common soldiers in the Civil War. In it he observed pointedly that around 200,000 blacks had fought for the Union. "Those few who had the opportunity to participate in battle under reasonably propitious circumstances," he asserted, "seem to have given a creditable account of themselves, and some displayed great gallantry."[17]

Wiley's efforts to draw blacks into the centennial commemoration may appear somewhat tokenistic in the wake of the civil rights movement, but at a time when massive resistance was at its height, his calls for a black presence within the centennial establishment were relatively bold—the work of a committed white liberal as well as a southern historian writing for a national audience.[18] As early as April 1956, over a year before the establishment of a federal commission, Wiley proposed that a grand seminar should lay plans for the upcoming commemoration. "I think it would be desirable to have the Negroes represented among the participants," he advised, adding that John Hope

16. Meier and Rudwick, *Black History*, 110.

17. Bell I. Wiley, "A Time of Greatness," *Journal of Southern History* 22 (1956): 32.

18. Wiley had no qualms distancing himself from partisans of the Lost Cause in the tense racial climate of the mid-1950s. Commenting on an attack by the Nashville historian Stanley Horn on novelist McKinlay Kantor's critical account of the infamous Confederate prison at Andersonville, he told Ralph Newman that Horn "seems to be carrying an oversize Rebel chip on his shoulder. His line will please the UDC's and a lot of die-hard Rebel patriots, but to the overwhelming majority of Southern scholars, and to many laymen, it will brand him, in my firm opinion, as a strongly biased historian." Wiley to Ralph G. Newman, Oct. 3, 1955, folder on "Civil War Book Club," box 184, Wiley Papers.

Franklin, soon to take up a tenured post at Brooklyn College, would be an ideal choice, being "one of the most highly respected and most articulate of the Negro scholars."[19] As a member of the CWCC, Wiley subsequently urged the appointment of a handful of blacks to the agency's advisory council and articulated his belief in an inclusive commemoration of the Civil War.[20]

If Walker Percy's jibe that African Americans were to be the "ghost at the feast" was close to the mark, it was not strictly accurate.[21] A few blacks such as Madaline A. Williams in New Jersey, John Hope Franklin in New York, and Charles Wesley in Ohio were active participants in the centennial in their capacity as members of northern state commissions. Even though their appointments resulted from the limited political influence that blacks exerted in those states, their presence alone virtually guaranteed some commitment to racial themes on the part of their respective agencies. Wesley, for example, wrote a short pamphlet on the role of Ohio blacks in the Civil War that appeared in 1962 as a publication of the state historical society.[22] The New Jersey commission evinced its heightened racial consciousness by giving a black politician a leading role in its commemoration of Lincoln's preinauguration visit to Trenton. The New York agency committed itself to a full-scale commemoration of emancipation at the beginning of 1961, and its chairman, Bruce Catton, began to stress this theme publicly at the same juncture.[23]

Meanwhile the ASNLH, for all its weaknesses still the foremost institution for black history, did what it could to use the centennial to further its own long-running objectives. It disseminated information about the race's involvement in the Civil War in various ways. Its chief scholarly organs, the *Journal of Negro History* and the *Negro History Bulletin,* featured several articles relating

19. Wiley to Richard B. Harwell, April 19, 1956, folder on "General Correspondence, 1955–1957," box 184, Wiley Papers.

20. Wiley was particularly concerned that Charles H. Wesley, "a highly respected person among scholars among both races . . . and . . . a splendid gentleman," be appointed to the advisory committee. Wiley to Ulysses S. Grant III, Jan. 20, 1958, folder on "General Correspondence, 1958," box 184, Wiley Papers. Wesley subsequently accepted a request to serve in this capacity.

21. Walker Percy, "Red, White, and Blue-Gray" (1961), in *Signposts in a Strange Land,* ed. Patrick Samway (New York: Farrar, Straus, and Giroux, 1991), 82.

22. Charles H. Wesley, *Ohio Negroes in the Civil War* (Columbus: Ohio State University Press for the Ohio Historical Society, 1962).

23. First Assembly of New York Civil War Centennial Commission, April 17, 1961, minutes, box 1, office files 1961–64, A1444-78, Records of the New York Civil War Centennial Commission, New York State Archives (hereafter NYCWCCR); Bruce Catton, "Where the Great Change Took Place," *New York Times Magazine,* Feb. 5, 1961, 11.

to the centennial in the early 1960s. Prominent ASNLH members including Professors Wesley, Franklin, and Quarles delivered numerous public lectures and wrote important books, essays, and school texts stressing the centrality of race to the Civil War experience. Franklin, for example, lectured on "Abraham Lincoln and the Politics of War" at the Brooklyn Public Library in early 1961, and Quarles penned a generally positive account of the relations between the wartime president and African Americans.[24]

None of these historians was a radical. The most well known of them, John Hope Franklin, was noted for his insistence that blacks should shed their introverted mentality born of segregation and prove their talents by securing entry into mainstream academic life.[25] It was precisely because they were integrationists that they regarded the centennial as an opportunity to remind whites and blacks alike of a historic moment when their nation had been compelled to transform slaves into citizens. They were confident that they were contributing to the ongoing freedom struggle, which had now entered its critical direct-action phase. Thus they consistently disseminated the main strands of the black counter-memory to a public that, owing to the consciousness-raising activities of the civil rights movement, was more receptive than it had been since the 1870s to the idea that slavery was a brutal institution, that it had been the primary factor in causing the Civil War, that blacks had played an active role in their own liberation (aided and abetted by sympathetic abolitionists as well as the immortal Lincoln), and—a theme of striking contemporary relevance—that the war had confirmed federal suzerainty over the states. The North's victory, contended Franklin in the second edition of *From Slavery to Freedom* published in 1963 (the year the Kennedy administration belatedly introduced a comprehensive civil rights bill into Congress), meant victory for a perpetual Union: "all states were bound henceforth to recognize the superior sovereignty of the federal government."[26]

Support for the resurgent black counter-memory came from parties inside and outside the academy. The ASNLH encouraged grassroots discussion of

24. *New York Amsterdam News*, Jan. 7, 1961, 16; Benjamin Quarles, *Lincoln and the Negro* (New York: Oxford University Press, 1962).

25. "You know of the extremely high standards that I require of Negroes who would be worthy of the esteem of their fellows," wrote Franklin in the midst of the centennial, "but I do not require this as a condition for their enjoyment of civil rights." John Hope Franklin to Allan Nevins, Aug. 27, 1962, folder 1, box 76, Allan Nevins Papers, Rare Book and Manuscript Library, Columbia University.

26. John Hope Franklin, *From Slavery to Freedom: A History of American Negroes*, rev. ed. (New York: Alfred A. Knopf, 1963).

Civil War issues by members of its local affiliates and backed special centennial events such as the New York Public Library's exhibition on "The Negro
in the Civil War" and ambitious plans by the Chicago-based American Negro
Emancipation Centennial Authority (ANECA) to promote public awareness
of 1963 as the centenary of the Emancipation Proclamation.[27] Activities like
these were given greater prominence by the backing of black businessmen,
newspapers, and radio stations. They did not, moreover, go unsupported by a
growing number of sympathetic white scholars who intensified the search for
a usable past as the black freedom struggle progressed. James M. McPherson,
a young Princeton historian who had participated in civil rights demonstrations in Baltimore while a graduate student under C. Vann Woodward,
wrote *The Struggle for Equality,* a detailed study of the antislavery movement
during the Civil War and Reconstruction published during the penultimate
year of the centennial. McPherson made explicit his presentist motivation by
dedicating the book to "all those who are working to achieve the abolitionist goal of equal rights for all men."[28] Liberal white historians were joined by
some white-owned businesses and white politicians who had a vested interest
in being seen to advance African-American objectives. In Chicago, home to a
million blacks, the A&P grocery chain contributed to a money-raising drive
launched by ANECA to fund its grandiose project for an exposition of black
progress to mark the centenary of emancipation. Founded by a local public
relations expert, ANECA enjoyed support not only from local black minis-
ters and civic leaders including Rev. Joseph H. Jackson, the influential head
of the National Baptist Convention who served as its president, but also from

27. Wesley was a trustee of ANECA. *Chicago Defender,* Jan. 28–Feb. 3, 1961, 6.

28. James M. McPherson, *The Struggle for Equality: Abolitionists and the Negro in the Civil
War and Reconstruction* (Princeton: Princeton University Press, 1964), unnumbered dedication
page. Other historians of the middle period writing in the late 1950s and early 1960s underscored
what they saw as a connection between the Civil War era and the contemporary freedom struggle.
See, for example, William Dusinberre, *Civil War Issues in Philadelphia, 1856–1865* (Philadelphia:
University of Pennsylvania Press, 1965), 190, and William E. Gillette, *The Right to Vote: Politics
and the Passage of the Fifteenth Amendment* (Baltimore: Johns Hopkins University Press, 1965),
9–11. In remarks at a session devoted to *The Struggle for Equality* at the November 2003 Southern
Historical Association meeting in Houston, James McPherson stated explicitly that his interest in
the abolitionists stemmed from a combination of Woodward's socially aware teaching and scholarship on Reconstruction and his own commitment to the goals of the developing civil rights
movement. "[M]y interest in the American Civil War was not stimulated by the centennial commemorations from 1961 to 1965," he stated categorically in a subsequent private communication.
McPherson to the author, Nov. 10, 2003.

Chicago's Democratic boss, Mayor Richard J. Daley, a man heavily reliant on black client politicians and black votes.[29]

The effectiveness of these efforts is unclear. Although significant numbers of African Americans must have read or heard about the centennial during the early weeks of 1961, most were probably focused either on the continuing fight against segregation or on the prosaic task of simply getting by in urban America or the rural South. Two things, however, helped to bring the centennial to the attention of growing numbers of blacks: first, a dawning realization that segregationists were using the event to pursue their own political ends; second, the role played by the civil rights movement in stimulating popular interest in African-American history.

The extent of the white South's initial domination of the centennial took most African-American leaders by surprise. The Civil War was slated to be a prominent theme in Negro History Week in February 1961, but it was not the only item on the agenda at the various local events organized by the ASNLH and other black community organizations. However, media accounts of the celebrations in Montgomery and Jackson and, even more important, of the segregation crisis in Charleston rapidly convinced black leaders that the spurious notion of a consensual commemoration of the Civil War was playing into the hands of bitter-enders. As we have seen, the national NAACP gave strong support for a boycott of the federal commission's fourth national assembly. The involvement of the nation's oldest civil rights organization was probably a major factor in President Kennedy's decision to intervene in support of a compromise that did at least signify his readiness to divorce the United States government from segregation.

With their consciousness raised to new heights by the spring of 1961, African Americans and their white allies were ready to contest the memory of the Civil War as vigorously as any devotee of the Lost Cause. On March 4, *The Crusader,* an uncompromising newssheet edited by maverick black activist Robert Williams in Monroe, North Carolina, informed readers of the "Centennial of Shame." The U.S. government, warned Williams, was preparing "to pay homage" to a region that had once "threatened to destroy the Union for the sake of slavery . . . [T]he North is fast becoming a running dog for the southern way of life . . . At this time the entire Colored world can get a good look at the true attitude of the nation that is out to enforce this special brand of democracy on a world still struggling to cast off its chains of bond-

29. *Chicago Defender,* Oct. 22–28, 1960, 7; Jan. 28–Feb. 3, 1961, 6; March 11–17, 1961, 2.

age."[30] Black historian Lawrence D. Reddick, a confidant of Martin Luther King who had lost his teaching post in Montgomery because of his vocal support of civil rights, delivered an angry speech to a gathering of teachers in New York shortly after the CWCC had reluctantly agreed to accept the naval-base solution to the problem of segregated facilities at its national assembly in Charleston. The Civil War festivities, he insisted, were perpetuating historical myths about the white South, myths that were "part of the psychological and political resistance" to the new administration's attempts to promote social progress.[31] It was time, he said, for a bonfire to be made of the Confederate symbols then being displayed throughout the South.

The conviction that segregationists were warping the nation's past elicited a stream of criticism from liberals of every hue. Brooklyn-born Howard N. Meyer, a former special assistant to U.S. attorneys general Francis Biddle and Tom Clark, penned a magazine article attacking the pernicious effects of the lilywhite orthodox narrative of the Civil War. The essay, driven by Meyer's interest in republishing the memoirs of a northern abolitionist, as well as by his support for the civil rights movement, also assailed centennial planners for trying to suppress all references to the moral and political issues at stake in the Civil War in a vain attempt to promote national unity. An official CWCC brochure about the conflict, he wrote, failed to mention blacks at all, let alone the fact that they had constituted 12 percent of the Union armed forces and 18 percent of the North's total casualties. Noting that the recent observances in Charleston had failed to stress the seditious nature of the attack on Fort Sumter, Meyer insisted that the war should be commemorated in such a way as not to deprive it of all meaning. "It does not serve America well, in the world of 1961," he observed, "to ignore the evil and iniquity of slavery in marking the Centennial of the conflict."[32] This essay was given wide publicity by the National

30. *The Crusader,* March 4, 1961, 4, Special Collections, Duke University Library. I am grateful to Joe Street for this citation.

31. *New York Times,* April 23, 1961, sec. 1, 74.

32. Howard N. Meyer, "Did the South Win the Civil War?" *Negro Digest* 13 (1961): 8. This was a November reprint of the article originally published in *Commonweal* in June 1961. Because of his growing interest in, and sympathy for, the developing civil rights movement, Meyer had been excited to track down a rare copy of Thomas Wentworth Higginson's classic *Army Life in a Black Regiment* (1870) in a Portland, Maine, bookshop. Sensing its importance to the struggle (Higginson had recruited a regiment of black Union troops in South Carolina), the New Yorker secured its republication by Collier Books in 1962. Meyer to the author, March 12, 2005. "Two hundred thousand Negroes fought in that war," Meyer told a local newspaper on the pending appearance

Council of Churches, a staunch supporter of the civil rights movement, and warmly welcomed by the veteran black labor leader A. Philip Randolph. "There is no doubt," commented Randolph (echoing the plangent complaints of Frederick Douglass in the postbellum era), "that this whole Civil War Centennial commemoration is a stupendous brain-washing exercise to make the Civil War leaders of the South heroes on a par with the Civil War leaders of the North, and to strike a blow against men of color and human dignity."[33]

While the angry black response to the events of early 1961 helped to deprive the centennial of legitimacy in the eyes of many Americans (and thereby contributed significantly to reform of the CWCC), it is unlikely that the majority of blacks were unduly exercised by these squabbles over historical memory. But if African Americans remained as dimly aware of their history as whites were about their own past, the efforts of scholars like Quarles and Franklin did combine with the spectacular progress of the civil rights movement to stimulate popular interest in black history. During late 1961 and 1962 the black monthly magazine *Ebony* ran a series of articles by the journalist Lerone Bennett. Each brisk essay detailed the positive role played by blacks in seminal American events such as the Revolution, the Civil War, and Reconstruction. The author's stress on black agency was a genuine revelation to many readers and struck a deep chord in individuals whose political consciousness had been raised to new heights by the freedom struggle. One Chicago resident praised the series for its stress "on the role of the Negro, himself, in the struggle for freedom and equality . . . The part played by the Negro in liberating himself is a story seldom told and largely unknown."[34] Marie Josey from Brooklyn wished that *Ebony* circulated among whites. "When I was in high school," she wrote, "I realized how very little they knew about the history of the Negro in this country. All they knew was the Negroes were 'docile' slaves. I must confess that this was my conception of the Negro until I started

---

of the reprint, "but you never hear of them. We buried their achievements, as we buried those of other leading Negroes immediately after the war, when we defeated slavery but accepted segregation." *Long Island Press*, July 8, 1962, clipping in folder on "Colored Organizations," box 69, subject files 1957–66, CWCCR.

33. Randolph read an extract from Meyer's essay in *Interchurch News*. A. Philip Randolph to Meyer, July 13, 1961, frames 106–7, reel 2, Bayard Rustin Papers (UPA microfilm, 1988). In thanking Meyer for sending him a copy of the article, Martin Luther King Jr. paid tribute to his correspondent's "determined efforts to bring to the light of day the injustices and distortions practiced in our time." King to Meyer, Jan. 31, 1962, folder on "Colored Organizations," box 69, subject files 1957–66, CWCCR.

34. *Ebony*, July 1962, 13.

subscribing to your magazine."[35] James E. Haynes wrote from Cleveland to describe Bennett's work as "bread and water to a thirsty people." It would, he contended, "not only strengthen our beliefs and determinations in the North, but lend encouragement and moral support to our stride-breaking brothers in the South."[36] A Los Angeles man said he had been so inspired by what he had read that he was thinking about taking a course in history. "I have always loved the subject," he reflected, "but since leaving high school I guess I have been too lazy to do anything about it."[37]

From mid-1961 onward, blacks began to engage more positively with the centennial, their response paralleling the growth of the civil rights movement in the early years of the decade. Their engagement took two forms. The first, essentially cultural, involved continuing efforts to empower the black counter-memory on the basis of a discernible growth of popular interest in the black past. The ASNLH therefore redoubled its efforts to promote awareness of Civil War themes among African Americans. Insisting (not unlike a more radical black activist, Malcolm X), that "[t]he control of the presentation of history is so often the control of the future of a people," the association's president, Charles H. Wesley, called on blacks to forge ahead with plans to collate and disseminate information about the race's experience in the Civil War.[38] Community meetings, study groups, museum exhibits, essay contests, and the unveiling of plaques should all be used, he urged, to counter the white South's apparent stranglehold over the centennial. Astutely, he pointed out that as time went on the very chronology of the war would begin to work against those who reveled in past Confederate triumphs. From the start of 1961, observed Wesley, there had been "a preoccupation with the glorification of the drama of the War as it opened in 1861 with Southern dominance and victories . . . What will we see when General Grant marches through the Wilderness and General Sherman marches to the sea!"[39] The second way in which blacks participated in centennial affairs was more overtly political.

35. *Ebony,* Aug. 1962, 13.

36. *Ebony,* Oct. 1962, 13.

37. *Ebony,* Aug. 1962, 13.

38. Wesley, "Civil War and the Negro-American," 95. Wesley's comment can be compared with the statement of Malcolm X's ill-fated Organization of Afro-American Unity in June 1964 that "[w]e must recapture our heritage and our identity if we are ever to liberate ourselves from the bonds of white supremacy. We must launch a cultural revolution to unbrainwash an entire people." *By Any Means Necessary: Speeches, Interviews and a Letter by Malcolm X,* ed. George Breitman (New York: Pathfinder Press, 1970), 54.

39. Wesley, "Civil War and the Negro-American," 78–79.

Here their interest focused on commemorating what members of the race had always regarded as the supreme event of the Civil War: Lincoln's Emancipation Proclamation. Efforts to mark its centenary with a view to publicizing the gap between the promise and reality of life in America, however, remained heavily dependent for success on the response of powerful white elites.

EMANCIPATION BLUES

The burden of developing an official commemoration of the Emancipation Proclamation rested principally on the shoulders of three government parties: the CWCC, a handful of northern state centennial agencies, and the U.S. Civil Rights Commission. The results were extremely disappointing, primarily because these bodies were controlled by whites possessed of limited empathy for blacks and pursuing a range of agendas that did not match exactly those of the civil rights movement.

Federal interest in commemorating emancipation had diverse political roots. In early December 1961, several weeks after Congress had discussed but failed to pass a resolution setting up a special commission to develop plans to mark the upcoming centenary of Lincoln's edict, Louis Martin penned a memorandum on the subject to President Kennedy's closest adviser, Theodore Sorensen. Noting that several "Negro groups" such as the Chicago-based ANECA were planning their own commemorations, Martin—the only African American on the Democratic National Committee—drew Sorensen's attention to "the possibility that those who are interested in a fast buck will exploit this type of thing." It would be much better, he argued, if the federal government got involved, either by creating a special committee or through "the orbit" of the CWCC now that it possessed, in Allan Nevins, "a new Chairman who can read or write." By no means the first African American to use foreign policy as leverage in the fight for civil rights, Martin added, "Negroes in America and the peoples of Africa and other non-white areas would be interested in anything the Administration did about this matter. There are some political values here which I am sure you recognize."[40] Sorensen certainly did see the political utility of Martin's suggestion. "I think this is worth following

40. Louis Martin to Theodore Sorensen, Dec. 6, 1961, folder on "Emancipation Proclamation Anniversary, April 24–August 24, 1962," box 20, Lee White Papers, White House Staff Files, John F. Kennedy Presidential Library.

up," he wrote in the briefest of memoranda to the president's future civil rights adviser, Lee White.[41]

CWCC officials had already decided that some formal recognition of the abolition of slavery was essential if they were to restore public faith in the centennial project, even though they remained acutely conscious of the need to retain the support of the southern commissions. Within a week of setting out his inclusive vision for the observances, Nevins had secured the support of his reconstituted commission for a suitably dignified ceremony on September 22, 1962, to mark the issuing of Lincoln's preliminary Emancipation Proclamation.[42] The project received enthusiastic backing from the administration, with Lee White assuring Nevins that President Kennedy would "be happy to participate" in the ceremony.[43] While it is possible that White had in mind a symbolic gesture in favor of African-American civil rights, the CWCC certainly did not see the projected emancipation ceremony in this light. As befitted a liberal anticommunist Democrat, Nevins was determined "to give the commemoration an international character as recalling a great world event."[44] When John A. May inquired if the reorganized CWCC would try to use the emancipation centenary to promote civil rights, Nevins strove to downplay the project's domestic significance:

> My own feeling is that we ought to lift this particular commemoration far above the immediate and temporary political or social contentions which, as you rightly say, should be excluded from all observances. For this reason, I have favored treating the wartime emancipation as one event in a worldwide movement, stretching over the centuries, for the liberation of

41. Sorensen to Lee White, Dec. 12, 1961, ibid. Harris Wofford left the White House staff in the middle of 1962 "primarily because of the affirmative pull of the Peace Corps, and of Africa" but also because he sensed that his role as a buffer between the president and civil rights leaders was not actually aiding the cause of racial equality. In addition, he had been subjected to criticism in the black press for "wearing a Confederate general's uniform to a high-spirited New Frontier costume party." Harris Wofford, *Of Kennedys and Kings: Making Sense of the Sixties* (1980; reprint, Pittsburgh: University of Pittsburgh Press, 1992), 164–65.

42. Nevins to Arthur M. Schlesinger Jr., Dec. 13, 1961, folder on "Civil War Centennial Commission," box WH3B, Arthur M. Schlesinger Jr. Papers, White House Files, JFK Library.

43. White to Nevins, Feb. 6, 1962, folder FG633, box 198, White House Central Files, JFK Library.

44. Nevins to Edmund C. Gass, Dec. 22, 1961, folder on "Nevins, Allan—Oct. 13, 1961," box 134, subject files 1957–66, CWCCR.

the colored peoples of the globe from servitude . . . By selecting a theme of these large proportions, and choosing appropriate speakers, we can elevate our commemoration far above petty contentions of the day. In giving it a world-wide significance, we can perhaps at the same time accomplish something for the standing of the United States in the family of nations.[45]

In common with his fellow Civil War historian Bruce Catton, the new CWCC chairman regarded the emancipation centenary not primarily as a chance to promote the cause of African-American rights (though he was personally sympathetic to that cause) but as a means of fighting the cold war. Thus, instead of making the abolition of slavery in the United States the centerpiece of the event as most blacks might have expected him to do, Nevins planned to highlight the proclamation's contribution to a broader and ongoing trend of "colored" freedom. If this clever manipulation of Civil War memory evinced a deplorable lack of understanding of the live black counter-narrative, it certainly gelled neatly with John F. Kennedy's desire to win over hearts and minds in the developing world and the CWCC's desperate need to keep the southern centennial commissions on board. It came as little surprise, then, that Nevins did not consider inviting a single African American to speak at the Lincoln Memorial in September, preferring instead to contemplate giving the job to trusted foreigners such as the Colombian president, the prime minister of Nigeria, and the Indian ambassador to Washington.[46] Ironically, the cold war underpinnings of the emancipation event were articulated most clearly by the only black member of the CWCC. In a resolution submitted to an executive committee meeting on January 30, Roy Davenport, a Kennedy loyalist, placed Lincoln's proclamation in the context of human rather than black freedom:

> Time has given the Emancipation Proclamation a significance far broader than it had when issued. Originally, it connoted one kind of freedom for one group of people in a country. Today its significance transcends these limitations.
>
> The true significance of the Proclamation today lies in its spirit of freedom for all men everywhere. In the context of today's processes of complex social adjustments throughout the world, this means freedom from

45. John A. May to Nevins, Dec. 13, 1961; Nevins to May, Dec. 26, 1961, folder on "South Carolina Civil War Centennial Commission—1961," box 125, subject files 1957–66, CWCCR.

46. Nevins to Schlesinger, Dec. 13, 1961, folder on "Civil War Centennial Commission," box WH3B, Schlesinger Papers.

the restraining effects of ignorance, fear, hunger, and disease. It also means freedom of the human mind and spirit in all fields of creative endeavor, including the arts, the sciences and technology.[47]

The thinly disguised anticommunism of Davenport's resolution left little doubt that the CWCC was not going to be become a vehicle for civil rights. As James Robertson testily informed a white female correspondent in January, he and Nevins had made it clear that the centennial would be "free of political and social problems that confront us today." It would "do a grave injustice to the more than 618,000 Americans who gave their lives in that struggle of a century ago if we were to convert a commemoration of their deeds and sacrifices into a program to eliminate modern day problems that might ultimately restir again the bitter feelings and violence that swept this Nation to war in 1861."[48]

Notwithstanding Nevins's cold war emphasis and Robertson's successful attempts to limit the "political" content of the emancipation ceremony in order to assuage the fears of southern centennial chiefs, the CWCC could not ignore blacks entirely in its plans for September 22. To do so would have sparked another disastrous round of criticism from the national press. Tokenism and stereotyping, however, were to be the order of the day. A young black musician, Ulysses Kay, was commissioned to compose a short musical piece especially for the ceremony, and subsequently a decision was taken to invite the renowned African-American soprano Mahalia Jackson to sing a solo.

While plans for the ceremony progressed relatively smoothly during the spring and early summer of 1962, tensions occasionally surfaced inside the CWCC over the degree to which the agency should suppress the racial dimensions of the Emancipation Proclamation. When Nevins suggested preparation of an official pamphlet on the edict, his southern lieutenants (reared in a tradition that stressed the pragmatic origins of Lincoln's antislavery policy) urged restraint. James Robertson professed to be "enthusiastically" in favor of such a booklet but added that he was "somewhat alarmed" by Nevins's contention that "the 'implications of emancipation for the future should be emphasized.'"[49] Staff member Ed Gass concurred. After calling the idea "excellent,"

---

47. CWCC, executive committee minutes, Jan. 30, 1962, folder on "Executive Committee Meetings—Awards," box 60, subject files 1957–66, CWCCR.

48. James I. Robertson Jr. to Rose J. Knight, Jan. 10, 1962, folder on "Complaints: re Commission 1962–63," box 69, subject files 1957–66, CWCCR.

49. Robertson to Nevins, April 3, 1962, folder on "Nevins, Allan—Oct. 13, 1961," box 134, subject files 1957–66, CWCCR.

he told the commission's chairman: "I would hope that in a short introduction you might be able to emphasize the historical aspects of the material contained therein rather than any association the data might have toward modern-day problems." Failure to heed this advice, he suggested, would damage relations with the southern commissions "and others who do not possess our—shall I say—liberal thinking on historical facts."[50] The southerners got their way. The agency did issue a booklet on the centenary of emancipation, but it merely contained a small selection of documents without commentary.[51]

Although segregationists continued to fret about what President Kennedy might say in his September 22 address, they were generally pleased with the CWCC's efforts to—in their parlance—depoliticize the emancipation ceremony and had no occasion to disrupt the agency's unremarkable fifth national assembly in Columbus, Ohio, in May 1962. "There was a very close feeling of unanimity among the Southern folk at Columbus," reported Sidney Roebuck, head of the Mississippi commission. "Mr. Robertson sensed this, and he stayed with us very closely. He said that some of the northern radicals were trying to stir up a fight, but that he and Mr. Nevins were determined that this would not happen."[52]

The CWCC's hopes for a successful (and uncontroversial) observance of the preliminary Emancipation Proclamation were threatened by some last-minute drama. The first problem was President Kennedy's late decision not to attend the ceremony. In spite of frequent contacts between the White House and CWCC officials over the course of 1962, Theodore Sorensen called Nevins in California on August 22 to report that a "mix up" had occurred and that the president could not participate. The following day a two-man CWCC delegation, Fred Schwengel and James Robertson, went to the White House and spoke to Sorensen and two other presidential aides, Kenneth O'Donnell and Arthur Schlesinger. O'Donnell claimed that he had not known of the event until the previous day and that unfortunately Kennedy had already accepted another commitment. Schwengel pleaded with the aides to reconsider. The program, he said, afforded "a great opportunity to the President to not only speak to the American people but to the world in an excellent setting to

50. Gass to Nevins, April 5, 1962, box 11, reading file 1958–66, CWCCR.

51. CWCC, *Emancipation Centennial, 1962: A Brief Anthology of the Preliminary Proclamation* (Washington, DC: Government Printing Office, 1962).

52. Sidney T. Roebuck to Sam Dickinson, May 16, 1962, folder on "Arkansas—State Chairman," box 707, Records of the Mississippi Commission on the War Between the States, Record Group 19, Mississippi Department of Archives and History (hereafter MCWBTSR).

present the message our country has to tell on freedom."[53] His effort was in vain. Although the president did agree to make a videotaped address for the occasion, he was not present at the Lincoln Memorial on September 22. Instead the CWCC had to content itself with an address from Nevins's political associate, Adlai Stevenson, and a guest appearance from Attorney General Robert F. Kennedy.

What looked at first sight to have been poor management by the White House was, in all likelihood, a carefully calculated decision. Kennedy's leading advisers probably reasoned that too close an association with civil rights might damage the Democratic cause in the forthcoming midterm elections. Racial tensions were increasing by the day as an African American, James Meredith, sought admission to the University of Mississippi with the assistance of the federal courts. Reformers meanwhile were urging the president to issue a Lincoln-style "emancipation" order banning segregation in federally financed housing. Indeed, some hoped Kennedy would use the CWCC ceremony as a platform for this measure—speculation that induced the chairman of the Republican National Committee to predict that the White House would "cheapen" a historic occasion with "a political publicity play."[54] Against this backdrop Kenneth O'Donnell, noted for regarding civil rights as a political liability, may have taken the lead in canceling the president's plans.[55] This was James Robertson's presumption. "It seems obvious to me," he told Nevins angrily, "that Mr. O'Donnell willfully juggled the President's schedule (or else removed our service from it) for reasons that are probably political."[56]

The irate Virginian had another major concern in the weeks leading up to the ceremony. In mid-September, Bishop Smallwood E. Williams, a black Baptist minister who headed the Washington, DC, affiliate of the SCLC, announced a boycott of the proceedings with the backing of Dr. Martin Luther King. The CWCC's failure to place a single black speaker on the emancipation program had proved offensive to civil rights activists in the capital, and their vocal opposition threatened to bring down a storm of negative publicity on the commission.[57] The embarrassing controversy led to a hastily arranged

53. Schwengel to Kenneth O'Donnell, Aug. 24, 1962, folder 2, box 76, Nevins Papers.

54. *New York Times*, Sept. 22, 1962, 12.

55. Harris Wofford described O'Donnell as "the guardian of the presidential gate" who would plead constantly, "We have to save the President's time—does he have to see King now?" Wofford, *Of Kennedys and Kings*, 165.

56. Robertson to Nevins, Aug. 27, 1962, folder on "Nevins, Allan—Oct. 13, 1961," box 134, subject files 1957–66, CWCCR.

57. *New York Times*, Sept. 18, 1962, 25.

meeting between CWCC personnel, black leaders, and Justice Department officials. The resulting agreement provided for the appointment of an African American to the speakers' roster and the seating of blacks on the main platform. The name of the respected federal district judge Thurgood Marshall was quickly appended to the list of orators—a partial victory for the civil rights movement, which was now growing in confidence and impatience.[58]

In view of the problems involved in putting the event together, the emancipation ceremony in Washington on September 22, 1962, was, from the organizers' perspective, a minor success. The presence at the Lincoln Memorial of political celebrities such as Robert Kennedy and Governor Nelson Rockefeller helped to guarantee network television coverage. Only a small crowd—no more than 4,000—actually turned up to watch, but as many as 20 million domestic television viewers may have seen the hour-long ceremony in the comfort of their own homes.[59] After the call to order by Allan Nevins and a solemn invocation, Mahalia Jackson sang the national anthem accompanied by the U.S. Marine Band. Archibald MacLeish then recited his new poem "At the Lincoln Memorial: A Poem for the Centennial of the Emancipation Proclamation," the band played Ulysses Kay's "Forever Free: A Lincoln Chronicle," Governor Rockefeller presented New York's original draft of the preliminary edict, Thurgood Marshall made some brief remarks, and Adlai Stevenson, recruited at the last minute by Nevins, delivered a short speech.[60] President Kennedy's videotaped message was then shown and, after a solemn benediction, Mahalia Jackson sang what Arthur Schlesinger later described as a "final glorious rendition" of the "Battle Hymn of the Republic."[61]

In his recorded address the president made clear the contemporary racial significance of the Emancipation Proclamation. Referring pointedly to the abolition of "the evil of human slavery," Kennedy was at pains to stress that

58. New York Times, Sept. 19, 1962, 27.

59. Robertson to CWCC members, Dec. 28, 1962, folder on "Civil War Centennial Commission," box WH3B, Schlesinger Papers.

60. Engaging Stevenson's services proved to be a morning's work for Nevins. He "would have said no to anybody but me," boasted the CWCC chairman from his home in California. Nevins to Robertson, folder on "Nevins, Allan—October 13, 1961," box 134, subject files 1957–66, CWCCR. Nevins contributed material to the ambassador's speech. See Adlai Stevenson to Nevins, Sept. 5, 1962, box 29, Nevins Papers.

61. Schlesinger to Mahalia Jackson, Oct. 16, 1962, folder on "Emancipation Proclamation 9/6/62–10/18/62," box WH9, Schlesinger Papers. An official program of the event is located in the same folder. For an account of the emancipation ceremony, see New York Times, Sept. 23, 1961, sec. 1, 1, 50.

while blacks had fought tirelessly for freedom over the past hundred years, the task initiated by Abraham Lincoln was far from finished: "Much remains to be done to eradicate the vestiges of discrimination and segregation, to make equal rights a reality for all of our people, to fulfill finally the promises of the Declaration of Independence. Like the proclamation we celebrate, this observance must be regarded not as an end, but a beginning. The best commemoration lies not in what we say today, but in what we do in the days and months ahead to complete the work begun . . . a century ago." [62] No doubt these fine words would have carried even greater weight had Kennedy actually been present. Nevertheless, followed as they were by Mahalia Jackson's powerful rendering of the "Battle Hymn," they drew strength from the deep well-spring of America's civil religion.

Adlai Stevenson's keynote address, by contrast, was a curious rhetorical concoction that made nods in the direction of civil rights but focused primarily on broader cold war themes. Hailing the Proclamation as "the redemption of young America's promise" and a central event in "the globe-circling spread of our spirit of national independence and individual freedom," the UN ambassador reminded his audience that "freedom is again at stake. This time the whole worldwide society of men is perilously divided on the issue. National independence has swept the earth like wildfire, but individual freedom is still the great unfinished business of the world today." Although Stevenson then alluded to the burdens of racial discrimination in America, his subsequent observation that Lincoln's greatness lay in his capacity "to see human affairs and human emotions in all their complexity and ambiguity" seemed to preclude easy solutions to the country's racial problems. It was much more important, he suggested, that Americans' "sense of our own failures and weaknesses in the struggle for freedom does not mean, for one instant, any faltering in the sacrifices which are necessary to ensure that the Western democracies and the unaligned peoples of the world have the shield against aggression that they need, and the aid necessary to uphold it." [63] Stevenson's address lacked the moral clarity of Kennedy's pithier statement on civil rights. If its thinly disguised preoccupation with foreign policy imperatives did not signify that a totemic event in African-American history had been entirely appropriated by powerful elites, it certainly helped to dilute the moral force of the overall

62. *Public Papers of the Presidents of the United States: John F. Kennedy, 1962* (Washington, DC: Government Printing Office, 1963), 702–3.

63. Press release 4044, Sept. 21, 1962, folder on "Emancipation Proclamation 9/6/62–10/18/62," box WH9, Schlesinger Papers.

ceremony. But, then, that was precisely what Nevins and Robertson had in-tended all along.

Perhaps one can sympathize with their dilemma to an extent, for unduly antagonizing the southern commissions would have destroyed the centennial as a national event. Their efforts to limit the "political" content of the emanci-pation ceremony certainly paid off. John May was the only hardline segrega-tionist present at the Lincoln Memorial, and he pronounced himself relatively pleased with the low-key proceedings. "I must say in all fairness," he reported to Sidney Roebuck, "that 'Bud' Robertson and the Commission itself, did a wonderful job in holding the radicals down as much as possible." Black activ-ists, he said (referring to Smallwood Williams's group), had demanded, but failed to secure, equal time for Martin Luther King with Adlai Stevenson. "The Negro[e]s," he added, "objected to Stevenson vigorously, which surprised me, and Stevenson made a fairly good speech. Mahalia Jackson was featured doing several songs, and when Nelson Rockefeller and Bobby Kennedy got through 'kissing her ass' I felt so sorry for Mahalia that before I left Washington, I sent her a tube of Nupercainal."[64]

Colonel May also told Roebuck that he thought "Nevins, Schwengel, and Company" were "thoroughly disgusted . . . because the Negro[e]s did just what we predicted—attempted to take over the celebration." He was correct. In their private correspondence CWCC officials revealed their hostility toward rising black assertiveness, derisively referring to Bishop Williams as "De Law'd" and "Holy Daddy" and denigrating both the standard of Mahalia Jackson's per-formance and her allegedly exorbitant claim for expenses.[65] Their temper was not improved by criticism of the ceremony in the black press. The *Baltimore Afro-American,* for example, described it as "a sordid example of white su-premacist thinking," the CWCC having "thought it would be just dandy if colored Americans were restricted with the old plantation pattern of singing and dancing."[66] After all his hard work over the previous nine months, James

64. May to Roebuck, Sept. 24, 1962, folder on "South Carolina State Chairman [July 1960–Nov. 1962]," box 721, MCWBTSR. Some readers will recognize Nupercainal as a popular brand of hemorrhoidal ointment.

65. Gass to Nevins, Sept. 22, 1962, folder 2, box 76, Nevins Papers; Nevins to Gass, Sept. 30, 1962, and Robertson to Nevins, Sept. 25, 1962, folder on "Nevins, Allan—Oct. 13, 1961," box 134, CWCCR. As noted, Kennedy aide Arthur Schlesinger was more charitable in his assessment of Mahalia's Jackson's performance. She and her associates, he commented, "rendered valuable ser-vices to the Commission and the Nation." Schlesinger to Gass, Oct. 1, 1962, folder on "Emancipa-tion Proclamation 9/6/62—10/18/62," box WH9, Schlesinger Papers.

66. *Baltimore Afro-American,* Sept. 29, 1962, 5.

Robertson was moved to describe the whole event as "in many respects . . . a disgusting spectacle."[67]

The September 22 ceremony was not the only federal commemoration of emancipation in the early 1960s. During the spring the CWCC's heavy dependence on the southern commissions had actually resulted in a conscious policy decision to delegate commemoration of the centenary of the full proclamation (January 1, 1963) to the U.S. Civil Rights Commission.[68] Set up in 1957 to collect data and make policy recommendations, the commission lacked the requisite statutory power and funding to make a decisive breakthrough in the civil rights sphere. However, its very existence appeared to signal the U.S. government's determination to enforce existing constitutional rights after World War II. In May 1962 John F. Kennedy asked John A. Hannah, the president of Michigan State University and head of the commission, to produce a detailed report on civil rights in America provisionally entitled "One Hundred Years of Progress." Designed to coincide with the forthcoming centenary of emancipation, the report should, in Kennedy's words, "prove an important contribution to a national and international understanding of the progress we have made, the factors which have made this possible, and the road we still have to travel." The federal government, he added, had "a grave responsibility to bring home to the nation the full meaning of the Emancipation Proclamation," and the Civil Rights Commission should take "a leading role" in

67. Robertson to May, Sept. 25, 1962, box 11, reading file 1958–66, CWCCR. "One point so many people miss with the Centennial," recalls Robertson, "is who was foot-dragging. We at CWCC did everything we could to get the civil rights and Centennial movements together at least in part. Yet black leaders made it painfully evident that they wanted nothing whatsoever to do with the Centennial. They did not like the intent, they were scornful of Abraham Lincoln, and they viewed Centennial activities as a threat to their own programs." Black hostility to Adlai Stevenson at the time of the emancipation ceremony, he asserts, was caused by the paucity of African Americans on the ambassador's staff. Robertson to the author, Dec. 1, 2005.

68. This decision originated at a March 1962 conference between Robertson, Harris Wofford, Roy Davenport, and a second African American, Undersecretary of State Carl Rowan. Having explained the resistance of the southern commissions to an emancipation commemoration, Robertson was pleased to report, "They all recognize our problem, and the danger, of our participating in such a function. All have absolved us of any active role in the planning or staging of these ceremonies." Robertson to Nevins, March 21, 1962, folder on "Nevins, Allan—October 13, 1961," box 134, subject files 1957–66, CWCCR. Primary responsibility for emancipation planning was thus hived off to the U.S. Civil Rights Commission. See Schlesinger to JFK, memorandum ("Emancipation Proclamation Commemoration Problems"), Aug. 30, 1962, folder on "Emancipation Proclamation 1/1/62—8/31/62," box WH9, Schlesinger Papers.

promoting this objective.[69] The prominent black historian John Hope Franklin was engaged to write the report—another sign of the administration's escalating commitment to attaining equal rights for African Americans. Or so it seemed.

President Kennedy's reference to the promotion of "a national and international understanding of the progress" made by the United States in the field of civil rights betokened something other than an unalloyed moral commitment to racial justice on the part of the administration. Aware of their leader's determination to show a progressive face to the outside world at a time of intense competition between the superpowers, Kennedy aides fully understood the import of segregation and racism to Soviet propaganda and the concurrent need to prove America's vaunted commitment to freedom. In the spring of 1962 Herbert Mitgang of the *New York Times* wrote to the White House suggesting that if a team of Lincoln scholars could be sent to Asia, Africa, and South America in September they "could tell the world about the new America in connection with the hundredth anniversary of the Emancipation Proclamation." Arthur Schlesinger quickly transmitted this idea to Edward R. Murrow, the director of the United States Information Agency (USIA), adding that even if it were not taken up he hoped "we have some plan for the systematic exploitation abroad of the Emancipation Proclamation Centennial."[70] Murrow's response was favorable. "In regard to the general exploitation of the centennial of the Emancipation Proclamation," he replied, "I have cranked it into our planning operation which will develop the appropriate guidance and programming in cooperation with the other elements of the Agency."[71] The foreign policy considerations evident in this exchange dominated the thinking of all those federal employees engaged in planning emancipation-related events in 1962–63. Allan Nevins was open about his motives, describing the September 22 commemoration as one that could "be used most effectively by the USIA, and which will stand as an adequate interpretation of the national and international significance of the Emancipation Proclamation."[72]

69. JFK to John A. Hannah, May 23, 1962, folder on "Emancipation Proclamation Centennial Planning Committee Materials 1961–1963, Part 4," box 5, U.S. Commission on Civil Rights 1958–63, Berl I. Bernhard Papers, JFK Library.

70. Schlesinger to Edward R. Murrow, May 16, 1962, folder on "Emancipation Proclamation 1/1/62–8/31/62," box WH9, Schlesinger Papers.

71. Murrow to Schlesinger, May 21, 1962, folder on "Emancipation Proclamation 1/1/62–8/31/62," box WH9, Schlesinger Papers.

72. Nevins to Schlesinger, Sept. 5, 1962, folder on "White House 1961, 1962, 1963," box 105, subject files 1957–66, CWCCR.

The bureau certainly made the best of the opportunities presented by the centenary of abolition. It subsequently distributed information packs on the CWCC ceremony to foreign media outlets and ensured that USIA libraries abroad were equipped with books and lectures about the Civil War and black emancipation.[73]

Most African Americans, of course, regarded the hundredth anniversary of the Emancipation Proclamation not primarily as a chance to score points in the propaganda war against the Soviet Union but as a means of underlining the urgent need to terminate a great moral wrong at home. The tension between these two rather different (though not unconnected) agendas was apparent not only in the angry response of African Americans to the white-dominated ceremony at the Lincoln Memorial but also in an unsavory spat arising out of John Hope Franklin's draft report for the Civil Rights Commission. Instead of heralding the progress made by blacks and other minority groups in the United States (especially since World War II), Franklin chose to write something more akin to a jeremiad detailing the historic impact of American racism on nonwhites in no uncertain terms. Charged with overseeing production of a text that was to have both external and internal functions, the commissioners and their staff were appalled. Allan Nevins was one of the strongest critics. In spite of his avowed sympathy for civil rights, Nevins claimed that Franklin was culpable of using "partisan" and "inflamed" terminology, had glossed over the failure of "the Negro governments" during Reconstruction, ignored "the temporary inferiority of the Negro" in the late nineteenth century, and confused general racism with civil rights abuse. "Your text," he told Franklin, "is a little too much a history of general outrages, violence, terrorism and prejudice; too often we are not given a specific violation of recognized civil rights." As befitted an employee of the federal government, as well as the co-author of a popular consensus-era textbook entitled *America: The Story of a Free People,* Nevins was keen to point out that "you should not treat as illegal in 1880 what had become plainly illegal by 1960. To do this would be to falsify your history, and to make the picture appear darker than it actually was."[74] Rev. Theodore Hesburgh, the president of Notre Dame University and

73. USIS Feature F-62-383 and "USIA Activities in Connection with the Civil War Centennial" in folder on "Publications," box 28, subject files 1957–66, CWCCR.

74. Allan Nevins and Henry Steele Commager, *America: The Story of a Free People* (Boston: Little, Brown, 1942). Nevins's report on Franklin's draft is enclosed in Nevins to Berl I. Bernhard, Sept. 9, 1962, folder on "Emancipation Proclamation Centennial Planning Committee Materials, Part 2," box 5, U.S. Commission on Civil Rights 1958–63, Bernhard Papers.

a prominent member of the Civil Rights Commission, concurred. Franklin's text, he wrote, was "entirely too negative."[75]

Although John Hope Franklin may have misunderstood his brief (or at least underestimated the relevance of the report to the political needs of the Kennedy administration), he bridled at the suggestion from the commission's White House staff director, Berl I. Bernhard, that his manuscript "would not inspire further progress because it reflects a lack of National concern and infinitesimal progress." His counter-assertion of September 24, 1962, exposed the gap between black and liberal white perceptions of the race question. "As I told you in December and on several subsequent occasions," he wrote to Bernhard, "The history of the Negro and civil rights in the United States is not a 'pretty picture.' I would have thought that in a country like ours, with its great vigor and its determination to do what is right, a knowledge of the facts would inspire it to correct its injustices and make further progress . . . Where conditions have improved and where situations have been corrected, I have not only described them, but I have shown how and why the improvements have been made. If I were to go beyond that and transform the report into a platform, I would be writing a tract and not a history."[76]

Of course, the Civil Rights Commission was looking for precisely what Franklin was reluctant to deliver: an upbeat document that would in part sanction the existing civil rights policy of the Kennedy administration. While it did prepare a more politically useful report with the help of a team working under Charles Wesley at Central State College in Ohio, the agency's efforts to mark the centenary of the Emancipation Proclamation delivered few concrete achievements.[77] Notwithstanding innovative suggestions such as the construc-

75. Theodore Hesburgh to Bernhard, Sept. 4, 1962, folder on "Emancipation Proclamation Centennial Planning Committee Materials 1961–1963, Part 3," box 5, U.S. Commission on Civil Rights 1958–63, Bernhard Papers.

76. Franklin to Bernhard, Sept. 24, 1962, folder on "Emancipation Proclamation Centennial Planning Committee Materials 1961–1963, Part 2," box 5, U.S. Commission on Civil Rights 1958–63, Bernhard Papers.

77. Although the final report admitted the persistent gap between "aspirations and actual practices," it also noted "the tremendous strides" made in civil rights since 1863: "In the decades since the Second World War the pace of progress has accelerated until today, for all the contradictions, all the transitional dislocations, all the temporary setbacks and stalemates, governments at all levels as well as private associations and individuals are pressing determinedly and successfully toward the goal of equality before the law and equal opportunity for all." U.S. Commission on Civil Rights, *Freedom to the Free: Century of Emancipation, 1863–1963—A Report to the President by the United States Commission on Civil Rights* (Washington, DC: Government Printing Office, 1963), 2, 3.

tion of a national museum of African-American history, the cash-strapped commission had to settle for more mundane accomplishments, notably the issuing of a commemorative stamp, an emancipation exhibit at the National Archives, and a special proclamation from John F. Kennedy released on December 28, 1962.[78] Noting that slavery was an "iniquitous institution" and that the securing of equal rights "is one of the great unfinished tasks of our democracy," the president proclaimed that the Emancipation Proclamation expressed "our Nation's policy, founded on justice and morality" and called upon his fellow Americans to cooperate with government in commemorating the centennial.[79] These were more fine words, but they fell short of the decisive action against segregation and injustice for which civil rights leaders were calling.

African American attempts to mark the proclamation themselves were even more stymied by an absence of money than those of the Civil Rights Commission. ANECA's plans for a grand centennial exhibition to display the race's progress over the previous one hundred years was the most ambitious black-run project. However, in spite of the support of well-known African Americans such as Jackie Robinson and Joe Louis, it stood little chance of reaching its target budget of $6.3 million without substantial financial backing from whites. Although black political clout in the Chicago area helped secure a grant of $150,000 from the state of Illinois, organizers regarded this as a mere step in the right direction and sought additional funds from the New York Civil War Centennial Commission.[80]

On the face of things ANECA might have expected to gain a serious hearing from this source. Black voters were a significant factor in New York politics, and the state's liberal Republican governor, Nelson Rockefeller, was a visible supporter of Martin Luther King in particular and the civil rights movement in general. The local centennial commission headed by Bruce Catton had been reasonably forthright in its condemnation of the CWCC during the Charleston crisis and began serious preparations to commemorate the

78. Cornelius Cotter to Bernhard, memorandum, Sept. 27, 1962, folder on "Emancipation Proclamation Centennial Planning Committee Materials 1961–1963, Part 3," box 5, U.S. Commission on Civil Rights, 1958–63, Bernhard Papers; Bernhard to White, memorandum, Jan. 10, 1963, folder on "Emancipation Proclamation Planning Committee Materials 1961–1963, Part 1," box 5, U.S. Commission on Civil Rights, Bernhard Papers.

79. JFK, Proclamation 3511: Emancipation Proclamation Centennial, Dec. 28, 1962, *Public Papers of the Presidents: John F. Kennedy, 1962* (Washington, DC: Government Printing Office, 1963), 910.

80. Thomas E. Mulligan Jr. to Paul B. Hanks Jr., Oct. 25, 1961, box 2, office files 1961–64, A1444-78, NYCWCCR.

Emancipation Proclamation during the summer of 1961. It was guaranteed a leading role in forthcoming observances by the fact that the state owned an original copy of Lincoln's preliminary edict. This fortunate accident resulted in a decision to make the document the centerpiece of a permanent emancipation shrine in the state education building in Albany. Governor Rockefeller, moreover, seemed delighted to bask in his role as the guardian of the Emancipation Proclamation, overseeing its appearance, for example, at the CWCC ceremony in September 1962. Unhappily for ANECA, rhetorical and practical aid for commemorative activities on the part of white liberals in New York did not necessarily translate into financial backing for its exhibition.

In the fall of 1961 William Rowe, a leading member of ANECA's New York affiliate, approached the state government for financial assistance.[81] Invited to comment, Thomas ("Ed") Mulligan, chairman of the Catton commission, replied that his own agency had emancipation matters in hand and that enterprises such as the projected shrine would cost much less than any ANECA project. As far as he was concerned the scheme was "a promotion—pure and simple—to hold up New Yorkers with the threat that if they don't support the program they are discriminating."[82] In a formal reply to "Billy" Rowe early in the year, Mulligan declined the opportunity to advance funds, insisting that the New York legislature could not be expected to provide money for activities that duplicated those of his commission.[83]

While the widespread concerns about the financial viability of ANECA may have been justified, one can surely empathize to some extent with the exhibition's planners.[84] Given the limited nature of funding available within the black community, their ambitious scheme was bound to rest on shaky financial ground without governmental support. As was revealed also by the CWCC's efforts to marginalize African Americans at the Lincoln Memorial and the Civil Rights Commission's treatment of Franklin's report on Negro progress, avowedly progressive whites were reluctant to surrender control of the nation's history to their black wards. ANECA's weeklong Negro Progress Exposition did open at McCormick Place in Chicago on August 16, 1963. It was a relatively conservative affair featuring exhibits on emancipation and contemporary black

81. William L. Rowe to Ogden Reid, Oct. 4, 1961, microfilm, reel 24, 136282-78, Nelson A. Rockefeller Papers, New York State Archives.

82. Mulligan to Hanks, Oct. 25, 1961, box 2, office files 1961–64, A1444-78, NYCWCCR.

83. Mulligan to Rowe, Jan. 26, 1962, box 2, office files A1444-78, NYCWCCR.

84. John Hope Franklin was one of several blacks concerned about ANECA's finances. See also Isabelle Savell to Chuck Palmer, Oct. 26, 1961, box 2, office files A1444-78, NYCWCCR.

life as well as a beauty contest and music by Duke Ellington.[85] While it testified to the growing political and financial clout of the North's black middle class, the exposition was completely overshadowed by one of the great set-piece events of the southern civil rights movement: the March on Washington.

FREE AT LAST: MARTIN LUTHER KING AND CIVIL WAR MEMORY

As white liberals struggled to retain their authority over historical memory, the black-led civil rights movement proceeded to undermine their efforts by making history in the present. A profoundly patriotic movement, it sought not social revolution but moral reformation: to make Americans live up to their fine ideals. For African Americans the real prize was not some showy national commemoration of the Emancipation Proclamation but the more fundamental goal of racial equality. However, because the movement was attempting to expose the gap between words and deeds, the advent of the Civil War centennial furnished mainstream black leaders and organizations with an opportunity to exert leverage on national politics. As Frederick Douglass had understood, the Civil War could be regarded convincingly—in racial terms—as a genuinely inclusive historical moment, a time when blacks and whites had, for disparate motives, combined to fight the nation's secessionist enemies and when the principle of equal rights had been enshrined in the U.S. Constitution. Although the NAACP adopted the slogan "free by '63" to highlight the contemporary political significance of the emancipation centennial, it was Douglass's integrationist heir, Martin Luther King, who most effectively deployed historical memory as a weapon in the fight for equal rights.

The son of a relatively well-to-do black minister in Atlanta's Sweet Auburn district, King developed a profound awareness of the African-American counter-memory from an early age. As a teenager he delivered a prize-winning oration on "The Negro Constitution" at a high-school contest sponsored by the black Elks. In it he observed that "after tumult and war, the nation in 1865 took a new stand—freedom for all people. The new order was backed by amendments to the national constitution making it the fundamental law that thenceforth there should be no discrimination anywhere in the 'land of the free' on account of race, color or previous condition of servitude." Even though, he wrote, "Black America still wears chains," the struggle for enforcement of the Civil War amendments continued: "We believe . . . that we may conquer southern armies by the sword, but it is another thing to conquer

85. *Chicago Defender,* Aug. 17–23, 1963, 1, 2; Aug. 24–30, 1963, 6.

southern hate, that if the franchise is given to Negroes, they will be vigilant and defend even with their arms, the ark of federal liberty from treason and destruction by her enemies." He concluded with an optimistic flourish: "The spirit of Lincoln still lives."[86]

Perhaps Martin Luther King's signal contribution to the civil rights movement was, as Richard Lischer has intimated, his concerted effort to elevate interminable local battles against segregation into "holy crusades of mythic proportions."[87] He succeeded to a remarkable degree, largely by highlighting America's dismal performance as a covenanted nation. Here, the historical themes that he had enunciated in his youthful oration were of enormous utility, for they furnished rich "evidence" of the extent to which the nation had departed from its original goals (as those goals had been reaffirmed in the 1860s). Abraham Lincoln, the Great Emancipator, remained a critical ally. Seeking to encourage, cajole, and shame the White House into providing decisive assistance for the black freedom struggle, King drew on a suggestion emanating from the U.S. Civil Rights Commission to urge President Kennedy to emulate Lincoln by issuing his own emancipation edict—in this instance, to end segregation.[88] In October 1961 he spoke to Kennedy on the subject in the Lincoln Room of the White House. The president responded cautiously but indicated his willingness to consider "a written explanation of the 'Second Emancipation' proposal."[89] On May 17, 1962, an SCLC representative duly submitted to the president an "Appeal . . . for a National Rededication to the Principles of the Emancipation Proclamation and for an Executive Order Prohibiting Segregation in the United States of America."[90]

King's "Appeal" played adeptly on President Kennedy's concern for his place in history. It also highlighted the relevance of the Civil War centennial to the contemporary freedom struggle. "Mr. President," the document began sonorously, "sometimes there occur moments in the history of a nation when it becomes necessary to pause and reflect upon the heritage of the past in or-

86. Martin Luther King Jr., "The Negro and the Constitution," [May 1944], in *The Papers of Martin Luther King, Jr., Volume 1: Called to Serve, January 1929–June 1951*, ed. Clayborne Carson (Berkeley: University of California Press, 1992), 110–11.

87. Richard Lischer, *The Preacher King: Martin Luther King, Jr. and the Word that Moved America* (Oxford: Oxford University Press, 1995), 121.

88. David J. Garrow, *Bearing the Cross: Martin Luther King Jr. and the Southern Christian Leadership Conference* (1986; London: Jonathan Cape, 1988), 161.

89. Ibid., 169–70.

90. Ibid., 199.

der to determine the most meaningful course for the present and the future." The centenary of the Emancipation Proclamation, it claimed, was "a peculiarly appropriate time" for Americans to rededicate themselves to the founding principle of equality before the law. King went on to set the proclamation in historical context. With the help of Bruce Catton's writing, he reminded Kennedy how, after "Robert E. Lee's grey-clad Army of Northern Virginia" had been repulsed at the Battle of Antietam, President Lincoln had issued his edict bringing slavery to an end. King then proceeded to connect explicitly the past with the present: "The struggle for freedom, Mr. President, of which the Civil War was but a bloody chapter, continues throughout our land today. The courage and heroism of Negro citizens at Montgomery, Little Rock, New Orleans, Prince Edward County, and Jackson, Mississippi is only a further effort to affirm that democratic heritage so painfully won, in part, upon the grassy battlefields of Antietam, Lookout Mountain, and Gettysburg." Here then was "a unique opportunity" for Kennedy, "to initiate a dramatic and historic step forward in the area of race relations."[91]

Wary of alienating southern Democrats ahead of the 1962 congressional elections, the president ignored the attached calls for executive action against discrimination even in the limited sphere of public housing. However, the "Appeal" did not curtail Martin Luther King's efforts to use history as a weapon of protest. Indeed, outwitted personally by segregationists in Albany, Georgia, and frustrated generally by continuing evidence of massive resistance in the Deep South, he became increasingly convinced that federal intervention constituted the only effective means of destroying Jim Crow. Although the decisive breakthrough did not come until the SCLC's direct-action campaign in Birmingham in the spring of 1963, King's attempts to secure federal aid continued to encompass a range of rhetorical strategies. In this respect the African-American memory of the government's suppression of southern rebellion proved to be extremely useful.

On September 12, 1962, the nation's foremost civil rights leader attended a special dinner hosted by New York's Civil War Centennial Commission to commemorate the signing of the preliminary Emancipation Proclamation.

91. Martin Luther King Jr., "An Appeal to the Honorable John F. Kennedy[,] President of the United States[,] for a National Rededication to the Principles of the Emancipation Proclamation and for an Executive Order Prohibiting Segregation in the United States of America," May 17, 1962, folder on "Emancipation Proclamation Centennial Appeal to President Kennedy re: Civil Rights, May 17, 1962," box 5, U.S. Commission on Civil Rights, 1958–1963, Bernhard Papers.

The guests at the Park Sheraton Hotel in Manhattan feasted on breast of capon, vegetables, salad, and ice cream and then attended to remarks delivered by, among others, Bruce Catton, Martin Luther King, and Governor Nelson Rockefeller.[92] Speaking on the verge of a serious desegregation crisis in Oxford, Mississippi, King sought to further his cause with a carefully honed statement that mixed sectionalism and ridicule in equal measure. Recent events, he asserted, showed that the discredited Confederacy still retained "a veto power over the majority of the nation." The South, he added, pouring scorn on the administration's failure to confront segregation, was "an autonomous region whose posture toward the central government has elements as defiant as a hostile nation. Only the undeveloped or primitive nations of the world tolerate regions which are similar, in which feudal autocrats or military governors hold sway over the federal power. It is a condition unknown to modern industrial societies except our own." In a barbed comment that might have been regarded as a supplement to his recent "Appeal," King added that only great presidents were genuinely tortured by racial issues. "No president," he insisted, "can be great or even fit for office, if he attempts to accommodate injustice to maintain his political balance."[93] The next day, as if to underline the contemporary validity of Civil War allusions, Governor Ross Barnett of Mississippi appeared on television to denounce federal attempts to integrate the state university. Shortly afterward the president and his attorney general, Robert F. Kennedy, were forced to dispatch U.S. troops to Oxford in order to protect James Meredith from baying segregationists.

If this incident suggested that decisive government intervention on the side of the civil rights movement was triggered largely by the violent actions of segregationists rather than the oratory of black leaders like Martin Luther King, it would be wrong to discount the growing influence of the black counter-memory during the early 1960s. By the time of the Ole Miss crisis, President Kennedy had begun to doubt whether his understanding of the Civil War period was accurate. He started reading the books of C. Vann Woodward to acquaint himself with the latest scholarship. In the wake of the disorder in Birmingham and elsewhere during the spring and summer of 1963, he told Arthur Schlesinger that he no longer understood white southerners. "I'm

92. Emancipation Proclamation dinner, menu and program, Sept. 12, 1962, box 2, office files, 1961–64, A1444-78, NYCWCCR.

93. Martin Luther King Jr., Address to the New York Civil War Centennial Commission, Sept. 12, 1962, box 3, series 3, Martin Luther King Jr. Papers, Martin Luther King Jr. Center for Nonviolent Social Change.

coming to believe," he said, "that Thaddeus Stevens was right. I had always been taught to regard him as a man of vicious bias. But, when I see this sort of thing, I begin to wonder how else you can treat them."[94]

The Kennedys were less eager than King to adopt a sectional tone in their speeches, but the civil rights leader's historically informed analysis was a compelling one. They recognized that the racially exclusive consensus of the 1950s was breaking down rapidly and that careful allusions to the Civil War could help to promote and legitimize the kind of racial change necessary to preserve domestic peace and take the sting out of communist propaganda. Thus references to the unfinished work of emancipation peppered their speeches in late 1962 and 1963. Attorney General Robert Kennedy, for example, told an audience at the opening of a centennial exhibit at the National Archives on January 4, 1963, that "no single deed has done more than Lincoln's signing of the Emancipation Proclamation to redeem the pledge upon which this republic was founded—the pledge that all men are created equal, are endowed equally with unalienable rights and are entitled equally to life, liberty and the pursuit of happiness." There was, he asserted, an urgent connection between the lifting "from all our citizens [of] the degrading burdens of intolerance, bigotry and discrimination" and the successful promulgation of democratic ideas abroad: "Other countries have discrimination, intolerance and bigotry, too. But because we are a free society—open for all the world to see—and because we ourselves were born of revolution, people of these lands look to us to see whether we can eradicate these plagues."[95] Eight weeks later the president described the Emancipation Proclamation in his civil rights address to Congress as "only a first step—a step which its author unhappily did not live to follow up, a step which some of its critics dismissed as an action which 'frees the slave but ignores the Negro.'"[96] Admittedly, as black leaders like King were quick to point out, these were words, not deeds. (Even the president's civil rights speech retained the administration's familiar emphasis on voluntarism and gradualism.) Yet, they were not *empty* words. The Kennedys genuinely wanted an end to flagrant racial injustice in America, if only because that injustice

94. JFK, quoted in Hugh Brogan, *Kennedy* (London: Addison Wesley Longman, 1996), 167.

95. Robert F. Kennedy, Remarks at the Opening of Exhibit on the Emancipation Proclamation, Washington, DC, Jan. 4, 1963, folder on "Emancipation Proclamation Centennial Planning Committee Materials 1961–1963, part 1," box 5, U.S. Commission on Civil Rights 1958–63, Bernhard Papers.

96. JFK, Special Message to the Congress on Civil Rights, Feb. 28, 1963, *Public Papers of the President: John F. Kennedy, 1963* (Washington, DC: Government Printing Office, 1964), 222.

undermined America's global influence and disturbed domestic peace. In all likelihood, many of their anxious listeners (including some southern whites) were persuaded by these powerful resorts to history and thereby rendered more receptive to the comprehensive civil rights legislation subsequently induced by the movement.

That 1963 had been billed by civil rights groups like the NAACP as the year of full emancipation continued to inform the rhetoric of Martin Luther King, even in the wake of his success in Birmingham. At the start of the most famous performance of his life, his "I Have a Dream" speech delivered to a rapt interracial throng at the Lincoln Memorial on August 28, he anchored his predominantly linear address on the rock of America's Civil War past. Merging his voice with that of the Great Emancipator before whose marble form he stood, he echoed the opening words of the Gettysburg Address, imparting at once deep historical legitimacy to his message: "Fivescore years ago, a great American, in whose symbolic shadow we stand today, signed the Emancipation Proclamation. This momentous decree came as a great beacon light of hope to millions of Negro slaves who had been seared in the flames of withering injustice. It came as a joyous daybreak to end the long night of captivity."

King, however, immediately revealed that he had come to Washington not primarily to laud the Emancipation Proclamation but to criticize America for not fulfilling the promise of that hallowed edict. In a masterful passage steeped in repetition and rhythmic predicates, he used the advent of the centennial to illustrate the abysmal lack of progress on civil rights since 1863: "But one hundred years later, the Negro still is not free; one hundred years later, the life of the Negro is still sadly crippled by the manacles of segregation and the chains of discrimination; one hundred years later, the Negro lives on a lonely island of poverty in the midst of a vast ocean of material prosperity; one hundred years later, the Negro is still languished in the corners of American society and finds himself in exile in his own land." At this point King looked further back in time, drawing on "the magnificent words" of the Constitution and the Declaration of Independence for his celebrated metaphor of the "bad check," an unpaid promissory note whose funds blacks were ready to collect. From the past King moved seamlessly to the present, calling on his followers "to remind America of the fierce urgency of now." And then, departing dramatically from his prepared text, he spelled out his compelling dream of the future, the development of the beloved Christian community "deeply rooted in the American dream that one day this nation will rise up and live out the true meaning of its creed—we hold these truths to be self-evident, that all men are created equal." For his rousing finale he collapsed past, present, and future by envisioning the millennial moment "when all of God's children—black men and white men, Jews and Gentiles, Catholics and Protestants—will be able to join hands and to sing in the words of the old Negro spiritual, 'Free at last, free at last; thank God Almighty, we are free at last.'"[97]

The March on Washington, of course, was not an official centennial event. However, King's acclaimed speech, which outshone anything uttered at the same venue the previous September, confirmed the inability of the various Civil War commissions to monopolize the memory of America's bloodiest conflict. Although most CWCC officials and government elites outside the agency worked to ensure that relatively little of the rich black counter-memory came to public view in the early 1960s, the determination of civil rights activists to contest the centennial revealed the war's continuing significance to African Americans as a politically charged totem of equal citizenship and federal power. During the early days of the 1960 Greensboro sit-ins, members of the college football team at all-black North Carolina A&T formed "a flying wedge" to protect demonstrators as they entered downtown stores to protest Jim Crow facilities. Carrying small American flags, they pushed confidently past jeering whites on the sidewalk. "Who do you think you are?" shouted the onlookers. "We the Union Army," retorted the footballers.[98] Three years later John Lewis, the chairman of the Student Nonviolent Coordinating Committee (SNCC), channeled his frustration at the government's failure to protect civil rights workers in the field into an angry speech preceding King's oration at the March on Washington. Even though he agreed to soften his address after last-minute criticism from movement insiders, a preedited draft of the speech was distributed among the crowd on the Mall. "We won't stop now," read Lewis's thundering peroration, "All of the forces of Eastland, Barnett, Wallace, and Thurmond won't stop this revolution. The time will come when we will not confine our marching to Washington. We will march through the South, through the Heart of Dixie, the way Sherman did. We shall pursue our own 'scorched earth' policy and burn Jim Crow to the ground—nonviolently. We shall fragment the South into a thousand pieces and put them back together

97. Martin Luther King Jr., "I Have a Dream," in *A Testament of Hope: The Essential Writings and Speeches of Martin Luther King Jr.,* ed. James M. Washington (San Francisco: HarperSanFrancisco, 1991), 217–20.

98. William H. Chafe, *Civilities and Civil Rights: Greensboro, North Carolina, and the Black Struggle for Freedom* (Oxford: Oxford University Press, 1980), 119.

in the image of democracy. We will make the action of the past few months look petty. And I say to you, WAKE UP AMERICA!"[99]

Here was proof, if proof were needed, that African Americans possessed a vital past that was at least a match for the white supremacist version trumpeted by segregationists and their allies inside and outside the centennial establishment.

99. John Lewis, "Original Text of Speech to be Delivered at the Lincoln Memorial," Aug. 28, 1963, in Clayborne Carson et al., eds., *The Eyes on the Prize Civil Rights Reader: Documents, Speeches, and Firsthand Accounts from the Black Freedom Struggle, 1954–1990* (New York: Penguin, 1991), 165. Lewis's controversial speech went through a number of drafts and received input from several civil rights activists. When SNCC members Courtland Cox and James Forman advised him to bolster his "revolution" motif with an analogy, Tom Kahn, a white Howard graduate, suggested a reference to Sherman's March to the Sea in 1864. The decision to conduct this gratuitous assault on Lost Cause sensibilities may have been understandable in the light of SNCC's daily encounters with violent segregationists, but it was deemed too outspoken for the March on Washington by A. Philip Randolph and other moderate black leaders at the Lincoln Memorial. In deference to Randolph, Lewis agreed to strike it out along with comments critical of the Kennedy administration. John Lewis with Michael D'Orso, *Walking with the Wind: A Memoir of the Movement* (San Diego: Harcourt Brace, 1999), 218–19, 225–27.

6

Winding Down

The Forgotten Centennial, 1962–1965

MOST AMERICANS LOST interest in commemorating their Civil War after the initial burst of enthusiasm in 1961. The CWCC's new leadership team was more attuned to contemporary political currents than its predecessor, but the agency's limited moves toward greater racial inclusiveness did nothing to reinvigorate the centennial. Commemorative events did not cease completely. Most major, and many minor, battles fought between 1862 and 1865 received some kind of formal recognition. Some were reenacted before thousands of paying spectators, notwithstanding the CWCC's hostility toward sham battles after the publicity disaster at Manassas. But as media interest in the once heavily touted heritage fest waned dramatically, most people were too preoccupied with the troubling present to get unduly excited about the nation's sanguinary past. In part the declining interest was a predictable consequence of the influence now exercised by the historians who headed the CWCC. Allan Nevins and James Robertson largely succeeded in their efforts to transform the centennial into a consensual scholarly exercise, which they, like the leading northern commissions, conceived as a more fitting and enduring tribute to the Blue and the Gray than the discredited, not to say ephemeral, bread-and-circuses policy associated with Karl Betts.[1] While this strategic shift made for a duller commemoration of the Civil War (suggesting that a popular yet dignified observance of that conflict was not possible in the early 1960s), it may have served an unheralded political function by helping to divorce the centennial from the increasingly violent campaign that southern segregationists were waging against the civil rights movement. Because bitter-enders frequently used Confederate-style rhetoric and symbols to resist attacks on Jim

---

1. "Dr. Nevins and I," James I. Robertson Jr. recalls, "were more concerned [than Betts and Grant] with scholarly contributions that would live beyond the hoopla of the moment." Robertson to the author, Dec. 1, 2005.

Crow, one might have expected them to continue using the centennial, at least selectively, as a mobilizing tool, just as they had done in Montgomery and Jackson in the spring of 1961. This did not happen. By the time the last major centennial event was staged at Appomattox Court House in April 1965, the centennial had been largely forgotten. Given the extent of racial strife and sectional friction in the early 1960s, this was, perhaps, a cause for relief rather than regret.

SEGREGATION NOW, SEGREGATION FOREVER

Although a full-scale repeat of the Civil War was never a real possibility during the Kennedy years, Adam Fairclough rightly contends that it is by no means inconceivable that the South could have become a Northern Ireland–style morass during this period.[2] Some southern politicians did nothing to hinder the growth of conditions in which resentment and violence could breed, adhering to the view that they could best serve themselves and their embattled section by posing as defenders of the Lost Cause. This conviction had a long (if far from respectable) pedigree in the Deep South. Scapegoating the federal government for the social ills of the present and the injustices of the emotion-laden past often played well in the region, no more so than after the *Brown* decision. One of the foremost exponents of Confederate theater was Governor Ross Barnett of Mississippi, a rabble-rousing segregationist who proved to be a persistent thorn in the side of the Kennedy administration. As his participation in Jackson's secession-day parade revealed, Barnett understood that the centennial could be put to good political use at home. On November 3, 1961, he welcomed members of the Confederate States Civil War Centennial Conference to a meeting in downtown Jackson. Cognizant that his audience shared his views on states' rights and racial equality, the governor underscored his belief that the centennial constituted an ideal opportunity not only to stress the resourcefulness, steadfastness, and courage of Civil War–era southerners but also to "focus a respectful attention upon the progress of the Southern States of the present." After joking that everyone except "freedom riders" was warmly invited to come south for commemorative events, he came to the crux of his remarks. "Among the cherished traditions which Southern men and women have always supported," said Barnett, "is local control of local affairs. Our forefathers knew and Southerners today know that no matter how wise and well meaning the National Government might be it can not administer

2. Adam Fairclough, *Better Day Coming: Blacks and Equality, 1890–2000* (New York: Viking Penguin, 2001), 264.

local and State affairs as wisely as those Americans on the scene, living with the problems." The delegates, he concluded, would surely concur "that the fate of this nation may well depend on the determination and the fortitude with which Southern men and women resist this trend toward centralization."[3]

While there was more froth than substance to the centennial antics of many white southern politicians in the early 1960s, "memories" of the Lost Cause continued to bolster Jim Crow in the face of the growing threat posed by the civil rights movement, the Justice Department, and some federal judges. Barnett himself was deadly earnest in his belief that the region's past could be used to rally popular opposition to what he regarded as federally sponsored race-mixing. The dangers of his quasi-Confederate posturing and the potential for linkage between centennial observances and white supremacist violence became evident during fierce rioting that occurred on the campus of the University of Mississippi in late September 1962. Determined to be seen to resist federal efforts to secure James Meredith's entry into Ole Miss, Governor Barnett ordered public officials to execute state segregation laws even at the risk of incarceration by U.S. authorities. The action immediately prompted Governor John Patterson of Alabama to counsel the White House against dispatching troops. "We stand united in this fight," warned Patterson, "and will continue to resist all unlawful encroachments by the federal government."[4] Although the Alabaman's warning was undermined rapidly by southern governors' failure to concert action in defense of Mississippi, it was pointed enough to underline the close connections that many southerners perceived between past and present struggles.

Throughout the night of September 30, 1962, and for most of the following day, angry whites, stirred by Barnett's defiance and their own revulsion at forced integration, wreaked havoc on the university campus at Oxford while federal marshals (eventually reinforced by regular army troops) endeavored to protect Meredith and restore a semblance of order. The journalist Fred Powledge watched as a retired army general, Edwin A. Walker, tried to rally the mob by clambering onto a Confederate war memorial and shouting

3. Ross R. Barnett, speech to Confederate States Civil War Centennial Conference, Nov. 3, 1961, folder on "Confederate States Centennial Conference (11 States)," box 107, subject files 1957–66, Records of the Civil War Centennial Commission, Records of the National Park Service, Record Group 79, National Archives (hereafter CWCCR).

4. *Montgomery Advertiser,* Sept. 28, 1962, A1. For a full account of the dramatic events at Ole Miss, see Taylor Branch, *Parting the Waters: America in the King Years, 1954–63* (New York: Simon and Schuster, 1988), 662–72.

encouragement. Powledge, who received a beating himself, saw segregation-ists wave a Confederate battle flag as they met oncoming troops with jeers of "Yankee go home" and "Why don't you go to Cuba?"[5] By the time the riot-ing had been quelled, two people were dead and 160 U.S. marshals had been injured.

In Jackson white residents had been similarly outraged by the efforts of the federal authorities to secure Meredith's admission to Ole Miss. On the day before the campus riot, demonstrators thronged the streets of the capital to display their solidarity with the governor. Many held aloft Confederate ban-ners or sported Confederate uniforms. Those dressed as Rebels were mem-bers of Mississippi Grey units activated as a promotional move by the state's centennial commission. They had purchased their specially manufactured cotton tunics, hats, and trousers at a cost of $21.50 during the previous year's observances of secession. Official figures indicated that there were over 3,200 members of Mississippi's centennial militia by 1962. Apparently some of these men considered themselves as ready to defend the white South against federal assault as their forebears had been a century ago.[6]

Segregationists were genuinely appalled by President Kennedy's reluctant decision to send troops into a southern city to enforce a federal court man-date. Sidney T. Roebuck, the Barnett loyalist who headed Mississippi's centen-nial agency, interviewed a white youth claiming to have personal evidence of federal brutality at Ole Miss. He immediately dispatched this news to another of the state's leading segregationists, James O. Eastland, who chaired the U.S. Senate Judiciary Committee. The wealthy plantation owner assured Roebuck that his committee would investigate thoroughly the "outrageous" happenings at Oxford. Sharing Roebuck's "concern and indignation over these events," he promised "to try to see that the truth is known."[7]

Much as Jefferson Davis abetted the cause of emancipation by heading an unsuccessful proslavery rebellion against the United States, Ross Barnett's rash

5. *Atlanta Journal*, Oct. 1, 1962, 1.

6. Mississippi Commission on the War Between the States, *Join the Mississippi Greys: A Guide for the Organization of Units of Mississippi's Centennial Military Force in Memoriam* (n.p., n.d.), folder on "Mississippi State Commission," box 117, subject files 1957–66, CWCCR; *Report of the Mississippi Commission on the War Between the States* (Jackson: University Press of Mississippi, 1962), 10.

7. Sidney T. Roebuck to James O. Eastland, Oct. 5, 1962, Eastland to Roebuck, Oct. 9, 1962, folder on "E–Misc. [Jan. 1961–June 1964 and undated items]," box 711, Records of the Mississippi Commission on the War Between the States, Record Group 19, Mississippi Department of Ar-chives and History (hereafter MCWBTSR).

attempt to prevent the integration of the state university actually did more to help the cause of civil rights than that of segregation. While national opinion was overwhelmingly supportive of the president, even moderate segregationists found Barnett's Lost Cause posturing counterproductive, embarrassing, and irresponsible in the context of the cold war and the South's pursuit of economic growth.[8] However, the events at Ole Miss highlighted once again the power of Confederate memory in the rearguard fight to save Jim Crow. Federal support for James Meredith did not deter other prominent southern segregationists from using the centennial as a platform to advance their political interests. George C. Wallace, John Patterson's successor as governor of Alabama, soon supplanted Barnett as America's most visible purveyor of neo-Confederate symbolism and rhetoric.

Wallace had a very clear idea about the central place occupied by the Civil War in both the history of the South and in the region's highly racialized politics of the early 1960s. His great-grandfather had been wounded fighting for the Confederacy at Lookout Mountain in 1863, and Wallace, in common with many members of his generation, treasured vivid boyhood memories of listening to the tall tales of Confederate veterans. From personal experience he understood the close correlation between the Lost Cause and Jim Crow. And, after his gubernatorial defeat in 1958 at the hands of the demagogic Patterson, he knew the power of white supremacist appeals to sway ordinary voters. Elected governor in late 1962 as a committed defender of the established order, he was inaugurated early the following year to the sound of Rebel yells. A Confederate band played marshal music at the ceremony, which also featured a gray-clad company of reenactors representing the celebrated Montgomery Rifles.[9] Wallace's notorious "segregation now, segregation forever" inaugural was delivered on the same spot at the state capitol where Jefferson Davis had accepted the provisional presidency of the proslavery republic in February 1861. One of his first acts as governor was to rename the Alabama Highway Patrol the "Alabama State Troopers" and to require the placement of a Confederate battle flag on the bumper of each patrol car. In the days leading up to his stage-managed resistance to court-ordered integration of the state university, he quoted Alabama's fire-eating secessionist William Lowndes Yancey and had the Rebel banner flown over the state capitol in order to intimidate

8. See, for example, *Washington Post*, Oct. 2, 1962, A12; *Birmingham News*, Oct. 1, 1962, 18.

9. Alabama Civil War Centennial Commission, minutes of the meeting held Dec. 7, 1962, folder 6, Administration Files, Alabama, Governor (1963–1967: Wallace), SG14027, Alabama Department of Archives and History (hereafter AlaG).

Attorney General Robert Kennedy, who traveled to Montgomery in a vain effort to defuse the crisis at Tuscaloosa. The governor also exhibited an interest in preserving the heritage of the Confederacy. In January 1965 he asked Albert B. Moore, the historian who headed Alabama's centennial agency, to investigate the possibility of securing state ownership of Yancey's run-down old home outside Montgomery with a view to restoring it.[10]

When Pennsylvania's Gettysburg centennial commission invited state governors to participate in observances to mark the hundredth anniversary of the nation's most famous battle, Moore urged Wallace to attend. The latter's presence might not only reenergize the centennial in Alabama but also present the charismatic and politically ambitious segregationist with valuable national media exposure. The governor was eager to go. Within weeks of his "stand at the schoolhouse door" in Tuscaloosa, George Wallace journeyed to Gettysburg, where the Pennsylvanians had planned a series of events to commemorate the three-day battle. On July 1 he placed a wreath on the monument to the Alabamans who had fallen on the field, remarking "that descendants of both sides of the Civil War will soon be united in a common fight to end the growing power of a central government." Later that day he joined eight of his fellow governors in a dignified ceremony at the Eternal Light Peace Memorial. Rebel yells could be heard as he stepped forward to lay his floral tribute to the Gettysburg dead. "This is a solemn occasion," he told watching newsmen. "We stand with the descendants of brave men who fought for the North and South, and we will stand for defense of the Constitution."[11] On July 2, flanked by two state troopers, he reviewed a two-hour parade through the town by over 6,000 men, women, and children clad in blue, gray, and the uniforms of modern military organizations.[12]

On one level Wallace's appearance at the Gettysburg commemoration struck a discordant note. It came at a historic moment in U.S. history, when the Kennedy administration, fearful of worsening racial conflict and emboldened by significant backing from the American public in the wake of blanket media coverage of the SCLC's Birmingham campaign, had finally announced its determination to strike down Jim Crow by introducing a comprehensive civil rights bill into Congress.[13] Wallace's public attack on the federal government

10. George C. Wallace to Albert B. Moore, Jan. 13, 1965, folder 8, SG22401, AlaG.
11. *Montgomery Advertiser*, July 2, 1963, 1–2.
12. *New York Times*, July 3, 1963, 28.
13. On the origins of the 1964 Civil Rights Act, see Adam Fairclough, *To Redeem the Soul of America: The Southern Christian Leadership Conference and Martin Luther King Jr.* (Athens: Uni-

(integral to his support for segregation) conflicted with the emancipationist interpretation of the Civil War that was becoming increasingly influential outside the South owing to the activities of the civil rights movement. Although African Americans did not play a prominent role in the events at Gettysburg, this civil rights interpretation received prominence in several speeches delivered at the battlefield, including that of Richard Hughes, the Democratic governor of New Jersey, who insisted that "[t]he Civil War was not fought to preserve the Union 'lily-white' or 'Jim Crow' . . . [I]t was fought for liberty and justice for all." [14] Wallace, of course, was contemptuous of northern liberals like Hughes. He had gone to Gettysburg in part to strengthen his southern base and to refute any complacent notions of a civil rights consensus. He made a point of mingling with Confederate reenactors who participated in a rerun of Pickett's charge on July 3 and two weeks later was testifying before the Senate Commerce Committee against the new civil rights bill.[15] However, the governor was no ordinary southern politician. More charismatic and politically savvy than Ross Barnett, whose defiance during the Ole Miss crisis had emphasized his narrow sectional appeal, Wallace harbored broader ambitions. As his tributes to the southern *and* northern dead at Gettysburg suggested, he was starting to re-brand himself as a credible national conservative—a rightwing southerner who could transcend his regional base by appealing to the inchoate racial and antistatist fears of many northern, as well as southern, whites.

---

versity of Georgia Press, 1987), 133–35; and Mark Stern, *Calculating Visions: Kennedy, Johnson, and Civil Rights* (New Brunswick, NJ: Rutgers University Press, 1992), 81–92.

14. Speech of Governor Richard Hughes, New Jersey Civil War Centennial Commission press release, folder on "Gettysburg Rededication, July 1, 1963," box 3, Records of the New Jersey Civil War Centennial Commission, New Jersey State Archives (hereafter NJCWCCR). Gettysburg speeches by Notre Dame president Rev. Theodore Hesburgh and Pennsylvania's Republican governor, William Scranton, also contained references to the unfinished struggle for civil rights. See *New York Times*, June 30, 1963, sec. 1, 39; July 2, 1963, 14.

15. For a transcript of Wallace's testimony, see Wallace, "Statement Before Senate Committee on Commerce re Senate Bill 1732," July 15, 1963, folder 18, SG22362, AlaG. Around 30,000 people watched the reenactment of Pickett's charge. Five hundred troops on each side participated in a sham battle given added authenticity by sound effects and smoke-machines. The Confederates halted below the summit of Cemetery Ridge where the final Rebel attack had petered out in 1863. The two groups then "lowered their arms, marched together to a spot behind the Bloody Angle, formed hollow squares, pledged allegiance to the national government, and raised the Stars and Stripes on a tall staff while a U.S. Navy band played the national anthem." *Charleston News and Courier*, July 4, 1963, B8.

Wallace's admirers in Alabama were ecstatic at the apparent success of his northern ventures. Albert Moore, writing after the trips to Gettysburg and Washington, expressed his pride in the governor's recent performances. "Many people over the country approve of your views as to the race issue and government in accordance with the Constitution," he commented. "All of them must realize that we have a man in our Governor's chair, one who has convictions and enough spunk to state them frankly anytime and anywhere." [16] For his part, Wallace was delighted by the almost adulatory reception he had received from many people at Gettysburg. "I don't know when I have ever enjoyed anything more," he told one correspondent. [17] His ability to reach out to nonsoutherners was demonstrated the following year when he entered the race for the Democratic presidential nomination. Performing surprisingly well, he won sizable shares of the vote in primary elections in Wisconsin, Indiana, and Maryland on a platform that fused none-too-subtle racism with appeals to old-time religion and his now familiar attacks on the dangers of centralized government. [18]

The centennial-related activities of leading segregationists like Barnett and Wallace underscored the live political significance of Civil War memory in the early 1960s. But while both men may have yearned to ground a successful counterattack against the forces of big government and civil rights in the glorious heritage of the Confederacy, history proved to be of limited utility in the struggle to preserve and, in Wallace's case, to nationalize southern values. Waning popular interest in the centennial, particularly in the South where enthusiasm had been most evident, testified to the relative bluntness of Lost Cause memory as a weapon of struggle, especially in the face of contemporary political and social change.

LOSING INTEREST

The speed with which white southerners in particular lost interest in the centennial requires an explanation, for had the region's centennial agencies so desired, they could have played a role in attempting to create the kind of paramilitary quasi-Confederate movement that Barnett and Wallace seemed

---

16. Moore to Wallace, July 19, 1963, folder 20, SG22362, AlaG.

17. Wallace to Mrs. Pat Bailey, July 15, 1963, folder 20, SG22362, AlaG.

18. On Wallace's 1964 campaign, see Dan T. Carter, *The Politics of Rage: George Wallace, the Origins of Conservatism, and the Transformation of American Politics* (New York: Simon and Schuster, 1995), 202–22.

eager to mobilize. They were creatures of segregationist regimes in the Deep South and were staffed by white supremacists like Sidney Roebuck and Albert Moore, committed allies of the administrations that employed them.

Southerners' interest in the Civil War, it should be emphasized, did not disappear entirely during the last three years of the centennial. The most active state agencies, such as those in Virginia, Mississippi, Alabama, and Tennessee, collaborated with the NPS and interested local groups (principally chambers of commerce, patriotic organizations such as the UDC and the SCV, and county historical societies) to sponsor a range of centennial events between 1962 and 1965. Even Georgia's lackluster commission managed to oversee a series of successful Chickamauga days, each devoted to a state possessing a monument on the battlefield that had provided the Confederacy with one of its few major victories in the second half of the Civil War.[19] Such efforts meant that many salient military events were marked in some significant formal way between early 1962 and the spring of 1965. Exceptions included Missionary Ridge—commemoration of which was abandoned in the immediate aftermath of President Kennedy's assassination in November 1963—and the sanguinary succession of exchanges that occurred between Lee and Grant in Virginia during the final year of the war. Confederate defeats, however, were not passed over automatically.[20] Reenactments were staged at many of the chief sites of Grant's and Sherman's decisive campaigns in Mississippi and Georgia respectively as well as at Franklin and Nashville, Tennessee.[21] Turnout at these events was modest but by no means derisory. As many as 12,000 people watched a

19. Stanley R. Smith to Moore, Feb. 6, 1963, folder on "Confederate States CWCCs: Alabama CWCC, 1960–64," box 1, RCB 7548, Records of the Georgia Civil War Centennial Commission, Record Group 079-01-001, Georgia State Archives (hereafter GaCWCCR); Beverly M. DuBose Jr. to Carl Sanders, Dec. 30, 1963, folder on "Correspondence of Beverly M. DuBose, 1963," GaCWCCR, RG 79-2-2.

20. Tennessee Civil War Centennial Commission, minutes of the meeting held Nov. 30, 1964, microfilm, frame 534, reel 6, Records of the Tennessee Civil War Centennial Commission, Tennessee State Library and Archives (hereafter TCWCCR).

21. The Georgia CWCC chairman estimated the attendances at Resaca and New Hope to be 3,000 and 1,500 respectively. DuBose to Frank Veale, June 23, 1964, folder on "Correspondence of the Chairman Beverly M. DuBose, 1964," GaCWCCR, RG 79-2-2. The sham battle at Kennesaw Mountain caused greater problems because "more people attempted to witness the reenactment than the available roads could comfortably accommodate, with the result that a large number were never able to reach the reenactment site." Over 2,000 men participated in the battle itself. DuBose to Jack Spalding, July 7, 1964, ibid.

reprise of the Battle of Brice's Crossroads in Mississippi in early June 1964.[22] An estimated 5,000 spectators turned up in freezing conditions to watch the reenactment at Franklin at the end of the year.[23]

Although sham battles drew the largest crowds, southern centennial exercises took many forms. April 1965, for example, witnessed several grassroots events organized by coalitions of civic groups in Alabama. In Russell County locals organized a day of ceremonies to mark the centenary of the Battle of Girard (a minor action before the final Union assault on Mobile). Boys from units of the Phenix City high school ROTC marched and drilled in Confederate garb on the grounds of the county courthouse, pledges of allegiance to the United States were recited, and salutes made to the Confederate flag. After the school glee club sang "Dixie" and the "Star Spangled Banner," the focus of attention switched to religious observances held at the grave of the unknown soldier in Lakeview Memorial Gardens. There, veterans belonging to the American Legion presented memorials to the Confederate dead and the dead of all American wars. The inhabitants of Dallas County, still reeling from the SCLC's recent and highly successful voting rights campaign in the area, participated in another representative community affair on April 2. The county Civil War centennial commission joined forces with the UDC and the chamber of commerce to coordinate a program of events commemorating the Battle of Selma. The day began with a meeting at the white high school auditorium at which the school band played patriotic music and J. Ed. Livingston, chief justice of the state supreme court, delivered an address entitled "Courage, Heroism, and Self Denial: One Hundred Years Ago and Today." Livingston distributed framed certificates of achievement and gold pins to students who had won an essay contest sponsored by the centennial group. The following day the Tuscaloosa County historical society sponsored a reenactment of a Civil War skirmish that was "watched with interest by a small rain-soaked assemblage."[24]

None of the commemorative events that took place in the South during the last three years of the centennial were value-free. As well as providing segregationist leaders like Judge Livingston with a platform for their outspoken views on states' rights, they gave ordinary white southerners further opportunities

22. Roebuck to Smith, June 10, 1964, folder on "Georgia-Miscellaneous [Jan. 1962–April 1964 and undated items]," box 712, MCWBTSR.

23. *Franklin Review-Appeal*, Dec. 3, 1964, A6.

24. Alabama Civil War Centennial Commission, "News Letter," 6 (May 28, 1965), in folder 8, SG22401, AlaG.

to demonstrate their heightened sense of regional identity at a time of acute political crisis in the région. Public memorialization of the Battle of Selma, for example, allowed white residents of Dallas County to reassert their continuing commitment to traditional values following the torrent of national criticism that descended on their community in the aftermath of "Bloody Sunday."

However, while the centennial did not go away, it impinged but dimly on the consciousness of most southern whites after 1961. By the winter of 1961–62, even though tourist interest in the Civil War remained buoyant, state centennial agencies were reporting a discernible reduction in interest among local people. After dispatching a questionnaire to county commissions in late 1961, Virginia's state centennial agency, by far the best funded and most active body of its kind in the region, indicated that popular enthusiasm for the commemoration was patchy at best. "General apathy and public lack of interest was reported by several [county] committees," it concluded, "but the majority reported interest continuing." [25] Elsewhere, the situation appeared to be even more serious. A high school principal who chaired the Cumberland County centennial committee in east Tennessee reported on May 31, 1962, that "there is practically no interest here among the people in general, but a few of us are doing what we can." [26] The mayor of Lexington, Mississippi, had no more encouraging news for his state commission in July. "We have not been able to work out plans for a centennial celebration here," he wrote. "I am sorry but I prefer not to go into it without better prospects for it being a success." [27] By the end of the year Sidney Roebuck was writing to other commission chairmen in the South soliciting their views on the "serious problem" of "how to maintain public interest in the Centennial." [28]

Roebuck's peers had several answers for him. John May of South Carolina, recuperating from a serious heart attack, replied somewhat unhelpfully "that the lesson we wish to teach to future generations is that the South fought a war of principle. And although we were out numbered we were never really defeated, and that the principle for which we stood should be adhered

25. "Analysis of Replies to Local Committee Questionnaire," encl. in James J. Geary to members of Virginia Civil War Centennial Commission executive committee, Dec. 26, 1962, folder on "National Civil War Centennial Commission," box 2, Records of the Virginia Civil War Centennial Commission, Library of Virginia (hereafter VaCWCCR).

26. B. M. Carr to Campbell H. Brown, May 31, 1962, microfilm, frame 639, reel 1, TCWCCR.

27. W. B. Kenna to Mississippi Commission on the War Between the States, July 27, 1962, folder on "Miscellaneous [Feb. 1962–Sept. 1963]," box 714, MCWBTSR.

28. See, for example, Roebuck to Peter Zack Geer, Nov. 1, 1962, folder on "Confederate States CWCCs: Alabama CWCC, 1960–64," box 1, RCB 7548, GaCWCCR, RG 079-01-001.

to by future generations."[29] More usefully (though hardly optimistically), the Arkansan Sam Dickinson said that he considered it unlikely that public interest could be sustained in the centennial. "I know of nothing of a historical nature," he continued,

> that has ever held public attention for a sustained period. News indexes reveal less and less reference to Civil War commemorations over the country. Television stations in Little Rock regularly give time for talks on Arkansas history, and during recent months they have asked that the Civil War not be included because people are tired of the subject.
>
> With Russians in Cuba and Kennedy's forces at Ole Miss, the public, I fear, is not likely to give much thought to Civil War observances from here on out. So long as the international situation is tense newspapers will have to give a lot of space to it and consequently will have to eliminate matters of no great passing importance from their columns.[30]

The Alabama chairman, Albert Moore, agreed with Roebuck that maintaining grassroots interest in the Civil War commemoration was "the foremost question now confronting the Centennial authorities in all of our states." Too many people, he thought, were resting on their laurels after the successes of 1961. He also provided independent confirmation of Dickinson's view that the centennial was being crowded out by more pressing events. "I believe," he commented, "that the civil rights and integration controversies have aroused prejudices that are adversely affecting the Centennial Commemoration of the Civil War." Continued Moore, "the critical international problems now confronting us are doubtless detracting interest from the Centennial commemoration. Many no doubt feel that we should focus our attention on the exceedingly difficult problems of the present instead of studying the past."[31]

Notwithstanding their labors over the next two and a half years, the southern state chairmen were never able to solve Roebuck's conundrum. They were

29. John A. May to Roebuck, Nov. 6, 1962, folder on "South Carolina State Chairman [July 1960–Nov. 1962]," box 721, MCWBTSR.

30. Sam Dickinson to Roebuck, Nov. 2, 1962, folder on "Arkansas—State Chairman," box 707, MCWBTSR. As if to give added substance to his remarks, Dickinson also told Roebuck that he had recently resigned from the Arkansas centennial commission.

31. Moore to Roebuck, Nov. 8, 1962, folder on "Alabama State Director [July 1960–Dec. 1962]," box 707, MCWBTSR.

certainly not helped by the parsimony of state legislatures at a time when the American economy was just emerging from recession. Although the Virginia commission remained relatively well funded owing to its positive contribution to state tourism, most others were operating, as Tennessee's director Campbell H. Brown put it, "on a shoestring."[32] Roebuck himself took a voluntary salary cut and moved into new quarters.[33] The Mississippi commission's office was closed in the spring of 1964, though technically the agency continued to operate for the remainder of the centennial.[34] By this time Florida's agency survived only as a committee of the state's Library and Historical Commission, and its counterpart in Louisiana had been dispatched by legislators in Baton Rouge.[35] Albert Moore was able to oversee a program of low-key events in Alabama with the help of a modest $28,000 legislative appropriation for 1963–64.[36] A reorganized Georgia commission remained afloat, though only by going cap-in-hand to the governor every time the energetic new director, Beverly M. DuBose Jr., sought to foster initiatives.[37] DuBose's pet scheme was the construction of three informative marker centers that would enable automobile tourists to re-live the Battle of Atlanta by driving around the increasingly built-up environs of the Georgia capital. But while initially he was hopeful of financial assistance from other agencies, he was forced to scale down his plans by word from the city's parks department that "only a limited amount of funds" was available for the project.[38] Promoting the centennial proved to be a major struggle for all southern organizers. Most politicians in the region were

32. Brown to Creed F. Bates, June 18, 1963, microfilm 1115, frame 1152, reel 6, Stanley F. Horn Papers, Tennessee Historical Society Collections, Tennessee State Library and Archives.

33. Roebuck to Dorsey J. Barefield, April 2, 1963, folder on "B—Miscellaneous [1963–1964]," box 707; Roebuck to William D. Neal, July 18, 1963, folder on "N—Miscellaneous," box 717, MCWBTSR.

34. Gladys Sladen to DuBose, July 1, 1964, folder on "Correspondence of the Chairman Beverly M. DuBose, 1964," GaCWCCR, RG 79-2-2.

35. Adam G. Adams to Robertson, Nov. 11, 1963, folder on "Florida Civil War Centennial Commission—1961," box 111, subject files 1957–66, CWCCR; *Baton Rouge Morning Advocate*, May 7, 1964, A1, clipping in folder on "Louisiana Civil War Centennial Commission—1961," box 114, subject files 1957–66, CWCCR.

36. Alabama Civil War Centennial Commission, minutes of the meeting held March 3, 1964, folder 7, SG22401, AlaG.

37. DuBose to Robertson, March 30, 1964, folder on "Correspondence of the Chairman Beverly M. DuBose, 1964," GaCWCCR, RG 79-2-2.

38. Jack C. Delius to DuBose, March 12, 1964, ibid.

unconvinced that it would attract enough tourists to warrant the investment of taxpayers' dollars—still less that it would stimulate much grassroots support for their own careers.

There are several reasons why the centennial quickly lost its power to mobilize white southerners after 1961. The diminishing funds available to the centennial commissions were significant, for in the early days of the commemoration these state agencies had played a critical role in fostering popular interest in the Civil War. However, there were clearly other factors involved. Public interest in history, even in the avowedly glorious heritage of the South, was always limited. Members of patriotic groups such as the UDC repeatedly complained about modern southerners' failure to pay due homage to the deeds of their Confederate ancestors. After the first explosion of popular enthusiasm during the centenary of secession, it was bound to be an uphill task keeping local whites focused on an event that was not only scheduled to last for four years but also, as Sam Dickinson and Albert Moore observed, clashed with a dramatic series of contemporary domestic and international crises. At least three other contributory factors drained the centennial of political relevance and vitality in the region.

First, as some segregationists (and the black historian Charles H. Wesley) recognized from the outset, the reality that the South had eventually lost the Civil War rendered the centennial a relatively ineffectual weapon in the armory of Jim Crow's defenders. Celebrating the process of secession at a time when most whites in the region were deeply concerned about the intrusion of the federal government into their lives made a good deal of political sense to bitter-enders. The same could not be said for commemorating Grant's Vicksburg campaign, Sherman's taking of Atlanta and subsequent march through Georgia and the Carolinas, or Lee's failure to withstand the siege of Petersburg. As most postbellum southerners themselves had understood, it was simply not possible to avoid the unpalatable fact that the Yankees had won the Civil War and that the dream of an independent southern nation had gone forever. James Geary discovered that his colleagues on the Virginia commission had little interest in marking what was virtually the final act of the southern rebellion, Lee's surrender at Appomattox Court House. Geary had great plans for this historic occasion, envisioning it as a consensus-drenched climax to the national centennial proceedings: a "massing of flags in a colorful pageant symbolizing the unity which came with the end of the Civil War."[39] How-

39. James J. Geary to Grover C. Steele, Dec. 20, 1963, folder on "Appomattox Centennial Plans," box 2, VaCWCCR.

ever, although these plans were already well advanced by the end of 1963, he failed to win support for them at a meeting of his agency's executive committee early in the new year. "One member," he reported, "felt that flags smacked of something of a joyful nature, a celebration. He said he would rather see the place draped in crepe."[40] Kermit Hunter, a professional playwright who had produced a draft script for the pageant, was understandably frustrated. A self-confessed southern liberal, he labeled the committee's negative response "abhorrent," adding: "I consider Appomattox a beginning, not an end, and I see no virtue in spending the rest of eternity moaning about the defeat. It was a victory, for America, but of course it is not America that we are concerned with here, and that makes me sad." Geary's colleagues, Hunter concluded, were a "collection of jerks": "I think that in their own way they are unpatriotic, that they are a detriment to American unity and progress, and the sooner they all die off, the better this nation will be."[41]

As well as highlighting the connection between southern military defeat and declining interest in the centennial, these comments suggested a second reason why the commemoration lost its appeal in the South as the 1960s wore on. Virtually all white southerners, regardless of their position on segregation, considered themselves loyal Americans. A celebration of Confederate heroism and sacrifice, therefore, was hardly likely to turn into a concerted campaign of violent resistance against the United States government, particularly when (as Fairclough observes) that government usually resisted the urge to impose its will by the use of troops.[42] The majority of local people lacked the desire and the excuse to push sectional tensions to breaking point, even though the Kennedy and Johnson administrations sorely tested their patience on civil rights issues. To some extent this was simply recognition of reality, a result of the vast growth in federal power since World War II. Southern governors, certainly most of those who participated in the Rebel pageantry of early 1961, were politically sagacious enough to know that as the final resort the federal government could use its military resources to enforce the law of the land— hence their reluctance to offer practical help to Ross Barnett during the Ole Miss crisis. But the South's relative quiescence was not just a matter of naked power relations or the Kennedys' softly-softly approach to civil rights. It was also a product of feeling and countervailing memories. Popular support for the centennial decreased partly because, in the wake of their successful

40. Geary to Kermit Hunter, Jan. 14, 1964, ibid.
41. Hunter to Geary, Jan. 15, 1964, ibid.
42. Fairclough, *Better Day Coming*, 264.

reintegration into the national fold at the turn of the century and their subsequent service in two world wars, southern whites regarded themselves as red-blooded American patriots engaged in a dangerous struggle with the forces of global communism. As Fred Powledge had observed, even the mob at Ole Miss had been infuriated that the federal troops dispatched to Oxford had not gone to fight the real enemy in Cuba. Clearly, sectional antagonism did increase during the first half of the 1960s under the press of events, and, as the Meredith crisis had revealed, raw patriotism was not necessarily regarded as incompatible with a determination to defend the existing racial order. Yet the very fact that some influential southern conservatives tried to channel centennial passions into the cold war struggle constituted a sure sign that Confederate memory was of limited utility to political elites in the region.

One instance of a well-known southern segregationist working to promote the centennial as a cold war exercise rather than a purely sectional commemoration was a speech delivered by Senator J. Strom Thurmond of South Carolina at the modestly attended "Confederate Day" ceremonies in Vicksburg on August 19, 1962. A keen exponent of Civil War history (he had a surprisingly positive view of Abraham Lincoln as a deeply religious man), the former Dixiecrat leader might have been expected to use this occasion to blast the Kennedy administration for its civil rights policies.[43] Instead, he used it to teach a contemporary military lesson. The Confederate defenders of Vicksburg in 1863, he argued, suffered defeat because they had failed to come to terms with the unorthodox campaign tactics of the enemy. This mistake, concluded the senator, had important lessons for modern America. "The communist offensive," he insisted, "is a war of maneuver. It is a war in which we are now engaged. While we must, of course, be prepared for any type of war, even to the extent of being prepared for a nuclear exchange if necessary; at the same time we must concentrate on the type of war which is now occurring. Unless we stem and reverse the tide of the cold war, we may well find ourselves encircled and left with no alternative but to make a final desperate stand, which, like that of the besieged Confederates within Vicksburg, was limited from the outset to at best a temporary postponement of ultimate defeat."[44]

43. For Strom Thurmond's views on Lincoln, see H. Alexander Smith to Ulysses S. Grant III, Aug. 11, 1958, folder on "Congressional Mail: Congress—Curtis Publishing Company," box 70, subject files 1957–66, CWCCR.

44. Thurmond, Address at Vicksburg National Military Park, Aug. 19, 1962, folder on "Mississippi Commission on the War Between the States—1962," box 117, subject files 1957–66, CWCCR.

Attempts by influential right-wingers like Thurmond to use the centennial as a weapon in the ongoing crusade against communism reflected and molded a steely grassroots Americanism that found political form not in the kind of violent Confederate revival feared by some black leaders in 1961 but in a surge of support for the brand of super-patriotic states' rights Republicanism that enabled Arizona senator Barry Goldwater to carry five Deep South states in the 1964 presidential election. Although Republican party-builders in the region were not averse to using Confederate symbols to promote their cause, the underlying thrust of their activities can hardly be described as nostalgic. Indeed, by promoting the development of a genuine two-party system in the region, those efforts were essentially modernizing. The southern Republicanism of Strom Thurmond (he publicly supported Goldwater's candidacy in 1964) certainly embraced opposition to civil rights legislation, but its basic dynamic was national in the sense that its hostility to communism, commitment to economic growth, prioritization of law and order over Jim Crow, and devotion to a particular definition of American freedom transcended an attachment to section.

Much the same could be said of the devotees of Governor George Wallace. Albert Moore was a firm supporter of both the governor and segregation. However, rather than simply using his position as chairman of Alabama's centennial agency to disseminate pride in the region's Confederate past, he worked to promote the original cold war objectives of the national commission. His instruction booklet, *Reasons for the National Commemoration of the Civil War,* published in 1963, paid homage to the courage and resolution of the Confederates. Yet it also informed Alabamans that southern defeat had given them "a legally indestructible Union" and that the centennial was making a vital contribution to national education. "To understand and cherish our great traditions," wrote Moore, "is our strongest defense against Communism or any other un-American 'ism.' If we do not understand and respect our traditions, we shall be easy prey for Communist brain-washers." [45]

Southern whites' deep-rooted pride in their country meant that over time growing numbers of people in the region began to find the combination of state-sponsored violence and mock-Confederate posturing both embarrassing and shameful. Even George Wallace discovered that his use of Rebel symbols did not go uncontested at home. This was particularly true of his decision to follow the example of South Carolina and use the centennial as an excuse for

45. Albert B. Moore, *Reasons for the National Centennial Commemoration of the Civil War: Its Basic Objectives and Potential Values* (n.p., 1963), 5, 10–11.

flying the Confederate battle flag atop the Alabama state capitol in Montgomery.[46] This gesture of defiance attracted criticism from significant numbers of
white southerners irked by the governor's apparent lack of national patriotism. One Baptist minister from Birmingham, for example, described himself
as an opponent of integration but attested that his grandfather had fought for
the Confederacy and died a bitter old man. "There is no place today for any
display that will arouse bitterness, old hatreds," he wrote. "We are Americans
first, Alabamans second, and rebels in the *past!*"[47] A female correspondent of
the *Montgomery Advertiser* concurred. Her late grandfather, another Confederate veteran, had "tucked away the Confederate flag" and proudly adopted the
Stars and Stripes after losing two sons in World War I. "He was a gentleman
of the old school," she added boldly, "and would be dismayed at the disgrace-
ful use of the Confederate flag by men who flaunt it for political expediency
and the ignorant element joined unfortunately by gullible children who follow
them blindly."[48] The most outspoken criticism came from another Alabama
woman who denounced the governor's policy as "childish, impudent, and ut-
terly stupid." Southerners, she insisted, had no alternative but to accept that,
in the wake of the 1964 Civil Rights Act, "changes in the 'Southern Way of Life'
are going to be made. PLEASE GOD, CAN'T WE ACCEPT THESE INESCAPABLE
CHANGES WITH SOME SHRED OF DIGNITY??"[49]

Governor Wallace was unrepentant. After one northern correspondent
wrote to protest the flying of the Confederate flag during school desegregation
demonstrations in Notasulga at the beginning of 1964, he insisted that it was
"not flown out of disrespect for the flag of the United States, but as a symbol
of resistance to what the people of that small town felt to be undue interference in their local affairs."[50] No people were more loyal to the Star Spangled
Banner "than the great Southern region of the country." He also told a worried
Mobile high school student that "the Confederate flag is part of the American
flag and part of the American heritage and tradition." Russian flags, he added,
"fly all around the United Nations but that doesn't mean that anyone has put
those flags above the American flag."[51] While such protestations of loyalty to
the United States revealed that segregationists like Wallace saw no conflict

46. Wallace to Mary M. Hyland, Jan. 9, 1965, folder 16, SG22387, AlaG.
47. Raymond T. De Armond to Wallace, Jan. 30, 1963, ibid.
48. *Montgomery Advertiser,* Feb. 13, 1964, 4.
49. Mona Smith Boner to Wallace, March 16, 1965, folder 16, SG22387, AlaG.
50. Wallace to L. F. Ryan Jr., Feb. 20, 1964, ibid.
51. Wallace to Hyland, Jan. 9, 1965, ibid.

between their actions and American superpatriotism, it is unlikely that they convinced many of the governor's critics, even those in his own state. That Wallace's use of the Rebel battle flag caused controversy inside the South furnished evidence that at least a significant minority of local whites were deeply unhappy with Confederate theatrics during the early 1960s. In a speech at Atlantic City in November 1962 the Georgia historian Bell Wiley assured his audience that "[w]e're beginning to get over the War now" and that "there is a move under way for Southerners to become Americans."[52] Wiley's remarks were not entirely wishful thinking. Without doubt the centennial suffered grievously from the ongoing process of political modernization in the South that was preeminently an effect of the civil rights movement.

A final reason for the relatively low-key nature of southern centennial events between 1962 and 1965 was the national commission's persistent determination not to antagonize the southern agencies. A chronic lack of funding and declining levels of popular interest did much to forestall any possibility of a quasi-Confederate revival in the Deep South linked to the region's centennial establishment. Nonetheless, the CWCC's resolute commitment to an intersectional observance of the Civil War can at least be credited with deterring segregationists like Sidney Roebuck and John May from fostering an embarrassing split within the national coalition—one that might have made white supremacy an even more important theme in southern commemorative activities than it actually was in the 1960s. As we have seen, however, there were serious costs attached to the CWCC's stress on maintaining consensus, not least a continuing reluctance to educate Americans about the racial significance of the Civil War.

THE CENTENNIAL TAKES A SCHOLARLY TURN

The CWCC's oversight of the centennial during the tenure of two professional historians, Allan Nevins and James Robertson, was characterized by an emphasis on scholarship that was in marked contrast to the more populist tone adopted by their predecessors. Rhetorically the reorganized commission was more attuned to the sensitivities of African Americans, but in practice the attitudes of the old and the new regimes to racial issues had more in common with each other than Nevins's initial statement of intent led people to expect.

Notwithstanding his interest in stimulating America's output of high-quality popular history, Allan Nevins possessed a realistic appraisal of what

52. Bell I. Wiley, Speech at New Jersey Education Association Meeting, [Nov. 1962], folder on "Wiley, Dr. Bell I.," box 12, NJCWCCR.

his commission could, and could not, do to instruct the general public about the nation's past. When CWCC member Fred Schwengel suggested that "the greatest contribution that we could make in this centennial is to instill in our young people an active interest in American history in general, and Civil War history in particular," Nevins demurred.[53] There was, he snapped, no statutory authorization for intrusion into the sphere of public education: "The school systems of our fifty states have tens of thousands of buildings, hundreds of thousands of teachers, and billions of dollars in funds. The Commission has one floor of an old building, a staff of five full-time workers, and a precarious allowance of $100,000 a year." Nevins objected personally to the congressman's contention that the commission had largely failed to educate Americans about the Civil War. "I am as much grieved as any American by the amount of ignorance of history shown both by young people and older people," he wrote. "But I refuse to believe that the Centennial Commission and its chairman can justly be held responsible." The real blame lay with the "ragged, uneven" quality of the public schools and the fact that so many youngsters "grow up in third-rate homes" or in communities without adequate library facilities. "Failure! Failure! Failure!" concluded Nevins sarcastically. "You don't know half of it. I have failed to wipe out illiteracy in Ecuador. I have failed to stop homicide in Chicago. And look at the Congo—what an awful failure there by the Chairman of the Centennial Commission!"[54]

Even though Nevins was not wholly averse to the idea that the CWCC had an educational mission (he wrote several official pamphlets on specific aspects of the war and sanctioned the production of a short text for students), his main interest was in promoting academic scholarship. This was understandable, not only in view of his own position as one of the country's leading authorities on the Civil War but also, as he told Schwengel, in the light of the limited funding available to his hard-pressed agency. On taking up office in December 1961 he quickly threw his considerable energies into two projects: the Impact series of Civil War monographs and the production of two definitive document collections—the private papers of Ulysses S. Grant and Jefferson Davis. Both of these projects were to cost him dearly in terms of time and stress.

Owing largely to the financial support proffered by New York publisher Alfred A. Knopf, Nevins was able to commission fifteen Impact volumes

53. Fred Schwengel to Allan Nevins, Feb. 1, 1963, folder on "Schwengel, Fred (Hon.)," box 136, subject files 1957–66, CWCCR.

54. Nevins to Schwengel, Feb. 9, 1963, folder on "Miscellaneous Correspondence, 1963," box 184, Bell I. Wiley Papers, Manuscript, Archives, and Rare Book Library, Emory University.

over the course of the centennial. As the series title implied, each contributing author was required to examine the significance of the Civil War in his or her specialist field of study. The chairman's commitment to greater social inclusiveness led him to commission works on women and blacks as well as on more conventional subjects such as European military thought, political and constitutional development, agriculture, and science and technology. The project was commendably ambitious but at best only partially successful. Despite suffering a heart attack in January 1963 and having important tasks to complete (editing a volume of President Kennedy's speeches and completing his own eagerly anticipated account of the Civil War), Nevins found that he had to devote much of his time to knocking the early volumes into shape. The promising young southern historian Mary Elizabeth Massey went well beyond the prescribed word limit, leaving Nevins to scrutinize her "ill written" manuscript line by line, "smoothing the English & removing the excess verbiage."[55]

At least Massey produced her volume on the role of women in good time. Other contributors were less efficient. The worst offender was Captain Cyril Falls, a military historian at the University of Oxford. Although Falls, an acquaintance of Nevins, produced a draft of his book on postbellum European military thought by the winter, readers found it poorly focused and inadequately researched—this in spite of the fact that Nevins had bombarded the Englishman with scholarly advice.[56] Falls rather lamely claimed that he had found it difficult locating sources in London. A trip to the British Library's newspaper annex to read the nineteenth-century French journal *Revue des Deux Mondes* had proved particularly fruitless. "I was told it was at Colindale," Falls informed Nevins, "and went up there to find a useless Negro in charge, and it was some time before the Librarian turned up and I learnt that it was at Bloomsbury."[57] Nevins was still dealing with the wreckage of this volume years after the centennial proper had ended. At the beginning of 1969, he could be found trying to persuade another Oxford historian, Michael Howard, to take on the job of completing the volume.[58] Howard apparently declined the

55. Nevins to Edmund Gass, Oct. 4, 1965, folder on "Civil War Centennial Commission—Impact Series," box 87, Allan Nevins Papers, Rare Book and Manuscript Library, Columbia University. See also Massey to Nevins, Sept. 26, 1965, ibid.

56. Nevins to Cyril Falls, Aug. 2, Aug. 5, 1963, folder on "Impact Volumes—Correspondence," box 87, Nevins Papers; Carl Haverlin report on Falls manuscript encl. in Justin G. Turner to Nevins, Feb. 11, 1966, ibid.

57. Falls to Nevins, Aug. 31, 1965, ibid.

58. Nevins to Michael Howard, Jan. 7, 1969, ibid.

task. Along with the vast majority of the other books in the series, the ill-fated monograph had not seen the light of day by the end of the decade.

In fairness to Cyril Falls, part of the problem may have lain with Nevins's original conception of the Impact series. The captain indicated at an early stage that he considered the war's influence "on military thought to be slight, even in Britain, France and Germany."[59] A number of other contributors expressed similar concerns.[60] By assuming an exaggerated significance for the American conflict, Nevins helped to create problems not only for some of his authors, but also—because he had to pick up many of the pieces—for himself.

The CWCC chairman discovered that the Grant Papers and Davis Papers were time-consuming also. Obtaining funding for these expensive endeavors was a major headache, for the commission had neither the money nor the statutory power to pump prime them effectively. Both Nevins and Robertson regarded them as central to the ultimate success of the centennial, not only because of their long-term contribution to scholarship but also because their publication would confirm the CWCC's overriding commitment to good feeling between the sections. The Grant Papers proved the easiest project to get underway. Nevins used his considerable influence to secure the formation of a nonprofit corporation, the Ulysses S. Grant Association, which would oversee publication of the Union commander's correspondence under the editorial guidance of John Y. Simon, a leading authority in the field. Critical funding was supplied by some of the main northern commissions and, more important, Ohio State University Press, which evinced an early interest in publishing the material. Even Ulysses S. Grant III overcame his bitterness at the treatment he had received in 1961 in order to place his grandfather's private family correspondence in the hands of the association.[61]

The Jefferson Davis project posed more difficult problems. The CWCC was not helped by the fact that a historian, Hudson Strode, had been given exclusive permission by the Davis family to use hitherto unseen correspondence in order to write a biography of the Confederate president.[62] Strode was intensely protective of the manuscripts in his possession and reluctant to release them

59. Ashbel Green to Nevins, Aug. 9, 1967, ibid.

60. William B. Bean to W. F. Norwood, Nov. 4, 1965, ibid.

61. Ulysses S. Grant III outlived the centennial, dying at his College Hill home in Clinton, New York, in August 1968.

62. The third and final part of Strode's biography was not published until 1964. Walter L. Brown, reviewing *Jefferson Davis: Tragic Hero*, observed that as "a disciple of Davis," Strode outdid "even the most devoted Daughter of the Confederacy." *American Historical Review* 70 (1965): 1251.

for publication until he had completed his revisionist tome. Lack of money, however, was the most serious problem. The project simply could not get started without financial backing from the southern commissions. Unfortunately, they had little surplus cash, and in the case of the Virginia commission (preoccupied with celebrating the peerless legacy of Robert E. Lee) the will to contribute was virtually nonexistent.[63] The major breakthrough came early in 1964 when persistent lobbying by the CWCC and its southern allies procured a grant of $20,000 from the Southern Company, a holding corporation for four regional power providers.[64] With crucial institutional backing from the well-endowed Rice Institute and a substantial contribution from the William Stamps Foundation of Houston in 1965, the viability of the project was assured.[65] Publication of the Davis Papers under the editorship of the prominent Rice historian Frank Vandiver from 1970 onward constituted one of the CWCC's major achievements—an enduring testimonial to the commission's persistent attachment to the core principle of intersectional amity.

African Americans (and, to an extent, the cause of historical knowledge) were the main victims of this attachment. Notwithstanding the ongoing activities of the civil rights movement and some vociferous black criticism of the CWCC's lukewarm commemoration of the preliminary Emancipation Proclamation, the federal agency made few attempts to highlight racial topics during the second half of the centennial. Even when individual members of the commission did take steps to alert the public to the racial import of the centennial, their efforts were relatively timid and sometimes unsuccessful.

Allan Nevins was particularly keen, for personal, political, and scholarly reasons, that the commission should ignore neither the role that blacks had played during the Civil War nor the relevance of Civil War themes to the burgeoning struggle for racial equality in the United States. His main initiative was a scholarly symposium to be held in Washington in January 1964 to mark the centenary of Lincoln's Gettysburg Address.[66] The CWCC chairman ensured that race would be one of the main themes of this colloquium by inviting Senator Paul H. Douglas of Illinois to deliver one of the papers. A liberal Democrat who happened to be a personal friend, as well as one of

63. Robertson to Geary, Oct. 21, 1962, box 12, reading file 1958–66, CWCCR.

64. Moore to Robertson, Feb. 28, 1964, folder on "Alabama Civil War Centennial Commission—1961," box 107, subject files 1957–66, CWCCR.

65. Frank E. Vandiver to Robertson, June 7, 1965, folder on "Jefferson Davis Papers," box 131, subject files 1957–66, CWCCR.

66. For a discussion of the first two volumes of Nevins's *War for the Union,* see pp. 251–52.

the strongest supporters of civil rights legislation in Congress, Douglas accepted his brief with a certain amount of trepidation. Nevins, however, lavished generous praise on the senator's address, which urged congressmen in favor of Kennedy's stalled civil rights bill "to observe the same energetic steadfastness in the cause of human freedom which the men of the Union displayed on Culp's Hill, Little Round Top, and at the clump of trees in the center of the Union lines where the final agonized gasp of the battle [of Gettysburg] was uttered."[67] Nevins pronounced Douglas's effort "both original in ideas and polished in style," adding that he was positive "that everybody who reads your paper will be inspired by your eloquent defense of civil rights and your highly justified remarks upon the bigoted southerners and reactionary Republicans who have united in opposing the needed reforms in this field."[68]

Although they were less willing than Allan Nevins to antagonize southern conservatives, Bruce Catton and Bell Wiley also tried to ensure that the agency did not pass over the racial significance of the Civil War at a time of successive domestic crises over civil rights. Wiley, for example, lobbied (albeit unsuccessfully) for a session on the role of African Americans in the Civil War at the CWCC's national assembly in 1963.[69] Catton urged strongly not only that this assembly should be held in Boston but also that it should provide the occasion for a ceremony to commemorate Colonel Robert Gould Shaw, the white officer who had led black troops in their heroic assault on Fort Wagner.[70] Catton duly spoke at Boston College on May 25, 1963, at a ceremony dedicated to Shaw's memory sponsored by the Massachusetts centennial commission. His speech came less than two months after Americans had been exposed to the

67. Paul H. Douglas, "The Significance of Gettysburg" in Allan Nevins, ed., *Lincoln and the Gettysburg Address: Commemorative Papers [by] John Dos Passos, Arthur Lehman Goodhart, Reinhold Niebuhr, Robert Lowell, Paul H. Douglas, David C. Mearns* (Urbana: University of Illinois Press, 1964), 115–16.

68. Nevins to Paul Douglas, Jan. 28, 1964, folder on "Lincoln and the Gettysburg Address Correspondence," box 85, Nevins Papers. Arthur Goodhart, an eminent law specialist at the University of Oxford in England, thought less well of Douglas's contribution because he feared that its stress on a contemporary political issue would render the papers redundant before their publication. See Goodhart to Nevins, Jan. 28, 1964, ibid.

69. Wiley to Nevins, May 25, 1962, folder on "Miscellaneous Correspondence, Civil War Centennial Commission, 1963," box 184, Wiley Papers. The itinerary of the Boston conference is contained in folder on "National Assembly—1963—program," box 54, subject files 1957–66, CWCCR.

70. CWCC, Minutes of Meeting, May 5, 1962, folder on "Minutes—Commission Meetings, Agendas etc.," box 184, Wiley Papers.

shocking media coverage of Martin Luther King's landmark campaign in Birmingham. Catton began by lauding the Yankee officer for sacrificing his life in the cause of black freedom, then proceeded to impart contemporary relevance to his address by arguing (for once not referring to the communist threat) that the quintessential American belief in unfettered human freedom was under attack in the present. "No one," he said,

> can read about what has happened in Birmingham without experiencing a great revulsion of feeling. But that revulsion will do nobody any good unless it reminds us to make certain that our own house is put in order. We are not better people than the ones who were black-jacked off of their own doorsteps by heavy-handed state troopers; we are just luckier than they are. We are still facing the challenge Robert Gould Shaw faced, and although we are not called on to do what he did we are at least obliged to reach into our own hearts and wrench out everything that may stand between us and complete acceptance of the universal dignity and equality of man. We are at least obliged to make clear to everyone which side we stand on—and to make this clear to the authorities in our own state as well as those of a state a thousand miles away.[71]

These were not the words of a radical. Indeed, any African Americans in the audience may have wondered at the speaker's preoccupation with white sacrifice. Nevertheless, this address was a relatively rare event in the history of the CWCC—a conscious attempt by one of its members to utilize the past in the service of contemporary racial equality.

Such occasions were few and far between because of the CWCC's determination to maintain the original centennial coalition intact. This meant continuing to suppress racial themes in order to prevent the southern commissions from abandoning the centennial. The goal was met primarily because Allan Nevins largely acquiesced in his young deputy's attempts to conciliate the southern segregationists. Inexperienced though he was in such matters, James Robertson proved to be a talented administrator and consummate broker after assuming responsibility for the day-to-day running of the national agency in late 1961. His former doctoral adviser, Bell Wiley, quickly reported that the new executive director was "acquitting himself well." Robertson, he told Nevins after a visit to CWCC headquarters, "works hard, maintains a

---

71. Bruce Catton, speech at Boston College, May 25, 1963, folder on "National Assembly, 1963," box 184, Wiley Papers.

cheerful outlook and wins friends for himself and the Commission by his open cordiality. He and Ed Gass work well together. The morale of the staff appears to be very good indeed."[72] Certainly Robertson did develop an effective working relationship with his fellow southerner. Edmund Gass was an accomplished Washington bureaucrat who, the former executive director remembers, "had contacts with federal agencies that facilitated many programs we undertook" and "possessed a warm and engaging personality."[73]

Thinking along similar lines so far as the welfare of the centennial was concerned, the two men labored tirelessly to turn the troubled agency from a bastion of Jim Crow into a vehicle fit for the moderate social reformism of the Kennedy years. Like Wiley, Robertson and Gass were both proud southerners who understood that Dixie must adapt in order to prosper. Strategically, Robertson occupied the crucial position. As Nevins's hands-on deputy in Washington, he was charged with overseeing a more inclusive and dignified commemoration—one that would not embarrass the liberal Democratic administration which he served. Generally speaking, Robertson was willing to perform the role allotted to him. He may not have been an enthusiastic supporter of the civil rights movement (few southern whites were), but he was genuinely in awe of Nevins, welcomed signs of political change in the South (notably Carl E. Sanders's triumph over his segregationist opponent in Georgia's 1963 Democratic gubernatorial primary), and was even more confident than Wiley that his homeland was changing for the better.[74] However, his commitment both to the chairman and to broader New South ideals did not render him impervious to the influence wielded by segregationists inside the region's centennial establishment. Robertson knew that men like John May and Sidney Roebuck had to be conciliated if the centennial were to survive, and he did not hesitate to use his southern credentials to promote this end. Although this conviction and behavior helped to eliminate whatever political heat was left in the centennial by late 1962, it prompted a modicum of friction between the CWCC's illustrious chairman and his southern lieutenant.

Tension was particularly apparent over the degree to which the agency should promote its official commitment, in line with that of other federal bu-

72. Wiley to Nevins, March 26, 1962, folder 2, box 76, Nevins Papers.

73. Robertson to the author, Dec. 1, 2005.

74. Robertson to Wiley, Sept. 14, 1962, box 12, reading file 1958–66, CWCCR. Sanders's victory over his bitter-end opponent, Marvin Griffin, in Georgia's fall 1963 Democratic gubernatorial campaign is evaluated in Harold Paulk Henderson, *Ernest Vandiver: Governor of Georgia* (Athens: University of Georgia Press, 2000), 172–75.

reaus, to equal rights. In late 1962 Nevins told Robertson that he was concerned about CWCC support for the approaching Vicksburg centennial of July 1963. Formulated as they were in the midst of escalating domestic tension over Jim Crow, Mississippi's ambitious plans to mark the most important Civil War event to have occurred on home soil portended another Charleston-style fiasco. Nevins therefore asked his deputy to take "the precautionary step" of writing to the authorities in Vicksburg to ensure that they were aware of "the possibility of embarrassment" in July and that they were working "to avoid any unfortunate contretemps." Lest he be misunderstood, the chairman added that the CWCC would be "gravely remiss if we do not place ourselves on record as expressing our firm conviction that adequate facilities in hotels and restaurants shall be given any colored people who care to visit the commemorative ceremonies."[75] Robertson wrote accordingly to the Mississippi executive director, Sidney Roebuck, in February 1963. Addressing himself familiarly to "Dear Sid," he explained that one or two questions had come from "official channels" about whether "adequate facilities" would be available for "the various races" at Vicksburg.[76] The Gettysburg folks, he added, were making loud noises about their own event in July, and he was keen to publicize the Vicksburg commemoration as much as possible. The letter illustrated Robertson's evolving diplomatic skills. As well as being assured of the Virginian's friendship and common southern lineage, Roebuck was being told that the racial concerns emanated from the White House and not the CWCC. Mention of the Gettysburg competition was designed to ensure compliance on the facilities issue without unduly alienating the sensitive Mississippian. Clever though it was, the missive did not have quite the effect it intended. Roebuck telephoned Robertson for clarification and, as he later reported to John May, was informed that "the Kennedys had stuck their nose into the matter." Roebuck then "said the people of Vicksburg would continue to maintain their customs regardless of whether or not we had a program at Vicksburg; that there were motels for both white and colored races in Vicksburg and that I felt that all of those who really wanted to attend the programs there could be accommodated." Robertson, he added, seemed to be "in total agreement with me in the matter."[77] Apparently believing that Roebuck would comply with

75. Nevins to Robertson, Dec. 18, 1962, folder on "Nevins, Allan—Oct. 3, 1961," box 134, subject files 1957–66, CWCCR.

76. Robertson to Roebuck, Feb. 5, 1963, box 13, reading file 1958–66, CWCCR.

77. Roebuck to John A. May, Feb. 19, 1963, folder on "South Carolina State Chairman [Jan. 1963–April 1964 and undated]," box 721, MCWBTSR.

the ambiguous requirement for "adequate facilities" for both races, Robertson followed up these contacts with a phone call to John Holland, chairman of the Mississippi commission who was also the mayor of Vicksburg. He found Holland to be "a young and rather personable chap" who reassured him "that no discrimination or segregation of any sort will be practiced or tolerated during the Vicksburg ceremonies."[78]

Although the disparity between the responses of the two segregationists may be accounted for partly by the fact that Holland was more moderate than Roebuck on matters of race and that the Vicksburg ceremonies would take place mainly in the federally owned National Military Park, these explanations hardly justified Robertson's confidence in the Mississippians' good faith.[79] Nevins, certainly, was not persuaded. In June he asked his deputy if firm assurances had been given that "a fair and acceptable provision of food, drink, and shelter will be available for Negro visitors [to Vicksburg]." If they had not been received, added the chairman, he was ready to relay agency policy on this matter in letters to Mayor Holland and the local newspaper: "It is important that we place ourselves fully on record, so that if any difficulty arises we can point to our efforts."[80] Once again Robertson hastened to reassure his superior. All of the events, he wrote, would be staged on federal land and NPS officials in Vicksburg had told him "that certain hotels and motels will *quietly*—and unknown to the public—accept Negroes who are members of state commissions or serving in some other official capacity." Added Robertson grandiloquently, "I think this last-named development is truly one of the miracles of our century."[81]

On this evidence the Vicksburg commemoration appears to have justified James Robertson's hyperbole. It might even serve as a good case study of how, during the early 1960s, southern states' desire for material gain came to trump their attachment to segregation. The CWCC's executive director was certainly excited by his participation at the Vicksburg centennial, which took the form of solemn commemorative services on the battlefield, an academic seminar on the Union siege, a salute to the ladies of the Confederacy, a gala Confederate

78. Robertson to Nevins, Feb. 14, 1963, box 12, reading file 1958–66, CWCCR.

79. According to Ed Bearss, the NPS research historian at Vicksburg, Roebuck was "far to the right of Johnny Holland." Bearss, taped comments to the author, Jan. 2004.

80. Nevins to Robertson, June 11, 1963, folder on "Nevins, Allan—Oct. 31, 1961," box 134, subject files 1957–66, CWCCR.

81. Robertson to Nevins, June 18, 1963, ibid.

ball, and guided tours of all the main historical sites.[82] On his return to Washington, he reported happily to Nevins that "not one incident of discrimination
or racial disturbance occurred" at the event. The Mississippians "seemed to go
out of their way to be cordial and hospitable to the one or two Negroes who
attended the seminars and commemorative ceremonies on the battlefield."[83]
The chairman was unpersuaded. Although he did consent to write a note of
congratulations to John Holland, he also reported that a delegation of the Illinois centennial commission headed by Governor Otto Kerner had decided
to spend only a day in Vicksburg because it had been told that its single black
member could only be lodged in segregated accommodation.[84]

These proceedings did not reflect well on the CWCC. At a time of rising
public awareness about the indignity of segregation, the commission made
only half-hearted efforts to flag its opposition to the practice. While Allan
Nevins might have done more to clarify what he meant about ensuring "adequate facilities" for blacks, his deputy either allowed himself to be hood-
winked by the Mississippians or was less perturbed than he might have been
about the problems African-American visitors might face once they left the
boundaries of the Vicksburg Military Park. The commemoration passed off
without incident largely because the federal authorities and the Illinois centennial commission chose not to force the segregation issue.

While James Robertson had better luck trying to secure guarantees about
desegregated accommodation when he was organizing the 1964 national assembly in Atlanta, he remained consistently sensitive to perceived slights
against the southern memory of the Civil War and suspicious of even limited
attempts to incorporate racial themes into the centennial.[85] In so doing he was
continuing to ensure minimal black participation in commemorative events
and doing little to promote the admittedly elusive cause of historical truth.

82. "Siege of Vicksburg Centennial," June 30–July 4, 1963, official program, folder on "Mississippi CWCC," box 3, VaCWCCR.

83. Robertson to Nevins, July 8, 1963, folder on "Nevins, Allan—Oct. 31, 1961," box 134, subject
files 1957–66, CWCCR.

84. Nevins, written comments on verso of Robertson to Nevins, June 18, 1963, ibid.

85. DuBose to Robertson, Feb. 6, Feb. 14, 1964, folder on "Correspondence of the Chairman
Beverly M. DuBose, 1964," GaCWCCR, RG 79-2-2. DuBose's assurances about the integration of
facilities in Atlanta were not matched by evidence of his own racial moderation. When Robertson
intimated that the only black CWCC member, Roy Davenport, might be among the guests at a
private party to be hosted by the Georgia chairman, DuBose promptly canceled the function.
DuBose to Robertson, May 12, 1964, ibid.

When Nevins first mooted his idea of a symposium to mark the Gettysburg Address, for example, Robertson proffered a distinctly cool response. Such a program, he suggested, would offend the Pennsylvanians who were planning their own event. More germanely, he went on, Lincoln's remarks were "slanted for the Northern side," and therefore "such a program would make us appear again as if we were leaning heavily away from the South." There were, he alleged, "many Civil War students who do not share Fred Schwengel's and your enthusiasm for Lincoln in general and his Address in particular."[86] In this instance only Nevins's persistence finally overcame the evident distaste for his idea at CWCC headquarters.

Robertson's determination to mollify the southern commissions at the expense of a broad airing of racial themes was manifest on several other occasions during his tenure of office. For example, he was moved to reassure his fellow Virginian, James Geary, that there would be "no panel or formal discussion of the Emancipation Proclamation" at the 1963 Boston national assembly. Even though it was a glaring omission in view of Boston's prominent role in the antebellum antislavery movement, the program contained no session dedicated to this theme.[87] That same year Robertson decided to write a CWCC pamphlet on the Civil War for high school students. When Nevins and Wiley suggested that he should deal with the role of black Union troops, his reaction was only grudgingly compliant. "I plan to add a paragraph or two about them in 'The Common Soldiers' section," he replied: "In the full complexity of the war, the contributions of Negroes was [sic] relatively minor. But I agree that, for safety['s] sake, we had best call attention to their deeds."[88] Robertson proved at least as ready to accede to the comments of southern segregationists. Stanley Horn, chairman of the Tennessee commission, which had distanced itself from the CWCC since the troubles at Charleston, took particular exception to the draft's reference to the "murder" of the black Union garrison at Fort Pillow on the Mississippi.[89] Robertson responded by thanking him for

86. Robertson to Nevins, Jan. 4, 1963, folder on "Nevins Correspondence—1963," box 77, Nevins Papers.

87. Robertson to Geary, Dec. 3, 1962, folder on "National Civil War Centennial Commission," box 2, VaCWCCR; sixth national assembly program in folder on "National Assembly—1963—program," box 54, subject files 1957–66, CWCCR.

88. Robertson to Wiley, Aug. 15, 1963, box 13, reading file 1958–66, CWCCR.

89. Stanley F. Horn to Robertson, Aug. 14, 1963, frame 154, reel 2, Horn Papers. Modern historians generally accept that black troops were massacred by Confederates after the fall of the Union garrison at Fort Pillow on April 12, 1864. See esp. John Cimprich, *Fort Pillow, a Civil War Massacre, and Public Memory* (Baton Rouge: Louisiana State University Press, 2005).

his views and removing the "slip" from the text.[90] In truth, no one reading the resulting handbook would have known that racial issues were central to the coming and the outcome of the Civil War. Robertson fudged the causative role of slavery in a necessarily brief historiographical introduction and devoted as much space (one single paragraph) to black troops in the Confederacy as to the far greater numbers who fought for the Union.[91] He also went out of his way to balance northern and southern views of the war, incorporating Stanley Horn's defense of Jefferson Davis, highlighting the horrors of northern prison camps to neutralize his description of the notorious Confederate stockade at Andersonville, and describing Robert E. Lee as being "most remembered for an almost flawless character."[92]

By looking out for southern interests in his capacity as executive director, James Robertson helped to sustain the centennial as a consensual exercise in public history. In so doing he can be credited with reducing the centennial's political value to hardline segregationists. For as long as the southern commissions felt assured that the CWCC would not become a mouthpiece for civil rights, they had little incentive to foster a rabidly pro-Confederate centennial—one that would have run counter to the "national" line of the CWCC and conceivably might have strengthened white resistance to the civil rights movement. But African Americans paid a price for Robertson's desire to conciliate the Confederate States Conference. Small wonder, then, that black participation in the centennial remained minimal, notwithstanding the interest in black history generated by the civil rights movement of the early 1960s.

A STILLNESS AT APPOMATTOX

By the spring of 1965 the centennial was a low-key affair. Some of the state commissions, notably that of New York, had either ceased to function or, as in the case of the Mississippi agency, were limping along to little purpose without the necessary government funding.[93] Public interest in the Civil War, of

---

Cimprich notes, "Despite the roughly equal numbers of black and white Federals, the death rates by race alone were 65 percent for blacks and 29–33 percent for whites (including thirteen officers of black troops)" (85). The scholarship of Dudley Cornish and Albert Castel had begun to build a strong case for the existence of a massacre at Fort Pillow before the centennial began (119).

90. Robertson to Horn, Aug. 20, 1963, frame 155, reel 2, Horn Papers.

91. James I. Robertson Jr., *The Civil War* (Washington, DC: CWCC, 1963), 5–6, 57–58.

92. Ibid., 45–47, 53, 55.

93. New York's centennial agency fell victim to legislative budget cuts in the spring of 1963. See Nelson A. Rockefeller to Nevins, May 28, 1963, and Thomas E. Mulligan to Robertson, [May

course, had not gone away. Demand for Robertson's free student handbook was high, the popular history magazine *Civil War Times Illustrated* boasted a growing subscription list, and the number of round tables was increasing rapidly.[94] Attendance at Richmond's Centennial Center remained buoyant, and tourists continued to flock to battlefields like Gettysburg, Chickamauga, and Vicksburg.[95] Grassroots commemorations persisted in states that had been touched by the final stages of the war, and several military engagements were marked with a colorful reenactment that would have gladdened the heart of Karl Betts. Had he lived, however, it is unlikely that the CWCC's controversial executive director would have been impressed with the overall state of the centennial at its close. What had once been conceived as a major national pageant had become, at best, a footnote to the 1960s.

With the country preoccupied by recent events in Selma and the inexorable military build-up in southeast Asia, it was hardly surprising that the media paid little attention to what was virtually the last act of the centennial: a suitably dull ceremony held under lowering skies at Appomattox Court House in April 1965, less than a month after the introduction of a comprehensive voting rights bill into Congress. The Virginia commission had got its wish for a low-profile event to coincide with the hundredth anniversary of the demise of the embryonic southern nation. One reporter observed that only around 5,000 people were present, many of them battle reenactors dressed in period costume. Some of the spectators burst into applause when the U.S. Marine Band broke into "Dixie," but the general air was more respectful than defiant.[96]

The reality of Lee's defeat and the decisive actions of the civil rights movement gave white southerners little stomach for the last rites of the Confederacy. In fact, in the aftermath of the SCLC's Selma campaign, southern newspapers greeted the close of the observance with a measure of relief. Among the most

1963], folder on "New York Civil War Centennial Commission—1962," box 121, subject files 1957–66, CWCCR.

94. Robertson to May, Oct. 31, 1963, box 12, reading file 1958–66, CWCCR; *Civil War Times Illustrated* 2 (April 1963): [2].

95. More than 78,000 people visited the Centennial Center during the summer months of 1964. Virginia CWCC, Centennial Newsletter, Sept. 1964, folder on "Virginia Civil War Centennial Commission—1962—Information," box 129, subject files 1957–66, CWCCR. Attendance at Gettysburg rose annually from 1.7 million visits in 1961 to 2.3 million in 1965. See NPS tabulations in folder on "National Park Service," box 27, subject files 1957–66, CWCCR.

96. Robert Cook, "From Shiloh to Selma: The Impact of the Civil War Centennial on the Black Freedom Struggle in the United States, 1961–65," in Brian Ward and Tony Badger, eds., *The Making of Martin Luther King and the Civil Rights Movement* (Basingstoke, UK: Macmillan, 1996), 145.

trenchant remarks were those of the *Birmingham News,* an increasingly out-spoken critic of Governor George Wallace:

> Four years ago we began a Civil War Centennial memorialization. It foundered and we have not heard much about it in some time. Perhaps it was just as well. The time during which the centennial observance fell has been a troubled time, and the trouble is not over yet.
>
> Today we can think back in a quiet tribute to the courage and sacrifices of those who fell during the terrible four years, men in blue as well as gray. The Union was preserved. Though Southern advocacy lingers, surely none can regret the victory did assure the Union, without any right of secession. Had that not been the outcome, we would not be strong enough today to stand for our own and the freedom of others throughout the world.[97]

This reassertion of the orthodox line on the Civil War peddled remorselessly by the CWCC since the late 1950s spoke volumes. While the centennial had evoked bitter "memories" of the War Between the States, it seemed even more evident at the close than it had been at the beginning of the commemoration that many white southerners were reluctant to allow those remembrances to obstruct the progress of either the region or the wider American nation. As the use of Confederate symbols to contest black political and cultural influence in the South revealed, deep-rooted resentments spawned by the Civil War did not simply disappear. When, in early 1965, the *Columbia State* issued a special edition to coincide with the centenary of the burning of the South Carolina capital, one local woman thanked the editor for revealing "the extent of the carefully planned destruction and petty malice shown by Sherman and his merciless assault on the people of South Carolina."[98] What was waning, however, was the power of such memories to move large numbers of whites in the region to take actions that ran counter to their interests in the second half of the twentieth century.

The Civil War centennial was not the bringer of change. This was the work of the civil rights movement in combination with economic development and the belated intervention of the federal government. However, the commemoration did uncover the limits of segregationist resistance in the 1960s even if,

97. *Birmingham News,* April 9, 1965, 10.

98. Lulu Crosland Ricaud to William D. Workman Jr., Feb. 17, 1965, folder on "The State, Special Editions, The Burning of Columbia, Reader Response," William D. Workman Jr., Papers, Modern Political Collections, South Caroliniana Library, University of South Carolina.

as in the case of Ross Barnett and George Wallace, it sometimes helped to fuel it. The reality was that growing numbers of whites, even in the Deep South, grudgingly became reconciled to the demise of Jim Crow. Two weeks before the closing ceremony at Appomattox, the *Birmingham News* had responded to the police attack on peaceful civil rights demonstrators in Selma by criticizing Alabama's political leaders for endangering the state's future.[99] Although this viewpoint prompted plenty of negative responses, several readers wrote in with a reality check. "We have listened so often to Gov. Wallace make alibis and proclaim 'segregation forever,'" said one of them, "that many of us apparently believe that it can last forever and that it is our inherited right to deny the Negro his right to vote. I have lived in Alabama all my life, and I love the South; but I feel I live in America—not the Confederacy. If it is wrong to discriminate in America, it is wrong in Alabama."[100] It is doubtful whether the CWCC's small contingent of progressive white southerners ever read this comment. Had they done so, they surely would have felt that their considerable labors were paying off and that at last their beloved Southland was beginning to move forward without entirely jettisoning its fevered past.

99. *Birmingham News,* March 28, 1965, 1.
100. *Birmingham News,* April 7, 1965, 10.

7

An Opportunity for Warmth

The Civil War Centennial as an Exercise in Consensus Culture

ALTHOUGH THE VARIOUS Civil War centennial commissions—national, state, and local—took the lead in supervising commemorative activities across the United States, they had no monopoly on how the most traumatic event in the country's history was sold to Americans in the late 1950s and 1960s. Government elites seeking to use the centennial as a tool of consensus soon discovered that the Civil War was subject to multiple interpretations and that other groups, notably blacks and white southerners, were no less determined to co-opt the plastic past for their own ends. Joining in the cultural struggle for the memory of the Civil War were a plethora of other interested parties including television producers, Hollywood moviemakers, historical fiction writers, and academics. Of course, many of their visual and written productions were driven by the desire for corporate and individual profit. However, in general their motives were more mixed than those of the manufacturers of those tacky centennial souvenirs so distasteful to many of the commemoration's organizers. Eager to entertain and sometimes to instruct, as well as simply to make a profit, they generated a sizable corpus of Civil War programs, films, and books. This cultural output did little to overturn existing popular preconceptions about the war, but under the influence of the ongoing civil rights movement, it did exhibit perceptible signs of an intellectual shift away from the racially exclusive consensus narrative of the Civil War that had underpinned segregation since the late nineteenth century.

THE WAR ON SCREEN

The Civil War centennial did not attract as much attention from the purveyors of television and silver-screen excitement as some commentators expected at the outset. In one sense, this was surprising. The Civil War was an undeniably dramatic event and one that exercised a demonstrable hold on the national psyche. Rendered colorful, tragic, and romantic as it had been in the lush 1939

MGM film version of *Gone with the Wind,* it had been shown to be, potentially at least, a highly marketable product. But herein lay a major problem. *Gone with the Wind* was a hard act to follow. Any Civil War movie was bound to seem tame alongside it. In addition, at $4.25 million, it had proved extremely expensive to make.[1] The studio had struck gold by turning it into one of the first genuine event movies, tying it closely to Margaret Mitchell's bestselling novel of the same name, marketing it effectively, and conducting a very public and lengthy search for the right actress to play the heroine, Scarlett O'Hara. Had the film included battle scenes it would have been even more costly. (Audiences watching *Gone with the Wind* experienced combat indirectly in shots of Scarlett walking among the wounded, Atlanta under siege, and Confederate troops on the retreat from the burning city.) By the 1950s, when Hollywood began to face rising competition from television, movie moguls had even less reason to invest in financially risky Civil War features that could not possibly live up to the most popular film of all time and would, in all likelihood, lose them a good deal of money.[2]

Cost was not the only reason why Hollywood studios were reluctant to touch the Civil War. Producers and their financial backers were also worried about alienating white southerners. While audiences below the Mason-Dixon line were smaller than those above it, takings generated in the South were often large enough to push films into the black. Thus, when director John Huston finally managed to persuade skeptical MGM executives to back his plans for a movie version of Stephen Crane's classic novel *The Red Badge of Courage,* he announced his determination to avoid the "North vs. South" aspects of the Civil War.[3] Most of the relatively few full-blown Civil War features made during the 1950s and early 1960s (and the more common westerns that incorporated wartime themes and characters) evinced an almost pathological concern on the part of studios and moviemakers to secure the patronage of southern whites. United Artists marketed John Ford's *The Horse Soldiers* (1959) with a trailer showing Federal cavalrymen backed by a choir singing

1. Bruce Chadwick, *The Reel Civil War: Mythmaking in American Film* (New York: Alfred A. Knopf, 2001), 188.

2. Over five million television sets were sold each year in the United States during the 1950s. George Lipsitz, *Time Passages: Collective Memory and American Popular Culture* (Minneapolis: University of Minnesota Press, 1990), 44.

3. Melvyn Stokes, "The Civil War in the Movies," in Susan-Mary Grant and Peter J. Parish, eds., *Legacy of Disunion: The Enduring Significance of the American Civil War* (Baton Rouge: Louisiana State University Press, 2003), 66.

the well-known Confederate song "the Bonnie Blue Flag."[4] Television executives were also nervous about the response in the South, particularly when massive resistance to school desegregation led citizens' groups in the region to mobilize against programs that they deemed incompatible with the southern way of life. The obvious response, which was to render any Civil War program sympathetic to the Confederacy, was not entirely unproblematic. CBS's *The Gray Ghost* (1957), an adventure series about John Mosby's Rebel partisans, was so pro-southern that it met stiff resistance from national advertisers concerned about its lack of appeal to nonsoutherners. The company first offered the tales of Mosby's derring-do on syndicated release only and then canceled the series completely.[5]

In the wake of this sobering experience, TV companies were slow to take advantage of the programming opportunities presented by the centennial. In early 1961 the scriptwriter Mort Lewis reported that media folk were moving in on the Civil War field "with the force, vigor and speed of an army of snails attacking a fortress of turtles." There were, he claimed, two reasons for this lack of interest among TV executives: first, a widespread feeling that Americans were not as obsessed about the Civil War as centennial organizers believed; and second, specific concerns about the reactions of southern whites. Both views, reckoned Lewis, were misguided, but, he added, "they are as genuine as Joe Johnston's Quaker guns at Manassas were to McClellan."[6]

Worries about the profitability and impact of Civil War productions resulted in a dearth of output on both the wide and the small screens. The relatively few TV programs and movies on the subject that did appear during the centennial years usually bent over backwards to be fair to both sides (but particularly the South) and, in spite of being designed to entertain rather than to instruct, carried an underlying political message entirely consonant with the dominant values of the 1950s. For the most part the message was blatantly consensual, a point illustrated by the title of NBC's *The Americans,* which premiered in January 1961. A saga of the Canfield brothers, one Confederate, the other a bluecoat, the series went out of its way not to offend southern whites. "Far more episodes focused on the brother in gray than the brother in blue," recalls one devoted fan. "The Confederate brother and his comrades always

---

4. Joseph McBride, *Searching for John Ford: A Life* (New York: St. Martin's, 2001), 595.

5. Allison Graham, *Framing the South: Hollywood, Television, and Race during the Civil Rights Struggle* (Baltimore: Johns Hopkins University Press, 2001), 4.

6. *New York Times,* April 12, 1961, 56.

kicked the stuffing out of swarms of Yankees and cheered while doing so. The brother in blue never seemed really interested in combat." [7]

Rather greater sectional balance was on display in *Quantrill's Raiders*. In this 1958 United Artists release directed by Edward Bernds, a Confederate officer played by Steve Cochran improbably abets the Union garrison in Lawrence, Kansas, to defend the town against William Quantrill's southern guerrillas. His developing romance with a local Yankee woman underscores the theme of sectional unity. A similarly hackneyed plot device was deployed in *The Horse Soldiers* when John Wayne (as Colonel John Marlowe, USA) falls steadily in love with a feisty southern belle in the same mold as Scarlett O'Hara. Director Sam Peckinpah, one of Hollywood's rising stars not usually renowned for his conventionality, pursued the theme of North-South reconciliation in *Major Dundee* (1965) by having Ben Tyreen, an honor-bound Confederate officer played by Richard Harris, hoist the Stars and Stripes as his final act in battle against the French in Mexico. Predictably, other films with Civil War content released during the centennial years—Disney's feel-good TV movie, *Johnny Shiloh* (1963), the MGM comedy *Advance to the Rear* (1964), or Universal's much-touted *Shenandoah* (1965)—did little to challenge audiences' preconceptions about the Civil War, certainly not to the extent of challenging the existing stereotype that the conflict had been a tragic brothers' war in which African Americans had played a negligible role.

Most disappointing for its neglect of the Civil War's racial themes at a time of expanding public concern about the state of domestic race relations was *The Horse Soldiers*. In the final stages of his career, veteran director John Ford was perfectly aware of the corrosive impact of racial prejudice on the American self. He had probed the subject to brilliant effect in his classic 1956 western *The Searchers* and, notwithstanding his evolution from New Deal liberal to nostalgic conservative, was more sensitive than many Hollywood people to the contemporary concerns of African Americans. For example, although many of the campaign sequences in *The Horse Soldiers* were shot in Mississippi and Louisiana during late 1958, Ford—worried that Althea Gibson, the black tennis star playing the part of loyal house servant Lukey, would receive unequal treatment on location—ensured that she did not have to leave Los Angeles to carry out her role.[8] No less pertinently, as a New England–born

---

7. William G. Piston to the author, Feb. 6, 2004. *The Americans,* directed by John Rich, starred Richard Davalos as Rebel brother Jeff and Darryl Hickman as Union corporal Ben.

8. Scott Eyman, *Print the Legend: The Life and Times of John Ford* (New York: Simon and Schuster, 1999), 467.

Irish American with a strong interest in United States history, Ford was better placed than anyone to make a great—perhaps *the* great—Civil War movie, one that made clear to American moviegoers not only that the war was more than just an unfortunate family quarrel but also that it was a contest of striking contemporary relevance.

Quite why Ford agreed to make a film of the script shown to him by ambitious screenwriters John Lee Mahin and Marty Rackin is difficult to say. Ford was an intelligent man, and the script in front of him was largely devoid of intellectual or artistic merit. Neither Mahin nor Rackin appears to have had more than a superficial understanding of the Civil War. Stirred by reading Harold Sinclair's 1956 story of Colonel Benjamin H. Grierson's Union incursion into Mississippi, they described the tale as having "all the dash and boldness of a commando raid." Both men felt "that the War between the States was the last of the gallant wars" and that there was "a chance in this epic story for a spectacle and an opportunity for warmth. It had the necessary elements for color and large screen. It had reality, which to us is the prime requisite of a great motion picture." Sinclair's novel, however, lacked one key ingredient. "Part of the mission in writing entertainment for a mass audience," claimed Mahin and Rackin, "is the injection of romance."[9] The result was Colonel Marlowe's slow-burning relationship with Constance Tower's southern lady, Miss Hannah Hunter of Greenbriar, set against a background of relatively sanitized sectional conflict.

Judging by the unremarkable content of the film, Ford's cold war patriotism appears to have got the better of him. Even though the movie had a predominantly northern focus in that it dramatized a Yankee raid, the motif of the doomed yet courageous South was evident throughout. Emotionally and intellectually sympathetic to the Union cause (he often boasted disingenuously that his father had fought for it), Ford had garnered respect for the Confederacy after his marriage to Mary McBride Smith, a defiant southerner who was a lifelong member of the UDC.[10] Thus, while Ford recounted the steady progress of Marlowe's Federals toward Baton Rouge, he simultaneously made the film a tribute to the Lost Cause. The southern war effort received legitimacy not only in the redoubtable character of Miss Hunter but also in Ford's depiction of an unsuccessful Pickett-style charge against the Federal troopers at Newton Station, his carefully crafted account of young southern cadets

9. John Lee Mahin and Martin Rackin, "The Horse Soldiers or Grierson's Raid," *Civil War History* 5 (1959): 183–84.

10. McBride, *Searching,* 24, 125.

marching out to confront the invaders, and the honorable conduct of a Confederate commander who offers assistance to wounded Federals in the final frames of the movie.

While such attention to sectional balance assuaged any concerns that studio executives might have had about marketing the picture, it did not make it a memorable one. Behind the scenes, *The Horse Soldiers* was an almost unmitigated disaster. Generous payments to the film's leading actors, John Wayne and William Holden, reduced the amount of money that could be lavished on the movie. Wayne's commitment was always limited because he was preoccupied with his own project, *The Alamo*. "Duke" made Ford's job even more difficult by engaging in heavy bouts of drinking with Holden. To cap matters, Ford, already fatigued by the arduous filming schedule (he was now sixty-four years old), blamed himself personally for the accidental death of his favorite stuntman, Fred Kennedy, and took to the bottle himself. By the close of the film he had lost all the interest he had once had in the project.[11]

As Mahin and Rackin later admitted, *The Horse Soldiers* was "an unfortunate picture. Bad movie."[12] But this judgment was not shared by the CWCC, which awarded it a special citation.[13] It is easy to understand why. The movie's respect for the Confederacy and its inattention to the black counter-narrative of the Civil War made it an ideal vehicle for Karl Betts and Ulysses S. Grant III, who spent the late 1950s fostering support for the centennial among southern whites. John Ford's evident unhappiness with the movie, however, may have stemmed partly from his suppression of racial themes at a time when Americans were becoming increasingly concerned about civil rights. The cinematographer William H. Clothier said that he had never "met any man who knew as much about the history of the Civil War as John Ford."[14] The celebrated director knew that slavery had played a critical role in the coming of the war, that large numbers of blacks had fought for the Union, and that these historical facts had profound relevance at the close of the Eisenhower era. An element of self-recrimination, therefore, may have contributed to his decision to make *Sergeant Rutledge* the following year. Casting the imposing black athlete Woody Strode as an officer in the 9th Cavalry, U.S. Colored Troops,

11. Ibid., 596–98.

12. Ibid., 594.

13. A photograph of General Grant presenting the award to Wayne and Holden was included in the commission's official report. See CWCC, *The Civil War Centennial: A Report to the Congress* (Washington, DC: Government Printing Office, 1968), 9.

14. McBride, *Searching*, 594.

Ford used the film not only to depict the tragic consequences of racial and sexual hysteria but also to show how nineteenth-century blacks had earned their citizenship rights by fighting against the republic's enemies (in this case the Indians).[15] He claimed to be very proud of the result. "They didn't want me to do that film," the former World War II filmmaker told an interviewer in 1966, "because they said a film about a 'nigger' wouldn't make any money and because it couldn't be distributed in the South. I got angry and told them that they could at least have the decency to say 'Negro' or 'colored man' instead of 'nigger,' because most 'niggers' were worth more than they were. I found that out when I debarked on Omaha Beach: there were dozens of bodies of blacks spread out on the sand. When I saw that, I understood that it was impossible not to consider them as full-fledged Americans."[16]

Unfortunately *Sergeant Rutledge* was, as predicted, a flop at the box office and did nothing to improve Ford's declining reputation in the United States. Even though it indicated the director's willingness to use history for overtly didactic purposes, Ford had already lost his opportunity to use popular interest in the Civil War centennial to make telling points to a wide audience. There can be few more poignant illustrations than *The Horse Soldiers* of the seductive appeal of the Lost Cause to the most well-intentioned Americans in the late 1950s.[17]

Not every Civil War–related movie released during the centennial period paid homage to the Old South. *Raintree County,* a turgid 1957 MGM film starring Elizabeth Taylor, was marketed unusually as a "Yankee version of the Civil War." The film, based on Ross Lockridge Jr.'s successful novel of the same name, subverted *Gone with the Wind* stereotypes by replacing Scarlett O'Hara with mentally unhinged plantation mistress Susanna Drake. Instead of the unbowed, stoical society depicted by Margaret Mitchell, the South featured here was the sick, racially obsessed one portrayed in the writing of Carson McCullers and Tennessee Williams. But while *Raintree County* had obvious

15. Ford's use of Indians as a device to highlight black patriotism may have resulted in another bout of personal recrimination. He certainly atoned for his negative portrayal of Native Americans in *Sergeant Rutledge* by making *Cheyenne Autumn* (1964), a worthy but overlong account of the sufferings of the Plains Indians at the hands of the federal government.

16. Gerald Peary, ed., *John Ford Interviews* (Jackson: University Press of Mississippi, 2001), 100.

17. Ford did contribute a twenty-two-minute Civil War segment to MGM's 1962 epic *How the West Was Won.* Although biographer Joseph McBride suggests that it furnished a cautionary note to the movie's expansionist bombast, the segment (which featured John Wayne as General Sherman) lacked significant intellectual or dramatic merit. McBride, *Searching,* 634.

contemporary resonance, it placed southern white womanhood, not African Americans, at the center of the historical narrative. The ongoing civil rights movement, however, was already educating Americans about the active role played by blacks in U.S. history. As it gathered pace in the early 1960s one might have expected the movement to exert increasing influence on the way the Civil War was interpreted by Hollywood.

In 1965 Universal Pictures released *Shenandoah*, a Civil War feature directed by onetime University of Virginia graduate Andrew V. McLaglen. Aware that the war was no guarantee of box office success, the studio's executives sought to maximize audiences on both sides of the Mason-Dixon line by utilizing the same strategies employed by United Artists in *The Horse Soldiers*. First, they looked for star names that would bring in the crowds. The quintessential liberal hero, James Stewart, was cast as Charlie Anderson, the widowed patriarch of a nonslaveholding Virginia family striving to remain neutral in a war growing ever closer to their well-tended homestead. Doug McClure, familiar to television audiences in his role as Trampas in *The Virginian*, played a Confederate officer wooing Anderson's daughter, Jennie. The actors playing Anderson's sons, Jacob and James, were Glenn Corbett, star of the TV series *Route 66*, and Duke's scion, Patrick Wayne, hailed by the movie's trailer as "Rising Star of *McClintock.*"

Second, Universal found a screenplay that it hoped would not offend northerners or southerners at a time of acute racial tension in the United States. James Lee Barrett, one of Hollywood's leading screenwriters, fashioned a strong plot line. As the story unfolds, the hardworking, independent-minded Andersons are drawn inexorably into the conflict with tragic consequences for individual family members. At the outset Charlie Anderson tells his combative sons that as nonslaveholders they have no business fighting in a war to protect slave property. But when his youngest boy is mistaken for a Confederate soldier and captured by the Yankees, he and his offspring begin a long and apparently fruitless search. In the picaresque second half of the movie the Andersons burn a Federal train carrying Rebel prisoners while son James and his wife, left to take care of the farm, are murdered by deserters. After a second son, Jacob, is accidentally shot by a raw Confederate recruit, an upbeat resolution is achieved by the return of the lost boy in the final scene of the movie. The film's treatment of both sides is sectionally balanced. Unsympathetic Federal characters such as a purchasing agent and a Union officer who refuses to allow the Andersons to search the train for their son are balanced by George Kennedy's dignified performance as Colonel Fairchild, who signs an order for the bòy to be released if he is found. Although the Andersons are southerners who end up opposing the Federals, viewers are invited to regard them primarily as honest, God-fearing Americans caught up in a tragic situation beyond their control. The death of Jacob at the hands of the young Confederate not only highlights the senselessness of fraternal conflict but also establishes a certain distance between the Andersons and the Rebel cause.

Described in a publicity leaflet as "basically a sensitive story of the terrible futility of war" (though trailed as a movie that "Shakes the Screen with Its Thunder"), *Shenandoah* purveyed mixed messages throughout.[18] The Andersons' core values—hard work, independence, devotion to family, and reverence for God—are depicted as timeless American ones. Charlie Anderson, played in familiar homespun fashion by Stewart, is a decent man with whom we are asked to empathize. But only up to a point. For while Charlie's impulse to protect his sons from the war is entirely understandable, the narrative makes it impossible for us to avoid the conclusion that this desire is impractical, perhaps even (from a civic point of view) selfish. The sympathies of both McLaglen and Barrett appear to lie not only with Charlie but with two other characters whose influence on the elderly father is, like that of events, essentially educative.

At one point in the film the Anderson farm is visited by a group of Rebel soldiers trying to recruit the sons into Confederate service. When Lieutenant Johnston asks, "When are you going to take this war seriously, Mr. Anderson?" Charlie responds stubbornly that "this war is not mine and I take no note of it." To which the officer retorts, "Maybe you'll take notice of it when the Yankees drop a cannonball on your front parlor." Although Charlie insists that his sons belong to him and not to the state, this encounter is swiftly imbued with retrospective pathos when, in succeeding frames, the Rebel patrol is ambushed by Federals and the bodies are discovered by the Andersons. The audience's dawning realization that its sympathies should not lie entirely with the embattled family is intensified by Charlie's conversation with Tom, a local doctor who delivers his first grandchild. Virginia is losing this war, Charlie says rhetorically. The physician nods gravely and explains that he has one son buried in Pennsylvania after falling at Gettysburg, another who has just returned from the army with tuberculosis, and a third who rides with the

18. *Shenandoah* (undated publicity leaflet), folder on "National Assembly, June 1964/May 1965," box 184, Bell I. Wiley Papers, Manuscript, Archives, and Rare Book Library, Emory University.

formidable guerrilla fighter Nathan Bedford Forrest. Anderson is thus left to ruminate on what looks suspiciously like a Hollywood lesson in civic responsibility. Issued when growing numbers of fathers (and mothers) were being asked to send their sons to Vietnam in the service of the U.S. government, this lesson seemed strangely at odds with the studio's admittedly half-hearted attempt to market *Shenandoah* as an antiwar film.

Given that the civil rights movement was reaching the peak of its influence when the movie was released, one might have expected McLaglen and Barrett to advertise the patriotic role played by blacks in the Civil War. However, because the film was obviously made for white audiences, North and South, race was hardly more integral to *Shenandoah* than it had been to *The Horse Soldiers*. There was one exception. Gabriel (Eugene Jackson Jr.), a young and apparently well-treated slave belonging to one of the Andersons' neighbors, is told by Federal troops that he is free. Though we do not know it immediately, he sets off to join the Union army. What might have been an opportunity to promote understanding rather than warmth is then squandered toward the close of the movie. Gabriel reappears on the battlefield dressed in Union blue and carrying a rifle, but instead of killing Confederates (which is partly what black soldiers in the Union army were recruited to do), he rescues his wounded friend, the Andersons' missing son now fighting for the Confederacy, and, off-screen, escorts him home to the final, heartwarming family reunion. While Gabriel's Union service is at least acknowledged, the impact on viewers is softened, perniciously so, by the redeployment of the enduring southern half-truth that slaves remained loyal to their masters during the Civil War. The cursory amount of time devoted to Gabriel's wartime exploits simply adds to the impression that McLaglen and Barrett were reluctant to pay more than lip service to the activities of the modern civil rights movement.

One viewer who was not unduly bothered about this was the CWCC's executive director, James Robertson. "I freely confess," he told David Polland of Universal Pictures in April 1965, "that I have maintained a consistently negative attitude toward Hollywood's past treatments of the Civil War. Too many films were historically inaccurate, amateurishly done, and void of both the real tragedy and the deep sentiments of that era." By contrast he considered *Shenandoah* "without qualification to be the best Civil War drama ever put on film. Its battle scenes are more authentic than those in 'The Red Badge of Courage'; its plot and characters are more original than the ingredients of 'The Horse Soldiers.' In my opinion the human warmth, simple emotionalism and rich portrayal of an embattled American generation cause 'Shenandoah' to eclipse easily that so-called 'classic' treating of the war, 'Gone with the Wind.'" [19]

Only one centennial-era movie actually set during the Civil War made it clear to audiences in the early 1960s that African Americans had played a central role in the War of the Rebellion. Californian Sam Peckinpah's second feature film, *Major Dundee,* was grievously flawed as a result of producer Jerry Bresler's decision to make severe cuts before the movie saw the light of day. However, even though the promising young director was reputedly ready to "fucking" kill Bresler after seeing the final version, his "hopelessly fragmented and at times incoherent" tale of a demented Union officer's punitive expedition into Mexico in the final months of the Civil War had a certain integrity about it.[20] Peckinpah clearly intended Dundee's band of white U.S. army regulars, U.S. Colored Troops, disgruntled Confederates, and Indian guides to stand as a microcosm of American society—tough, quarrelsome, and ethnically plural yet ultimately united in its struggle against external enemies: in this case the French expeditionary force dispatched to Mexico by Emperor Napoleon III. Charlton Heston, who played the major, had been intrigued by the possibility of using the film to probe the dynamics of Civil War conflict, while the director himself was eager to assault the romantic cavalry epics of John Ford by injecting more realistic violence into his vision of the West.[21] Bresler's cuts defeated the latter goal, but Peckinpah's film did contain one scene that acknowledged race hatred and class friction as integral factors in the Civil War.

In camp after crossing the Rio Grande, Dundee's rag-tag, multicultural company is soon at war with itself. When one of the Confederates orders a black soldier, Aesop (Brock Peters), to take off his boots, the Union trooper refuses. After a white clergyman intervenes on the side of the African American, the Rebels go for their guns—a move that prompts the white bluecoat sergeant to yell, "you southern trash, sit down." A miniature sectional conflict is averted only by the action of Dundee's rival, Major Ben Tyreen, CSA. Tyreen, a beau sabreur of common birth who has already put down one of his Rebel comrades as a "red-necked peckerwood," acts quickly to prevent the

19. James I. Robertson Jr. to David Polland, April 27, 1965, folder on "Robertson, James I.—Personal 1963–1964," box 135, subject files 1957–66, Records of the Civil War Centennial Commission, Records of the National Park Service, Record Group 79, National Archives.

20. David Weddle, *Sam Peckinpah: If They Move . . . Kill 'Em!* (1994; London: Faber and Faber, 1996), 252.

21. Ibid., 229, 233.

imminent clash by complimenting "Mr. Aesop" on the way he and his men handled the day's river crossing. At the end of this tense scene Major Dundee, a southern Unionist who has no sympathy for abolitionism, tells Tyreen that the gesture was necessary but that he is sorry it was so painful for him. When the "plumed cavalier" replies warmly that southerners can take care of their own, Dundee shoots back, "If you can you waited too long to do it. All you people. All the way down the line." Freighted with contemporary significance, this remark could not have been lost on American cinemagoers at the time of the ill-fated movie's release in the spring of 1965.

Although Peckinpah's film would not have been a masterpiece even without Jerry Bresler's clumsy intervention, its honest depiction of the violence underlying relations between the various groups and individuals in Dundee's troop conveyed a more convincing picture of what had happened in the United States between 1861 and 1865 than the cozier variant peddled by Ford in *The Horse Soldiers,* McLaglen in *Shenandoah,* and, of course, the CWCC throughout its existence. This said, the sobering fact remained that a hundred years after Appomattox no one in Hollywood was prepared to make a sustained and meaningful statement about the Civil War that penetrated to the core of that vicious conflict.

FICTION FIGHTS THE CIVIL WAR

In 1956 Ralph Newman, founder of the Civil War Book Club in Chicago, observed that around 100,000 books (fiction as well as history) had been written about the war. Someone, he noted (Carl Sandburg perhaps), had suggested "that if you wanted to build an all-inclusive collection of every Civil War title known, you would have to shelve the Grand Canyon to make a place to put it."[22] If these marks of public interest in the war must have been grist to Newman's mill, the advent of the centennial promised even better business for authors, publishers, and booksellers. Writing five years later, at the outset of the centennial proper, James Robertson calculated that over 300 Civil War books had been published in the previous eighteen months. However, the poor quality of many of these titles meant that he regarded this figure as a cause for concern rather than a reason to celebrate. Unless the present trend was halted, he wrote, "the real contributions to Civil War history will be lost in the avalanche and the reading public may grow weary of searching for works of real historical and literary value." Insisting that "the literary forces now marshaled have a greater potential for destruction than did the armies of Lee, Grant, John-

---

22. Ralph G. Newman, "For Collectors Only," *Civil War History* 2 (1956): 97.

ston and Sherman," Robertson concluded: "Authors, publishers, and readers all have obligations to one another in perpetuating the true saga of the Civil War. And all assuredly owe an inestimable debt to those men of Blue and Gray who demonstrated a courage, fortitude, and devotion to duty so characteristic of America. We *must* keep that image alive—and undistorted."[23]

The anxiety of the young University of Iowa professor about standards was fully justified, for the quality of the vast literary output of the centennial years was extremely uneven. However, as far as Civil War fiction was concerned, this was actually no great surprise. Contemporary literary critics seemed agreed that the sectional conflict had produced no literature of any great worth. As Robert A. Lively put it in 1957: "The plain fact is that the mass of Civil War novels flows out in that sluggish stream which has been described as 'sub-literary.'"[24] Yet Lively went on to contend correctly that historical fiction was not without its importance, owing to its reflection of "persistent sectional traditions" and role as an underrated provider of education about the war itself.[25] As Ralph Newman indicated, the Civil War had furnished a compelling subject for American writers over the years. The centennial period witnessed publication of scores of new novels that allow us an opportunity to gauge the impact of political and social change on the popular fiction of the 1960s.

A glance at this work reveals the extent of that impact to have been decidedly limited. The majority of the themes covered by the writers of Civil War stories in the centennial period were familiar, hoary ones that had underpinned the mainstream interpretation of the Civil War for decades. A modicum of sectional bias was often apparent, but authors appear to have realized that an excess of regional zeal was bound to limit the size of their readership and therefore to have tempered their advocacy of either cause accordingly.

Among the most common themes in the popular fiction of the centennial was that of the kindly Mr. Lincoln, a centerpiece of national mythology long accepted, if not always endorsed enthusiastically, by large numbers of southern whites. Readers of all ages in the early 1960s could find the nation's wartime savior in a variety of situations. In Natalia M. Belting's *Indy and Mr. Lincoln* (1960), young Abe rescues a naughty white pig from the mud at the expense of ruining his Sunday best. "I reckon, Indy," says the lanky railsplitter, "the only way folks will be able to tell us apart is by the length of our

---

23. James I. Robertson, "The Continuing War," *Civil War History* 7 (1961): 81–82.

24. Robert A. Lively, *Fiction Fights the Civil War* (Chapel Hill: University of North Carolina Press, 1957), 4.

25. Ibid., 5.

legs." [26] Another children's book, Helen Kay's *Abe Lincoln's Hobby,* which appeared the following year, also featured animals—in this case cats who laugh until Lincoln's death deprives them of the one person whose humorous stories could make them smile. [27] Teens who read Irene Hunt's award-winning *Across Five Aprils* (1964) encountered the merciful, "sad-eyed" president through the home-front experiences of Illinois farm boy Jethro Creighton. When one of Jethro's elder brothers deserts from the Union army, the lad writes to Lincoln and receives word of an amnesty for those who have left the front without permission. [28]

A similar tactic benefits Linden Cleave in David Divine's *Thunder on the Chesapeake* (1961), an overwrought account of the *Monitor-Merrimac* duel in 1862. Lindie (a devout Virginia secessionist who is ravished by her would-be Rebel lover, Revell Jordan, as the aptly named *USS Congress* burns in Hampton Roads) espies Lincoln on a visit to Norfolk and is struck by the dark eyes "filled with an illimitable sadness." In spite of her experience at the hands of Jordan, Linden acts swiftly when he is captured by the Federals. She visits the White House, obtains a personal interview with the president, and emerges with release papers. Lincoln's only request is that the young woman should return home and help him in his task of making "the Nation come together again." Fortunately for Linden, Stephen Knott, a thoroughly decent U.S. naval officer who has long been a rival for her affections, accompanies her on the voyage home. They gaze out at Old Glory flapping proudly on the shore at Hospital Point. "Lin, you've got to accept it now," says Stephen. "Yes, I know," replies Linden implausibly as she reflects on the president's contention that a house divided against itself cannot stand. "This is going to be the greatest country that the world has ever known—if it holds together." [29]

Abe Lincoln's boundless charity was not the only commonplace theme of Civil War fiction during the early 1960s. Others, no less potent, included Rebel fortitude in the face of insuperable odds and the fidelity of blacks to southern whites. Toward the close of *The Dram Tree* (1961), Hamilton Cochran's bodice-ripping yarn of Confederate blockade-running, the central character Jeffrey Ryall and his beautiful companion, Tina Tyler, are present at the Federal attack on Fort Fisher in early 1865. Although the Rebels are outnumbered

26. Natalia M. Belting, *Indy and Mr. Lincoln* (New York: Henry Holt and Company, 1960), unnumbered page.

27. Helen Kay, *Abe Lincoln's Hobby* (Chicago: Reilly and Lee, 1961), unnumbered page.

28. Irene Hunt, *Across Five Aprils* (Chicago: Follett, 1964), 69, 159–75.

29. David Divine, *Thunder on the Chesapeake* (New York: Macmillan, 1961), 287, 365, 382, 388.

by four or five to one, the lovers strive valiantly to fight off the assault (Tina herself kills a marauding Yankee with a pistol), then escape from the fort and are given shelter by Sam and Liza Brown, free blacks who know Ryall's uncle. Revived with the aid of Liza's nourishing chicken broth, the lovers finally take their leave. "Thank God for people like you," says Tina as the Browns raise their arms in a parting salute. The novel ends with Jeff musing over the dram tree outside Wilmington, how it has "stood against storms and lightning and floods, strong, enduring and proud, just like the spirit of North Carolina all through history." The elderly pilot, Cappy, agrees: "The folks of the Old North State has got some git-up-and-go to them. They ain't going to sit around and moan and sulk just cause we lost the war."[30] Scarlett herself could not have put it better.

Signs of the reigning orthodoxy were apparent throughout the popular fiction of the centennial years. Frances Parkinson Keyes, a well-known southern novelist, stressed the ease of life for blacks under slavery in *Madame Castel's Lodger* (1962), her sprawling tribute to Confederate general P. G. T. Beauregard. "[T]he dusky residents" of the Beauregard plantation in Louisiana, Keyes told her readers, thieved without fear of punishment, possessed chicken coops and gardens, were visited regularly by the plantation mistress, and benefited from the communal nursery, where an "aged and capable Negress watched over the welfare of the pickaninnies whose mothers were working in the fields."[31] Southern writers who rejected the class-bound Old South tradition embraced by Keyes made it clear that most Confederate soldiers had not gone to war to preserve slavery. William Humphrey's *The Ordways* (1965), a fictionalized history of a family from northeast Texas, dwells respectfully on the character of grandfather Thomas Ordway. Thomas, blinded by shrapnel at Shiloh, had not joined the Army of Tennessee to defend slavery (any more than Union soldiers had gone to war to destroy it). Hating the peculiar institution because of the power it gave to southern elites, he fought not for an abstraction—his state or the Confederacy—but to defend his home.[32] In this he apparently had much in common with Johnny McLeod, the hero of Maggie Davis's *The Far Side of Home* published in 1963. Davis, a feature writer for the *Atlanta Journal and Constitution* who acknowledged the assistance of Bell Wiley, set out to write a novel of the common southern soldier. Encumbered

---

30. Hamilton Cochran, *The Dram Tree* (Indianapolis: Bobbs-Merrill, 1961), 285–86.

31. Frances Parkinson Keyes, *Madame Castel's Lodger* (New York: Farrar, Straus and Cudahy, 1962), 37.

32. William Humphrey, *The Ordways* (New York: Alfred A. Knopf, 1965), 39–40.

with an ear wound sustained during the battles for Atlanta, McLeod, a private in Hood's army, returns home to Jonesboro. There he fulminates against the source of the family's ills: "[T]he most damned fool thing that ever sent a nation to war was that property that started this one, and don't you believe it didn't . . . property that most of us never had any truck with! Niggers! A rich man's war and a poor man's fight! That's the gospel. Black property never meant a thing to most people in this state, only about a hundred or so that call themselves planters, aristocrats, what-have-you . . . I went off the same as the rest, I didn't have any niggers, didn't intend to have any, and wouldn't fool with them if I did, and yet I wasn't by God going to let some damned pinch-nosed Yankee come down here and throw things in an uproar over niggers."[33]

Authors who wrote from a northern point of view focused less on slavery as a cause of the war than on broader themes such as the coming-of-age experience and the tragedy of internecine struggle. *Johnny Shiloh: A Novel of the Civil War,* a popular 1959 offering from James A. Rhodes and Dean Jauchius, tells the story of Johnny Klem, a ten-year-old drummer boy devoted to the cause of the North, who escapes from home to accompany his state's Blue Raiders on their campaigns through Secessia.[34] Despite being appalled by the behavior of individual members of the regiment—especially the loathsome Long Charley—Johnny maintains his faith in the Union and grows up in the service of the same, impressing General Grant with his courage under fire at Shiloh, killing his first Rebel at Chickamauga, and swigging whisky after the assault on Lookout Mountain. Donald Honig's *Walk Like a Man* (1961) narrates the education of Jeffrey Taylor, a young New Yorker who, ignorant of what the war is about, pursues secretive Uncle Clay into Virginia. On the journey he meets a Union officer who explains why his men are fighting. "[O]ur country is our greater home," says Captain Morris, "and I'll wager you, Jeff, you've never taken thought to see how much you love it or how desperately you would fight to defend it."[35] At the close of the novel, Jeffrey discovers that Clay is a Confederate spy and completes the transition from ignorance to knowledge, from youth to manhood, by shooting him dead.

33. Maggie Davis, *The Far Side of Home* (New York: Alfred A. Knopf, 1963), 191–92.

34. James A. Rhodes and Dean Jauchius, *Johnny Shiloh: A Novel of the Civil War* (New York: Bobbs-Merrill, 1959). Rhodes, Ohio's longest-serving governor (1963–71, 1975–83), was state auditor when he co-wrote *Johnny Shiloh*. A Republican, he courted controversy in 1970 by sending National Guard troops to quell an antiwar disturbance on the campus of Kent State University. Four students were killed in the ensuing violence.

35. Donald Honig, *Walk Like a Man* (New York: William Sloane, 1961), 142.

Although books written from a northern perspective contained material likely to annoy some southern readers, most were written in the grip of
the lilywhite nationalist consensus. Johnny Shiloh was no hater of Rebels. At
Pittsburg Landing the boy-hero gives water to a dying Confederate. He asks
God to "[h]elp that feller" and muses that Rebs are no different from Yankees.
"'We're killing our own,' he muttered at last, and he was shaking. 'Killing our
own. And now I ain't sure why.'"[36] Lying in a hospital bed after the Union
defeat at Chickamauga, his friend, the giant blacksmith Gabe Trotter, is in a
similarly reflective mood: "There could be no right in this war . . . No justice.
No goodness. This was a fight between brothers. This was the story of Cain
and Abel. It was wrong."[37] Some pro-Union novels made brief allusions to the
role of slavery in causing civil war and to the antiblack sentiments of southern soldiers, but, crucially, they counterbalanced antislavery references with
consensus-oriented comments on the racism of the North and the hypocrisy
of radical abolitionists.[38] While readers learned that Gabe Trotter joined the
Blue Raiders "because he couldn't reconcile slavery with his religion," they
also witness through Johnny Shiloh's eyes the rape of a black girl by members of the regiment. "'They're only criminals,' Long Charley growled. 'Good
for one thing,' the red-faced corporal grunted. Then they all laughed. All but
Johnny."[39] On the road south Major Hank Stephens, the leading character in
John Brick's *The Richmond Raid* (1963), watches as a hapless black guide is
hanged by Union troops for leading them astray. "He was only a harmless
fool," says Stephens in muted opposition.[40] On the midwestern home-front,
Irene Hunt's Jethro Creighton is alarmed at the growing spirit of vindictiveness in the North—a spirit urged on by the radical Republicans "who resented

36. Rhodes and Jauchius, *Johnny Shiloh,* 86.

37. Ibid., 198.

38. Most Union troops harbored racist views. My point here is that under the influence of
Lost Cause ideology and consensus orthodoxy, writers of historical fiction in the early 1960s were
reluctant to consider that a minority of northern soldiers found slavery morally distasteful before
they joined up and that far greater numbers grew to hate the institution as the war progressed. It
was not unknown for antislavery attitudes, normally arising out of religious belief, to translate
into humanitarian concern for blacks. See Reid Mitchell, *Civil War Soldiers* (1988; reprint, New
York: Penguin, 1997), 117–31; James M. McPherson, *For Cause and Comrades: Why Men Fought
in the Civil War* (Oxford: Oxford University Press, 1997), 117–30; and, for cast-iron proof, David
C. Rankin, *Diary of a Christian Soldier: Rufus Kinsley and the Civil War* (Cambridge: Cambridge
University Press, 2004).

39. Rhodes and Jauchius, *Johnny Shiloh,* 102.

40. John Brick, *The Richmond Raid* (Garden City, NY: Doubleday, 1963), 154.

the President's spirit of clemency as violently as they resented the tenacity of the South."[41] Depressed by the way Unionists applaud the burning of Columbia, Jethro visits the offices of local newspaper editor Ross Milton. Milton is equally worried about the revenge mentality abroad in the North and, though elated by Illinois's ratification of the Thirteenth Amendment, is concerned by the complexity of racial issues. What will happen to the freedpeople, he asks the lad? "What will become of men and women who have known nothing but servitude all the days of their lives? They are without experience, without education; they'll be pawns in the hands of exploiters all over the nation. You watch this thing, Jeth, you watch the abolitionists who have ranted against the South; see if they extend the hand of friendship to the uneducated, unskilled men who will come to the north looking to them as a savior."[42]

When Jethro accepts the wisdom of these comments by recalling the antiabolitionist comments of his southern cousin, readers are left in little doubt that Milton is articulating the views of the book's author. An elementary school teacher in the notoriously racist Chicago suburb of Cicero, Irene Hunt harbored orthodox views about the abolitionists which were not only grounded in longstanding scholarly wisdom but which may also have reflected her own anxieties about contemporary racial problems in the urban North.

The best single clue to the persistence of the racially charged consensus narrative in the Civil War fiction of the early 1960s was the widespread dearth of credible African-American characters. An awareness of black agency, however, generated by a combination of personal experience and contemporary events, was evident in at least two novels—both of them the work of white southerners.

John William Corrington's *And Wait for the Night* (1964) was an angry text. The author, a thirty-two-year-old Rice graduate and member of the English faculty at Louisiana State University, conceived his first novel as a "deeply felt tribute to the fathers," a story "about the time they [the Yankees] occupied my country and tore it up so badly that, when things more or less settled down, no one in my family managed to get to college between 1866 and 1951."[43] The unfolding narrative (which follows the main character, Major

41. Hunt, *Across Five Aprils*, 195.

42. Ibid., 214.

43. John William Corrington, *And Wait for the Night* (New York: G. P. Putnam's Sons, 1964), comments on back of dust jacket. Corrington, a friend of LSU's prominent Civil War historian T. Harry Williams, found his sectional consciousness raised by reading *The Angry Scar*, Hodding Carter's bitter novel of life in the postbellum South. William Parrill, "After the Confederate War: A

Edward Sentell, from the siege of Vicksburg to the postbellum Union occupation of his home town of Shreveport) is burdened with a labored plot
and a host of stock characters. The latter include Colonel Jonathan Lodge, a
wrathful Yankee officer whose abolitionism is rank hypocrisy; Amos Stevens,
a decent pro-Confederate planter who is served by his faithful black attendant, Rye Crowninshield, secretly liberated by his master before the war; and
Bouvier, a virulently racist comrade of Sentell who joins the Klan-style resistance to Reconstruction. The novel is raised above the average in part by Corrington's rejection of the cozy trope of the brothers' war. He opens his story at
the siege of Vicksburg with Sentell, Bouvier, and their colleague, Masterson,
pouring a withering fire into a Yankee salient created by the explosion of a
mine under the city's fortifications. Unusually for any artistic production of
the centennial years, readers were allowed to smell the stench of death. As
"the casual slaughter" continues, "Sentell began to see bodies, parts of bodies. The Federals lay on top of one another like cornstalks fallen under the
scythe, like grass cut and bundled carelessly, left to rot by the mower's hand." [44]
This Peckinpah-like willingness to convey the ferocity of battle is imbued with
greater meaning by Corrington's honest acknowledgment that white supremacism underpinned the Confederate cause in the Civil War and that some black
men had actually fought with the North to kill southern whites. When the
firing at the crater stops, the Rebels are confronted by a handful of survivors.
The latter "stood straight and defiant and stared up at them as if the difference between death and imprisonment was really no difference at all, and
that however the Southerners might decide it, there would be no begging, no
more bowing, and smirking, no more deference at all ... 'Niggers,' Masterson
said.—'Niggers.'" [45]

No less remarkably for a centennial-era work of historical fiction, *And Wait
for the Night* also includes a genuinely active black character, Rye Crowninshield's son, Phillipe, who absconds from his master at Antietam, joins the
Union army, and returns to Shreveport, the setting for much of Corrington's
later prose, at the head of 300 U.S. Colored Troops from the garrison at Little
Rock. Even though he is under no illusions about the Federals, Phillipe un-
derstands the significance of a uniform and a gun. March straight, he tells his
men as they prepare to parade through the streets. "What you got to show is

Conversation with John William Corrington (1932–1988)," in *John William Corrington: Southern
Man of Letters,* ed. William Mills (Conway: University of Central Arkansas Press, 1994), 184–85.

44. Corrington, *And Wait,* 40, 41.

45. Ibid., 45.

you know what freedom is for." As the story unravels, tensions in Shreveport increase. Colonel Lodge looks for any excuse to grind the treasonous residents into the dirt while they in turn resent the prospect of blacks lording it over them. Amos Stevens, however, refuses to acquiesce in Bouvier's plans for an attack on Phillipe ("There will be no night-riding against one of my people"). And Sentell, a spokesman for the New South, helps to save the black man's life by warning him of the guerrillas' impending attack. After his narrow escape from death, Phillipe tells his father, "See what your white people tried to do to me?" To which Rye responds by holding Amos's hand to his chest and saying, "Dis is my white people here." [46]

It would be easy to take this closing retort as evidence of Corrington's innate conservatism. The same could be said for Sentell's wartime prediction that the United States is likely to become "a single monolithic giant of a nation with its heart in New York, its brain in Washington and its cells, the states themselves, only ciphers, only shadow governments to pass dicta from the central rulers to the people ruled." [47] However, Corrington's decision, grudging though it may have been, to give blacks an authentic-sounding voice indicated that the book was not, as one reviewer suggested, "a Ku Klux tract," but rather the work of a promising young southern author. [48] Corrington may have been steeped in the mythology of the nineteenth-century South and too quick to blame avowedly hypocritical Yankees for the triumph of modernity over tradition in America, yet patently he was suspicious of Lost Cause dogma, cognizant of the need for interracial cooperation within the region, and more aware than most of his peers that blacks had played a positive role in U.S. history.

It was a more prominent southern writer, Robert Penn Warren, who composed the most profound work of Civil War fiction of the early 1960s. Entering his mid-fifties when the centennial began, Warren was widely regarded as one of the modern South's most perceptive commentators and talented writers. Notwithstanding his impeccable Confederate credentials—Grandfather Penn had ridden with Forrest—Warren's sensitivity to the burdens of history rendered him a rigorous critic of both his native region and modern American society in general. [49] A public opponent of segregation, he was suspicious

46. Ibid., 345, 433, 495

47. Ibid., 48–49.

48. Parrill, "After the Confederate War," 186.

49. For Warren, his allegedly antislavery grandfather was "history," "the living symbol of the wild action and romance of the past." *Talking With Robert Penn Warren,* ed. Floyd C. Watkins, John T. Hiers, and Mary Louise Weaks (Athens: University of Georgia Press, 1990), 2.

nonetheless of easy solutions to the South's racial problems and insistent on the need to devise answers in the light not of abstractions but of social and cultural realities.

In 1961 he published *The Legacy of the Civil War,* a book the iconoclastic literary critic Edmund Wilson adjudged "the most intelligent comment . . . that has yet been brought forth by this absurd centennial."[50] His primary insight was that the war, "that mystic cloud from which emerged our modernity," had allowed North and South to evade self-criticism. White southerners, he contended, used the Civil War as "the Great Alibi." Confederate mythology enabled them to turn defeat into victory and defects into virtues. Foremost among these defects, insisted Warren, was the majority population's treatment of race. Did whites ever realize, he pondered, that the events at Little Rock and elsewhere were obscene parodies of the meaning of history? But northerners were no less culpable, he wrote. For them the Civil War was the "Treasury of Virtue," a dimly understood conflict that allowed them to feel good about themselves for no particular reason.[51] Only blacks, he contended, remembered "the Big Sell-Out," the North's abandonment of the former slaves in the 1870s.[52] True, the abolitionist cause was just, he admitted, "But who can fail to be disturbed and chastened by the picture of the joyful mustering of the darker forces of our nature in that just cause?"[53] Reminding Americans at a time of sham battles that the war was extremely costly in terms of "real blood, not tomato catsup," Warren concluded that the war's essential contemporary meaning was that it held in suspension "so many of the issues and tragic ironies—somehow essential yet incommensurable—which we yet live."[54]

Warren explored some of these themes in *Wilderness: A Tale of the Civil War,* also published in 1961. The allegorical novelette was a difficult book written in Warren's spare, allusive style. It found little favor with some reviewers, one of whom charged the author with "sententious solemnity and mass appeal sexuality."[55] The key to understanding the story lies in Warren's contention in *Legacy* that America's racial strife resulted from an absence of rigorous self-criticism on the part of northerners and southerners. In *Wilderness* he uses

50. Edmund Wilson, *Patriotic Gore: Studies in the Literature of the Civil War* (New York: Oxford University Press, 1962), xxxi.

51. Robert Penn Warren, *The Legacy of the Civil War: Meditations on the Centennial* (New York: Random House, 1961), 53–57.

52. Ibid., 68.

53. Ibid., 23.

54. Ibid., 50, 108.

55. John Blotner, *Robert Penn Warren: A Biography* (New York: Random House, 1997), 349.

the wartime experiences of Adam Rosenzweig, a naïve, club-footed Bavarian Jew who comes to the United States to fight for freedom, in order to chart the character's intellectual transition from deluded romantic to clear-sighted realist. Warren conceived this transition to be imperative for societies and individuals alike.

Even though the book was really no more about the Civil War than the poet Robert Lowell's contemporaneous critique of modern American values, "For the Union Dead" (1960), the sectional conflict provided Warren with the tools to press his thesis. Adam's intellectual journey is driven largely by a cumulative awareness of northern hypocrisy and flawed humanity (black as well as white). As soon as he arrives in New York he is swept up in the antiblack draft riots of July 1863. (Initially he thinks the city must be under attack by Rebels.) Saved from death by Mose, the black servant of his rich uncle, Aaron Blaustein (a cynical figure contemptuous of civic duty and the *Plattdeutsch* who ran at Chancellorsville), Adam sets out for the front with Mose and a brooding white southerner, Jedeen Hawksworth, another of Blaustein's employees whom the German ingénue takes to be an opponent of slavery. Along the road and on arrival in northern Virginia, Adam discovers that nothing is quite what he has assumed. Federal troops abuse women and use contrabands for sport. Jedeen turns out not to be an abolitionist. A southern woman tells Adam, "Killen [is] what they is fightin fer. They all done got the habit."[56] Most important, perhaps, Mose, a significant character in the book, is shown to be a genuinely human figure rather than the idealized figment of Adam's abolitionist zeal. Having already alienated Adam by lusting openly after a white woman, the African American forfeits any residual trust by being unmasked as a Union deserter and then murdering Jedeen for his money. Alone in the Wilderness surrounded by the noise of battle, Adam feels betrayed by everyone he has known. Yet cumulatively his experiences have brought him to a state of elation: "He felt that he was on the verge of a great truth. He felt that everything he had ever known was false."[57] Liberated from his romantic ideas, he knows now that persistent self-criticism is the only solution to self-delusion. He knew at that moment "that he would have to try to know what a man must know to be a man. He knew that he would have to try to know that

56. Robert Penn Warren, *Wilderness: A Tale of the Civil War* (New York: Random House, 1961), 266.

57. Ibid., 303.

the truth is unbetrayable, and that only the betrayer is ever betrayed, and then only by his own betraying."[58]

Of course, as both *Legacy* and *Wilderness* revealed (and as at least one critic pointed out), Warren was unable completely to transcend his regional attachment.[59] The Lost Cause trope of northern hypocrisy remained central to most white southerners' understanding of the war, and this quintessentially southern author relied heavily upon it to promote his deeper agenda. His interpretation of the Civil War was shaped inevitably not only by his southern upbringing but also by the existing state of historical knowledge about topics such as abolitionism. However, at the same time that Warren penned his pleas for the relentless scrutiny of myth masquerading as history, some American historians were beginning to ask new and searching questions about the received wisdom on the Civil War.

(RE)WRITING CIVIL WAR HISTORY

In 1960 one of the country's most respected historians, C. Vann Woodward, dedicated his influential book *The Burden of Southern History* to Robert Penn Warren. Woodward, like Warren and many of his fellow southern liberals, regarded special pleading by North or South as extremely dangerous. "We are," he wrote, "presently approaching the centenary of the Civil War. Simultaneously we are approaching the climax of a new sectional crisis—a crisis that divides the country along much the old sectional lines, over many of the same old sectional issues. It would be an ironic, not to say tragic, coincidence if the celebration of the anniversary took place in the midst of a crisis reminiscent of the one celebrated." He continued: "The historian who, in these circumstances, writes the commemorative volumes for the Civil War centennial would seem to have a special obligation of sobriety and fidelity to the record. If he writes in that spirit, he will flatter the self-righteousness of neither side. He will not picture the North as burning for equality since 1863 with a hard, gem-like flame. He will not picture the South as fighting for the eternal verities. He will not paint a holy war that ennobled its participants. And he will try to keep in mind the humility that prevented the central figure in the drama

---

58. Ibid., 310.

59. Warren, commented a hostile British reviewer of *Legacy*, "tries to give what he probably conceives to be a middle-of-the-road account of the Civil War, but the old partisanship shows through in the very choice of language." Peter d'A. Jones, "The Struggle for the Union Continues," *New Republic*, May 15, 1961, 17.

[Lincoln] from ever falling in with the notion that he was the incarnation of the Archangel Michael."[60]

Over the next five years many well-known historians, some of them members of the CWCC, took Woodward's advice to heart, attempting to write accounts of the Civil War period without surrendering to the temptation of sectional bias. But as the civil rights movement grew in vitality, some of Woodward's peers rejected his cautious message. At a critical moment when nonviolent protesters were risking their lives to challenge what passed for the conscience of America, activist scholars seized on history as a weapon of social reform and elevated nineteenth-century abolitionists to the level of heroes. The civil rights crusade had a dramatic impact on how familiar topics in nineteenth-century U.S. history were interpreted by historians. Although an unabashed presentism and ingrained nationalism rendered their work problematic, some professional Civil War scholars in the late 1950s and 1960s did more than any contemporary film director or fiction writer to ensure that it would never again be possible to launch a bland, racially exclusive commemoration of America's most damaging contest.

The three major historical blockbusters of the period, however, were written in the lingering grip of consensus orthodoxy. Of these the least heralded at the time was Shelby Foote's *The Civil War: A Narrative*. In 1954 Foote, a Mississippi-born novelist whose great-grandfather had fought at Shiloh and chased Grierson's raiders across the Magnolia State, secured a commission from Random House to compose a three-part history of the war. Writing 500 words a day, he completed two massive volumes of what he called his "American iliad" during the centennial period.[61] Hailed by one commentator as "the single outstanding achievement of the Centennial observance," the project's strengths lay in the lyrical quality of the author's prose, his eye for arresting detail, and his determination to probe the Confederate side of the story without eulogizing the Lost Cause.[62] Less impressive, thought some reviewers, was his overriding concern with military events. Biographer C. Stuart

60. C. Vann Woodward, *The Burden of Southern History* (Baton Rouge: Louisiana State University Press, 1960), 86–87.

61. Shelby Foote, *The Civil War: A Narrative, Volume 1: Fort Sumter to Perryville* (New York: Random House, 1958); *Volume 2: Fredericksburg to Meridian* (New York: Random House, 1963); C. Stuart Chapman, *Shelby Foote: A Writer's Life* (Jackson: University Press of Mississippi, 2003), 165.

62. Louis D. Rubin Jr., "General Longstreet and Me: Refighting the Civil War," *Southern Cultures* 8 (Spring 2002): 44.

Chapman has argued convincingly that this massive work became Foote's "escape from a new civil war."[63] Organizing his material around the reconciliatory theme of battlefield heroism allowed the Mississippian to avoid engaging with unsettled (and unsettling) issues rooted in the persistence of Jim Crow. In spite of being privately opposed to the worst excesses of massive resistance, Foote's southern pride and racial fears prevented him from supporting the civil rights movement. When, for example, a mob thwarted efforts to integrate the University of Alabama in January 1956, Foote decried the "rocks and eggs" of the segregationists yet assailed the "ruthless Madison Avenue methods of the NAACP."[64] Although an afterword in volume two of *The Civil War* contained sarcastic thanks to Governors Barnett, Wallace, and Faubus for "helping to lessen my sectional bias," the text itself contains few references to slavery's role in causing the Civil War or the wartime actions of African Americans.[65] While many of his peers utilized insights derived from the present to shed light on the past, Foote used the past to avoid the present. Although his undoubted achievement, finally completed in 1974, did not go entirely unrecognized in the centennial years, not until "Red" Warren recommended him to the documentary filmmaker Ken Burns in 1986 did Shelby Foote begin to reap the rewards that he and many others believed were due to him.[66]

Before agreeing to serve as chairman of the CWCC, Allan Nevins completed two parts of his multivolume *The War for the Union*.[67] In these impressive books, enriched by their author's purposeful prose and unrivaled mastery of political events, the journalist-turned-historian articulated a strong, if overstated, central thesis: that the Civil War's importance in U.S. history lay primarily in its contribution to the large-scale organizational skills of the American people. A nationalist scholar writing in the mold of James Ford Rhodes, Nevins (as his actions as head of the centennial agency clearly revealed) was con-

63. Chapman, *Shelby Foote,* 165.

64. Ibid., 175.

65. Foote, *Civil War* 2: 971.

66. Chapman, *Shelby Foote,* 258–59. Warren's admiration for *The Civil War* was not reciprocated. According to Chapman, Foote "disliked Warren's philosophically driven novels claiming that they 'stink too much of the lamp'" (259). Foote's mellifluous appearances on Burns's popular PBS documentary on the Civil War in 1990 generated the sale of 400,000 volumes of his trilogy by mid-1991. "Ken," Foote told Burns, "you've made me a millionaire" (263).

67. Allan Nevins, *The War for the Union, Volume 1: The Improvised War, 1861–1862* (New York: Charles Scribner's Sons, 1959) and *The War for the Union, Volume 2: War Becomes Revolution* (New York: Charles Scribner's Sons, 1960).

sistently aware of the cold war context in which he wrote. His insistence in the preface to volume one that the war had been "a people's war" was loaded with significance at a time when American democracy was competing against Soviet totalitarianism, as was his conviction that the conflict had brought essential discipline and cohesion to a once "inchoate nation."[68]

Nevins's preoccupation with American nation-building and lack of interest in battlefield events automatically limited the amount of space he devoted to the Confederacy in these volumes. However, his bias toward the northern cause, evident in his previous books, may have been intensified by his irritation at the way segregationist violence embarrassed the United States in the arena of international public opinion. He pulled no punches in his analysis of the outbreak of civil war, for he not only gave credence to the claim that a group of southern radicals had conspired to break up the Union (a view rejected by Rhodes) but also placed primary blame on the Confederate leadership for the outbreak of the conflict at Sumter. Yet he did make more than passing nods to the traditional orthodoxy. Even though his heroes were men like Lincoln, Edwin Stanton, and Montgomery Meigs who imposed system on an unsystematic nation, he could still describe Robert E. Lee as "a man of lionhearted qualities," and Charles Sumner, the nineteenth-century Senate's foremost advocate of black rights, as "an egotist who let vanity override common sense."[69] The concluding chapter of volume two, devoted to the process by which blacks were recruited into the Union army, showed signs of a glimmering awareness of black agency among consensus historians, but it would be stretching a point to claim that African Americans were a centerpiece of Nevins's grand narrative.

In terms of its contemporary impact, the most important of the three epic histories released during the centennial period was Bruce Catton's *Centennial History of the Civil War*.[70] Catton, as we have seen, was a prominent member of the centennial establishment, an officer of both the CWCC and New York's own "Catton commission." The senior editor of *American Heritage Magazine* was also one of the United States' most accomplished exponents of popular history. The secret of his success lay in his ability to make America's past accessible and interesting to nonacademic readers, largely by combining a poetic prose style with compelling narrative drive and a gift for personalizing

68. Nevins, *War for the Union*, 1: v.

69. Ibid., 2: 131, 203.

70. Bruce Catton, *The Centennial History of the Civil War, Volume 1: The Coming Fury* (Garden City, NY: Doubleday, 1961), *Volume 2: Terrible Swift Sword* (Garden City, NY: Doubleday, 1963), *Volume 3: Never Call Retreat* (Garden City, NY: Doubleday, 1965).

historical experience.[71] Raised in the solid Republican community of Benzonia, Michigan, before World War I, Catton was ideally placed to tap the heavy demand for loyalty-building Civil War books during the 1950s. He recalled growing up among the local Union veterans and refighting the sectional conflict with his friends in a downtown park. He possessed a conservative attachment to home and country, tinged with nostalgia, that informed his Homeric conception of the American past and connected him to the lost veterans of his youth and the cold war–era nationalism of his readers. "Maybe," he wrote in an autobiographical work published in 1972, "the warmest, most uncritical, patriotism on earth is the feeling a small-town man develops for what he can see when he looks out of his bedroom window."[72]

Commissioned in the mid-1950s by the *New York Times* and publisher Doubleday, Catton's *Centennial History* was a major achievement on the part of the author and his highly capable research staff headed by E. B. "Pete" Long. The three handsome, readable tomes—each one eagerly awaited by the media and general public—appeared successively in 1961, 1963, and 1965. Most reviewers heaped fulsome praise on what one described as "an all-time great in the field of Civil War history, and perhaps one of the giants of all historical writing and research."[73] It is true that not everyone was impressed. Shelby Foote's Greenville friend, Walker Percy, commented acidly that Catton treated the Civil War as "a kind of mystical experience, a national rite of passage in the course of which a lot of sweaty young men killed each other with unsurpassed dedication and skill and in so doing presided over the rebirth of the American character."[74] But the trilogy sold well in the United States and abroad and introduced huge numbers of people, young and old, to the Civil War for the first time.

Primarily a work of attempted synthesis bolstered by a substantial amount of illustrative primary material, *The Centennial History* broke no new ground. Like Foote, Catton did emphasize the primary strategic significance of the western theater (an arena that was still relatively neglected by scholars) and met with some success in balancing his largely familiar account of Union ma-

71. David H. Potter, "The Sound of Bugles: Prelude to Fratricide," *Saturday Review*, Nov. 18, 1961, 20–21.

72. Bruce Catton, *Waiting for the Morning Train: An American Boyhood* (Garden City, NY: Doubleday, 1972), 70.

73. Le Roy H. Fischer, review of *Terrible Swift Sword*, in *Civil War History* 10 (1964): 103.

74. Walker Percy, "Red, White, and Blue-Gray" (1961), in *Signposts in a Strange Land*, ed. Patrick Samway (New York: Farrar, Straus, and Giroux, 1991), 78.

neuvers with developments in the Confederacy. However, he struggled to explain why the war had occurred in the first place and was far more at home with the conflict's military aspects than its political or social dimensions. The main reason why causation posed such a problem for Catton in the first volume of his history, *The Coming Fury,* was his failure to critique effectively the conventional wisdom on slavery and abolitionism. He had no difficulty declaring slavery immoral or contending that white southerners, nonslaveholders and slaveholders alike, had seceded primarily to preserve white supremacy. However, his debt to Craven-style revisionism meant that he endorsed the dubious notion that slavery was dying out in the 1850s, that northern abolitionists were politically irresponsible, and that Republicans had been largely devoid of humanitarian sympathy for blacks. Consequently (although his argument was not entirely consistent), he appeared to fall back on the increasingly outmoded and certainly oversimplistic view that the Civil War had resulted from a disastrous miscalculation by a blundering generation of politicians, North and South. Only "a hard-boiled realist" like Stephen A. Douglas, he asserted, had had the wit to try and find a workable alternative to intersectional violence.[75]

If Catton's explanation of the war's origins was unconvincing, he prepared a stronger thesis for the second and third volumes of his narrative. Expounded previously in *This Hallowed Ground,* this was his contention that the inexorable press of events had transformed a limited war for the Union into a revolutionary struggle for human freedom. It was hardly a profound insight, but at the time of the civil rights movement, Catton's largely celebratory account of how the nation had triumphed over slavery struck a chord with contemporary readers. His activities as a member of the centennial establishment suggest that he was eager to impress this politically resonant theme on the public. It was his good fortune that *Terrible Swift Sword,* the volume in which he explained the genesis of the Emancipation Proclamation, appeared in the same year as the Birmingham crisis and the introduction of a comprehensive civil rights bill. Few readers in 1963 could have misunderstood the relevance of Catton's comment that "[t]he people who were about to be freed were slaves and they were Negroes; but also, quite unexpectedly, they had become Americans, and Americans they would always be—then, thenceforward and forever . . . To define freedom anew for the Negro was to redefine it for everybody, and

75. Catton, *Centennial History,* 1: 98.

the act which enlarged the horizon of those in bondage must in the end push America's own horizon all the way out to infinity."[76]

If this portentous passage appeared to confirm the impact of the ongoing civil rights (and cold war) struggles on Catton's uneasy mix of revisionist and nationalist historiography, the same could be said for his portrayal of radical antislavery Republicans. For decades, politicians like Thaddeus Stevens and Charles Sumner had been vilified by southern whites and northern conservatives. By the time Catton brought his third volume to a conclusion, he was ready to paint a more balanced picture of these men. "They had their full share of hate and vindictiveness, to be sure," he averred, "but they were also passionately interested in freedom."[77] The extent to which America's bestloved Civil War historian had departed from consensus orthodoxy should not be exaggerated. His narrative remained respectful of the Confederate cause throughout and contained only limited allusions to the importance of race and black agency during the war. This said, the *Centennial History* was clearly a transitional work in the sense that its progress revealed how the old revisionism (which stressed the human cost of the war at the expense of its achievements) was being superseded by a new nationalist historiography that lauded not only the saving of the Union but also the shining promise of racial equality embedded in texts such as the Emancipation Proclamation and the Gettysburg Address. The unfolding orthodoxy, however, was not primarily the work of well-known Civil War scholars like Catton or Nevins. Younger historians outside the centennial establishment took the lead in finally discrediting the crumbling scholarly consensus that had underpinned the existence of segregation for more than half a century.

Barely a week after the centennial proper began in January 1961, Dwight Dumond, a prominent historian of abolitionism, told Allan Nevins of his concerns about racial unrest in the South. He felt, he wrote, "a terrible urgency about this rottenness in the South, its destruction of democratic institutions and our influence abroad, and the need to do something more. We must go back to basic principles. My forthcoming history of the antislavery movement will help."[78] This crusading zeal motivated many liberal and left-wing U.S. historians in the early 1960s, who probably agreed with T. Lawrence Connelly's

76. Ibid., 2: 371.

77. Ibid., 3: 461.

78. Dwight L. Dumond to Allan Nevins, Jan. 13, 1961, folder 2, box 76, Allan Nevins Papers, Rare Book and Manuscript Library, Columbia University.

view that the centennial was a cross between a joke and an embarrassment.[79] The results were not always well received—the respected southern Civil War historian David Potter was decidedly unimpressed with Dumond's "polemical," and unashamedly pro-abolitionist, book.[80] However, their efforts transformed the way several major topics in Civil War history were interpreted in the academy.

The destruction of Beardian economic determinism and the revisionists' blundering generation thesis had been well underway before the advent of the centennial. Both of these schools had played into the hands of southern partisans by stressing, respectively, the amorality of northern industrial civilization and the sectionally irresponsible actions of the abolitionists. By the end of the 1950s, economic historians had disproved the Beards' model of a unitary capitalist class in the North. Meanwhile, the cumulative efforts of black and white historians, aided by events, had consigned the magnolia-scented interpretation of slavery to the dustbin of American scholarship. Once the peculiar institution had been shown to be brutal and exploitative and the civil rights movement had uncovered the historical durability of southern racism, it was almost inevitable that the fanatical abolitionists of yesteryear would start to be reinterpreted as modern-day freedom riders. While traces of the old revisionism could still be found in the work of major historians like Catton and David Donald, by 1965 growing numbers of professional scholars concurred with Martin Duberman's assertion, in a landmark collection of essays on the antislavery struggle, that there was now sufficient evidence "for believing that those who protested strongly against slavery were not all misguided fanatics or frustrated neurotics."[81]

79. T. Lawrence Connelly, *Will Success Spoil Jeff Davis? The Last Book about the Civil War* (New York: McGraw-Hill, 1963). "[T]he disease Centennialism is the uncontrolled desire to commemorate," observed Connelly in his debunking examination of Civil War fever. "There is something magic about the figure 100, possibly the fact that it so closely resembles a one dollar mark" (31). For a more labored spoof of the centennial, see Edmund G. Love, *An End to Bugling* (New York: Harper and Row, 1963).

80. David M. Potter, review of Dumond, *Antislavery: The Crusade for Freedom in America* (1961), in *American Historical Review* 67 (1962): 1064.

81. Martin Duberman, "The Northern Response to Slavery," in Duberman, ed., *The Antislavery Vanguard: New Essays on the Abolitionists* (Princeton: Princeton University Press, 1965), 412. Duberman's collection contained essays by Staughton Lynd and Howard Zinn, two leftist scholars active in the civil rights movement. See Lynd, "The Abolitionist Critique of the United States Constitution" (209–39), and Zinn's provocatively titled "Abolitionists, Freedom-Riders, and the Tactics of Agitation" (417–51). For evidence of persistent revisionism, see David Donald, *Charles*

Closely connected with these realigning historiographical shifts was a radical revision of the orthodox view of Reconstruction. An essential weapon in the segregationists' fight to preserve Jim Crow, the hackneyed tale of white suffering at the hands of mercenary carpetbaggers and ignorant blacks was virtually turned on its head by what looked like a new account that lauded the efforts of radical Republicans and their abolitionist allies to promote equal rights for African Americans in the 1860s, denigrated the efforts of President Andrew Johnson to obstruct this goal, and highlighted the positive achievements of the much-maligned Reconstruction-era governments in the South. This emerging interpretation, which of course owed a formidable debt to the efforts of Carter G. Woodson, W. E. B. Du Bois, and other earlier historians to sustain the black counter-memory of the Civil War, was the work of a diverse group of scholars: principally African Americans like John Hope Franklin and Benjamin Quarles and progressive whites broadly sympathetic to the goals of the civil rights movement—notably, Eric L. McKitrick, John H. and LaWanda Cox, James M. McPherson, Kenneth M. Stampp, and a gifted British historian, William R. Brock.[82] Through their efforts, undergirded by civil rights activists in the field, the academy began to regard what C. Vann Woodward dubbed "the First Reconstruction" (to distinguish it from the post-*Brown* "New Reconstruction") as a tragedy not because it had taken place but because it had not gone far enough.[83]

The Civil War itself attracted a vast amount of scholarly attention in the first half of the 1960s. Surprisingly, perhaps, this outpouring did not produce the kind of paradigmatic shift that occurred in the interpretation of slavery, abolitionism, and Reconstruction. In part this was because the majority of scholarly books on the war targeted the military aspects of the conflict.

Sumner and the Coming of the Civil War (New York: Alfred A. Knopf, 1960), an unflattering portrayal of the antislavery politician's alleged psychological inadequacies.

82. John Hope Franklin, *Reconstruction after the Civil War* (Chicago: University of Chicago Press, 1961); Benjamin Quarles, *Lincoln and the Negro* (Oxford: Oxford University Press, 1962); Eric L. McKitrick, *Andrew Johnson and Reconstruction* (Chicago: University of Chicago Press, 1960); John H. Cox and LaWanda Cox, *Politics, Principle, and Prejudice, 1865–1866: Dilemma of Reconstruction America* (New York: Free Press of Glencoe, 1963); James M. McPherson, *The Struggle for Equality: Abolitionists and the Negro in the Civil War and Reconstruction* (Princeton: Princeton University Press, 1964); Kenneth M. Stampp, *The Era of Reconstruction, 1865–1877* (New York: Alfred A. Knopf, 1965); William R. Brock, *An American Crisis: Congress and Reconstruction, 1865–1867* (New York: St. Martin's; London: Macmillan, 1963).

83. C. Vann Woodward, *The Strange Career of Jim Crow* (New York: Oxford University Press, 1955), 9.

Historians therefore continued to debate familiar issues such as the leadership roles of Abraham Lincoln and Jefferson Davis, the relative importance of the eastern and western fronts, the tactical and strategic abilities of Grant and Lee, and the reasons for Union victory and Confederate defeat. However, American scholars' growing interest in grassroots social history did promote a number of important studies that heralded a more comprehensive understanding of the war. A new preoccupation with interdisciplinarity and quantitative techniques prepared the ground for a more sophisticated assessment of political partisanship in the middle period. Younger scholars, following the lead set by Lee Benson in a pathbreaking history of partisanship in Jacksonian New York, began to probe the sources of political combat in the 1850s and discovered that the traditional preoccupation with elites had distorted understanding of what really mattered to ordinary Americans in the 1850s.[84] Joel H. Silbey, a graduate of the University of Iowa in 1963, argued convincingly that the slavery question had not monopolized antebellum political debate as most older scholars had assumed. A caustic critic of Bruce Catton, he contended that "[t]he Civil War has had a pernicious influence on the study of American political development that preceded it"—a statement that could have been taken as a rejection of everything the centennial stood for.[85] The so-called new political history allowed scholars, for the first time, to formulate convincing definitions for hitherto ambiguous (and loaded) political labels. Even the radical Republicans emerged as an analytically useful political grouping—a fact of great importance for the study of Republican policymaking during the Civil War and Reconstruction.[86] While a striking new explanation for the outbreak of war failed to emerge from the deluge of centennial-era literature, by 1965 a growing number of American historians—certainly of those outside the South—endorsed the view that moral opposition to slavery had been an integral component of Republican party ideology and that the South's determination to protect the peculiar institution resulted directly in

84. Lee Benson, *The Concept of Jacksonian Democracy: New York as a Test Case* (Princeton: Princeton University Press, 1961).

85. Joel H. Silbey, "The Civil War Synthesis in American Political History," *Civil War History* 10 (1964): 140. In a critical review of William and Bruce Catton, *Two Roads to Sumter* (1963), Silbey attacked the elder Catton's tendency "to simplify complexities for the sake of readability" and "to seek out the dramatic incident and personality to heighten the story and its flow." *Civil War History* 10 (1964): 104.

86. Among the most important early quantitative analyses of the Civil War and Reconstruction-era Congresses was Glenn M. Linden, "Congressmen, 'Radicalism,' and Economic Issues" (Ph.D. thesis, University of Washington, 1963).

civil war. For the moment at least, the civil rights movement appeared to have handed the North victory in a revitalized academic struggle over the war.[87]

Ironically, however, the efforts of liberal and left-leaning historians to overturn the politically charged orthodox interpretations of abolitionism and radical Republicanism often had the unintended result of perpetuating the marginalization of blacks in the dominant narrative of the Civil War. In the early 1960s it was still left to African Americans themselves to take the lead in highlighting the actions of their nineteenth-century forebears: not just Lerone Bennett, whose writings in *Ebony* had an immediate impact on black readers, but also historian Benjamin Quarles, who built on his earlier work to draw a strong portrait of Frederick Douglass in his contribution to Martin Duberman's collection of essays on the antislavery movement. "[H]ere was no stammering fugitive from the South," he wrote; "here was no shiftless former slave unable to cope with the responsibilities of freedom. Here was a different brand of Negro." Tellingly (in the same year as Selma), Quarles also trumpeted Douglass as an integrationist and a patriot, a man who once declaimed, "We are Americans, and as Americans we would speak to Americans."[88] In 1962 Quarles had made Douglass an important player in his account of President Lincoln's evolving relationship with blacks. Broadly favorable to Lincoln, Quarles was nevertheless at pains to point out that the Emancipation Proclamation had been prompted by the flight of thousands of slaves from the farms and plantations of the Union-occupied South. It was, he wrote, "an accessory after the fact: Negroes had been making themselves free since the beginning of the war."[89] Some white historians, among them Leon F. Litwack, Larry Gara, James McPherson, and Joel Williamson, did attempt to incorporate blacks more centrally into the narrative, helping (alongside the radicalization of the ongoing freedom struggle) to draw readers' attention to the essential role played by

87. Even as the civil rights movement reached the peak of its achievements, some white historians remained particularly skeptical about regarding antislavery Republicans as freedom fighters. See, for example, Robert F. Durden's dissenting contribution, "Ambiguities in the Antislavery Crusade of the Republican Party," to Duberman, *Antislavery Vanguard*, 362–94, and William Gillette, *The Right to Vote: Politics and the Passage of the Fifteenth Amendment* (Baltimore: Johns Hopkins University Press, 1965), 9–11. Their findings contributed to the subsequent emergence of the free-labor paradigm, which effectively synthesized the new work on Civil War–era politics. See Eric Foner, *Free Soil, Free Labor, Free Men: The Ideology of the Republican Party Before the Civil War* (New York: Oxford University Press, 1970).

88. Benjamin Quarles, "Abolition's Different Drummer: Frederick Douglass," in Duberman, *Antislavery Vanguard*, 129, 131.

89. Quarles, *Lincoln and the Negro*, 187.

nineteenth-century blacks in their own liberation.[90] Although most scholars of the Civil War era would not fully recognize the reality of black agency until the academy had absorbed the effects of Black Power, the advent of a new trend was clearly apparent in some writings of the early 1960s.

Judging by its principal manifestations in film and fiction, the Civil War centennial did little to alter existing popular preconceptions about the conflict. For most Americans, certainly a majority of those living outside the South, the war remained essentially an entertaining hobby: a colorful, romantic, action-packed event with little or no contemporary political relevance. This said, some professional historians shared with segregationists and black activists a sharper awareness of the close linkage between culture and politics. Because it took time for their insights to be assimilated by TV producers, moviemakers, and fiction writers, their work did not alter significantly the way most people conceptualized the Civil War in the early 1960s. However, they chipped away at the lilywhite consensus orthodoxy that had underpinned the idea of the centennial in the first place and thereby helped to lay the foundations for more racially inclusive interpretations of the American past. Whether the greater inclusiveness evident in mature later works such as James McPherson's *Battle Cry of Freedom* (1988) carried with it vastly enhanced explanatory power is debatable. The updated nationalist interpretation of the Civil War regnant by the close of the twentieth century exhibited some of the flaws of the old narrative that it had largely replaced, claiming, for example, to find evidence of American virtue (this time in the shape of emancipation, civil rights, and patriotic sacrifice) in the midst of a season of ferocious domestic bloodletting which many Civil War–era folk had regarded as devoid of meaning. Revisionism declined steeply in influence after 1960, but, as Edward L. Ayers has intimated, modern historians neglect some of its insights at their peril.[91]

90. Leon F. Litwack, "The Emancipation of the Negro Abolitionist," in Duberman, *Antislavery Vanguard*, 137–55; Larry Gara, *The Liberty Line: The Legend of the Underground Railroad* (Lexington: University of Kentucky Press, 1961); McPherson, *Struggle for Equality*; Joel Williamson, *After Slavery: The Negro in South Carolina during Reconstruction, 1861–1877* (Chapel Hill: University of North Carolina Press, 1965).

91. Edward L. Ayers, "Worrying About the Civil War," in Karen Halttunen and Lewis Perry, eds., *Moral Problems in American Life* (Ithaca: Cornell University Press, 1998), 145–65.

Conclusion

THANK GOD IT'S FINISHED:
THE CENTENNIAL AND THE WIDER WORLD

ON FRIDAY, APRIL 30, 1965, around 800 delegates gathered in Springfield, Illinois, to attend the eighth, and last, national assembly of the CWCC. The prevailing atmosphere was reflective rather than celebratory, fittingly so in view of the power shift that had taken place within the agency since mid-1961. Also symptomatic of that shift was the paucity of southern delegates in Springfield. No one was present from Tennessee, Alabama, or Mississippi, and even Virginia failed to send an official delegation. Democrats were prominent on the list of speakers, indicative of the fact that custody of the centennial had passed from Eisenhower Republicans to Johnson-era liberals.

Those in attendance listened to prominent historians and politicians discourse on a range of Civil War topics. Allan Nevins jetted in from England (where he occupied the Harmsworth chair at Oxford University) to update the meeting on the latest historiography. Shelby Foote took time out from writing the third volume of his magnum opus to speak compellingly about the Civil War in fiction. Senator Paul Douglas read a paper on "Lincoln: World Symbol of Freedom." Bruce Catton delivered the post-banquet address on May 3, an eloquent recounting of "the events that made our American Civil War unique as well as tragic."[1] In addition to hearing talks the conferees enjoyed a number of trips. On Saturday morning they were bused to the restored Lincoln home where Illinois congressman Paul Findley presided over the site's dedication as a National Historic Landmark. The following day some of them attended Sunday morning service at First Presbyterian, the Lincoln family church. This was definitely no place for Lost Cause devotees. Some members of the

---

1. Wayne C. Temple, "Last Assembly of the Civil War Centennial Commission," *Lincoln Herald* 5 (1965): 87.

congregation were moved to tears by the minister's reading of Walt Whitman's elegiac poem "When Lilacs Last in the Dooryard Bloomed"; most recovered their composure quickly enough to join the choir in a stirring rendition of the last stanza of the "Battle Hymn of the Republic."

The mood lightened that afternoon when delegates were driven to a nearby cinema to watch a preview of *Shenandoah*. Don't miss this "truly . . . great movie" advised one of the lucky viewers. "Its equal may not be seen for several years. Take several handkerchiefs with you. But if you seek smut, sex or abnormalities, you will not find these factors in this picture."[2] On Tuesday, May 4, the group journeyed to Oak Ridge Cemetery for one of the last public acts of the CWCC. Delegates joined members of the Illinois legislature to witness floral wreaths from Adlai Stevenson and Governor Kerner carried into Lincoln's tomb and placed on the sarcophagus of the Great Emancipator. At the close of the proceedings there was general agreement that of all the agency's meetings the Springfield assembly had been "the most successful and probably the best attended."[3]

If those present could have been forgiven for breathing a sigh of relief that the Civil War centennial had ended on a high note, not a few delegates enjoyed reading the irreverent sentiment, "Thank God it's Finished!" contained on the back of matchbooks circulating at the Springfield meeting.[4] For the plain fact was that the centennial had not been a success. Conceived originally as a cold war pageant that would unite Americans by encouraging them to recall the heroic deeds of their forefathers, the project had fallen foul of what historians Maurice Isserman and Michael Kazin have termed hyperbolically, "The Civil War of the 1960s."[5] Centennial planners made the critical mistake of underestimating the destabilizing impact of the civil rights movement on the lilywhite consensual memory that national and local elites sought to purvey to the public. While one can empathize with Karl Betts in his determination to organize a popular commemoration of the war, his willful refusal to acknowledge the legitimacy of the black counter-memory at a time of rising concern over civil rights almost guaranteed the kind of disastrous racial incident that nearly torpedoed the centennial at Charleston.

2. Ibid., 86.

3. Ibid., 90.

4. Harold M. Hyman, review of Martin Duberman, ed., *The Antislavery Vanguard* (1965), in *American Historical Review* 71 (1966): 688.

5. Maurice Isserman and Michael Kazin, *America Divided: The Civil War of the 1960s* (Oxford: Oxford University Press, 2000).

Intelligent historians such as Bell Wiley, Allan Nevins, and James Robertson deserve some credit for salvaging the project as an admittedly low-key national event, but the price of retaining the allegiance of the southern commissions remained the relative marginalization of African Americans. Efforts to deemphasize race in favor of cold war themes persisted long after historians assumed control of the CWCC, notably in planning and staging the Emancipation Proclamation ceremony in September 1962. Caught between seemingly irreconcilable strains of southern white and black collective memory, the reorganized national commission continued to pursue a consensual agenda that paid little more than lip service to the notion that blacks had been central players in the Civil War.[6] Consensus also reigned beyond the confines of

6. This did not prevent CWCC leaders from trying to play up their racial liberalism after the centennial had closed. The agency's final report, James I. Robertson Jr. told Ed Gass in December 1965, "should skirt all controversial issues" and emphasize "the grandeur and impact of the Emancipation Proclamation program . . . with a complete disregard of those incidents that came close to giving you and me stomach ulcers." Robertson to Edmund C. Gass, Dec. 1, 1965, folder on "Robertson, James I.—Personal 1963–64," box 135, subject files 1957–66, Records of the Civil War Centennial Commission, Records of the National Park Service, Record Group 79, National Archives (hereafter CWCCR). Allan Nevins also had a clear eye for his regime's historical reputation. "Somewhere in the [report's] later treatment of the Commission's work," he told Gass, "it might be stated that while Mr. Robinson [sic] and Mr. Nevins made every effort to treat Southern representatives and Southern points of view tactfully, they were adamant in their insistence on the observance of federal law and in their support of the purposes of the Kennedy and Johnson Administrations with reference to full Negro rights. They stated again and again that, as the Negro soldiers had played a great and gallant part in the Civil War, their services should be fully and warmly honored." Allan Nevins to Gass, April 25, 1966, folder on "Civil War Centennial Commission—Permanent File," box 88, Allan Nevins Papers, Rare Book and Manuscript Library, Columbia University. The published report noted Karl Betts's responsibility for "the Charleston blunder" but simply described the Emancipation Proclamation ceremony as "an impressive and moving event." Nevins's foreword, however, emphasized that "[t]hose members of the Commission best versed in history were . . . anxious that the commemorations of a war that resulted in emancipation, and in the guaranties of the 13th, 14th, and 15th amendments upon freedom, civil rights, and suffrage, should be held in such manner as to strengthen the social and moral solidarity of the Republic." CWCC, *The Civil War Centennial: A Report to the Congress* (Washington, DC: Government Printing Office, 1968), 1, 12, 18. Ed Gass died tragically before the final report was published. Other key CWCC members enjoyed mixed fortunes after the close of the centennial. Nevins continued to write until his death in 1971. The last two volumes of his *War for the Union* were published posthumously in the same year. Bell Wiley retired from Emory in March 1974. Subject to increasing bouts of depression, he died of a heart attack in 1980. James Robertson went on to pursue a successful academic career as a popular teacher of U.S. history at Virginia Tech. He

the centennial establishment. In TV series such as *The Americans,* in movies like *The Horse Soldiers* and *Shenandoah,* in most of the popular fiction of the early 1960s, the Civil War remained what it had been since the beginning of the century: fraternal, tragic, romantic, and, for the most part, racially exclusive. Only in the realm of political rhetoric (particularly that of the civil rights movement) and the work of growing numbers of professional historians was there hard evidence that the black counter-memory was gaining strength in the ongoing contest for the meaning of the Civil War.

No matter how egregious the marginalization of African Americans, we should pause before writing off the centennial as an unmitigated disaster. The commemoration spawned a number of important academic publications: scholarly editions of the papers of Jefferson Davis and Ulysses S. Grant, a two-volume bibliography of Civil War materials, some high-quality monographs in the CWCC's Imprint series, the National Archives' invaluable guide to the wartime record of the United States government, several useful state-sponsored books and pamphlets on local history, and well-crafted popular works such as Bruce Catton's bestselling trilogy. The arrival of the centennial not only induced the National Park Service to improve its Civil War sites as part of its Mission 66 program but also, through a combination of public and private efforts, helped to save battlefield land from the threat of development. Two new battlefield parks, Wilson's Creek in Missouri and Pea Ridge in Arkansas, were created as a result of the public interest generated by the centennial, and another 3,000 acres were added to existing military parks.[7]

While some professional historians found sham battles embarrassing, many Americans shared President Kennedy's well-known love of them. For children especially, the Civil War centennial—in all its guises—was an immensely exciting event in which they participated with great enthusiasm. William Garrett Piston, now a prominent military historian of the Civil War, was an eight-year-old boy growing up in east Tennessee when the centennial began in early 1961. He and his friends were hooked from the start. Even though he was the only kid on the block who possessed an official *Gray Ghost* pistol and holster set, everyone had a toy musket and rubber bayonet with which they refought the Civil War, much as Catton and his friends had reenacted it in Michigan half a century earlier. "The Centennial," Piston recalls, "was such a wonderful visual experience. Every newspaper and magazine was flooded with pictures. We

---

published a well-received study of Stonewall Jackson in 1997 and six years later was a historical consultant for Ron Maxwell's Civil War movie, *Gods and Generals,* the prequel to *Gettysburg.*

7. CWCC, *Report,* 34–35.

traded bubblegum cards. Every restaurant's placemat had a Civil War theme and every packet of Dixie Crystal sugar on the table told a Civil War story on the back. I earned a badge in Cub Scouts for my Civil War scrap book, which included the texts of articles by Bruce Catton clipped from the newspaper."[8]

If this testimony suggests that Karl Betts's encouragement of commercialism can be accorded some credit for generating popular enthusiasm for the centennial, it is also important to note that his agency's overriding preoccupation with consensus was far from exceptional. In the second half of the twentieth century, national elites across the globe sought to instill unity among their populations by sponsoring consensus-oriented commemorations of past events.

In 1950 the new apartheid regime in South Africa committed itself to a grandiose nationwide festival to mark the three hundredth anniversary of Jan Van Riebeeck's landing at the Cape.[9] South Africa had a relatively weak national history, and the idea of a cultural celebration of the country's European origins proved especially alluring to the racist Afrikaner government at a time when nonwhites were mobilizing to contest its political legitimacy. The Federation of Afrikaans Cultural Associations set up a central executive committee to help plan an extensive schedule of commemorative events. Convinced that the festival should be a "symbol of national unity," the committee oversaw the building of a stadium and exhibition halls as well as the preparation of historical pageants across South Africa that would culminate in a grand historical procession through Cape Town. In an effort to guarantee the widest possible support for the commemoration among the dominant race, moves were undertaken to include English-speaking whites in what was conceived as a popular celebration of racial unity and white supremacy. Although blacks were not excluded completely (separate planning for them was devolved to the government's Native Affairs Department), the fact that their Bantu pavilion and Zulu kraal were to be built alongside displays of white industrial progress illustrated how the exhibition site was intended to showcase the triumph of European civilization over African barbarism.[10]

8. William G. Piston to the author, Feb. 6, 2004.

9. On the Van Riebeeck commemoration, see Ciraj Rassool and Leslie Witz, "The 1952 Jan Van Riebeeck Tercentenary Festival: Constructing and Contesting Public National History in South Africa," *Journal of African History* 34 (1993): 447–68.

10. A comparison can be drawn with the effort to contrast white progress with nonwhite backwardness at the 1893 World's Columbian Exposition in Chicago, though here, too, the organizers' plans did not go uncontested by blacks. See Alessandra Lorini, *Rituals of Race: American Public Culture and the Search for Racial Democracy* (Charlottesville: University Press of Virginia, 1999), 33–48.

The drive for consensus was no less evident in France during the 1980s when the government of President François Mitterrand created the Mission du Bicentenaire to organize celebrations to coincide with the two hundredth anniversary of the Revolution.[11] Just as the CWCC had peddled sectional reconciliation in order to render Civil War memory useful to Americans, the Mission endeavored to reduce France's most violent and divisive historical event to its lowest common denominator. Rather than tackling the blood-soaked republican constitution of 1793, planners made the 1789 Declaration of the Rights of Man the centerpiece of their efforts. Quite apart from its relatively consensual origins (even liberal aristocrats had supported it), the Declaration had the added advantage of being couched in universal language that, much to the ire of British prime minister Margaret Thatcher, could only enhance France's self-image as the principal source of modern democracy. Even though it was better funded and more interventionist than the CWCC, the Mission looked to develop a popular grassroots commemoration by fostering the formation of local organizing committees through a network of correspondents.

In spite of the very different contexts in which they took place, neither the South African nor the French event achieved the consensual goals of the elites who planned them. On the Cape nonwhites were quick to recognize the political nature of a cultural festival. The antiapartheid Non-European Unity Movement (NEUM) initiated a successful boycott of the Van Riebeeck commemoration, resulting in paltry black involvement throughout and similarly dismal Malay and Coloured interest in the separate pageants staged for these groups in the new stadium. Nonwhites not only avoided the racially exclusive version of the past that was being thrust down their throats but also mobilized actively behind an alternative counter-memory. At the end of March 1952 several thousand people attended a mass meeting in Cape Town to hear Unity Movement speakers talk about the nonwhite builders of the nation and denounce Jan Van Riebeeck as the prime architect of slavery in southern Africa. Antigovernment newspapers such as the NEUM's *Torch* and the pro-ANC *Guardian* explained to readers how the commemoration was designed to belittle and exoticize nonwhites.

If anything, the bicentennial of the French Revolution proved to be even more politicized than the van Riebeeck tercentenary. While the moderate left and right appeared content to coalesce around a fraternal commemoration

---

11. The following discussion draws heavily on Steven Laurence Kaplan, *Farewell Revolution: Disputed Legacies, France, 1789/1989* (Ithaca: Cornell University Press, 1995).

based on the Declaration, those on the radical wings of the spectrum derided
the notion of a bread-and-circuses jamboree intended to augment the prestige of Mitterrand and his socialists. Ultra-rightists, many of them supporters
of Jean-Marie Le Pen's *Front National,* assailed the focus on human rights as
a stalking horse for pro-immigration policies. On the left, Communist party
activists insisted that the Mission's abjuration of the Jacobin Terror deprived
the commemoration of its proper educative function: namely, its potential to
teach the people that social equality could not be achieved without revolutionary struggle. *Vive 89,* the Communists' long-established vehicle for propagat-
ing a radical memory of the French Revolution, organized numerous activities during the bicentennial to educate working-class Frenchmen and women
on what it saw as the true meaning of the Revolution. To make matters even
more difficult for the Paris-based Mission, the Vendée region—site of some
of the worst violence in late-eighteenth-century France—and the conservative wing of the Catholic Church championed a potent counterrevolutionary
memory that made it impossible for elite politicians like Mitterrand to ignore
the downside of 1789. In spite of its problems (exacerbated by the tragic deaths
of its first two heads), the Mission managed to organize a successful and relatively value-free bicentennial parade down the Champs Elysées on July 14,
1989. But by that time any illusions that modern France was united over the
meaning of the Revolution had been dispelled completely.

The parallels between these two commemorations and the Civil War centennial in the United States are obvious. In South Africa impoverished racial
minorities organized in a not dissimilar manner to African Americans in
order to contest a white supremacist cultural festival that was likely to stoke
their oppression. In France, the Vendéens shared some white southerners'
distaste for an event intended to enhance the prestige of metropolitan elites
rather than respect painful regional memories rooted in a historic moment
of national fracture. The efforts of the Communists to torpedo consensus
with their revolutionary memory of the past resembled the efforts of African
Americans to contest the centennial with their own emancipationist reading
of the Civil War. Just as the French radicals sought to liberate the arch-Jacobin
Robespierre from the isolating grip of the center, so did African Americans
and their liberal and leftist allies attempt to overturn regnant negative images
of those other Jacobins, Thaddeus Stevens and Charles Sumner. Distant from
one another in terms of time and geographical space, each of these ceremonies
provided compelling evidence that human memory is far too fickle and fis-
siparous to provide reliable support for national commemorations insecurely
rooted in an elusive popular consensus.

The dramatic collapse of communism in Russia and eastern Europe shortly after the French bicentennial threw into relief the diffuseness of historical memory and the difficulties inherent in using the past as a means of reordering strife-torn and ethnically plural societies. The toppling of socialist rule in what Betts and Grant would have regarded as "captive nations" unleashed a stream of previously suppressed memories, some of them generated by the searing experiences of Soviet occupation, others rooted in a mythic past of peasant community and religious devotion. Unfortunately for the nation-building elites of the late twentieth-century, the sheer diversity of these memories precluded the easy imposition of consensus. In the Ukraine, for example, Jewish "memories" of sufferings incurred during the great seventeenth-century rebellion of Hetman Bohdan Khmelnytsky rendered problematic the development of a modern nation-state grounded in past Cossack glories.[12] Even in the liberated Baltic states, where personal narratives of Soviet oppression constituted the woof and warp of national identity, the presence of significant minorities of ethnic Russians hampered the emergence of a unitary past. In Russia itself, the demise of communism and the rapid break-up of the Soviet empire combined with economic collapse to yield at least three divergent popular responses to historical memory in the 1990s: a determination on the part of human rights organizations, professional historians, and, in large measure, the Orthodox Church to commemorate the victims of Stalinism; a commitment by many older people to uphold the comforting memories of collective struggle in the years of Soviet power and the Great Patriotic War against Nazi Germany; and a discernible desire on the part of many younger Russians to ignore the past entirely. Thus, while the yearning of one commentator for "an integral and uncontradictory conception" of the nation's past was entirely understandable, such a consensus seemed unlikely to develop in spite of the increasingly authoritarian tendencies of the Putin regime.[13]

In the days when rivalry between the United States and the old Soviet Union was at its height, the CWCC had been desperately slow to sense the dangers of imposing a consensual interpretation of the Civil War on a diverse populace. But, as the direct-action campaigns of the civil rights movement gathered pace during the early 1960s, the impossibility of persisting with a genuinely grassroots exercise in public history became apparent to wiser heads inside the

12. Alexander J. Motyl, *Dilemmas of Independence: Ukraine After Totalitarianism* (New York: Council on Foreign Relations Press, 1993), 86.

13. Catherine Merridale, "Redesigning History in Contemporary Russia," *Journal of Contemporary History* 38 (2003): 18.

agency. While Michael Kammen overstates the extent to which Allan Nevins (and by extension the racially blinkered, consensus-oriented, cold war liberalism he represented) accommodated the black counter-memory after 1961, perhaps the efforts of Nevins and Robertson to impart a greater degree of dignity to the centennial justified the verdict delivered by John Y. Simon in the fall of 1965.[14] "It is too easy," contended the Ohio State historian, "to be critical of the USCWCC by exploring the wide gap between the goal of a centennial for all Americans and the modest reality. It is more pertinent to observe that its career fell in a period when controversies over the place of the Negro in American society and federal-state relations recreated many of the disharmonies of the previous century. The Civil War was a pulsating force in the American present and only the dead past will rest quietly for graveside services of commemoration. Because the centennial had come too soon, the work of the USCWCC cannot be labeled as either success or failure but as an impossibility."[15]

By the time Simon made this generous assessment of the CWCC, the elite memory of the Civil War had begun to change. The replacement of the existing orthodoxy by a new and more inclusive (but no less nationalist) interpretation of the war indicated that an important shift in American values was taking place in the first half of the 1960s. That this process was not the work of the CWCC does nothing to undermine the fact that the centennial, broadly conceived, was a notable chapter not only in the history of U.S. cold war culture but also in the making of the modern South.

GETTING OVER IT? THE POSTCENTENNIAL SOUTH AND THE LIMITS OF CIVIL WAR MEMORY

In April 2003, following a concerted protest campaign by the NAACP, the Georgia legislature proposed abandoning completely the saltirewise Confederate battle flag that had angered many African Americans since its revival as a totem of white supremacism in the 1950s. If the voters acquiesced, the existing state flag would be replaced with a compromise design that, it was hoped,

14. Kammen reasonably credits Nevins with organizing a "dignified ceremony" at the Lincoln Memorial on September 22, 1962. However, in noting the CWCC chairman's determination to commemorate the Emancipation Proclamation in the face of southern recalcitrance, he fails to make clear Nevins's cold war motives or the existence of African-American disquiet at the commission's plans. Michael Kammen, *Mystic Chords of Memory: The Transformation of Tradition in American Culture* (New York: Alfred A. Knopf, 1991), 599.

15. John Y. Simon, "A House Divided: Reflections on the Civil War Centennial," unpublished paper delivered Oct. 1965, box 25, subject files 1957–66, CWCCR.

would offend no one.[16] The decision was greeted with relief by a white Republican member of the legislature, Senator Don Balfour of Snellville. Balfour was quoted by the *New York Times* as saying that his constituents were fed up with the debate over symbols. "'The biggest thing they tell me about the flag is 'Get over it,'" he said. "This will finally, once and for all, get us over it."[17]

Although the burden of the past weighs heavier on the South than any other region of the United States—much heavier than Senator Balfour wished to allow—the centennial furnished a modicum of proof that Civil War memory was less of a barrier to social and political change in the region than many contemporary observers believed. One reason for this was the sheer diversity of historical experience in the South. Most local centennial planners assumed that their constituency was a monolithic group of whites possessing direct kinship links to the Confederacy. Not only did this assumption ignore the majority of blacks who had no allegiance to this tradition but it also marginalized the past of those predominantly Upper South residents who possessed ties to the Union instead of, or in addition to, the Confederate cause. Historian William Garrett Piston is a case in point. As a youngster he was not so enthralled by the centennial that he failed to detect the pro-southern slant of TV programs like *The Americans*. Importantly, his consciousness was raised by his paternal grandfather, a Maine Yankee, who told him what his teachers had singularly failed to explain: namely, that many east Tennesseans had remained loyal to the Union during the war. The recollection reveals, first, how in the early 1960s individuals and families had their own live memories of the Civil War that could cut across the powerful pro-Confederate memory held by large numbers of southern whites. Second, it suggests how these heterodox memories could limit assent to majoritarian values, thereby ensuring that the dominant approach to the Civil War in the region was not an entirely controlling one.

Another thorny problem for unreconstructed southern patriots during the centennial years was that many people either had no interest in Confederate history or were willing to put the past behind them in order to build a truly modern South. As we have seen, state agencies in the region had to work hard

16. Although the predominantly blue flag adopted by the Georgia legislature in 2001 had sported a diminished St Andrew's Cross, the decision to retain a symbol so closely associated with slavery and segregation resulted in continued African-American demands for change. For a full account of the flag controversy in Georgia, see John M. Coski, *The Confederate Battle Flag: America's Most Embattled Emblem* (Cambridge, MA: Harvard University Press, 2005), 252–63.

17. *New York Times*, April 27, 2003, 28.

to stimulate local commemorative activities. In part this was because guardians of the Lost Cause like the United Daughters of the Confederacy and Sons of Confederate Veterans initially feared that the centennial was a stalking horse for Yankee triumphalism. Yet even when white supremacist control of the event was assured, organizers often discovered popular interest in their Confederate love-fest to be only patchy or temporary. Worse still, from the vantage point of bitter-enders, was the crucial readiness of southern whites like Bell Wiley, Ralph McGill, Frank Smith, James Robertson, and Ed Gass to embrace a New South free from the stultifying encumbrance of racial segregation. Notwithstanding disturbing signs of a Rebel resurgence in 1961 and 1962, at no stage during the centennial period did southern whites—many of whom had vivid personal memories of serving the United States in wartime—act in unison to make the past serve their needs in the present.

Although their decision, ultimately, to adjust to reconfigured power relations is essential to an understanding not only of the centennial but also of the South's relatively quiescent response to the federal civil rights legislation of the mid-1960s, white southerners were not the primary architects of reform during that turbulent decade. Civil rights activists working at all levels of the American polity generated so much pressure on Jim Crow institutions and customs that most whites in the region were virtually compelled to accept the idea of change. Movement protests imparted renewed potency to the black counter-memory of the Civil War, ensuring that the federal government could no longer ignore its contemporary ramifications.

We must not, however, exaggerate the extent to which reinvigorated memories of emancipation and black service in the Union armies altered both federal policy and popular awareness of the role that African Americans had played in the nation's history. Effective civil rights laws were the product of direct-action protests and government fear of social disorder, not of fundamental shifts in historical memory (though the black counter-narrative did help to legitimize federal legislation by grounding it in a sacred past inhabited by the peerless Lincoln). The influence of the counter-memory on popular culture, moreover, was severely limited, not only in the early 1960s but beyond the centennial. Even when, in 1989, Hollywood finally got around to making a movie about the wartime service of African Americans, Edward Zwick's account of the attack on Fort Wagner, *Glory*, failed to inspire a rash of copycat films.[18] True, Ken Burns's popular TV documentary, *The Civil War* (1990), built

18. For an insightful analysis of *Glory*, which stresses the movie's role in diminishing the trauma associated with defeat in Vietnam, see Jim Cullen, *The Civil War in Popular Culture: A*

on the latest scholarship in order to give greater coverage than the CWCC to slavery, emancipation, and black troops, but the tragic brothers' war trope remained central to the director's liberal, patriotic vision of the American past. Just as no one had suggested a centennial commemoration of Reconstruction, Burns passed up the opportunity to educate or reeducate millions of viewers about the racial struggles integral to an understanding of the immediate postbellum era. When Americans witnessed cinematic recreations of battle in Ron Maxwell's *Gettysburg* (1993) or the ferocious fighting at the Crater in Anthony Minghella's *Cold Mountain* (2003), they encountered few visual or aural signposts to the black counter-memory.[19] The United States now has a monument devoted to the memory of the African-American soldiers who fought for the republic in the 1860s, but few whites ever see it in its place outside the U Street metro station in Washington, DC.

The crucial point is not that the emancipation narrative continues to lack visibility outside the academy but that the civil rights movement gave blacks genuine political power which could be exerted when necessary in the heavily ritualized realm of what Alessandra Lorini has termed "American public culture."[20] It also imparted a degree of legitimacy to the counter-memory that made the latter progressively more difficult for whites to contest. In March 2004 Georgians voted to accept their new compromise flag by a margin of three to one.[21] Most whites who voted in the majority probably supported the new design because they understood that African Americans would not let the matter die—that to go on flying the battle flag in any form would result in renewed pressure from the NAACP, constant turmoil over the issue, and plenty of financially damaging external opprobrium. Similar reasoning resulted in the dedication of a statue of black tennis legend Arthur Ashe on Richmond's

Reusable Past (Washington, DC: Smithsonian Institution Press, 1995), 139–71. The black actor Denzel Washington, who played one of the leading roles in the film, confessed that he had never heard about African Americans fighting in the Union army. Bruce Chadwick, *The Reel Civil War: Mythmaking in American Film* (New York: Alfred A. Knopf, 2001), 281.

19. William Blair, "The Brothers' War: Gettysburg the Movie and American Memory," in Blair and William Pencak, eds., *Making and Remaking Pennsylvania's Civil War* (University Park: Pennsylvania State University Press, 2001), 245–59. Several commentators noted the absence of blacks in the movie version of *Cold Mountain,* among them Greg Tate in "Blacked Out," *Village Voice,* Feb. 4–10, 2004, http://www.villagevoice.com/issues/0405/tate.php (accessed Oct. 10, 2004).

20. Lorini defines American public culture rather high-mindedly as "a space where conflictual definitions of democracy can converse." Lorini, *Rituals,* xiii.

21. Coski, *Confederate Battle Flag,* 263.

Monument Avenue in July 1996.[22] It also brought down the Rebel banner from the South Carolina capitol in 1998 and occasioned the construction, on the statehouse grounds, of a permanent historical monument to local blacks. Of course, these developments did not indicate the complete success of the civil rights movement in the sphere of cultural politics. Georgia's "compromise" flag bears a close resemblance to the Confederacy's first national banner, the Stars and Bars, which was less threatening to blacks than the St. Andrew's Cross but still a repository of whiteness. The battle flag also remains a very visible sight on the capitol lawn in Columbia. Yet it would be wrong to belittle entirely these small signs of change. For they indicate not only that the black counter-memory now has a degree of leverage in the South that it did not possess in the 1960s, but also that some southern whites are not entirely obsessed with the past and, for a variety of reasons, are prepared to follow the sage counsel of Senator Balfour. While it is certainly true, as Tony Horwitz has shown, that Confederate theater and white racism have not gone away, the fact that the Lost Cause looks more like today's counter-memory than the black emancipation narrative testifies to the achievement of the civil rights crusade.[23]

W. Fitzhugh Brundage has contended rightly that "[t]he depth and tenacity of a historical memory within a society may serve as one measure of who exerts social power there."[24] On this basis alone, African Americans have yet to reach the Promised Land. This said, during the late 1950s and early 1960s segregationists like Ross Barnett and George Wallace struggled in vain to mobilize southern whites on the basis of a supposedly common and glorious past. That they failed was due largely to the perseverance of the civil rights movement, the faltering intervention of the federal government, and the resignation of many southern whites. If the Civil War centennial tells us anything, it is that seemingly entrenched historical memories are not always a match for the onrush of time, encompassing as it does a plethora of countervailing personal experiences, sometimes bewildering social and economic change, and persistent political struggle.

22. Brian Black and Bryn Varley, "Contesting the Sacred: Preservation and Meaning on Richmond's Monument Avenue," in Cynthia Mills and Pamela H. Simpson, eds., *Monuments of the Lost Cause: Women, Art, and the Landscapes of Southern Memory* (Knoxville: University of Tennessee Press, 2004), 234–50.

23. Tony Horwitz, *Confederates in the Attic: Dispatches from the Unfinished Civil War* (New York: Vintage, 1999).

24. W. Fitzhugh Brundage, "Introduction" to Brundage, ed., *Where These Memories Grow: History, Memory, and Southern Identity* (Chapel Hill: University of North Carolina Press, 2000), 11.

BIBLIOGRAPHY

MANUSCRIPT SOURCES

Alabama Department of Archives and History, Montgomery
Alabama Department of Archives and History Records.
Patterson, John, Governor of Alabama, Administration Files.
Wallace, George C., Governor of Alabama, Administration Files.

Bethesda, MD
Rustin, Bayard, Papers, UPA microfilm, 1988.

College of William and Mary, Williamsburg
Tuck, William M., Papers. Special Collections, Earl Gregg Swem Library.

Columbia University, New York
Nevins, Allan, Papers. Rare Book and Manuscript Library.

Emory University, Atlanta
Wiley, Bell I., Papers. Manuscript, Archives, and Rare Book Library.

Georgia State Archives, Atlanta
Georgia Civil War Centennial Commission Records.

John F. Kennedy Presidential Library, Boston
Bernhard, Berl I., Papers.
Kennedy, John F., Papers.
President's Office Files.
Schlesinger, Arthur M., Jr., Papers.
White House Central Subject Files.
White House Staff Files.

Library of Virginia, Richmond
Virginia Civil War Centennial Commission Records.

Mississippi Department of Archives and History, Jackson
Mississippi Commission on the War Between the States Records.

National Archives, College Park, MD
U.S. Civil War Centennial Commission Records. National Park Service Records.

National Archives, Washington, DC
U.S. House of Representatives Records. Committee on the Judiciary. 85th Congress.

New Jersey State Archives, Trenton
New Jersey Civil War Centennial Commission Records.

New York State Archives, Albany
New York Civil War Centennial Commission Records.
Rockefeller, Nelson A., Papers.

South Carolina Department of Archives and History, Columbia
South Carolina Department of Archives and History Records. Office of the Director,
    Agencies, Commissions, and Organizations File.

South Caroliniana Library, University of South Carolina, Columbia
Dorn, William Jennings Bryan, Papers. Modern Political Collections.
Hollings, Ernest F., Papers. Modern Political Collections.
Johnson, Olin D., Papers. Modern Political Collections.
Long, L. D. and J. C., Vertical File. Modern Political Collections.
McCray, John H., Papers.
Workman, William D., Jr., Papers. Modern Political Collections.

State Historical Society of Iowa, Des Moines
Iowa Civil War Centennial Commission Records.

Tennessee State Library and Archives, Nashville
Horn, Stanley F., Papers. Tennessee Historical Society Collections.
Tennessee Civil War Centennial Commission Records.

PRINTED PRIMARY SOURCES

Garrow, David J., Gerald Gill, Vincent Harding, and Darlene Clark Hine, eds. *The Eyes
    on the Prize Civil Rights Reader: Documents, Speeches, and Firsthand Accounts from
    the Black Freedom Struggle, 1954–1990.* New York: Penguin Books, 1991.
King, Martin Luther, Jr. *The Papers of Martin Luther King, Jr., Volume 1: Called to Serve,
    January 1929–June 1951.* Clayborne Carson, ed. Berkeley: University of California
    Press, 1992.

———. *A Testament of Hope: The Essential Writings and Speeches of Martin Luther King, Jr.* James M. Washington, ed. San Francisco: HarperSanFrancisco, 1991.

Public Papers of the Presidents of the United States: Dwight D. Eisenhower, 1959. Washington, DC: Government Printing Office, 1960.

Public Papers of the Presidents of the United States: John F. Kennedy, 1961. Washington, DC: Government Printing Office, 1962.

Public Papers of the Presidents of the United States: John F. Kennedy, 1962. Washington, DC: Government Printing Office, 1963.

Public Papers of the Presidents of the United States: John F. Kennedy, 1963. Washington, DC: Government Printing Office, 1964.

Robertson, James I., Jr. *The Civil War.* Washington, DC: U.S. Civil War Centennial Commission, 1963.

U.S. Civil War Centennial Commission. *Guide for the Observance of the Centennial of the Civil War.* Washington, DC: Byron S. Adams, 1959.

———. *Emancipation Centennial, 1962: A Brief Anthology of the Preliminary Proclamation.* Washington, DC: Government Printing Office, 1962.

———. *The Civil War Centennial: A Report to the Congress.* Washington, DC: Government Printing Office, 1968.

U.S. Commission on Civil Rights. *Freedom to the Free: Century of Emancipation, 1863–1963—A Report to the President by the United States Commission on Civil Rights.* Washington, DC: Government Printing Office, 1963.

Wilson, Elena, ed. *Edmund Wilson: Letters on Literature and Politics, 1912–1972.* New York: Farrar, Straus and Giroux, 1977.

NEWSPAPERS AND MAGAZINES

Atlanta Constitution
Atlanta Journal
Baltimore Afro-American
Birmingham News
Boston Globe
Charleston News and Courier
Chicago Defender
Civil War Times (Civil War Times Illustrated)
Ebony
Franklin Review-Appeal
Jackson Clarion Ledger
Montgomery Advertiser
New Republic

New York Amsterdam News
New York Times
Saturday Review
The State (Columbia)
United Daughters of the Confederacy Magazine
Washington Post

BOOKS

Bartley, Numan V. *The Rise of Massive Resistance: Race and Politics in the South During the 1950s.* Baton Rouge: Louisiana State University Press, 1969.

———. *The New South, 1945–1980.* Baton Rouge: Louisiana State University Press, 1995.

Belting, Natalia M. *Indy and Mr. Lincoln.* New York: Henry Holt and Company, 1960.

Blair, William. *Cities of the Dead: Contesting the Memory of the Civil War in the South, 1865–1914.* Chapel Hill: University of North Carolina Press, 2004.

Blair, William, and William Pencak, eds. *Making and Remaking Pennsylvania's Civil War.* University Park: Pennsylvania State University Press, 2001.

Blight, David W. *Frederick Douglass' Civil War: Keeping Faith in Jubilee.* Baton Rouge: Louisiana State University Press, 1989.

———. *Race and Reunion: The Civil War in American Memory.* Cambridge, MA: Belknap Press of Harvard University Press, 2001.

———. *Beyond the Battlefield: Race, Memory, and the American Civil War.* Amherst and Boston: University of Massachusetts Press, 2002.

Blotner, Joseph. *Robert Penn Warren: A Biography.* New York: Random House, 1997.

Bodnar, John. *Remaking America: Public Memory, Commemoration, and Patriotism in the Twentieth Century.* Princeton: Princeton University Press, 1992.

Branch, Taylor. *Parting the Waters: America in the King Years, 1954–63.* New York: Simon and Schuster, 1988.

Brick, John. *The Richmond Raid.* Garden City, NY: Doubleday, 1963.

Brock, William R. *An American Crisis: Congress and Reconstruction, 1865–1867.* New York: St. Martin's; London: Macmillan, 1963.

Brogan, Hugh. *Kennedy.* London and New York: Addison Wesley Longman, 1996.

Brundage, W. Fitzhugh, ed. *Where These Memories Grow: History, Memory, and Southern Identity.* Chapel Hill: University of North Carolina Press, 2000.

———. *The Southern Past: A Clash of Race and Memory.* Cambridge, MA: Belknap Press of Harvard University Press, 2005.

Campbell, Jacqueline Glass. *When Sherman Marches North from the Sea: Resistance on the Confederate Home Front.* Chapel Hill: University of North Carolina Press, 2003.

Carter, Dan T. *The Politics of Rage: George Wallace, the Origins of the New Conservatism, and the Transformation of American Politics.* New York: Simon and Schuster, 1995.

Catton, Bruce. *The Centennial History of the Civil War.* 3 vols. Garden City, NY: Doubleday, 1961–65.

———. *Waiting for the Morning Train: An American Boyhood.* Garden City, NY: Doubleday, 1972.

Chadwick, Bruce. *The Reel Civil War: Mythmaking in American Film.* New York: Alfred A. Knopf, 2001.

Chafe, William H. *Civilities and Civil Rights: Greensboro, North Carolina, and the Black Struggle for Freedom.* New York: Oxford University Press, 1980.

Chapman, C. Stuart. *Shelby Foote: A Writer's Life.* Jackson: University Press of Mississippi, 2003.

Chappell, David L. *Inside Agitators: White Southerners in the Civil Rights Movement.* Baltimore: Johns Hopkins University Press, 1994.

Cimprich, John. *Fort Pillow, a Civil War Massacre, and Public Memory.* Baton Rouge: Louisiana State University Press, 2005.

Cochran, Hamilton. *The Dram Tree.* Indianapolis: Bobbs-Merrill, 1961.

Connelly, T. Lawrence. *Will Success Spoil Jeff Davis? The Last Book About the Civil War.* New York: McGraw-Hill, 1963.

Corrington, John William. *And Wait for the Night.* New York: G. P. Putnam's Sons, 1964.

Coski, John M. *The Confederate Battle Flag: America's Most Embattled Emblem.* Cambridge, MA: Belknap Press of Harvard University Press, 2005.

Cosman, Bernard, and Robert J. Huckshorn, eds. *Republican Politics: The 1964 Campaign and Its Aftermath for the Party.* New York: Frederick A. Praeger, 1968.

Cox, John H., and LaWanda Cox. *Politics, Principle, and Prejudice, 1865–1866: Dilemma of Reconstruction America.* New York: Free Press of Glencoe, 1963.

Cox, Karen L. *Dixie's Daughters: The United Daughters of the Confederacy and the Preservation of Confederate Culture.* Gainesville: University Press of Florida, 2003.

Crawley, William Bryan. *Bill Tuck: A Political Life in Harry Byrd's Virginia.* Charlottesville: University of Virginia Press, 1978.

Cullen, Jim. *The Civil War in Popular Culture: A Reusable Past.* Washington, DC: Smithsonian Institution Press, 1995.

Dallek, Robert. *John F. Kennedy: An Unfinished Life, 1917–1963.* 2003; UK edition, London: Penguin Books, 2004.

Daniel, Pete. *Lost Revolutions: The South in the 1950s.* Chapel Hill: University of North Carolina Press, 2000.

Davis, Maggie. *The Far Side of Home.* New York: Macmillan, 1963.

Desmond, James. *Nelson Rockefeller: A Political Biography.* New York and London: Macmillan, 1964.

Divine, David. *Thunder on the Chesapeake.* New York: Macmillan, 1961.

Donald, David. *Charles Sumner and the Coming of the Civil War.* New York: Alfred A. Knopf, 1960.

Duberman, Martin, ed. *The Antislavery Vanguard: New Essays on the Abolitionists.* Princeton: Princeton University Press, 1965.

Dukore, Bernard F. *Sam Peckinpah's Feature Films.* Urbana and Chicago: University of Illinois Press, 1999.

Duncan, Harley. *West of Appomattox.* New York: Appleton-Century-Crofts, 1961.

Ellis, L. Ethan. *Steps in a Journey Toward Understanding: Activities of the New Jersey Civil War Centennial Commission in 1961 at Trenton, Charleston and Salem Church.* Trenton: New Jersey Civil War Centennial Commission, 1963.

Ely, James W., Jr. *The Crisis of Conservative Virginia: The Byrd Organization and the Politics of Massive Resistance.* Knoxville: University of Tennessee Press, 1976.

Eyman, Scott. *Print the Legend: The Life and Times of John Ford.* New York: Simon and Schuster, 1999.

Fabre, Geneviève, and Robert O'Meally, eds. *History and Memory in African-American Culture.* New York: Oxford University Press, 1994.

Fahs, Alice, and Joan Waugh, eds. *The Memory of the Civil War in American Culture.* Chapel Hill: University of North Carolina Press, 2004.

Fairclough, Adam. *To Redeem the Soul of America: The Southern Christian Leadership Conference and Martin Luther King, Jr.* Athens: University of Georgia Press, 1987.

———. *Better Day Coming: Blacks and Equality, 1890–2000.* New York: Viking Penguin, 2001.

Foner, Eric. *Free Soil, Free Labor, Free Men: The Ideology of the Republican Party Before the Civil War.* New York: Oxford University Press, 1970.

———. *Politics and Ideology in the Age of the Civil War.* New York: Oxford University Press, 1980.

Foote, Shelby. *The Civil War: A Narrative.* 3 vols. New York: Random House, 1958–74.

Foster, Gaines M. *Ghosts of the Confederacy: Defeat, the Lost Cause, and the Emergence of the New South, 1865 to 1913.* New York: Oxford University Press, 1987.

Franklin, John Hope. *Reconstruction After the Civil War.* Chicago: University of Chicago Press, 1961.

———. *From Slavery to Freedom: A History of American Negroes.* Revised edition. New York: Alfred A. Knopf, 1963.

Fried, Richard M., *The Russians Are Coming! The Russians Are Coming! Pageantry and Patriotism in Cold-War America.* New York: Oxford University Press, 1998.

Gallagher, Gary W., and Alan T. Nolan, eds. *The Myth of the Lost Cause and Civil War History*. Bloomington and Indianapolis: Indiana University Press, 2000.

Gara, Larry. *The Liberty Line: The Legend of the Underground Railroad*. Lexington: University of Kentucky Press, 1961.

Garrow, David J. *Bearing the Cross: Martin Luther King, Jr. and the Southern Christian Leadership Conference*. 1986; U.K. edition, London: Jonathan Cape, 1988.

Gillette, William E. *The Right to Vote: Politics and the Passage of the Fifteenth Amendment*. Baltimore: Johns Hopkins University Press, 1965.

Glassberg, David. *American Historical Pageantry: The Uses of Tradition in the Early Twentieth Century*. Chapel Hill: University of North Carolina Press, 1990.

Goggin, Jacqueline. *Carter G. Woodson: A Life in Black History*. Baton Rouge: Louisiana State University Press, 1993.

Goldfield, David R. *Still Fighting the Civil War: The American South and Southern History*. Baton Rouge: Louisiana State University Press, 2002.

Graham, Allison. *Framing the South: Hollywood, Television, and Race During the Civil Rights Struggle*. Baltimore: Johns Hopkins University Press, 2001.

Grant, Susan-Mary, and Peter J. Parish, eds. *Legacy of Disunion: The Enduring Significance of the American Civil War*. Baton Rouge: Louisiana State University Press, 2003.

Grantham, Dewey W. *The Life and Death of the Solid South: A Political History*. Lexington: University of Kentucky Press, 1988.

Guelzo, Allen C. *The Crisis of the American Republic: A History of the Civil War and Reconstruction Era*. New York: St. Martin's Press, 1995.

Hale, Grace Elizabeth. *Making Whiteness: The Culture of Segregation in the South, 1890–1940*. New York: Pantheon Books, 1998.

Halttunen, Karen, and Lewis Perry, eds. *Moral Problems in American Life*. Ithaca: Cornell University Press, 1998.

Hanchett, William. *The Lincoln Murder Conspiracies*. Urbana and Chicago: University of Illinois Press, 1986.

Hartje, Robert G. *Bicentennial USA: Pathways to Celebration*. Nashville: American Association for State and Local History, 1973.

Henderson, Harold Paulk. *Ernest Vandiver: Governor of Georgia*. Athens: University of Georgia Press, 2000.

Hendricks, Randy. *Lonelier than God: Robert Penn Warren and the Southern Exile*. Athens: University of Georgia Press, 2000.

Honig, Donald. *Walk Like a Man*. New York: William Sloane Associates, 1961.

Horwitz, Tony. *Confederates in the Attic: Dispatches from the Unfinished Civil War*. 1998; New York: Vintage Books, 1999.

Humphrey, William. *The Ordways*. New York: Alfred A. Knopf, 1965.

Hunt, Irene. *Across Five Aprils.* Chicago: Follett Publishing Co., 1964.

Isserman, Maurice, and Michael Kazin. *America Divided: The Civil War of the 1960s.* New York: Oxford University Press, 2000.

Jacoway, Elizabeth, and David R. Colburn, eds. *Southern Businessmen and Desegregation.* Baton Rouge: Louisiana State University Press, 1982.

Kachun, Mitch. *Festivals of Freedom: Memory and Meaning in African-American Emancipation Celebrations, 1808–1915.* Amherst: University of Massachusetts Press, 2003.

Kammen, Michael. *Mystic Chords of Memory: The Transformation of Tradition in American Culture.* New York: Alfred A. Knopf, 1991.

Kaplan, Steven Laurence. *Farewell Revolution: Disputed Legacies, France, 1789/1989.* Ithaca: Cornell University Press, 1995.

Kaser, James A. *At the Bivouac of Memory: History, Politics, and the Battle of Chickamauga.* New York: Peter Lang, 1996.

Kasson, Joy S. *Buffalo Bill's Wild West: Celebrity, Memory, and Popular History.* 2000; New York: Hill and Wang, 2001.

Kay, Helen. *Abe Lincoln's Hobby.* Chicago: Reilly and Lee, 1961.

Kennedy, John F. *Profiles in Courage.* New York: Harper, 1956.

Keyes, Frances Parkinson. *Madame Castel's Lodger.* New York: Farrar, Straus and Cudahy, 1962.

Lassiter, Matthew D., and Andrew B. Lewis, eds. *The Moderates' Dilemma: Massive Resistance to School Desegregation in Virginia.* Charlottesville: University Press of Virginia, 1998.

Levine, Bruce. *Confederate Emancipation: Southern Plans to Free and Arm Slaves During the Civil War.* Oxford: Oxford University Press, 2006.

Lewis, George. *The White South and the Red Menace: Segregationists, Anticommunism, and Massive Resistance, 1945–1965.* Gainesville: University Press of Florida, 2004.

Lewis, John, with Michael D'Orso. *Walking with the Wind: A Memoir of the Movement.* 1998; San Diego: Harcourt Brace, 1999.

Linenthal, Edward Tabor. *Sacred Ground: Americans and Their Battlefields.* Urbana and Chicago: University of Illinois Press, 1991.

Lipsitz, George. *Time Passages: Collective Memory and American Popular Culture.* Minneapolis: University of Minnesota Press, 1990.

Lischer, Richard. *The Preacher King: Martin Luther King, Jr. and the Word That Moved America.* New York: Oxford University Press, 1995.

Lively, Robert A. *Fiction Fights the Civil War: An Unfinished Chapter in the Literary History of the American People.* Chapel Hill: University of North Carolina Press, 1957.

Lorini, Alessandra. *Rituals of Race: American Public Culture and the Search for Racial Democracy.* Charlottesville: University of Virginia Press, 1999.

Love, Edmund G. *An End to Bugling.* New York: Harper and Row, 1963.

Lowell, Robert. *For the Union Dead.* London: Faber and Faber, 1965.

McBride, Joseph. *Searching for John Ford: A Life.* New York: St. Martin's, 2001.

McConnell, Stuart. *Glorious Contentment: The Grand Army of the Republic, 1865–1900.* Chapel Hill: University of North Carolina Press, 1992.

McFeely, William S. *Grant: A Biography.* New York: W. W. Norton, 1981.

McKitrick, Eric L. *Andrew Johnson and Reconstruction.* Chicago: University of Chicago Press, 1960.

McMillen, Neil R. *The Citizens' Council: Organized Resistance to the Second Reconstruction 1954–64.* Urbana and Chicago: University of Illinois Press, 1971.

McPherson, James M. *The Struggle for Equality: Abolitionists and the Negro in the Civil War and Reconstruction.* Princeton: Princeton University Press, 1964.

———. *Battle Cry of Freedom: The Civil War Era.* New York: Oxford University Press, 1988.

———. *For Cause and Comrades: Why Men Fought in the Civil War.* New York: Oxford University Press, 1997.

———. *Crossroads of Freedom: Antietam.* Oxford: Oxford University Press, 2002.

McPherson, James M., and William J. Cooper Jr., eds. *Writing the Civil War: The Quest to Understand.* Columbia: University of South Carolina Press, 1998.

Madden, David, and Peggy Bach, eds. *Classics of Civil War Fiction.* 1991; reprint, Tuscaloosa: University of Alabama Press, 2001.

Maltby, Richard. *Harmless Entertainment: Hollywood and the Ideology of Consensus.* Metuchen, NJ: Scarecrow Press, 1983.

May, Lary, ed. *Recasting America: Culture and Politics in the Age of Cold War.* Chicago: University of Chicago Press, 1989.

Meier, August, and Elliott Rudwick. *Black History and the Historical Profession, 1915–1980.* Urbana and Chicago: University of Illinois Press, 1986.

Mills, Cynthia, and Pamela H. Simpson, eds. *Monuments of the Lost Cause: Women, Art, and the Landscapes of Southern Memory.* Knoxville: University of Tennessee Press, 2004.

Mills, William, ed. *John William Corrington: Southern Man of Letters.* Conway: University of Central Arkansas Press, 1994.

Mitchell, Dennis J. *Mississippi Liberal: A Biography of Frank E. Smith.* Jackson: University Press of Mississippi, for the Mississippi Historical Society, 2001.

Mitchell, Reid. *Civil War Soldiers.* 1988; reprint, New York: Penguin, 1997.

Motyl, Alexander J. *Dilemmas of Independence: Ukraine After Totalitarianism.* New York: Council on Foreign Relations Press, 1993.

Navasky, Victor S. *Kennedy Justice.* New York: Atheneum, 1971.

Nevins, Allan. *The War for the Union, Volume 1: The Improvised War, 1861–1862.* New York: Charles Scribner's Sons, 1959.

————. *The War for the Union, Volume 2: War Becomes Revolution.* New York: Charles Scribner's Sons, 1960.

————, ed. *Lincoln and the Gettysburg Address: Commemorative Papers [by] John Dos Passos, Arthur Lehman Goodhart, Reinhold Niebuhr, Robert Lowell, Paul H. Douglas, David C. Mearns.* Urbana: University of Illinois Press, 1964.

Novick, Peter. *That Noble Dream: The "Objectivity Question" and the American Historical Profession.* Cambridge: Cambridge University Press, 1988.

Percy, Walker. *Signposts in a Strange Land.* Patrick Samway, ed. New York: Farrar, Straus and Giroux, 1991.

Perry, Gerald, ed. *John Ford Interviews.* Jackson: University Press of Mississippi, 2001.

Pressly, Thomas J. *Americans Interpret Their Civil War.* Princeton: Princeton University Press, 1954.

Quarles, Benjamin. *Lincoln and the Negro.* New York: Oxford University Press, 1962.

Rankin, David C. *Diary of a Christian Soldier: Rufus Kinsley and the Civil War.* Cambridge: Cambridge University Press, 2004.

Reardon, Carol. *Pickett's Charge in History and Memory.* Chapel Hill: University of North Carolina Press, 1997.

Rhodes, James A., and Dean Jauchius. *Johnny Shiloh: A Novel of the Civil War.* New York: Bobbs-Merrill, 1959.

Roper, John Herbert, ed. *C. Vann Woodward: A Southern Historian and His Critics.* Athens: University of Georgia Press, 1997.

Rowan, Carl T. *South of Freedom.* 1952; reprint, Baton Rouge: Louisiana State University Press, 1997.

Runte, Alfred. *National Parks: The American Experience.* Lincoln: University of Nebraska Press, 1979.

Salter, John R., Jr. *Jackson, Mississippi: An American Chronicle of Struggle and Schism.* 1979; reprint, Malabar, FL: R. E. Krieger, 1987.

Shaffer, Donald R. *After the Glory: The Struggle of Black Civil War Veterans.* Lawrence: University Press of Kansas, 2004.

Silber, Nina. *The Romance of Reunion: Northerners and the South 1865–1900.* Chapel Hill: University of North Carolina Press, 1993.

Sosna, Morton. *In Search of the Solid South: Southern Liberals and the Race Issue.* New York: Columbia University Press, 1977.

Spears, Jack. *The Civil War on the Screen and Other Essays.* South Brunswick, NJ: A.S. Barnes, 1977.

Stampp, Kenneth M. *The Era of Reconstruction, 1865–1877.* New York: Alfred A. Knopf, 1965.

Stern, Mark. *Calculating Visions: Kennedy, Johnson, and Civil Rights.* New Brunswick, NJ: Rutgers University Press, 1992.

Teel, Leonard R. *Ralph Emerson McGill: Voice of the Southern Conscience.* Knoxville: University of Tennessee Press, 2001.

Thelen, David, ed. *Memory and American History.* Bloomington and Indianapolis: Indiana University Press, 1990.

Thomas, Christopher A. *The Lincoln Memorial and American Life.* Princeton: Princeton University Press, 2002.

Thornton, J. Mills, III. *Dividing Lines: Municipal Politics and the Struggle for Civil Rights in Montgomery, Birmingham, and Selma.* Tuscaloosa: University of Alabama Press, 2002.

Toplin, Robert Brent, ed. *Ken Burns's "The Civil War": Historians Respond.* New York: Oxford University Press, 1996.

Vandiver, Frank E., ed. *The Idea of the South: Pursuit of a Central Theme.* Chicago: University of Chicago Press, 1964.

Ward, Brian, and Tony Badger, eds. *The Making of Martin Luther King and the Civil Rights Movement.* Basingstoke, U.K.: Macmillan; New York: New York University Press, 1996.

Warren, Robert Penn. *The Legacy of the Civil War: Meditations on the Centennial.* New York: Random House, 1961.

———. *Wilderness: A Tale of the Civil War.* New York: Random House, 1961.

———. *Talking with Robert Penn Warren.* Floyd C. Watkins, John T. Hiers, and Mary Louise Weaks, eds. Athens: University of Georgia Press, 1990.

Weddle, David. *Sam Peckinpah: If They Move . . . Kill 'Em.* 1994; U.K. edition, London: Faber and Faber, 1996.

Weeks, Jim. *Gettysburg: Memory, Market, and an American Shrine.* Princeton: Princeton University Press, 2003.

Wesley, Charles H. *Ohio Negroes in the Civil War.* Columbus: Ohio State University Press, for the Ohio Historical Society, 1962.

Wiggins, William H., Jr. *O Freedom! Afro-American Emancipation Celebrations.* Knoxville: University of Tennessee Press, 1987.

Wiley, Bell Irvin. *The Bell Irvin Wiley Reader.* Hill Jordan, James I. Robertson Jr., and J. H. Segars, eds. Baton Rouge: Louisiana State University Press, 2001.

Williamson, Joel. *After Slavery: The Negro in South Carolina During Reconstruction, 1861–1877.* Chapel Hill: University of North Carolina Press, 1965.

Wilson, Edmund. *Patriotic Gore: Studies in the Literature of the American Civil War.* New York: Oxford University Press, 1962.

Winter, Jay, and Emmanuel Sivan, eds. *War and Remembrance in the Twentieth Century.* Cambridge: Cambridge University Press, 1999.

Wofford, Harris. *Of Kennedys and Kings: Making Sense of the Sixties.* 1980; reprint, Pittsburgh: University of Pittsburgh Press, 1992.

Woodward, C. Vann. *The Strange Career of Jim Crow.* New York: Oxford University Press, 1955.

——. *The Burden of Southern History.* Baton Rouge: Louisiana State University Press, 1960.

——. *Thinking Back: The Perils of Writing History.* Baton Rouge: Louisiana State University Press, 1986.

ARTICLES

Bailey, Fred Arthur. "The Textbooks of the 'Lost Cause': Censorship and the Creation of Southern State Histories." *Georgia Historical Quarterly* 75 (1991): 507–33.

Brundage, W. Fitzhugh. "Commemoration and Conflict: Forgetting and Remembering the Civil War." *Georgia Historical Quarterly* 82 (1998): 559–74.

Cook, Robert. "(Un)furl That Banner: The Response of White Southerners to the Civil War Centennial of 1961–1965." *Journal of Southern History* 68 (2002): 879–912.

Franklin, John Hope. "A Century of Civil War Observance." *Journal of Negro History* 47 (1962): 97–107.

Gondos, Victor, Jr. "Karl S. Betts and the Civil War Centennial Commission." *Military Affairs* 27 (1963): 51–70.

Grant, Ulysses S., III. "Civil War Fact and Fiction." *Civil War History* 2 (June 1956): 29–40.

Grow, Matthew J. "The Shadow of the Civil War: A Historiography of Civil War Memory." *American Nineteenth Century History* 4 (2003): 77–103.

Kelley, Robin D. G. "'We Are Not What We Seem': Rethinking Black Working-Class Opposition in the Jim Crow South." *Journal of American History* 80 (1993): 75–112.

Mahin, John Lee, and Martin Rackin. "The Horse Soldiers or Grierson's Raid." *Civil War History* 5 (1959): 183–87.

Merridale, Catherine. "Redesigning History in Contemporary Russia." *Journal of Contemporary History* 38 (2003): 13–28.

Meyer, Howard N. "Did the South Win the Civil War?" *Negro Digest* 13 (1961): 3–10.

Nora, Pierre. "Between Memory and History: Les Lieux de Mémoire." *Representations* 26 (1989): 7–24.

Olick, Jeffrey K., and Joyce Robbins. "Social Memory Studies: From 'Collective Memory' to the Historical Sociology of Mnemonic Practices." *Annual Review of Sociology* 24 (1998): 105–40.

Rassool, Ciraj, and Leslie Witz. "The 1952 Jan Van Riebeeck Tercentenary Festival: Constructing and Contesting Public National History in South Africa." *Journal of African History* 34 (1993): 447–68.

Rubin, Louis D., Jr. "General Longstreet and Me: Refighting the Civil War." *Southern Cultures* 8 (2002): 21–46.

Silbey, Joel H. "The Civil War Synthesis in American Political History." *Civil War History* 10 (1964): 130–40.

Silver, James W. "The Twenty-First Annual Meeting." *Journal of Southern History* 22 (1956): 59–81.

Smyth, J. E. "'Young Mr. Lincoln': Between Myth and History in 1939." *Rethinking History* 7 (2003): 193–214.

Temple, Wayne C. "Last Assembly of the Centennial Commission." *Lincoln Herald* 5 (1965): 83–90.

Thompson, Lawrence S. "The Civil War in Fiction." *Civil War History* 2 (March 1956): 83–95.

Vandiver, Frank E. "Notes and Comments: Harper's Interprets 'The South Today,'" *Journal of Southern History* 31 (1965): 318–23.

Wesley, Charles H. "The Civil War and the Negro-American." *Journal of Negro History* 47 (1962): 77–96.

Wiley, Bell I. "A Time of Greatness." *Journal of Southern History* 22 (1956): 3–35.

———. "Report of the Activities Committee to the Civil War Centennial Commission." *Civil War History* 5 (1959): 374–81.

Woodward, C. Vann. "Look Away, Look Away." *Journal of Southern History* 59 (1993): 487–504.

THESES

Allen, Kevin M. "The Civil War Centennial in South Carolina: A Case Study in the Construction of Memory, 1961–1965." M.A. thesis, University of South Carolina, 2001.

Baker, Bruce E. "Devastated By Passion and Belief: Remembering Reconstruction in the Twentieth-Century South." Ph.D. thesis, University of North Carolina, 2003.

INDEX